# The Sea-craft
# of Prehistory

# The Sea-craft of Prehistory

Paul Johnstone

Prepared for publication by
Seán McGrail

Harvard University Press
Cambridge, Massachusetts
1980

*Library of Congress Cataloging in Publication Data*

*Johnstone, Paul.*
*The seacraft of prehistory.*
*Includes bibliographical references and index.*
*1. Boats, Prehistoric.   I. McGrail, Sean.*
*II. Title.*
*GN799.B62J64       387.2'1       79-22548*

*ISBN 0-674-79595-4*

# Contents

|  |  | page |
|---|---|---|
| Foreword by Seán McGrail | | xiii |
| Introduction | | xv |
| Acknowledgments | | xvii |

**Part I**
**General Survey of Early Types of Water Transport**

| 1 | Earliest times | 3 |
|---|---|---|
| 2 | Raft and reed | 7 |
| | The single log · the log raft · the reed boat · Egypt · Mesopotamia · Africa · the Mediterranean · Europe to India · Tasmania · the Pacific · America · earliest use | |
| 3 | Bark | 17 |
| | Earliest use · evolution of bark craft · South America · Africa · North America · northern Europe and Asia · developments of the bark boat | |
| 4 | Skin | 26 |
| | Types of skin craft · Britain and Ireland · Scandinavia · southern and eastern Europe · southern Asia and India · Russia and the Arctic · America · military use of skin boats · distribution · origin of skin boats | |
| 5 | Dug-outs and the evolution of the plank-built boat | 45 |
| | Planked boat origins · the simple dug-out · making a dug-out · developments of the simple dug-out · multiple dug-outs · expanded dug-outs · stabilisers and outriggers · the evolution of planked boats | |

**Part II**
**Europe**                                                      *page*

6    The earlier Mediterranean                                    55
     The obsidian trade · what type of boat? · skin or
     basketry? · reed · the dug-out

7    The later Mediterranean                                      67
     Metal tools and trade · Crete · Egypt · ship-
     building techniques · evolution in the
     Mediterranean · mast and sail · the keel · the
     war-ship · literary evidence · anchors · evidence
     from wrecks · *'hupozoma'* or hogging truss?

8    The Atlantic                                                 85
     The ships of the Veneti · the Blackfriars 1 ship ·
     the Bruges boat · 'Celtic' ship-building · the
     Portuguese *saveiro* · the *hippos* · the gondola and
     the *dghaisa* · Mediterranean and Atlantic
     seaboard developments · sail · the evolution of
     planked craft · skin boats · reed craft

9    Scandinavia                                                  102
     Stone Age skin boats · the Bronze Age · an
     experimental skin boat · dug-outs · planked
     craft · sail · medieval developments in northern
     Europe

10   The British Isles: skin boats                               121
     Stone axe trade · Classical times · the Caergwrle
     bowl · the Broighter boat · the Bantry pillar ·
     from the Mesolithic to the medieval · Neolithic
     migrants · the building and use of skin boats ·
     Irish voyages to Iceland · skin boat survivals

11   The British Isles: wooden craft                             140
     Dug-outs · planked boats · the Brigg 'raft' · two
     Lincolnshire dug-outs · boat-building
     techniques · coins and carvings · distribution of
     skin and planked boats · the development of
     planked boats

12   European river craft                                        156
     Roman river craft · Roman guilds · 'Celtic'
     boats · types of river craft · canals and rivers ·
     propulsion

**Part III**
**Outside Europe**

*page*

13  The Indian Ocean and Arabian Gulf     171
Early Indus craft · Indus/Sumeria trade · reed
craft · Egypt and the Persian Gulf · wooden
boats · sewn boats · boat-building techniques ·
development of planked boats

14  China and Japan     185
CHINA: reed and skin · rafts and dug-outs · the
sampan · the junk · plank fastenings · masts ·
leeboards and rudders · sail · *yuloh* and
paddlewheel · the magnetic compass ·
development of sampan and junk · the dragon
boat
JAPAN: dug-outs · rafts · skin boats · bark
canoes · sewn boats · dragon boats · later
developments

15  The Pacific     200
Colonisation of the Pacific · Marquesas Islands ·
Heyerdahl's theory · Pacific craft · Maori war
canoes · other boat-building techniques ·
seamanship and navigation · the evolution of
Pacific craft · dug-outs and long-boats ·
outriggers · double canoes and rafts · chronology ·
Polynesia to America?

16  The Americas     219
THE AMERICAN CONTINENT: Birch bark · skin
boats · trans-oceanic voyages · rafts and sails
THE WEST INDIES: rafts · sail · reed craft · dug-outs

Abbreviations used in the notes     236

Notes     237

Index     255

# Illustrations

**Maps**

*page*

| | | |
|---|---|---|
| 1.1 | The Bering Strait | 5 |
| 1.2 | Sunda and Sahul Shelves | 6 |
| 4.1 | Distribution of skin boats | 38 |
| 4.2 | Britain and Ireland | 44 |
| 6.1 | Central and eastern Mediterranean | 61 |
| 8.1 | Distribution of megalithic monuments in Europe | 86 |
| 10.1 | Stone axe distribution in Britain and Ireland | 122 |
| 11.1 | Distribution of skin and planked boats in Britain and Ireland | 154 |
| 13.1 | Indian Ocean and Arabian Gulf | 183 |
| 15.1 | Pacific area, with certain radiocarbon dates | 202 |

**Figures**

| | | |
|---|---|---|
| 2.1 | Japanese raft from the Muromachi period | 8 |
| 2.2 | Model of raft from Arica, Chile | 8 |
| 2.3 | Frieze from Midau el-Tahrir, Kasr el-Nil | 9 |
| 2.4 | Fragments of linen from el-Gebelein | 10 |
| 2.5 | Jemdat Nasr seal | 11 |
| 2.6 | Silver model boat from Ur | 11 |
| 2.7 | Bark-bundle craft from Tasmania | 12 |
| 2.8 | Model of Chatham Island reed float (*waka-puhara*) | 13 |
| 2.9 | Excavated model of reed boat, Chile | 14 |
| 2.10 | Modern reed boats from Peru | 14 |
| 3.1 | Australian Aboriginal bark canoe | 18 |

*page*

| | | |
|---|---|---|
| 3.2 | Aboriginal bark painting | 18 |
| 3.3 | Bark canoes from Tierra del Fuego | 19 |
| 3.4 | Bushman painting, Basutoland | 20 |
| 3.5 | (a–f) Bark canoe building sequence | 22–3 |
| 4.1 | Rock carving from Bohuslän, Sweden | 29 |
| 4.2 | Rock carvings from Evenhus, Norway | 29 |
| 4.3 | Rock carving (?) from Val Camonica, Italy | 30 |
| 4.4 | Bow of a umiak | 30 |
| 4.5 | Inflated skin in use, China | 31 |
| 4.6 | Inflated skins used by Assyrian soldiers | 31 |
| 4.7 | Bronze Age rock carvings showing cleft bows, Norway | 32 |
| 4.8 | Cleft bows, Alaska and Aleutian Islands | 33 |
| 4.9 | Birch-bark canoe and kayak | 34 |
| 4.10 | Inflated skin floats, Valparaiso | 35 |
| 4.11 | Umiak frame | 35 |
| 4.12 | Umiak being covered | 36 |
| 4.13 | Eskimo kayak | 37 |
| 4.14 | (a) Painting from Las Figuras rock shelter, Andalusia | 43 |
| | (b) Ivory comb from the Iberian Bronze Age | 43 |
| | (c) Painting from Dolmen de Antelas, Portugal | 43 |
| 5.1 | The Pesse dug-out | 46 |
| 5.2 | The Llyn Llangorse dug-out | 47 |
| 5.3 | Multiple dug-out from Poland | 48 |
| 5.4 | Double dug-out from Finland | 49 |

ix

*page*

5.5 Building a Finnish dug-out – heating the boat 49

5.6 Building a Finnish dug-out – forcing out the sides 50

5.7 Building a Finnish dug-out – fitting washstrakes 50

5.8 Dug-out in Manila harbour, Philippines 51

5.9 The Kentmere boat 51

6.1 Phylakopi model boat 57

6.2 Contorniate coin 58

6.3 Ring from the island of Mochlos, Crete 58

6.4 Graffito from Bet She'arim, Israel 59

6.5 Painting on Cycladic vase, model Cretan dug-out and a reconstruction drawing by Landström 61

6.6 Phaistos disc 62

6.7 Carving from Naxos, Greece 63

6.8 Lead model boats from Naxos 64

6.9 Mosaic of a double-ended boat from Tunisia 65

6.10 Stele from Terenouthis 65

6.11 Engraving from 'Maison aux stucs', Delos, Greece 66

7.1 Minoan seal 68

7.2 Ship painting from Thera 68

7.3 Papyrus hunting craft 69

7.4 Cheops ship, external 69

7.5 Cheops ship, internal 70

7.6 Painting from Zawyet el-Mdin, Egypt 70

7.7 Dahshur boat 71

7.8 Relief from Mesopotamia 73

7.9 Egyptian woodworking 74

7.10 Naqada pot 76

7.11 Reconstruction drawing by Landström of early Egyptian boat 77

7.12 Cypriot vase with ship 78

7.13 Terracotta model from Amathous 78

7.14 Late Geometric vase from Dipylon, Athens 79

7.15 Reconstruction model of a round ship from Bet She'arim 79

7.16 Tomb painting of a long-ship from Jerusalem 80

*page*

7.17 Relief showing stern of Rhodian galley 83

7.18 Reconstruction drawings of ships on Trajan's Column, Rome, and the Triumphal Arch, Orange 84

8.1 Althiburus *ponto* 87

8.2 Blackfriars 1 ship during excavation 88

8.3 Blackfriars 1 ship – construction methods 89

8.4 Methods of fastening planking to frames with turned nails 90

8.5 A fragment of the Bruges boat 90

8.6 *Meia luas*, external 91

8.7 *Meia lua*, internal 91

8.8 *Saveiro* being launched 92

8.9 Early stage in building a *saveiro* 92

8.10 Making trenails 93

8.11 Aliseda brooch 94

8.12 Gallic coin with ship 94

8.13 Bronze relief on the Balawat gates 95

8.14 Khorsabad relief 95

8.15 Jal's eighteenth-century gondola 96

8.16 *Dghaisas* in Malta 97

8.17 A curragh under way 99

8.18 Oar of a *saveiro* 100

9.1 Rock carving from Evenhus, Norway 102

9.2 Rock carving from Vyg, northern Russia 104

9.3 Rock carving from Forselv, Norway 105

9.4 Eskimo drawing of umiak from Alaska 105

9.5 Harpooning scene on rock carving from Vyg, northern Russia 106

9.6 Rock carving from Gåshopen, Norway 106

9.7 Rock carving from Navestad Pyntelund, Norway 107

9.8 Rock carving from Bjornstad, Norway 107

9.9 Umiak with sun shining through it 108

9.10 Rock carving from Amoy, Norway 109

9.11 Chukchi sledge 109

9.12 Building an experimental skin boat 110

9.13 The experimental boat afloat 111

9.14 The experimental boat under way 111

*page*

9.15 Rock carving from Kalnes, Norway    111

9.16 Rock carving from Vyg, northern Russia    113

9.17 Rock carving from Nämforsen, Sweden    113

9.18 Roos Carr figures and boat    114

9.19 Loch Arthur dug-out    114

9.20 Hjortspring boat model    115

9.21 Nydam boat    115

9.22 Gokstad *faering* or ship's boat    116

9.23 Blind seam in a skin boat    117

9.24 Bronze Age engraving of a boat    118

9.25 Bremen cog    118

9.26 A seal of Harderwijk    119

9.27 A seal of New Shoreham    119

9.28 A Dorestadt coin    119

9.29 Utrecht ship    120

10.1 Caergwrle bowl – side view    124

10.2 Caergwrle bowl – underneath    124

10.3 Bronze Age shield from River Trent    125

10.4 Rock carving from Evenhus, Norway, boat with a disc    125

10.5 Rock carving from Amoy, Norway, boat with discs    125

10.6 Gold model boats from Nors, Denmark    126

10.7 Carving on west end of Lincoln Cathedral    127

10.8 Oculus on *meia lua*    127

10.9 Broighter boat model    128

10.10 Boat on the Bantry pillar    129

10.11 Curragh, Co. Kerry    129

10.12 Curragh under way    129

10.13 Captain Phillips's 'Wild Irish' wicker craft    130

10.14 Teifi coracle    130

10.15 (a, b) Two stages in building a Boyne coracle    134

10.16 (a–e) Stages in building a Kerry curragh    136–7

11.1 Liria craft    141

11.2 Bronze spearhead from North Ferriby and possible method of use    141

11.3 Sardinian bronze boat model    142

11.4 Ferriby boat 1    143

11.5 Ferriby boat 2    144

*page*

11.6 Ferriby boat 3    144

11.7 (a, b, c) Measured drawings of Ferriby boats 1, 2, 3    145

11.8 A reconstruction of Ferriby boat 1    146

11.9 A later reconstruction of Ferriby boat 1    147

11.10 The Brigg 'raft' in 1888    147

11.11 The Brigg 'raft' in 1974    148

11.12 The Brigg dug-out in 1886    149

11.13 Roman barge-shaped lamp    150

11.14 Underside of bow of *saveiro*    151

11.15 Coin of Allectus    151

11.16 Boat on Cossans stone    152

11.17 Carving in Jonathan's cave, East Wemyss, Fife    152

11.18 Jarlshof disc with boat    153

12.1 (a, b) Sections of Louvre relief    157

12.2 Vatican fresco of *codicaria*    157

12.3 Avignon barge    158

12.4 Moselle barge    159

12.5 Blessey bronze boat model    159

12.6 Coins of the Menapii    160

12.7 Boats in the Eadwine Psalter    160

12.8 Amiens boat    160

12.9 Badge of the Utricularii    161

12.10 Iron Age wooden cask    162

12.11 Ezinge chariot wheels    162

12.12 A Zwammerdam barge    163

12.13 Zwammerdam boat 3    164

12.14 The Bevaix boat    165

12.15 The Yverdon boat    165

12.16 Boat on Blussus's tombstone    166

12.17 The second Nemi ship    167

12.18 Boat on Sayala carving    168

13.1 Indus seal impression    171

13.2 Terracotta craft from Mohenjo-Daro    172

13.3 Graffito on an Indus potsherd    172

13.4 Model boat from Lothal    173

13.5 Craft in first Bahrain seal    174

13.6 Modern Bahrain reed boat    174

13.7 Rock carving from Egypt    175

13.8 Craft on second Bahrain seal    176

13.9 Craft on third Bahrain seal    176

13.10 al-Hariri's *Maqamat* illustration    177

13.11 *Masula* (sewn boat) from India    178

| | | *page* |
|---|---|---|
| 13.12 | Seventeenth-century drawing of *masula* | 179 |
| 13.13 | *Mahadalpura* boat | 179 |
| 13.14 | Andra coin with boat | 180 |
| 13.15 | *Beden-sayed* | 181 |
| 13.16 | Rafts with sail carved on the tomb of Amenophis II | 183 |
| 13.17 | Bowrey's 'cattamaran' | 184 |
| 14.1 | Ajanta painting | 185 |
| 14.2 | Northern Szechwan burial dug-out | 187 |
| 14.3 | Shang pictograph for boat | 188 |
| 14.4 | Typical modern Chinese sampan (model) | 188 |
| 14.5 | Formosan raft (model) | 189 |
| 14.6 | Foochow junk (model) | 193 |
| 14.7 | Yangtze dragon boat | 193 |
| 14.8 | Carving on an eagle bone from Sakhalin | 195 |
| 14.9 | Japanese drawing of a Russian kayak | 196 |
| 14.10 | Ainu bark boat | 197 |
| 14.11 | *Morota-bune* | 197 |
| 14.12 | Engraving on Oishi bronze bell | 198 |
| 14.13 | Commodore Perry's squadron at Kurihama, Tokyo Bay | 198 |
| 14.14 | Haniwa boat model | 199 |
| 15.1 | Sixteenth-century drawing of an outrigger canoe | 204 |
| 15.2 | Seventeenth-century drawing of a double canoe | 205 |
| 15.3 | Maori tree-felling technique | 207 |
| 15.4 | Maori log-rolling device | 207 |
| 15.5 | Maori method of tightening lashings | 208 |

| | | *page* |
|---|---|---|
| 15.6 | Maori and Fijian lashing methods | 209 |
| 15.7 | Maori war canoe (model) | 209 |
| 15.8 | Easter Island canoe | 210 |
| 15.9 | Wall painting from Niah caves, Sarawak | 212 |
| 15.10 | Small dug-outs excavated in Niah caves, Sarawak | 213 |
| 15.11 | Long-boat on bronze drum from Ngoc-lu, Vietnam | 214 |
| 15.12 | Double outrigger canoe | 215 |
| 15.13 | Dug-out with stabilisers | 215 |
| 15.14 | Borobodur ship carving | 216 |
| 15.15 | Log raft from the Solomon Islands | 217 |
| 16.1 | Canoes of Oonalashka | 220 |
| 16.2 | Boat carving on bodkin from Cape Krusenstern, Alaska | 221 |
| 16.3 | Fifteenth- or sixteenth-century umiak from Greenland | 221 |
| 16.4 | Valdivia pottery, Ecuador | 222 |
| 16.5 | A balsa raft | 224 |
| 16.6 | Madox's raft seen in 1582 | 225 |
| 16.7 | George van Spilbergen's raft | 226 |
| 16.8 | (a–f) Evolution of Oceanic sails | 226 |
| 16.9 | Benzoni's rafts (sixteenth century) | 227 |
| 16.10 | (a) Drawing of a *jangada* raft | 227 |
| | (b) Modern *jangada* off the Brazilian coast | 228 |
| 16.11 | Modern raft with *guares* | 228 |
| 16.12 | *Guares* or leeboards | 229 |
| 16.13 | Sailing raft from Gambier Island, Tuamotu Archipelago | 233 |
| 16.14 | Gold model raft from Lake Guatavita, Colombia | 233 |

# Foreword

Paul Johnstone long had my admiration and esteem, so that when Mrs Barbara Johnstone asked me to prepare *The Sea-craft of Prehistory* for publication, I was pleased to accept. In his many BBC Television productions, especially the *Chronicle* series, Paul presented archaeology in an entertaining and yet most instructive way, and his death in March 1976 was a great loss.

Paul had a special interest in boats, stemming from his wartime service in the Royal Navy, and from 1962 he contributed papers on the early history of boat-building and boat use to *Antiquity*, the *Mariner's Mirror* and the *International Journal of Nautical Archaeology*. Several of his *Chronicle* programmes were also about boats and ships: the Skuldelev ships, the Graveney boat and the Bremen cog, to name but three. During the last ten years of his life he compiled the material and formulated the concepts upon which this book is based, and by the time he died he had written over 150,000 words and amassed a considerable number of illustrations.

My main task has been to reduce Paul's text to publishable size, to select and identify the illustrations, and to revise references where new editions of works, such as Grahame Clark's *World Prehistory*, had become available.

In tackling the text reduction I was helped by the fact that several of the original eighteen chapters were complete articles in themselves, although they overlapped in time and in place with other chapters. I could therefore replace repetitive passages by cross-references. I was also able to delete material where the author's enthusiasm had taken him too far from his main theme of boat-building and boat use. In addition, I combined four chapters on skin boats into the present chapters 4 and 10, and I integrated a West Indies chapter with that on America. Throughout this task I aimed to retain the essential Paul Johnstone.

Paul's references to the dug-out canoe and his theories on its evolution and its place in the development of planked boats were scattered throughout the early part of the text. I thought it appropriate to bring these together in chapter 5. To this chapter, and also to chapters 8, 10, 11, and 12, I have added material from recent research where my specialist knowledge proved relevant, but I have sought to do this within the author's basic philosophy and argument. Throughout the book I have aimed to let Paul Johnstone's scholarship and distinctive approach stand on its own merits; I have not, for example, modified his interpretations on the occasions I hold somewhat different views.

Paul had difficulty in choosing a title which accurately reflected the scope of the book, for there is much in it about rivers and other inland waterways as well as the sea. Neither I nor the publisher have been able to think of a more appropriate title that was not too cumbersome, and therefore 'Sea-craft' it remains.

A glance at the contents page will reveal the emphasis placed on craft other than planked boats and dug-out canoes. These two types are in fact described and discussed in detail, but one of the great merits of Paul's work is the prominence he has given to craft of logs, reed, bark and skin which have often been undervalued, and indeed overlooked, by previous writers, but which must have been widely used in early times. An equally important prominence is given to elucidating the virtues and limitations of recent simple boat forms, with accounts of how they were built and used in conditions which allow parallels to be drawn with the prehistoric period.

Having finished this task, I am aware how widely Paul Johnstone read, in spite of his very busy life. It is also clear that he lost no opportunity to seek out material, both archaeological and ethnographic, which might help to explain the early history of Man the boat-builder and boat-user. I believe that this book will not only be of value to those working in the fields of nautical prehistory and archaeology, but will also help dry-land archaeologists and people with a general interest in history to appreciate the nautical aspects of antiquity.

I wish to thank Dr Derek Roe for advice on aspects of the first four chapters, Anne Yates who prepared the maps and the index, Marilla Fletcher who typed the revised parts of the text, and Camilla Raab of Routledge & Kegan Paul Ltd whose close reading of the script led to the correction of many inconsistencies and omissions.

Seán McGrail
Chilmark
July 1979

# Introduction

With the possible exception of an occasional wicker coracle, nothing but seagulls and shags disturbed the estuaries of the Thames, the Mersey and the Clyde.[1] So wrote Admiral Ballard as late as 1919 about the waters round Britain during the second millennium BC in an otherwise seamanlike and scholarly study of the Egyptian ships carved at Deir el-Bahri. 'It is simpler to conclude', said Lionel Casson, an authority to whom anyone interested in early seafaring is deeply indebted, in 1959, 'that the beads of Egyptian faience which have been found in Britain and the necklaces of green phosphate from the Near East which have turned up in prehistoric contexts in Brittany reached their destinations after long overland journeys.'[2]

The recent explosive sweep of archaeology has put those two cautious estimates of maritime prehistory very much in doubt. As Professor Stuart Piggott has said,[3] archaeology is now constantly and rapidly developing in a way more familiar to those who work in scientific fields than in the older disciplines. This dynamic accumulation of new information has set marine historians and pre-historians some interesting problems. In the past, great figures have worked on the available nautical evidence, and how much one owes them for this – Paris, Torr, Kirk, Casson, Anderson, Brogger and Shetelig, Adeney, Hornell and many more. But now we have the interesting situation that archaeology is evolving a more and more detailed world model, with many nautical implications which are often not reflected in the known nautical material. The early dates for the presence of man in Australia and the West Indies are two examples. Radiocarbon dating and wider investigations are establishing situations to which land-bridges during periods of lowered sea-levels are all too easy an answer and one which does not always have the proper geological support.

I have tried in this book to look at some of this new archaeological information and see how it can be related to existing nautical knowledge, and whether thereby the two can be mutually illuminated.

Anyone taking the whole world as his setting can justly be accused of rashness, if nothing worse. However, I thought it might be useful to try and collect together such relevant material as I could find, as it is often sparse and buried in other material, and it is surprising in how many otherwise excellent works one can look in vain in the index for any entry under boats, ships, canoes, dug-outs and so on.

I have also included a number of descriptions from recent or contemporary sources of the making of various types of primitive craft. These ethnographic examples have to be used extremely cautiously if parallels with early periods are sought. Nevertheless I think it can be useful to be reminded of the capacities, often far greater than one might imagine at first, of societies at different technological levels.

I have also been free-handed about what can be called a prehistoric ship. I have stopped short of the ships of Queen Hatshepsut, Greek and Roman galleys, the evolved ships of the Vikings, and all but the fringes of the Chinese material so admirably covered by Joseph Needham,[4] because all these are well written up by much better qualified people and they also come truly into historical contexts. On the other hand I have considered the ships of the Veneti, the Utrecht and Bruges boats, the 'Celtic' river vessels, and also the craft of the Dark Age Irish monks, because although all these also occur well within historic periods, they are closely related to pre-literate situations and it is often to archaeology that one has to turn for any additional information about them.

Something else this Introduction enables me to do is to thank the various people who have helped me, amongst them the Director and Librarian of the Institute of Archaeology, the Director and Librarian of the National Maritime Museum, the Keeper and Assistant Keeper of the Department of Egyptology at the British Museum, and the Director of the Hull Museum. Ted Wright, Ole Crumlin-Pedersen, Clinton Edwards, Sverre Marstrander, Detlev Ellmers, David Goddard, Beat Arnold, Valerie Fenwick, Angela Evans, Anna Ritchie, Alec Tilley, Lucien Basch, and Michael Katzev have all given me generous and helpful advice and information. Mrs Easy wrestled nobly with the vagaries of typing the manuscript. Above all I owe much gratitude to Professor Stuart Piggott and Professor Glyn Daniel for their interest and support over the years, all the more because it was given unstintingly to someone with no formal connection with archaeology. They may well shake their heads over the result, but without their encouragement this book would certainly never have been written. For its shortcomings and mistakes they are in no way responsible.

Barnes, 1975

# Acknowledgments

We would like to express our thanks for permission to reproduce the following material: the National Maritime Museum, London: Figs 2.1, 3.3, 4.10, 5.3, 5.8, 9.27, 11.9, 11.10, 11.11, 11.12, 13.15, 14.1, 14.4, 14.5, 14.6, 14.8, 14.9, 15.7, 15.12, 15.15, 16.1, 16.13; the Trustees of the British Museum: Figs 2.6, 7.6, 7.10, 7.12, 7.13, 8.13, 11.3, 11.15, 12.7, 15.11, 16.6; Crown Copyright. Science Museum, London: Figs 4.5, 14.3; the National Museum of Antiquities of Scotland: Figs 9.19, 11.7; the National Museum of Ireland: Figs 10.9, 10.15a, b, 10.16 a–e; the National Museum of Wales: Figs 5.2, 10.1, 10.2, 10.14; Exeter Maritime Museum and David Goddard: Fig. 8.8; Archaeology Museum, Kingston upon Hull: Fig. 9.18; County Museum, Lerwick, Shetland: Fig. 11.18; City of Sheffield Museum: Fig. 10.3; Department of Antiquities, Ashmolean Museum, Oxford: Figs 6.8, 7.1; the Master and Fellows of Magdalene College, Cambridge: Figs 10.13, 15.2; the British Broadcasting Corporation: Fig. 6.6; the National Monuments Record: Fig. 10.7; the Hudson's Bay Company: Fig. 4.9; the Mansell Collection: Figs 4.6, 12.2; David Attenborough: Fig. 15.14; Peter Marsden: Fig. 8.4; Peter Marsden and the editor of the *Mariner's Mirror* (the quarterly journal of the Society for Nautical Research): Fig. 8.3; Peter Marsden and the Press Association Ltd: Fig. 8.2; Jesco von Puttkamer and Adrian Cowell: Fig. 16.10a; Colin Renfrew: Fig. 14.14b; Michael Rice and Anthony James: Figs 13.5, 13.8, 13.9; David Wilson: Fig. 5.9; E. V. Wright: Figs 11.4, 11.5, 11.6, 11.7, 11.8, 13.11, 13.13; E. V. Wright, John Coates and the National Maritime Museum: Fig. 11.9; Cambridge University Press: Fig. 14.2; Jonathan Cape Ltd and Alfred A. Knopf Inc.: Fig. 4.3; the Egypt Exploration Society: Figs 7.9, 13.7; the editor of the *Mariner's Mirror*: Figs 14.7, 16.10a; the editor of the *Mariner's Mirror* and LeBaron Bowen: Figs 13.1, 13.3; the editor of the *Mariner's Mirror* and the Hakluyt Society: Figs 13.12, 13.17; Methuen & Co. Ltd: Fig. 4.1 and text quotations; Oxford University Press: Fig. 4.14a; the editor of the *Proceedings of the Prehistoric Society*: Figs 11.2a, b; Thames & Hudson Ltd: Figs 4.14c, 11.1; Williams and James (trustees for A. Evans): Figs 6.2, 6.3; the Trustees of the Australian Museum, Sydney: Fig. 3.2; the National Museum of Man of the National Museums of Canada, Ottawa: Figs 4.11, 4.12; Fred Bruemmer, Montreal: Fig. 4.13; the Canterbury Museum, Christchurch: Fig. 2.8; the Government Printing Office, Wellington: Figs 15.3, 15.4, 15.5, 15.6; the Board of the Burgomaster and Aldermen of the City of Antwerp: Fig. 8.5; Lucien Basch: Figs 6.11, 7.18; the National Museum of Denmark: Figs 9.20, 10.6; Egil Knuth, Copenhagen: Fig. 16.3; the National Board of Antiquities and Historical Monuments, Helsinki: Figs 5.5, 5.6, 5.7; Bibliothèque Nationale, Paris: Figs 2.7, 3.1, 8.12, 8.15, 12.6, 13.10, 15.1; Musée du Louvre, Paris: Figs 7.14, 8.14; Musée Archéologique de Dijon: Fig. 12.5; Roger-Viollet, Paris: Figs 6.9, 9.26, 12.3; Photographie Giraudon, Paris: Fig. 12.1; Staatliche Museen zu Berlin: Fig. 2.5; Museum für Völkerkunde,

Berlin: Fig. 16.12; Focke-Museum, Bremen: Fig. 9.25; Deutsches Schiffahrtsmuseum, Bremerhaven: Fig. 11.13; Mittelrheinisches Landesmuseum, Mainz: Figs 12.10, 12.16; Schleswig-Holsteinisches Landesmuseum für Vor- und Frühgeschichte, Schloss Gottorp: Fig. 9.21; Rheinisches Landesmuseum, Trier: Fig. 12.4; Soprintendenza alle Antichità (Egittologia), Turin: Fig. 2.4; Fototechna Unione, Rome: Figs 7.17, 12.17; Koninklijk Kabinet van Munten, The Hague: Fig. 9.28; Subfaculteit der Pre- en Protohistorie, Universiteit van Amsterdam: Figs 12.12, 12.13; Biologisch-Archaeologisch Instituut, State University, Groningen: Fig. 5.1; Centraal Museum der Gemeente Utrecht: Fig. 9.29; Universitetcts Oldsaksamling, Oslo: Fig. 9.8; Sverre Marstrander: Figs 4.7, 9.3, 9.4, 9.7, 9.9, 9.11, 9.24; Björn Landström: Fig. 6.5; International Book Production, Stockholm: Figs 6.1, 7.7, 7.11; Jean-Christian Spahni, Geneva: Figs 2.9, 2.10; the editor of *Helvetia Archaeologica*, Zurich: Fig. 12.15; the American Museum of Natural History, New York: Fig. 2.2; the Kelsey Museum, the University of Michigan: Fig. 6.10; the University Museum, University of Pennsylvania: Fig. 13.2; Clinton R. Edwards: Figs 15.13, 16.7, 16.9, 16.11; Clifford Evans and Betty J. Meggers: Fig. 16.4; Aldine-Atherton, Inc.: Map 1.2; Alfred A. Knopf, Fig. 16.2; Peabody Museum Publications: Figs 13.14, 16.8; Smithsonian Institution Publications: Figs 3.5a–f, 9.23; the Bernice P. Bishop Museum, Honolulu: Fig. 15.8; Museo del Oro, Banco de la República, Bogota: Fig. 16.14; the Egyptian Museum, Cairo: Fig. 2.3; Ahmed Youssef: Figs 7.4, 7.5; the Archaeological Survey of India: Fig. 13.4; the Director-General of Antiquities, Baghdad: Fig. 7.8; the Institute of Archaeology, the Hebrew University of Jerusalem: Figs 6.4, 7.15; the Israel Department of Antiquities and Museums: Fig. 7.16; the Tokyo National Museum: Fig. 14.14; Yokosuka City Museum: Fig. 14.13; the Sarawak Museum: Figs 15.9, 15.10; the publishers have taken all possible care to trace the ownership of copyright material and to acknowledge it fully.

# Part One

# General Survey of Early Types of Water Transport

# 1 Earliest times

Between 500,000 and 1,000,000 years ago, emergent Man made his way from the lightly wooded country of tropical Africa to the deserts of North Africa, the temperate woodlands of Europe and the forest tundra of Europe and Asia. There is little doubt about the starting-point of these travels since most authorities now agree that the first signs of human activity known to us, the manufacture of primitive stone tools, occurred in the African continent. This agreement extends also to the place for the evolution of *Homo erectus*. It was from Africa that this genus started to spread as an ancestral stock of modern man from Morocco to China and from South Africa to Germany.[1] It is hard to believe that in this progress all the water barriers encountered were crossed by swimming alone.

The meagre and often difficult archaeological evidence for this expansion, fossil bones, stone tools, occasional wood or bone implements, or the even rarer living site, throws little light on this point, except in one case. If one looks at the distribution of these Early Stone Age remains, they are more concentrated in Africa, western and eastern Europe and southern and eastern Asia. There is thus a gap of a sort through central Europe to the Adriatic and Mediterranean.[2] Furthermore, there are similarities between the north-west African finds and those in south-west Europe. All this may be due to the chances of archaeological survival, but it might also have some significance. Since the geological evidence[3] shows that the Straits of Gibraltar have been in

existence during the last two million or so years it looks as though there is at least a case for the first sea voyage having taken place in sight of the Pillars of Hercules.

There are problems, though, about this suggested drifting from Africa to Spain on a log or a piece of flotsam. One is the point at which the homonids learnt to swim. When our remote ancestors took to walking upright on two feet, they took an immensely important step towards the evolution of *Homo sapiens* by freeing the hands for tool-making and the consequent mental stimulation involved. At the same time they lost the faculty which four-footed animals have of being able to walk into water and then swim merely by continuing more or less the same action. The great apes in fact are prevented by their anatomical structure from using either an over-arm or a breast-stroke action and, not surprisingly, dislike and fear water. A good practical illustration of this is the shallow moat which sometimes confines these beasts on islands in zoos. The hominids must therefore have learnt to swim as a new achievement, and one would assume that no one would have attempted a crossing of the Straits of Gibraltar, even on some sort of float or raft, without this ability.

While, on the whole, Palaeolithic sites on the coast are rare, in England they seem frequently to cluster around rivers, such as the Thames and Medway in Kent or by lakes, like Hoxne in East Anglia. Remains of fish do not often occur on such sites,[4] so there must be more interest in the evidence from some Lower Palaeolithic sites in Africa and Spain which suggests that hunted beasts were deliberately driven into swampy areas on the edges of rivers and lakes where they could be trapped in the mud and caught.[5] For it cannot have been a long step in that situation to straddling a mass of floating reeds, or a floating log, and then turning eventually to the marine occupants of the lake, as well as the beasts floundering on its edges.

On the other hand, at least one study has emphasised the importance of the relative absence of fish from the Mousterian sites of Neanderthal man (70,000–30,000 BC), since the single specimens of fishes found at Salzgitter-Lebenstedt in northern Germany have to be set against the remains there of eighty reindeer and sixteen mammoths.[6] What is suggested is that Virchow's hundred-year-old diagnosis, that rickets accounted for the peculiar simian cast of some Neanderthal skeletons,[7] can now be much more strongly maintained by modern anthropological and medical knowledge. According to Ivanhoe, the extreme variability of some Neanderthal skeletons can be related to two things, latitude and climate. North of latitude 40°, the lack of solar ultraviolet light, particularly in a cold period when caves or tents or furs would reduce the skin's exposure to sunlight even further, necessitates an outside source of vitamin D. Two particularly rich sources are egg-yolks and fatty fish. While much of the evidence is negative, such as the absence of specialised fishing equipment or fish-remains at Mousterian sites, the general impression is certainly that Neanderthal man made very little use of fish. So it is not surprising that teeth and bone samples from Neanderthal fossil material have yielded unequivocal evidence of serious vitamin D deficiency and conditions practically specific of rickets.[8] Moreover the further a sample is from the Equator and the more positively it can be dated to periods of unfavourable climate, the more it shows these symptoms. Deformation from rickets would go a long way to explaining some of the Neanderthal characteristics, so instead of having him as an odd sort of throwback, he would fit much more easily into a gradual transition from *Homo erectus* to *Homo sapiens*.

While this is a controversial theory, there is another of Ivanhoe's conclusions that is widely accepted and relevant to possible early water travel. This is that the most important element of the more recent cultures (30,000 BC and later) was the development of fishing by means of an expressly developed tool assemblage which contributed substantially and routinely to the diet.[9] The presence of fish-bones like the vertebrae necklace from Barma Grande, of fishing equipment like the fish-gorge from La Ferrassie in the Dordogne, and of representations of fish such as the one on the Montgaudier baton are confirmatory evidence.[10]

So this then may well imply that while roughly in the Mousterian period there was little attempt to catch fish and therefore go on the water either accidentally or deliberately, a sharp change occurred during the succeeding period of the Upper Palaeolithic. As well as fishing being reflected in the finds of fish-bones and fishing tools of this period, it would also imply a much greater temptation to go beyond wading depth among the now rickets-free Aurignacian people in their unconscious hunt for fatty-fish oil.

What Grahame Clark and Stuart Piggott call the first great climax of human achievement occurred in the later stages of the Late Pleistocene between 35,000 and 10,000 BC,[11] when the Upper Palaeolithic peoples occupied the American continent and also Australia. Some writers have suggested that the first immigration from eastern Asia along the Pacific shores into America took place as much as 40,000 years ago, with another subsequently from central Siberia.[12] Both might presumably have used the land-bridge between the Chukchi Peninsula in Siberia and the Seward Peninsula in Alaska (see Map 1.1). The continental shelf there is both wide and shallow, and if the locking-up of waters in the glaciers lowered the sea-level by as little as 150 feet relative to today's level, it is calculated[13] that a 200-mile-wide bridge would have emerged. Nor would glaciation have blocked the way. Both sides of the Bering Strait and the land-bridge itself appear to have been free of permanent ice. On the other hand, the to-and-fro movements of animals and plant species alike would appear to have needed a

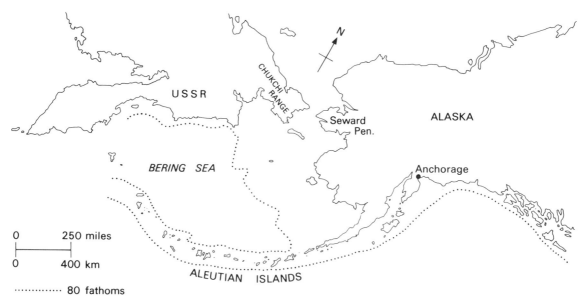

Map 1.1    *Siberia and Alaska and the Bering Strait*

longer and warmer link than geological evidence can supply at the moment, and, as we shall see, it is at least possible to suppose that the earliest inhabitants of America had craft capable of short sea crossings or island-hopping.

Man first came to Australia, too, by sea during this same period. After years of what D. J. Mulvaney once called 'exotic claims by Australian optimists', a series of radiocarbon dates from sites such as Lake Mungo and Kow Swamp have established not only that man reached Australia 40,000 years ago, but that one can also claim for Australia the earliest record of human cremation sites and some of the earliest occurrences of art.[14] As Mulvaney says, going simply by the growing body of evidence from south-east Asia and Australia, it is now possible to suggest that man may have possessed water-craft considerably earlier in his technological history than hitherto believed.[15]

Even though the shallow Sahul Shelf joined New Guinea to Australia and the Sunda Shelf linked Borneo and Java during one of the Late Glacial stages (Map 1.2), migrating man, in contrast to the uncertain progress of the first

Americans, would amost certainly have had to make a sea crossing of at least 180 kilometres on the Java–Timor island-hopping route and 95 kilometres on the Celebes–Moluccas one.[16]

In due course more detailed geochronological methods such as thorium-protoactinium dating,[17] deep sea cores and a better understanding of the effect of the orbital precession of the earth's long axis on the amount of radiation falling on the polar ice-caps may help to settle the problem of the rise and fall of sea-levels during the last 100,000 years. We will then know better whether the answer to such immigrations lies in land-bridges, which have perhaps on occasion been a little too easily called on to explain how they were achieved, or if in fact the evidence shows that early man must have travelled by water.

Man undoubtedly used water-craft during the Palaeolithic period, but we cannot say exactly what types of craft these were. Nevertheless, by examining the distribution of the earliest known examples of water transport, and by looking at the range of craft recently in use in pre-industrial societies, and knowing Palaeolithic man's technological capabilities, an informed estimate can be

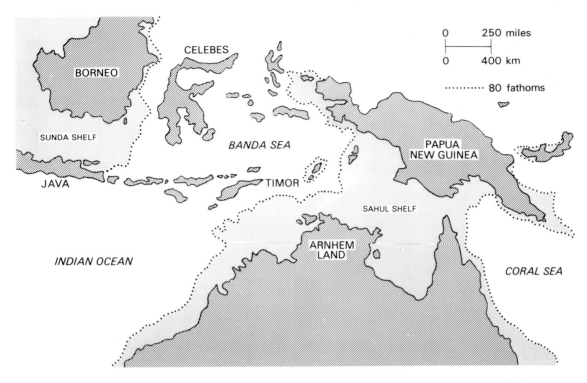

Map 1.2    *The East Indies, Papua New Guinea and northern Australia, with the Sunda and Sahul Shelves (after Butz* Environment and Archaeology, *1972)*

made of the craft probably used in the environment then prevailing. These matters are examined in the next three chapters. In the final chapter of Part I the dug-out canoe and its place in the evolution of the planked boat is considered.

# 2 Raft and reed

## The single log

Traditionally man's first craft is assumed to have been a floating log, the fortuitous gift of a swollen river – not that any evidence is ever likely to emerge to decide for or against this theory. Such a single unworked log has serious limitations, and real advance would not be possible until the development of some form of contrived craft. Although the use of fire was known, there is not much reason to suppose that these early hunters of the Lower Palaeolithic had either the tools or the margin of time available to stay in one place long enough for the fairly lengthy and elaborate operation of hollowing-out a dug-out. Similar considerations apply to the bark canoe. The abundance and wide distribution of flint scrapers suggest the skin clothing which must have made possible the northward advance into colder lands. Yet there is nothing in these collections which imply sewing or extensive fastening, so any rudimentary form of skin boat is ruled out at this early stage.

Thus it seems easier to say what early craft would not have been rather than what they were. However, an examination of the simple forms of water-craft used by people of the recent past may throw some light on this matter and show how early man may have progressed from the postulated single-log stage in his mastery of water transport.

Single logs ridden astride were still in use recently off the coast of Queensland, as they were in Ashanti,[1] and Belzoni saw one such craft in Egypt that had a cross-bar fitted at each end to give extra stability, and a mast and sail.[2] Olive MacLeod has described how the Buduma people of Lake Chad used to cross water on a single piece of ambach, which is the Arab name for *Herminiera elaphroxylon*, a shrub with very light buoyant stems.[3] These pieces are nearly 3 metres long, as thick as a man's leg, with one end slightly curved up to act as a prow. The traveller sat astride it and propelled himself by an over-arm paddling action. Similar floats were also used in Dahomey and the Upper Nile.

## The log raft

To join the two logs together with a creeper would certainly not be a very difficult next step. Indeed natural rafts of flotsam might have served as well, in the first place, as washed-away trees. The biologist H. H. Brindley has described[4] a raft of ambach logs which was used early this century for crossing the Nile in the Bari region of Uganda. This was so crude that it was made up each time it was needed from logs left lying about at crossing-places, and the traveller apparently always had to wait while this was done, as it was not permanent enough to be left ready for use. Brindley considered that the next stage of development was exemplified by a raft used by the Dakkas of the White Nile, which was also made of ambach strips but with a very simple shaping into boat form, the two sides being rounded off and the blunt bow having a slight rise.[5] A further advance was the ambach craft of the Shilluk people of the White Nile, which came to a pronounced point with a definite upturned bow. The final stage, also observed on the White Nile, was to add bundles to each side of a craft like this to give it more freeboard.

Nishimura has suggested a similar progression in the Far East from a first stage where logs are simply lashed side by side, a method that existed until recently in the Japanese highlands.[6] Then there are alternative stages. In one, cross-bars are added; in the other, layers running in opposite directions build up the height of the craft, as in the Far Eastern rafts of the Yalu and Amur Rivers.[7] The third and most advanced stage is when the cross-bars are inserted through holes in the logs, as in the rafts of Chiyoi Jyu Island,[8] or the balsa *prer* of the Palau Islands, west of the Carolines.[9] A 'freighter' type of raft[10] was well described by William Dampier in the 1680s making long voyages between Lima and the Bay of Panama.[11]

The bottom . . . is made of 20 or 30 great trees of about 20, 30, or 40 foot long . . . On top of these they place another shorter row of trees across them, pinn'd fast to each other, and then pinn'd to the undermost row . . . From this bottom the raft is raised to about 10 foot higher, with rows of posts sometimes set upright, and supporting a floor or two.

2.1   *Japanese raft from the Muromachi period with cross-bars inserted through the logs (National Maritime Museum)*

2.2   *Model of pre-Columbian raft excavated from a site near Arica, Chile, by Dr Junius Bird (American Museum of Natural History, New York)*

At the higher levels, only the side and end layers were added, so that a 'room', as Dampier called it, was left in the middle. The distinguishing feature of this 'freighter' raft seems to be its many layers.[12]

A tapered shape and an odd number of logs seem to be significant factors in traditional raft-making almost everywhere. They can be observed for instance in many Indian catamarans of logs lashed together, in the Japanese *nabe buta* of the Hida River,[13] in the sailing raft of Mangareva in the south Pacific observed by Captain Beechey when he discovered the island in 1825,[14] and in many South American examples, including the charming little pre-Columbian models (Figure 2.2) excavated by Junius Bird near Arica in Chile.[15]

Often with this tapered shape and uneven number of logs goes the practice of fastening the logs together with sharpened hardwood pins. Lionel Wafer, a surgeon and former shipmate of Dampier, described a Panamanian example in the seventeenth century:[16]

They take logs of wood not very big, and bind them together collaterally with Maho-Cords, making of them a kind of floor. Then they lay another Range of Log across these, at some distance from each other, and peg them down to the former with long Pins of Macaw-wood; and the wood of the Float is so soft, and tenacious withal, that it easily gives admittance to the Peg upon driving, and closes fast about it.

Dampier noticed the practice also, as did George Shelvocke off California in 1720,[17] and other examples have been reported from Africa, India, Australia, Melanesia, New Zealand and Brazil.

This leads Clinton Edwards to suggest that the

2.3   *Frieze from Midau el-Tahrir, Kasr El-Nil, Cairo, showing papyrus craft with fighting boatmen (Egyptian Museum, Cairo)*

combination of tapered shape and pinning invite inquiry as examples of possibly very old practices.[18] The 'possibly' in this sentence underlines the problem here. It is virtually out of the question to relate such practices to archaeological contexts. There is, however, plenty of literary evidence, as will be seen later, for ancient raft usage in the Mediterranean and by the Egyptians. In China, Ling Shun-Sheng thinks there is legendary evidence for the use of sailing rafts in the fourth millennium BC,[19] and Nishimura believed that the raft was the most likely craft in which Japan was originally reached.[20] In the Pacific a number of myths suggest that the raft was in use there before the outrigger and double canoe. In many other parts of the world, such as Australia, India, South America and the Caribbean, rafts were known to early peoples. So perhaps the best one can do is to say that this evidence confirms what is already generally accepted, the great antiquity of the raft. As Hornell observed of Indian rafts in general, however apparently crude they were, each part had its definite shape and position and, though there are a very large number of varied types, the design is still standardised within each locality.[21] This is another reflection of the great age of the raft and therefore the crucial part it played in man's early water-crossing, to say nothing of its later importance in Chinese, Pacific and South American seas.

## The reed boat

The reed-bundle or bark-bundle craft is a form of raft, but it has such individual characteristics and played such a considerable part in early maritime history that it is worth considering in a category of its own. It is, for instance, the most significant primitive craft in the area of Africa roughly confined between Lakes Victoria, Tana and Chad,[22] in a region associated with earliest man.

## Egypt

The significance of craft made from reeds is that the most simple form is a bundle. Equally their greater flexibility compared with logs has a great potential, which was in fact to be realised very significantly in early historical times. Undoubtedly the most important development of the papyrus or reed boat took place in ancient Egypt. This means, among other things, that there is a good pictorial record of the process. As Hornell has pointed out,[23] it is possible to see details like the rope lashings which held the bundles of papyrus together become conventionalised into painted lines on the wooden hulls of the ships of Rameses III or those in the Theban tombs, while the characteristic motif which originally came from the splay of the bundles of reeds beyond the end lashing became the papyrus umbel which was subsequently a hallmark of Queen Hatshepsut's sea-going ships.

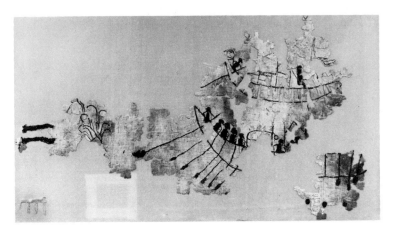

2.4  *Fragments of linen from El-Gebelein with reed craft (Soprintendenza alle Antichità Egizie, Turin)*

A factor besides sheer traditionalism which helped this process was the shortage of long timber in Egypt. This led eventually, when imported cedar of Lebanon was not available, to a complicated technique of using small pieces of acacia and sycamore, which Herodotus[24] likened to the laying of bricks in the building of a wall. It has also been suggested that in the early stages, as well as being copies from reed-bundle boats, Egyptian craft kept the long overhang fore and aft for the convenience of loading and unloading by running one end up the bank of the Nile.[25] This seems a good point because any similar feature is lacking in sea-going craft, where waves and beaching dictate a different design. Perhaps, however, it was found in time that while the overhang forward was convenient, it was safer if the after extremity was curved up to give some protection when running before the wind. Since reed structures are not self-supporting like wooden ones, the simplest way to achieve rigidity was to bend the aftermost reed bundle as far forward as it would go and then lash it to the hull. Such is the conservatism of sailors and ship-builders (a factor that runs constantly through this book), that this stern bent over towards the bow survived in the Mediterranean right through Greek and Roman times and even in recent Venetian small craft.[26]

Another feature of the reed boat was the bipod mast. Since there was no keel or even an extra strong member to take the strain of a mast foot, this thrust was halved by having two legs to the mast, each with a forked foot to straddle a bundle, a solution which was also reached in similar circumstances in South America. Unlike the outline of the hull, however, this feature did not long survive the changeover to a wooden hull.

## Mesopotamia

In the other great centre of civilisation in the ancient Middle East, Mesopotamia, there may have been a similar start to the story of water-craft there, but local circumstances soon led to a different development. On cylinder seals from the Jemdat Nasr period of about 3200 BC there are craft which have lashings holding down the recurved bow and stern which are so typical of reed-bundle craft (Figure 2.5). R. D. Barnett has pointed out that these were certainly in use in early Sumerian times, since the cuneiform sign for a ship is derived from this design.[27] But then the special local factor intervened. The availability of bitumen enabled the boat-builders of the Tigris and Euphrates to overcome one of the chief defects of the reed craft, the short-lived nature of its buoyancy. A reed framework covered with bitumen produced a combination of a flexible shape and a smooth featureless exterior without lashings, sewing, planks or cross-beam ends. This is well illustrated in the attractive silver model from Ur (Figure 2.6), and by the craft carved on a piece of

2.5   *Reed craft on a cylinder seal of the Jemdat Nasr period, c. 3000 BC (Staatliche Museen zu Berlin)*

2.6   *Silver model boat from Ur (British Museum)*

Babylonian terracotta in Rouen Museum (Museum no. 241).

Craft like this, either solid bundles or woven from reeds and covered with bitumen, were later described by Strabo,[28] and survived into fairly recent times for Sir Austen Layard to compare the *tiradas* or black boats of the Tigris and Euphrates of his day with those shown in the bas-reliefs of Nineveh, commenting with Victorian condescension, 'how little the barbarous inhabitants of these great swamps have changed after the lapse of nearly 3,000 years'.[29]

R. R. Chesney[30] gave a good description of the finishing work on one of these black boats made at Hit on the Euphrates in 1835. When the framework of interleaved branches and reeds was completed, some bitumen was warmed over a fire. Then, when sand and earth had been mixed into it to give the right consistency the mixture was applied inside and out with a wooden roller, giving ultimately a surface which was smooth, hard and waterproof.

## Africa

Away from the two great centres of ancient civilisation, it is perhaps worth including modern primitive examples in any survey of the distri-

bution of reed craft. South of the main African area of occurrence in the upper Nile, and in Lakes Victoria, Tana and Chad, there are the reed-bundle rafts used on the Okavango swamps of former Northern Bechuanaland.[31] These have a floor of four bundles of reeds with two larger bundles forming the sides and joining to give pointed and slightly upturned ends.

More significant perhaps are the reed boats shown in the well-known Tassili paintings in the Sahara. The fishermen among the primitive pastoralists who painted these used fish-hooks of stone and bone to catch their prey in the lagoons and rivers which still existed in the southern Sahara perhaps five thousand years ago.[32] Admittedly these craft date from much later than the Late Pleistocene expansion of mankind, but then they are comparatively evolved types with their blunt-ended crescent shapes and elaborate lashings. An interesting point in support of their identification as reed boats is the continued use and existence of reeds (*Typha* sp.) today in the Sahara, no longer for making boats but as a source of fuel and food.[33] In the moister Early Holocene, reeds could have been even more widespread, and the Tassili craft and modern survivals on the Ras ed-Dura lagoons in north-west Morocco and the River Lucus on the Moroccan Atlantic coast[34] could be relics of a widespread belt of usage across North Africa from the Nile to the Atlantic. It is not without significance either that today the Lake Chad area is the only one in Africa which matches the Upper Nile in diversity of surviving reed craft.[35]

## The Mediterranean

In the Oristano swamps of Sardinia fishermen use a one-man raft of two reed bundles with a third smaller one fastened vertically to make a beak-head.[36] (The reed boats of Corfu are discussed in chapter 6.)

In France there is an interesting hint from the Gallo-Roman period of reed boats there. It occurs in the text of the will of a Gallo-Roman man of the Lingones tribe who occupied the Langres region of the Haute-Marne.[37] In the last clause of the tenth-century AD transcript of this will he specifies the possessions he wants to be burnt with him including 'navem Liburnam ex scirpo', which presumably one would translate as 'a light reed boat'. The Illyrians of the Adriatic coast were the originators in the second century BC of the first *liburnian*, a type of fast war-ship, which eventually gave its name to any swift and light craft. *Scirpo* is a rush, rather different from the withies used to make the framework of a skin boat, so this may have been a bulrush craft.

## Europe to India

To the east, the fishermen in the swamps of Lake Balaton in Hungary have added a light wooden framework, but their craft is still basically a reed raft with an upturned stem.[38] Further east still, reed craft can be found, according to Hornell,[39] in a more or less continuous chain from Iraq to Iran, Afghanistan and on to India. Their presence in the Arabian Gulf and the Harappan (Indus) civilisation in the second millennium BC will be described in chapter 13.

## Tasmania

From the Indian subcontinent to the next occurrence to the south-east, in Tasmania, is not such a long gap as it might first seem. Pockets of Australoids are found in Ceylon and possibly southern India, to say nothing of the Andaman Islands and Malaya.[40] The Tasmanians must certainly have come originally from somewhere in south-east Asia, even if arguments still continue as to whether they crossed or avoided the Australian mainland in the process.[41] These now extinct

2.7 *Bark-bundle craft of Tasmania seen by Péron during his voyage of 1807 (from Lesueur and Petit's* Terre de Diémen, *Plate 10)*

*2.8    Model of a Chatham Island reed float (*waka-puhara*) (Canterbury Museum, Christchurch, New Zealand)*

aboriginal people were shown in Lesueur and Petit's Atlas to François Péron's 'Voyage of Discovery' of 1807 (Plate 10) using light skiffs made of bundles of bark: 'pirogues, formées chaume de trois rouleaux d'écories grossièment réunies par des lanières de même nature' (see Figure 2.7). Long poles or strips of bark were used as paddles and apparently quite long off-shore fishing voyages were made in these craft. Colonel Lane-Fox tells us that there was a model in the British Museum of a similar craft from Tasmania, made of rushes as well as rolls of bark, and with upturned ends. He adds that James Erskine Calder had told him of a Tasmanian craft he had seen made from bark rolls taken from the swamp tree (*Melaleuca* sp.).[42] Craft made from bark rolls or bundles are more akin to reed boats than the bark canoes discussed in chapter 3.

The Tasmanians are generally held to have been the most technologically primitive of all aboriginal peoples. If they were the principal users of bundle craft in Australia, it is at least not impossible that reed-bundle or bark-bundle craft may have been one of the earliest to bring migrants to Australia, being superseded in due course by bark canoes and then dug-outs.

### The Pacific

Further east in the Pacific, though this was an area where sea travel was dominated by the raft, the double canoe and the outrigger canoe, men could still turn on occasion, through lack of anything else, to the reed-bundle craft. Bishop Selwyn, describing how he crossed the Waitangi River in the South Island of New Zealand in 1844, speaks of

a craft formed of bundles of rushes bound tightly together in the form of a boat.[43] Under the care of a Maori guide, the difficult crossing of the torrential river was achieved with a 'rapid and prosperous passage'. There are a number of other early New Zealand descriptions of these *mokihi* or floats. Further east still, in the Chatham Islands, a shortage of timber drove the ancestors of the Moriori people from New Zealand to evolve the *waka-puhara* (Figure 2.8) made from stems of bracken and New Zealand flax.[44] On even more lonely Easter Island, where there was also a shortage of wood, the islanders used the *totora* reed to make canoes.

Moving back to Asia and on north-eastwards, reed crafts used by fishermen in the Syr–Darya regions, south of the Sea of Aral in the southern USSR,[45] are a link which takes us past ancient examples in China, like the *pu fa* or bulrush raft, and in Japan, like the *ashi-bune* or reed canoe (see chapter 14), and modern ones in Korea, to another crucial area, the American continent.

### America

Here one of the nautical problems presented by the archaeological record is the vast number of fish-bones found in some of the palaeo-Indian sites along the western coast of the continent.[46] These come from the middens of bands of hunter-fishers who must have foraged for small game and shellfish as well as sea-fish along the margins of the coast. The finding of nets and net-floats at the pre-pottery site (*c.* 2000 BC) of Huaca Prieta in Peru confirms the maritime nature of at least some of these early peoples.[47] Early historical sources and

2.9    *2,000-year-old model of a reed boat excavated by Professor J. C. Spahni from an Atacama burial site in Chile (J. C. Spahni)*

archaeological finds suggest that earlier forms of the modern reed fishing-boats of the Amara Indians of Lake Titicaca and parts of the Pacific coast of South America might have been used offshore to make these catches.

These modern South American reed boats are high points in a series which stretches most of the way down the west coast of the American continent, from those used by the Thompson Indians of British Columbia and the Klamaths of Oregon on to the Gulf of California, where the Seri Indians made probably the best known of the North American versions, and the middle Mexican coast.[48]

Figure 2.9 shows a miniature reed boat about 2,000 years old which was recently excavated in a

perfectly preserved condition in dry sand from a burial of the Atacama Culture near the mouth of the River Loa in northern Chile by Professor J. C. Spahni of Lima University.[49] It is obviously very similar to the modern reed boats still used on the Peruvian coast (Figure 2.10). There are also the pottery models of boats from the Peruvian Chimú Culture of about AD 1200, and the later Gallinazo and Mochica Cultures. The likeness of the Chimú model, with its lashed bundles of reeds, to the Tasmanian craft is strikingly apparent.

So efficient are these reed craft for their particular purpose that they seem hardly to have changed at all from the Spaniards' first reports of them to the present day.[50] Thus recent descriptions of how the Peruvian *caballitos* are made are an interesting guide to possible prehistoric practice. In one of the most complete accounts, the botanist Antonio Raimondi described both their construction and maintenance in 1859:[51]

The caballitos are formed of four bundles of reeds cut at one end and tapering to a point at the other. Two of these bundles are underneath and comprise the full length of the caballito, and the other two above are placed longitudinally over the first. The upper ones are shorter, thus leaving a cavity in which the fishermen place their catch . . . The position which the

2.10    *Modern reed boats on the Peruvian coast (J. C. Spahni)*

mounted man takes can be either seated with his legs extended forward, or on his knees. In difficult passages or when the sea is rough, he lowers his legs and sits astride; thus the name caballito.

Raimondi also observed one of the drawbacks of this type of craft.

This peculiar kind of boat lasts only a month, because little by little the reed absorbs water and gradually grows heavier. At times they take the bundles apart, and reassemble them when they have dried out a little. When they have been rendered useless for this purpose, they use the material for the construction of their houses.

Not that replacement offered much of a problem. According to Clinton R. Edwards, one of the leading authorities on these craft, at Huanchaco in Peru the cutting and planting of the *Scirpus* species are continuous more or less throughout the year. Cuttings from the base of the stalk, including the root crown, are thrust into the wet earth. They need no further tending and after six or seven months are ready for cutting just above the ground surface. The shorn root crown will respond to this treatment and grow again up to a dozen times.[52] After cutting, the reed stalks are left out to dry for two weeks before being used.

The relationship of these reed boats, whose antiquity is clearly established, to the various emigrations into America is hard to determine. Did a people moving south to the east of the Rockies turn towards the sea when game died out and there revive the only craft of which they had an ancestral memory? Alternatively, did they evolve afresh the one vessel which was feasible in the circumstances and within their technological capacity?

Or did they move quickly along the coast southward from Alaska in a period of warmer climatic conditions, keeping the tradition of these reed craft alive where suitable species of reeds were growing, but not stopping long enough to leave any evidence of their passing until they came to better conditions further south?

One way or another, Edwards does not accept an independent invention of these craft in the New World, judging them rather to be variations on a very ancient theme.[53] S. K. Lothrop, on the other hand, is very scathing and dismisses any form of sea travel as a possible factor in the southward movement of peoples through the American continent.[54] A point that is perhaps worth making here is that though reed-bundle craft are undeniably primitive and have their drawbacks, they are still very effective within their own limits. One witness to this was the Yankee sea captain, George Coggeshall, who made this entry in his journal in 1822 when off the coast of Peru.[55]

The ships that touch here cannot with any safety use their own boats and always employ the boats or canoes of the Indians, the surf being too high to venture off and on without the aid of these men, who are almost amphibious. They are trained to swimming from their infancy, and commence with a small 'Balsa' in the surf within the reefs, and by degrees, as they grow older and larger venture through the surf, and out upon the broad ocean . . . I have seen the men go off through [heavy surf] . . . and have with great anxiety observed them when a high rolling sea threatened to overwhelm them, watch the approaching roller, duck their heads down close to the reed boat, let the billow pass over them like a seal or a wild duck, and force their way with perfect confidence through the surf, where no white man would for a moment dare to venture.

Even today the fishermen on their caballitos venture several miles off-shore to the rich fishing-grounds on the edge of the Humboldt current.[56]

**Earliest use**

What one can say then is that the reed or bark-bundle boat has been distributed throughout most of the tropical and temperate world and that its use was certainly ancient in Egypt, Mesopotamia, the Harappan (Indus) civilisation, China, Japan, and South America and probably also in Australia. Though simple rafts certainly existed at the same time or even earlier, reed-bundle craft would often have been more practical, more handy and easier to construct. In areas where there was a shortage of wood, they would be dominant, and even technologically quite advanced peoples like the agriculturalists with their polished stone tools who occupied the Pacific islands might revert to them in these same arid circumstances. Hence their world-wide dispersal from the Mediterranean to the Americas.

This does not mean that one is suggesting there were direct links between ancient Egypt and Central America. It is just that the more early verified dates there are for the presence of Man in the American continent and Australia, the less surprising it is to find evidence for a common type of extremely simple craft which could be made with the slightest resources by wandering hunter-fishers.

Nevertheless modern ethnological evidence when used to argue about situations many thousands of years ago has to be treated with caution. Unfortunately, for certain periods, it is almost the only evidence and one has to hypothesise on very slight grounds. The area of the upper Nile and Lake Chad in Africa, where there are the greatest number of surviving reed-bundle rafts, is close to the area from which the hominids seem to have originated and started their spread round the world. If one accepts the somewhat controversial dating methods, then remains found in the Lake Turkana (Rudolf) area of Kenya, a tuff bed dated by the potassium-argon method at $2.6 \pm 0.26$ million years, 'have yielded the oldest known stone artefacts and hominid occupation sites'.[57] Egyptian and Mesopotamian evidence shows that reed-bundle boats were certainly considerably in evidence in the early stages of the civilisations of those two areas. Though Africa $2\frac{1}{2}$ million years ago was the earliest centre of human development, by the last interglacial it had become merely one of many occupied regions,[58] while areas of innovation moved to Asia and then to Europe. Africa might well therefore be the place to look for surviving relics of the earliest examples of practical deliberately-made water-craft and the prime primitive example there, the reed raft or boat, certainly has all the necessary requirements.

From there, these craft can be followed in an intermittent chain of modern survivals to Tasmania and to the west coast of South America. The reed or bark-bundle boat requires virtually no tools or technique to make, beyond the capacity to gather reeds or to peel bark, and to lash bundles together. It therefore seems reasonable, if one has to hypothesise about what boats were involved in man's earliest water journeys, that a very feasible alternative to the raft, which is so often assumed to be the only transport at this stage, would have been the reed or bark-bundle boat.

But the reed craft, for all its possible part in the first spread of the human race round the world, was in itself a blind alley in boat construction. It developed from a mere lake-side armful into the elaborate craft of the Egyptians and the Amara Indians of Lake Titicaca, but it could not go on increasing in size in its reed form without a proper framework, and its short life would have made that hardly worth while. Only off the west coast of South America, so well was it adapted to the local circumstances, did this particular type remain in existence on a large scale. Almost certainly it was the first craft to arrive there. Almost certainly it will be the last aboriginal craft to stay in use in South America, nosing through the surf on the coast, or the *totora* reed-beds along the shores of Lake Titicaca.[59]

# 3 Bark

Bark, like reeds and skin, was one of the most obvious materials for prehistoric man to use and, like those, it leaves very little trace in the archaeological record. However, we know that in various early societies throughout the world it has been recorded as being used to make shelters, roofs, flooring, pit-lining, tapers, torches, shoes, cradles, beehives, net floats, holsters, containers and, of course, boats.[1] Since many of these communities were wandering bands of hunter-fishers, it is quite likely that equivalent uses of bark were made in pre-agricultural times. Evidence that this was indeed so comes from the birch bark found in the Mesolithic sites of Star Carr in Yorkshire and Mullerup in Denmark, where it was stored in rolls ready for use, just as the modern Lapps do.[2] Other evidence for the early use of birch bark is the high standard its working had attained in Neolithic Switzerland, and the well-known drinking vessel from the oak coffin of Egtved in Denmark on whose base could still be found the remnants of a drink of cranberry wine flavoured with myrtle and honey.[3]

## Earliest use

James Hornell has argued that, rather than the lashed raft or the reed-bundle boat, the earliest of all contrived craft was probably the bark canoe.[4] It was much easier, he suggested, for early man, using crude stone tools, to strip the bark from a tree than to trim off the branches, fell it or hollow it out. The idea of doing this might have come first when

bark was pulled away in the search for grubs and insects, which would in turn lead to the making of rough containers of bark, and then on to the most primitive form of canoe, a trough of curled-up bark in roughly its original shape with the ends filled in by lumps of clay. Hornell quoted examples of these very crude craft made from a single sheet of bark (usually eucalyptus) in a trough shape, like those found in south-east South Australia, western Victoria and the Murray and Darling river basins of New South Wales.[5] Other similar examples come from Guyana and Brazil, Rhodesia and Tanzania.

This is certainly a suggestion to be considered. The fact that Australia and the American continent were occupied during the Late Pleistocene period by Upper Palaeolithic peoples might be used to support Hornell's arguments. The difficulties start if one attempts to project the bark canoe back and link it to the major dispersal of the Middle Pleistocene, or even earlier to the first crossing of the Straits of Gibraltar.

The bark canoe is by definition a product of appropriately wooded territories. As a means of coastal travel from south-east Asia, along the Javanese archipelago, it is feasible, and a bold crew might have survived an accidental crossing to Australia. The wetter conditions in Australia then[6] would have meant a humid or sub-humid climate, and a deciduous or rain-forest vegetation covered the whole route. Hornell may also be right in suggesting that the North American tradition of bark-canoe-building was derived from the

3.1  *Early nineteenth century Australian Aboriginal bark canoe, from Lesueur and Petit's Atlas to Péron's 'Voyage of Discovery'*

3.2  *Australian Aboriginal painting on bark showing a bark canoe (Trustees of the Australian Museum, Sydney)*

Tungus, Yakut and Goldi tribes of the Amur River in eastern Siberia.[7] Yet, whatever may be determined in the future about the exact effect of the various glaciations and pluvials of the Pleistocene, it can hardly be denied that much of the new occupation of land took place in semi-arid grassland and tundra areas, which rules out bark canoes. In fact man's advance to latitude 50° N was one of the outstanding facts of this period.

### Evolution of bark craft

Boats made of bark are still or have been recently in use in Africa, Asia, North and South America, and Australia.[8] For these Hornell worked out an internal chronology, that is to say a sequence of the progressively more elaborate stages through which bark craft seem to have evolved.[9] This started at a slightly more advanced level than the tied bark-bundle craft of the Tasmanians which are more akin to reed craft and probably belong to the very earliest stages of water travel. As we have seen, Hornell's first stage was a craft made from a single sheet of bark shaped like a trough.

In a more advanced version, the ends were bunched together and tied with creepers or fibre. Then, further north in Australia, a sign according to Hornell of increased development since the most primitive was nearly always to the south, came the sharp-ended one-piece canoe. This type was also used by the Lambas of Northern Rhodesia (Zambia), where the ends of the piece of bark were heated to make them pliable so that they could be bent back upon themselves and secured with skewers of wood. Both in Africa and Northern Australia the skewers of wood are replaced in some areas by sewing, and stretchers and thwarts make a further refinement. Finally, from the Gulf of Carpentaria comes an example where the main part of the hull is made of three strips of bark sewn together and, as well as gunwale poles and ties, a set of primitive ribs is inserted.

## South America

The Chilean bark canoes of the Yahgans and Alacalufs are similar. These craft were described by Miguel de Goicueta after the Spaniards' first contact with the aborigines' craft of the Chonos Archipelago,[10] and they seem to have changed little, apart from the addition of a crude sealskin sail, when in 1785 Vargas y Ponce recorded in excellent detail how they were made.[11]

The canoes . . . are composed of three pieces, the centre one forming the keel, stempiece, sternpost and bottom, and the other two the sides.

The industry with which they strip these trees is admirable, since for this task they have no instrument other than a somewhat pointed and shaped flint, with which they make cuts or incisions around the trunk, at each end, and then one from top to bottom which joins them. With much patience and skill they strip

3.3 *Bark canoes from Tierra del Fuego (National Maritime Museum)*

the bark in one whole piece from the trunk, of a length which will serve for the canoe. In some . . . this amounts to from 30 to 32 feet, including the curve of the centre piece which forms the bow and stern. The usual length of these fragile craft is from 24 to 26 feet, the beam four, and the depth from two to three feet.

So that the bark will assume the proper curve and shape, they place two heaps of stones at the ends, atop the exterior side of the bark . . . leaving [it] thus for two or three days in which it dries and assumes the proper shape for construction. Then they place the other two, which serve as the sides, almost perpendicular to the centre piece, joining them with stitches of dry reed and filling the seams with straw and mud to impede the entry of water as much as possible. In order to strengthen the sides they put from one end to the other of the canoe, very close together, sticks in the form of barrel staves, which take the shape of a semi-ellipsoid. They make the gunwale of each side with two thick and well-joined poles.

To the gunwales are fastened the ends of the curved pieces which form the floor timbers [and frames]. All this is tied with stitches and lashings of dried reeds. At certain distances they also place some transverse sticks which serve as thwarts.

At this stage the interior of almost the whole canoe is lined with pieces of the same bark, a foot wide, the ends of which are made fast to the gunwales. In order that they will easily assume the proper curve, they are heated by fire, and thus half dried out; in this manner they put them in place. In addition they form a kind of framework from the stern to the bow quarter, serving as a deck, suspended about a half-foot from the bottom, and leaving a space amidships from which to bail out the water. This framework consists of some sticks placed lengthwise which rest on others placed transversely. This and the rest of the canoe . . . is covered with bark . . . Many of these canoes can hold nine or ten Indians. They are propelled by oars in the form of paddles, which is the usual work of women. When they make a long voyage, which is almost always with a favourable wind or during a calm, they put a pole in the bow of the canoe, and attach to it a sealskin which has at its upper end a crosspiece in the form of a yard. They hold the lower corners of the skin in their hands . . . In the centre of the canoe they put some stones with many pieces of shell and sand, and on this base of cement they light their fire, maintaining it with sticks and branches.

On the other hand, in South America, as in Australia, simpler types were also found like the 'woodskin' of Guyana that Mrs Brindley saw in the 1920s. This consisted of a single sheet of bark which was rolled like a scroll and kept open by several thwarts, except at the ends where there was no filling or fastening, just the natural rolling-up of the bark and a slight sheer which lifted the bow and stern out of the water.[12]

## Africa

These canoes recall the description by Dr Livingstone of those by which he crossed the River Chikapa in central Africa. 'We were ferried over in a canoe made out of a single piece of bark sewed together at the ends, and having sticks placed in it at different parts to act as ribs. The word Chikapa means bark or skin, and this is the only river on which we saw this kind of canoe used.'[13] Similar canoes were still being used in 1956 by fishermen on the Pungwe River, Mozambique.[14]

Some Bushman paintings found in rock shelters in Natal and south-eastern Lesotho[15] show lively impressions of fishermen spearing their catch from some sort of craft (Figure 3.4), and are interesting for three reasons. First, the artist could never have seen a spawning run of yellowfish in those districts, so must have remembered it from an incident well to the north; second, one would like to know what sort of craft are being used; and third, excavations in one of the shelters have shown that, under the recent Bushman layers, the deposits go down 3 metres, revealing a collection of Late Stone Age tools which were used at least 20,000 years ago.

The craft, from their shape, are unlikely to have been dug-outs. But rather than bark as speculated by R. A. Jubb, either reed bundles or solid logs seem more likely to have been the material, since one of the few facts to be gleaned from this fascinating scene is that the fishermen appear to be standing on top of their craft. So they come more properly in the category described in chapter 2.

## North America

It was in North America that the bark canoe achieved the peak of its development, making it one of the most highly evolved of all primitive craft and one which, like the kayak, has had the compliment of being imitated and used for sport in contemporary society.

The first European accounts of the Indian canoe, by Jacques Cartier in 1535 and by Captain George Weymouth and Samuel de Champlain in 1603, are short of detail, and it is not until 1720–30 that any really informative accounts appear.[16] Even so, it is clear that this craft, made with Stone Age tools which from the first had received recognition from traders and settlers for its speed, strength and lightness, had achieved a high degree of refinement and variation before any European arrived on the scene.

The area where they were made was limited by the habitat of the paper birch, that is to say, a wide

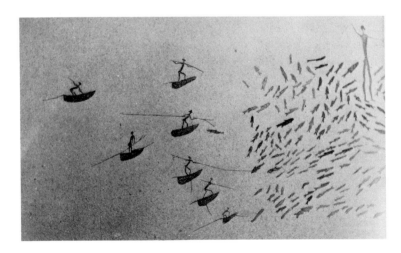

3.4  *Bushman painting found near the River Tsoelike, Tsatsalemeno, eastern Lesotho, copied by Patricia Vinnicombe (author)*

belt from Newfoundland to the Alaska coast. Spruce, elm, chestnut, hickory, basswood, cottonwood and other kinds of birch produced suitable bark, but all had some drawback in the way of available size, thinness, stretch, shrinkage and so on. To sew the bark together, the root of the black spruce was usually employed, though other roots and even rawhide were sometimes used. The gum most favoured to keep seams watertight also came from the black or white spruce, while white cedar produced the best ribs. Before the coming of the Europeans, stone tools were supplemented by fire, hot water helped to bend the wood, and awls made of splinters from the shank-bones of deer were used to make sewing holes. Drills of bone made the larger holes.[17]

When the Malecite Indians made a canoe, the gunwales were the first members to be formed. After the middle thwart had been fitted between them, the ends were then brought together and lashed, and the permanent thwarts fitted in place of temporary stays. Next, the assembled gunwales were laid on the building bed, into which twenty-six stakes were driven in pairs round the gunwale frame. After the canoe-builder was satisfied with this stage, the stakes and the gunwale frame were removed and the birch bark, white exterior side up, put in its place. On this the gunwale frame was then laid, and the bark outside its edges slashed at various points to allow the edges to be turned up neatly all round the frame. When everything had been properly aligned, the stakes were put back all round the turned-up bark shape and their tops fastened to each other in pairs. In the meantime, the women had sewn on any side pieces necessary to give the bark cover the right shape and size. The next stage was to clamp the bark against the outer stakes and fit battens along the inside. Then the gunwale frame was lifted up and secured by supports under the thwarts to give the right sheer, ready to have the bark cover secured to it, either by lacing, lashing, or fitting between gunwale and outwale. After the thwarts had then been fitted, and any gores sewn up, the canoe could then be lifted up bodily, turned upside down and put on two rests at a good working height, ready for the ends to be closed, and the stem-pieces fitted.

When the bark cover had been inspected and all sewing finished, the canoe was then put right way up ready for all seams to be payed with gum and for the internal sheathing and ribs to be fitted. The sheathing was first held in place by temporary ribs. Then when the sheer and the rough shape of the body had been checked, the permanent ribs (for a 6-metre-long canoe, more than fifty of white cedar heartwood, pre-bent to shape in boiling water) of five different lengths were forced into their notched positions under the gunwales. This was a most careful operation, in which a rib was rejected if it did not produce an even overall pressure on the sheathing when it had been driven home. After the headboards had been inserted and the gunwale caps pegged and lashed on, it only remained to gum all seams smoothly on the outside and apply whatever decoration was customary.[18]

This is a condensed account of an elaborate process which could have many variations in overall shape, in materials used, building techniques, stitching and lashing or order of procedure. But throughout the area where the birch-bark canoe was made (and Adney's hundred models give some idea of the possible varieties), the basic principle of the stressed rib and clamped sheathing applied, even in the so-called kayak-form canoes of Alaska and the North-West, or in the temporary 'emergency' skin boats used by the Indians when bark was not available.[19] According to Adney, virtually the same basic technique was used in making the latter as in the bark canoe. After the cover (perhaps three moose-skins sewn together) had been secured to the gunwale frame (which had been raised inside the stakes on the building bed in the usual way), stem-pieces, sheathing and ribs were then forced in, dictating the final shape as with the birch-bark canoe.

The bark canoe is primarily a river and lake craft. Though the North American version varied from small one-man hunting canoes to ones big enough to carry a ton of cargo, a large war-party or a family moving to a new living site, all were remarkably efficient craft for forest travel, being light enough to be carried overland for long distances even where trails hardly existed, capable of carrying heavy loads in shallow water and being

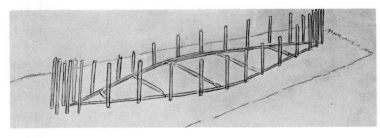

3.5   *Building an American Indian bark canoe (after Adney and Chapelle, The Bark Canoes and Skin Boats of North America, 1964):*
*(a) Stakes are temporarily located around gunwale frame*

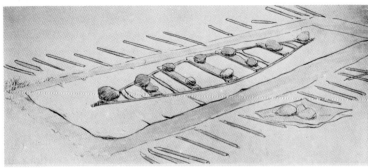

*(b) Stakes and gunwale removed; bark cover laid out and gunwale frame placed on it weighted with stones*

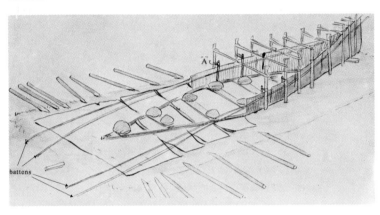

*(c) Gores are cut in the bark which is then shaped around the gunwale frame. 'A' shows the longitudinal battens secured by sticks lashed to stakes*

easily repaired on the way. Only the rather odd-looking canoes of the Beothuk tribe of Newfoundland seem to have been specifically designed for open-sea voyaging and are supposed to have reached outlying islands with runs of 60 miles or more, and to have crossed from Newfoundland to Labrador.[20] Their V-form and lack of bilge, provision for ballast and strongly flaring sides, all contrast with the more usual shape and, even if they do not depart from Indian building technique in any way, their shape suggests a different and specialised function. It is possible that a craft like this made one of the most startling of all canoe voyages. In 1508 a French ship picked up near the English coast 'a small boat made of bark and osiers, containing 7 men of medium height, darkish hue and attired in fish skins and plaited straw caps'.[21] On account of their broad faces and their habit of eating raw flesh and drinking blood these were considered to be Eskimos. From the sea-keeping point of view, this might well have been so. A boat could very well have been blown from Greenland, and enforced cannibalism might have kept its complement alive. On the other hand, if one accepts bark and osier at its face value, which are not known to have been used by Eskimos, this boat could have been some such canoe as that of the Beothuk, which had the shape

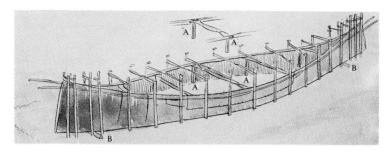

*(d) The bark cover is fully shaped and then sewn to the gunwale frame which has been raised to sheer level. 'A' shows sticks which fix the sheerline. 'B' are blocks which impose the rocker on the canoe*

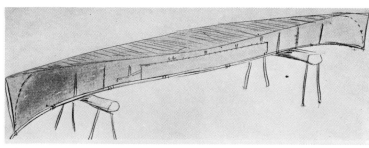

*(e) The canoe is placed upside down on trestles, where the ends are shaped and the sewing completed*

*(f) The canoe is now finished by fitting internal sheathing and ribs, and all seams are payed with gum*

to survive an evidently mild Atlantic crossing. However, this is hardly enough on its own to inflate the sea-going achievements of the bark canoe.

## Northern Europe and Asia

Turning to the ocean on the other side of the American continent, Hornell thought that the peculiar canoes of the Amur River in eastern Siberia, with their underwater pointed rams each end, were 'identical' with those used on the Kutenai River in British Columbia.[22] Chapelle, however, with his usual caution, points out that,

whatever the similarities of form, they are in fact constructed differently.[23] Yet the Siberian evidence does make a general point. The existence there of several types of bark canoe confirms the Australian and American evidence that bark was a material whose flexibility and long use led easily to many variations.[24] One should be cautious therefore of any suggestions of links or diffusion.

Though bark seems to have been much used in prehistoric Europe, as the already quoted rolls of birch bark from Star Carr and other sites demonstrate, there is very little other evidence for early bark boats. Grahame Clark[25] even goes so far as to say that apart from the 'very little boats, and very light' reported by Ohthere (a Norwegian who visited King Alfred) to have been carried overland by the Finns to make war on the Northmen, which might be either skin or bark, the only evidence one can cite for an early bark boat in Europe comes from Istorp in Västergotland, Sweden. This vessel was made from a single sheet of spruce bark which was sewn to the wooden frames by juniper thongs, and leather slips had been inserted between them to prevent chafing. This boat, solitary as it is, does give one slight clue to a possible reason for the rarity of bark boats in Europe. If the brief description by Humbla and von Post[26] indicates that the frames were solid and the outer cover was sewn to them, this would put it in the normal skin-boat-construction school, as opposed to the tension system of the North American Indians, the Yahgans and Alacalufs of Chile, and the Anula tribe of the Gulf of Carpentaria. Another distinction to be made is that the skin boat was as much a sea as a river boat, whereas the bark boat was far more suitable for inland waters. Possibly the explanation of the European situation lies here. The demand was more for coastal and island-reaching craft in the Postglacial period, a role which the skin boat was available to fill, as opposed to the North American situation where the skin boat was left at the post, as it were, and all the conditions favoured the evolution of the inland birch-bark canoe.

There is another area in Europe, though, where one would consider the inland waterways to be more like those of North America, and that is Finland. The interesting thing is that there are two types of craft here which might possibly explain the apparent absence of bark boats. One is the expanded softwood dug-out which is so light that contemporary Finns paddle it like a kayak. O. Crumlin-Pedersen's view that this craft is a crucial stage in the development of the classic Scandinavian ship of the Viking period is considered in chapter 9. Its appearance as far back as the Iron Age in the Baltic area might have helped to eliminate the conventional bark boat.

The other craft seems to have been described by both Olaus Magnus in the sixteenth century[27] and H. C. Folkard in the 1870s.[28] Olaus Magnus describes how the Lapps made their boats by joining together pieces of wood with sinews. Folkard's description of the boats used by the Lapps and Finns on their lakes and swift-flowing rivers is, as one would expect, rather more detailed. They were made of very thin planks of fir attached to a keel and ribs, the planks being sewn together with sinews of reindeer or fir root. The overall length of the keel was some 4 metres, coming to a high point at each end. There were only three or four ribs and they were very small. Folkard noted that one had to be very careful when stepping out, as any pressure on the sides would damage them. On the other hand, he reported them as being very light, flexible and strong and that they survived frequently striking rocks in passages through cataracts. Perhaps, then, the early Finns' boats were indeed made of bark, and these nineteenth-century Finnish sewn craft were the survivors of a boat form that had succeeded the bark boat in an area where one would expect conditions to have favoured its evolution.

## Developments of the bark boat

To summarise, the dominating factor with the bark boat was the presence of suitable trees – usually birch and beech – though the eucalyptus made a good alternative, as the canoe trees of Australia confirm. This means it would have been available for a good deal of the way during the human expansion during the Pleistocene period, to Australia, for instance. At the moment it is difficult to tie any of the stages of evolution, such as the insertion of bent twigs as ribs, to any particular piece of archaeological evidence. The very earliest stage, a single sheet of bark, a number of sheets skewered together, or rolls tied together as the Australian evidence shows, needed only the crudest of tools. Later stages, involving sewing, would of course demand awls or some other sort of piercing tool.

We may consider the possibility of developments from the bark boat by examining two situations where bark boats and planked boats co-existed. According to Brindley,[29] the sewn planked boats of the Ainu of the Kuril Islands are some 10 metres long, nearly 2 metres wide and over 1 metre deep, with a pointed stem and stern where the planking runs up in a sharp curve about 0.5 metres above the level of the gunwale. The seams of the planking are caulked inside by moss and covered by half-round battens kept in place by lashings of whale sinews or whalebone fibres. Gunwale timbers, knees (supporting timbers) and thwarts are all lashed similarly.

Bark canoes and *dalcas* also co-existed in western South America. *Dalcas* were boats made of sewn wooden planks which were used by the people of Chonos Archipelago and the Indians of Chiloé Island off Chile.[30] The first Spanish expedition to land on Chiloé, in 1558, did so in a fleet of *dalcas* and one of the Conquistadores, Alonso de Gongora Marmolejo, described them[31] as being made

of three planks, one for the bottom and one for each side, sewn with thin cords. In the seam formed by the planks they put a split cane lengthways and under it, above the seam, the bark of a tree which they call maque, which crushes easily as the stitches are taken . . . They are of some 30 to 40 feet long, with a beam of one yard, and narrow at bow and stern like a weaver's shuttle.

A later report in 1788 gives further details in that they have thwarts and floor timbers like those in other Indian canoes, but stronger.[32]

The interesting question is the relationship in these two cases between the planked boat and the bark canoe. The sewing, the shape and the caulking are all more or less identical. The difference is the substitution of wooden planks for bark slabs. In South America this alteration might reflect the acquisition of new types of tools like the hafted axe which the Chonos, the makers of *dalcas*, had possibly seen in use among more advanced peoples of the mainland.[33] On the other hand, it is not certain that planks could not have been worked with flints, shells and fire, in which case one is left with the question whether the *dalca* was an improved variant on the bark canoe, or (exactly the opposite) that the bark canoe was a poor imitation of the *dalca* by people lacking the necessary wood-working skills.

The latter alternative means ignoring or explaining away the very ancient shell middens on the islands of that part of the coast, since these certainly antedate the arrival of farming peoples with advanced enough skills to build the planked *dalca*.[34] It is possible that the Yahgans and Alacalufs, to reach the islands, used some craft even more primitive than the bark canoe – of which there is now no trace or evidence – but this seems unlikely. Clinton Edwards, rightly and cautiously, does not commit himself finally on this point,[35] but quotes in detail Cooper's thesis that under the pressure of local needs the Araucanians (farmers on the Chilean mainland), who seem to have been an intelligent innovating people, improved the bark canoe and thereby produced the *dalca*.[36] This may also have happened in Siberia and produced the plank boat of the Ainu of the Kurils.

These two areas of bark-boat development into a planked boat, if indeed this is what happened, appear to be isolated. As will be discussed in chapter 5, most authorities agree that the vast majority of planked boats were developed from the dug-out in one form or another.

# 4 Skin

The skin boat's place in prehistory has probably been examined even less than that of the reed boat. Unlike the dug-out, early examples of which have been excavated, neither of these two types is likely to survive in archaeological contexts.[1] But the reed boat at least had the advantage of being recorded in early historical times in the great civilisations of the Nile, the Euphrates and the Indus. The skin boat, on the other hand, tended to be used most on the edges of the populated world.

## Types of skin craft

However, if one combs through the available information, contemporary as well as ancient, there is sufficient evidence to come to certain conclusions. First, though, it is important to distinguish between the different types. There are five main kinds: the round skin boat, often called a coracle; the long skin boat, of which the curragh and umiak are examples; the kayak; the inflated skin float; and the raft made of a number of skin floats fitted into a framework. These five types of related craft are certainly distributed throughout the northern hemisphere, with some extension into the southern.

## Britain and Ireland

James Hornell, in his classic work, 'British coracles and Irish curraghs', has summarised much of the historical evidence for skin boats in western Europe.[2] Avienus's elaboration of the fourth or fifth century BC Massiliote *Periplus*, which gives an account of a coastal voyage from Atlantic Spain to Massalia (Marseilles), is probably the furthest back one can take the numerous references in classical writers to the busy sea traffic between the British Isles and Europe, and it was the survival of this tradition outside the limits of Roman nautical influence that led to the well-recorded skin-boat voyages of the Irish monks. Since Pliny, Solinus, Sidonius Apollinaris and Avienus seem to be writing about ocean voyages, one can assume these were made in curraghs, but that would not exclude the existence of British coracles on rivers well before Julius Caesar was impressed by them.

For earlier times, however, we must rely on indirect evidence. At Star Carr, the eighth millennium BC site near Scarborough in Yorkshire, the discovery of a paddle suggests that water travel had become normal among the hunters of this lake-side settlement.[3] However, we do not know what craft the paddle was used to propel. There were numerous rolls of birch bark, which suggests the possibility of birch-bark canoes, but, as we have seen, these are very rare in north-west Europe, and the Star Carr rolls showed no signs of having been sewn. Then there was evidence of tree-felling. Two birch trunks with their lower ends hacked into pencil-like points show that the stone axes of these people were capable of felling trees. Taking into account the two large wedges or chisels of deer antler found at Thatcham, Berkshire, it can be deduced that the Star Carr people had both adapted themselves to forest conditions and acquired possible means of making dug-outs.[4] On the other hand, the Star Carr hunters are shown by the finds there to have used skins in large numbers, and Grahame Clark suggests that, though there is no direct evidence, they probably wore the same sort of skin clothing as people in the circumpolar regions do now.[5] They had therefore the potential ability to make and use skin boats.

For lakes, slow-running rivers or even short coastal journeys, dug-outs would have been usable. But when it came to open-sea voyages in northern Europe, especially in the cold conditions which lasted for a time after the passing of the last glaciation, dug-outs would hardly have been satisfactory. Grahame Clark and Stuart Piggott say that skin boats could have been used in these times:[6] it is suggested here that it can be put more strongly than that.

A significant area in this argument is the one that stretches from Ireland to the west coast of Norway by way of Scotland. The sea which surrounded the living sites here was not the comparatively sheltered Mediterranean or English Channel but the cold, frequently disagreeable and always unreliable waters of the Irish Sea, the Minch and the Atlantic. Dryness at sea and seaworthiness were crucial factors in the evolutionary story of the skin boat. One of the most obvious pieces of evidence for this is simply where the boats were used. The west coast of Ireland, with its curragh tradition, and the west coast of Norway are both open to the worst the Atlantic can do. Craft that can stand up to these conditions have to be really seaworthy.

One of the best tributes to the qualities of the skin boat comes from Stefansson, describing the umiak in the north Atlantic. The usual one, he says,[7] is

thirty-five to forty feet long, big enough to carry two tons, and light enough for two men to carry. It is so strong and so fitted for rough handling that this was perhaps the chief reason why the Yankee whalers of north-western Alaska, when developing there a shore whaling industry during the last two decades of the nineteenth century, discarded the New Bedford whaleboat for the umiak when pursuing the blowhead.

One can imagine few men less likely to give an undeserved accolade to a craft than Yankee whalers!

Another American tribute to the umiak, also quoted by Stefansson, came from a Captain E. O. Jones, USN, one-time Commandant of the United States Coast Guard Academy.[8] He said that in his view, from what he had seen on ice patrols south of Greenland, the umiak 'was perfectly capable of remaining afloat in almost any weather'.

The Irish curragh has had many similar compliments. James Hornell says[9] that Aran Islands and Co. Kerry curraghs regularly weather storms that spell disaster to plank-built boats of considerably greater size. The fishermen of the Connemara mainland and the off-shore islands used to possess, besides their curraghs, a number of plank-built boats, but in a terrible storm in the early part of the century almost the whole fleet of wooden boats was lost with many lives, while the only curragh out that night came safely back. After that, they fell back on the curragh alone as the safest craft for inshore fishing.[10]

It seems more likely then that the Mesolithic Larnian peoples who lived on the coast of Ireland, and the Obanians who travelled out to the islands of Oronsay and Risga in Loch Sunart, Strathclyde, would have used skin boats (which they were as well equipped to make as are the Eskimo) rather than dug-outs. This suggestion is not based solely on sea-going conditions. An interesting confirmation comes from the finding in archaeological contexts of the bones of deep-water fish. Cod-bones are particularly significant here because, although cod have a complicated migratory cycle, they are not regularly present near inshore.[11] In Grahame Clark's view, the finding of the bones of cod, as well as those of conger, haddock, common sea-bream, ballan wrasse, the back ray, skate and sharks at Oban (Strathclyde) and Oronsay, confirms that the occupants of these sites in the Postglacial period must have undertaken deep-water fishing from boats, rather than from the shore.[12] Movius also noted an abundant supply of cod remains from the Early Postglacial site of Cushendun, Co. Antrim,[13] while a more recent find comes from the site of Morton, some 6 miles from St Andrews in Fife, Scotland.[14] In the sixth millennium BC, Morton was an island at high tide with temporary settlements of groups of hunter-gatherers who must have moved north not too long after the retreat of the ice. Of the fish-bones found at this site, a very high proportion were of cod, and of these many had come from large fish. From the presence of head-bones, as well as abdominal and caudal vertebrae, it could be assumed that whole fish were brought to the site and eaten. Other possible evidence for the use of boats here was the presence of many guillemot bones. These birds can be incapable of flight during the rapid moult after the breeding season, and so can be caught from a boat.[15]

By itself the Morton evidence might be considered equivocal as between skin boats and dug-outs. The Firth of Tay was the sort of sheltered area where dug-outs could have been used and there must almost certainly have been some variation and overlapping of types. On the other hand, Grahame Clark has pointed out that the absence of wood-working tools among the Obanians as well as the high percentage of skin-working tools on their sites argue against any use of dug-outs there.[16]

Then there is the interesting inference made by P. R. Ritchie that trade in stone tools was being carried out in Scotland in the Mesolithic period. In particular he has pointed out that bloodstone from Rhum has been found at Risga, Loch Torridon, Ardnamurchan on the mainland (Strathclyde) and in Skye. As well, Arran pitchstone has been found in a number of places in the east of Scotland.[17] The significance of polished stone axes of the Later Neolithic period as an indicator of sea-borne trade is more fully discussed in chapter 10. Here the importance of this Scottish trade is that it evidently took place in an earlier stage. The sea journey from Arran to the peninsula of Kintyre is short and sheltered and could have taken place in a small dug-out, but voyaging out into the Minch to Rhum is a rather different matter. It is also noteworthy that Grahame Clark suggests that, over on the coast of Norway, the important trade in stone axes from the island of Bømlo to the mainland was carried on by the Mesolithic

Nøstvet people, south of Oslo. As well as happening at a stage earlier than the Neolithic, this trade from Rhum and Bømlo took place in areas where subsequently skin boats were prominent.

So, in the broader picture, the ample presence of skin-working tools, the rough sea conditions and the large number of deep-sea fish-bones on Postglacial sites in a swathe from Cushendun to eastern Scotland, in an area where subsequently there was a powerful tradition of skin boats, surely suggest that the easily-made skin boat was more likely to have been the dominant type, especially bearing in mind the difficulties of making a dug-out with a Mesolithic tool assemblage. This suggestion also simplifies the question of the origin and dispersion of the Larnian and other early Postglacial peoples in Ireland. With skin boats capable of catching cod off-shore, they would not have been dependent on the often postulated land-bridges or lowered sea-levels for their original presence in Ireland or their subsequent dispersion.

## Scandinavia

At Ulkestrop in Denmark, a Postglacial island site in a lake has revealed not only a rectangular hut which had strips of bark half a metre wide inside it, but a paddle over 1 metre long made from hazel wood.[18] The fisherman and hunter who made his microlithic flint tools here must have lived a fairly similar life to the Yorkshiremen of Star Carr. Ole Klindt-Jensen thinks the craft used to reach this summer hunting-lodge was probably a skin one.[19]

The Mesolithic Ertebølle people of Denmark and the passage-grave people of southern Scandinavia are others who left fish-bone evidence of off-shore work in their middens, while the early agriculturalists of Gotland even buried fish-hooks in their women's graves. But the most considerable sea-fisheries in prehistoric Europe were those in Norway, the earliest site, at Viste near Stavanger, at least antedating the spread of farming there.[20]

The well-known rock carving from Bohuslän, north of Gothenburg in Sweden, which shows two men fishing with hook and line from a skin boat (Figure 4.1) is certainly much later than this, but as Brøgger and Shetelig said of Postglacial times in

4.1 *Late Bronze Age rock carving at Kville, Bohuslän, Sweden, showing two men fishing from a boat (J. G. D. Clark, Prehistoric Europe, 1952)*

Norway, 'it was the skin boat which made possible the settlement of the Western Isles'. In other words, these were boats which could sail or row the dangerous Maelstrom, between the Lofoten Islands, and the sea of Røst. Boats that were to be practical out there had not only to be light so that

they could ride the crest of the waves and thus avoid shipping too much water; they also had to be built strong and pliant so that they could take the heavy stresses of the sea.[21]

The often-quoted Norwegian Stone Age rock carvings from Evenhus (Figure 4.2) and Forselv show that the stretching process from coracle to a longer version had already begun by the time these carvings in the Arctic Art tradition were made.[22]

## Southern and eastern Europe

Much further south, in Spain, Strabo[23] describes how the Lusitanian mountaineers up to the time of the successful Roman general D. Junius Brutus, 136 BC, still used boats of tanned leather, while even earlier the Spanish mercenaries of Hannibal had crossed the Rhone on craft consisting of inflated skins with their shields placed on top.[24]

To the east, Anati has published among the many Italian rock carvings of Val Camonica, northern Brescia, a rather charming fishing scene which almost certainly shows a river coracle.[25] Anati puts this carving on the great rock at Naquane in the Late Iron Age, the second half of the first millennium BC. It illustrates very well an important characteristic of skin boats. The skin cover, as it dries out, shrinks and contracts, and

4.2 *Rock carvings of skin boats at Evenhus, Norway (author)*

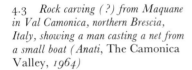

4.3   *Rock carving (?) from Maquane in Val Camonica, northern Brescia, Italy, showing a man casting a net from a small boat (Anati,* The Camonica Valley, *1964)*

4.4   *A umiak bow, showing the concave cone formed as the skin dries out and shrinks (National Museums of Canada, Ottawa)*

this is well seen, for instance, in the concave profile under an Eskimo umiak's bows (Figure 4.4). Where the framework is not as solid as in a umiak, you then get the bent-up look of the hull which the Val Camonica boat shares with the Welsh coracle.

Fish were apparently not a major element in the economy of the Camunian valley, but it is perhaps worth quoting here the advantages of fishing from a coracle, as described to James Hornell by the Welsh salmon-fishers of the upper Dee.[26]

A coracle draws so little water, between two and three inches only, that it can go almost anywhere, the paddler, using one hand only, can turn and twist it at will and shoot rapids and thread narrow channels in a way quite impossible in a canoe. When need be he may slip behind a boulder or a jutting rock, or hold on with paddle, gaff or foot and so fish places out of reach of the angler in waders or in any other craft but a coracle. In his basket boat the angler can snuggle in safely against a rocky ledge in a back eddy with foaming white water on one side or perhaps on both.

Besides illustrating vividly why the Italian Iron Age fisherman on the River Oglio should use a coracle, this quotation is extremely important as showing where and why the coracle might originally have developed and what are its basic virtues as compared to those of other primitive craft.

Anati's carving also makes much more sense of what seemed to James Hornell to be an obscure reference by Lucan to the Venetians on the River Po using boats made of willow covered with bulls' hides.[27] If they used them on the Po, it is near enough to the Oglio to reinforce the interpretation of the Val Camonica carving as a skin boat and confirm Lucan's observation.

Further east, one comes to the site of another reference to the use of skin floats to cross a river. The ethnographer Baron Nopsca[28] suggests that their introduction to the Upper and Lower Danube in the early Middle Ages was due to Tartar invasion, which was possibly the same reason for their presence until recently in Albania.[29]

## Southern Asia and India

This method of river crossing was also used in Mesopotamia, though there it certainly happened well before the time of the Tartars. The Tigris and Euphrates were in fact meeting-grounds where the

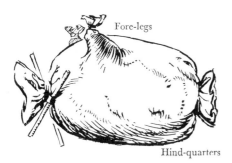
Fore-legs

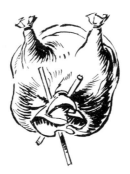

Hind-quarters

4.5 *An inflated bullock-skin, as used on the Huang Ho, China (Worcester, Sail and Sweep in China, 1966)*

traditional reed boat, the bitumen-covered *quffa* or local coracle, the inflated skin float, and the *kelek* or skin-float raft were all in use in very early historical times.

According to Hornell,[30] the skin float has been in more general use in recent times in Persia, central Asia and northern India and Pakistan than anywhere else, while its presence in other areas (see Figure 4.5) was probably helped by one of its outstanding characteristics, its military value. Besides Hannibal's armies, those of Pompey, Genghis Khan and Kublai Khan are all recorded as having made use of it,[31] and the famous Assyrian carving (Figure 4.6) in the British Museum shows that the forces of Ashur-nasir-pal II

did so too. But while obviously of great value to individual soldiers in crossing rivers, these skin floats needed to be fastened together within a wooden framework to achieve their greatest development. In this form they functioned in the Middle East, from the times at least of the Assyrians, to those of Sir Austen Layard, who used a buoyed raft of 600 skins to transport some of his largest trophies from Nineveh to Baghdad.[32]

Though Herodotus got some of his details wrong, he did manage to describe the principle behind the use of these craft, which seem even in his day to have taken a load of 150 tons.[33] After they had been carried downstream by the current through the rapids of the Tigris and Euphrates and

4.6 *Assyrian carving showing swimmers using inflated skins during an attack on a city by Ashur-nasir-pal II in 884 BC (Mansell Collection)*

had delivered their cargo, the rafts were taken apart, the wood and lashings sold, and the newly-tanned deflated skins taken back to their starting-place on donkey-back. Xenophon, the *Periplus* of the Erythraean Sea and Pliny[34] are other classical sources to mention these rafts, which were also used as far east as the Yellow River in China, though in Africa they seem only to appear in areas of strong Arab influence.

The use of inflated skins, however, does not prevent coracles existing side by side with them in some areas. The *quffas* of the Euphrates date back at least to the Assyrians. Coracles were also in recent use in the mountainous region of southern and eastern Tibet, in the upper reaches of some Chinese rivers and in the south of Mongolia.[35] Then an interesting and isolated appearance is in south-eastern India on some of the rivers of the Deccan and Madras. South and east from India the coracle does not appear. To the north and east, however, lies another of its great areas of development.

### Russia and the Arctic

The vast extent of the USSR contains much material that is highly relevant to the development of the skin boat. One example is the carvings of prehistoric skin boats in the Arctic Art style round Lake Onega, north-east of Leningrad, and the delta of the River Vyg. Another significant fact is that Siberia was virtually in a prehistoric state until colonised by the Russians in the seventeenth century. Even then, its huge extent and difficult climate limited the areas of development until recent times so that the territory is a splendid reserve of primitive craft.

The naturalistic Arctic Art of Russia is generally held to be related to that of northern Scandinavia. The boats carved on rocks on the eastern shores of Lake Onega and on the banks of the Vyg seem to be long for their beam and are distinguished by elks' heads on their prows. Since these sites are on inland waters, these craft could have been dug-outs. On the other hand, the close relationship of the carvings to those of the Arctic Art of Norway in which umiak-type craft are shown on several sites, the depth of freeboard (which seems too great for dug-outs but appropriate for high-riding skin boats), and finally the ram forefoot visible on a number of these craft argue against this. In a skin boat, one of the greatest drawbacks is the chance of holing the hull when beaching, the almost universal end of a voyage in days before harbours and slipways. The simplest way to guard against this is by having an extended forefoot, ram or double bow. While this particular device does not seem to have been present in the British Isles curragh sequence or in the Eskimo umiak, it reached fantastic proportions in the skin boats of the Scandinavian Bronze Age (Figure 4.7) and even survived in a stylised form in the bows of recent Alaskan and Aleutian skin boats (Figure 4.8).

Maringer and Bandi[36] think that the Komsa

4.7 *Norwegian Bronze Age rock carvings showing craft with cleft bows (Universitets Oldsaksamling, Oslo)*

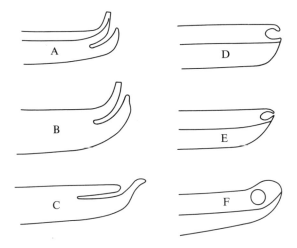

4.8 *Cleft bows on recent Alaskan and Aleutian skin boats (after Hornell,* Water Transport, *1970). A, Unalaska, Aleutian Islands; B, Aleutian Islands; C, Alaska; D, Bering Strait; E, Unaligmut, Alaska; F, Nunivak Island, Alaska*

Culture of northern Norway may be derived from Russia and have reached Norway via the coast of the White Sea, while Grahame Clark and Stuart Piggott[37] regard the Lake Onega, Vyg and Karelian carvings as offshoots from the Scandinavian group. Either way, the two seem to be related, and reports of further carvings in this style on the banks of the Rivers Yenisei and Lena, which flow into the Arctic Ocean,[38] suggest that the use of skin boats as reflected in these carvings was part of a circum-Polar tradition.

Less well known in the west are the rock carvings of boats from Kobystan in Azerbaijan, some 37 miles north of Baku. Soviet archaeologists suggest dates for the different styles, from 8000–6000 BC for the Mesolithic ones to 4000–3000 BC for the Late Neolithic and Bronze Age ones.[39] A cast of one of these carved rocks from the Historical Institute of Azerbaijan formed part of the exhibition of Historical Treasures of the Soviet Union which toured western Europe in 1967. On it was a large half-moon-shaped vessel which gave little indication of its nature, but two smaller vessels had double bows very reminiscent of some Scandinavian Bronze Age skin ones. The latitude of the site of these boats is some 46° N, which fits neatly

with Brindley's statement[40] that inflated skins and skin-float rafts are not found in Russia north of the Pamirs, that is, about latitude 40° N, north of which skin boats replace them.

Brindley's chief interest was, in fact, these boats and the elaborate mixture of other types that were still to be found in recent times in Siberia.[41] Kayak and umiak types, plain dug-outs and dug-outs with washstrakes sewn on each side, birch-bark canoes and more modern plank-built Russian types are all intermingled. However, some sort of a pattern can be seen among these. The skin boats, the *baidar* and *baidarka*, seem to have been used by the so-called palaeo-Siberians, the Chukchi to the north of the Gulf of Anadyr, the Koryaks and Kamchadals of the Kamchatka Peninsula, the Aleuts and Ostyaks of the many island groups, Kuriles, Prybilou, Nonivak, St Lawrence, Kodiak, Aleutians, round or near the Bering Strait and Alaska. There are also rather more uncertain accounts of Samoyeds and Lapps using two-seated *baidarkas* or kayaks. Broadly speaking, the Neo-Siberian tribes such as the Samoyeds, Yuraks, Dolgans, Tungus and Yakuts were later arrivals from the centre of the Eurasian land mass. The use of bark canoes on the Yenisei by the Samoyeds for fishing and fowling may reflect an adaptation of the skin boat for inland use in well-wooded country, or it may be a parallel though independent development.

It must be emphasised once again here that any deduction from contemporary craft about prehistoric equivalents should be treated cautiously. Nevertheless it does not seem too rash to consider that the *baidars* observed by Captain Joseph Billings when exploring the coasts of Siberia for the Empress Catherine II,[42] were the products of a very ancient tradition which probably went back beyond the arrival of Early Neolithic peoples there.

Together with the carvings of Karelia and Azerbaijan, these seem to be visible remains of what Marstrander calls a mighty tradition of boat-building which once extended in a belt from sea to sea across the central and northern parts of Europe and Asia.[43] The cleft-bow style which spans the two continents is a further link. While no recent

Scandinavian craft appear to have inherited this device from their ancient predecessors, the double bows still recently found in some Bering Sea craft are surely related, however degenerately, to the ones carved in hundreds on the rocks of Norway and Sweden and thereby encompass between them not only thousands of years but several thousands of miles.

## America

Across the Bering Strait, on the American continent, one has to begin any study of skin boats with the important distinction between the skin boats of the Eskimo and the Indians. The Eskimo build their umiaks by first completing a strong framework which can stand on its own and then sewing skins round it. The Indians, on the other hand, as with their bark canoes, used the covering to hold the framework together, for without it the frame would not hold together on its own. When suitable birch or other bark was not available for seasonal or geographic reasons, then this technique of placing the framework within the covering and securing everything by lashing the covering to the gunwales, inserting extra ribs as necessary, was simply applied to two or three moose-skins sewn together. In this way the Indian obtained what was virtually a skin version of his birch-bark canoe.

The bull-boat was an even more primitive affair.[44] It was essentially a one-skin coracle on a crude basket framework used for crossing rivers. Some were too small to carry even one paddler and were hauled along by a swimmer with his unwaterlogged possessions on board. These craft, once widely used by the buffalo-hunting Plains Indians, had a counterpart in the *pelota* of South America, which served the same purpose from Venezuela to Patagonia. Sometimes, though, these latter just took advantage of the natural curve of the animal's skin and relied on tying the four corners to keep a roughly oblong shape without any inserted framework at all.[45]

The inflated skin floats which were used off the west coast of South America between latitudes 10° and 35° S very much astonished Thomas Caven-

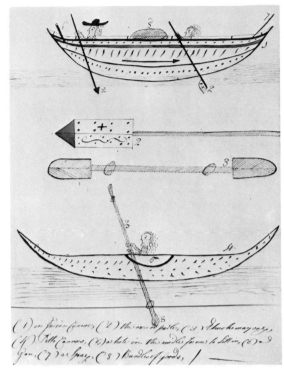

4.9 *Birch-bark canoe and kayak illustrated in James Isham's 'Observations on Hudson's Bay', 1743 (Hudson's Bay Company archive E2/2, fo. 6)*

dish on his round the world voyage of 1587.[46] In these extraordinary craft, inflated sealskins were fastened side by side, the bow ends close together, the stern ends diverging, and a small cane platform was placed on top.

But the supreme examples of skin-boat architecture on the American continent are the Eskimo umiak and kayak. They are so well known that their remarkable nature and seaworthiness need little underlining. Thanks to them, these originally Asian people, in their to-and-fro movements, were able to work their way east until they reached Greenland, thereby completing the circum-Polar girdle of skin-boat usage.

Eskimo building technique required a rigid frame with all parts fastened with pegs and lashings, to which the skin cover was secured and forced taut either by hauling on lacing or by the natural shrinking of the skin. The strength

4.10 *Early nineteenth century paired skin floats with platform in Valparaiso (National Maritime Museum)*

members of the umiak were the keelson and chine timbers which made a three-part rigid bottom to the craft. Across these went the floor timbers, while the frames went from the chine timbers up to the gunwales. Over the skeleton was put the cover of skins joined by cunning blind seams in which the needle never pierced the full thickness of the skin. This was made large enough to reach from gunwale to gunwale with a little over, so that the margin could be hauled down inside the craft and laced to a rising batten. After that, the cover was allowed to shrink until it became smooth and tight, when the seams would be rubbed with tallow and blubber, and oil would be applied to the rest.[47]

This is a different form of hull from the Irish curragh with its double gunwale, frames running the whole way from gunwale to gunwale and closely-spaced longitudinal stringers, though this too starts with a rigid framework. Part of the reason for this difference may be the type of covering used, since the seal- or walrus-skins of the Eskimo were much stronger than the cattle-hides of the Irish.[48]

On the other hand, the kayak is closer to the curragh in construction technique than the umiak, which has led to some interesting though rather profitless speculations about their relationship, since there is little positive evidence at the moment about the origin of the kayak. Its main strength comes from the gunwales to which the one-piece frames are attached. For these, driftwood, fir, pine, spruce or willow was used, while sinew was

4.11 *The framework for a Canadian Eskimo umiak (National Museums of Canada, Ottawa)*

4.12    *The skin cover being placed on the umiak frame (National Museums of Canada, Ottawa)*

generally used for lashing and sewing. According to Chapelle, because it is one of the most important tools in the Eskimo's fight for existence, the kayak has often to be designed for very particular requirements and so has developed greater variations in its form and size than the umiak.[49]

The difference between Indian and Eskimo craft is reflected in their use. Both the umiak and the kayak are essentially sea-going craft, and, to quote Chapelle, are 'exceptionally seaworthy'. As most Arctic waters are subject to violent storms, the Arctic skin boats have been developed with forms and proportions to meet this condition. In this matter, the light and flexible hull structure gives a special advantage. The kayak, in its highest state of evolution and in skilful hands, is perhaps the most seaworthy of all primitive small craft. The umiak is a close second, but, of the two, the kayak is safer under all conditions of Arctic travel.[50]

## Military use of skin boats

Finally, in this survey of where skin craft are found in time and place, one should note a practice which must surely give pleasure to any military historian, since it forms a link between Julius Caesar, Henry V and Wellington. In the Civil War, Caesar was able to extricate himself from a difficult position in Spain by ordering his troops to make coracles like those he recalled seeing in Britain some years before, and was thus able to

cross the River Sicoris near Lerida, when his enemies thought he was safely contained by its flooded waters.[51] Henry V, though one suspects he got the idea from his Welsh troops rather than from reading Caesar, ordered, according to Holinshed, among the military stores for his first expedition to France in 1414, 'boates covered with leather' for crossing over rivers.[52] Wellington showed both his usual grasp of the importance of adequate army transport and his caution by ordering that the twenty boats to be built for his Mysore campaign should be covered with '*double leather*' (the Duke's italics!) and sewn with thongs of such a size as to cover the gunwales of the boats all round.[53] Perhaps it also needs a military historian to decide whether it is significant that Hannibal, Genghis Khan and Pompey got their armies to use skin floats while Caesar, Henry V and Wellington used the solider, more stable, coracles.

## Distribution

This survey has ranged from Arctic Art carvings to modern ethnographical examples, reflecting in its patchiness the physically evanescent nature of this once widespread and crucial tradition. Even so, a geographical pattern does seem to emerge.

The areas where skin boats do not appear to have been used are most of Africa, the Mediterranean islands, south-east Asia and the East Indies, Australasia and the Pacific islands. Of the

4.13    *An Eskimo kayak (Fred Bruemmer)*

five types of skin craft, the raft of inflated skins seems to have the narrowest distribution, from Iraq and the Red Sea to China. The separate skin float, on the other hand, has been used from Spain across Eurasia to the west coast of South America. Its limitations, though, are north and south. It seems to have been found only between the latitudes of 40° N and 40° S. The kayak equally has a narrow distribution in latitude, though it has carried seal-hunters from Siberia to Greenland.

The round skin boat or coracle, in its different forms, is the most widespread of all. In some areas it has existed side by side with both the skin float and the skin float raft and it has certainly extended north and south of their limiting borders. It is pre-eminently a river craft particularly suited to fast-running mountain water. Its advantages for fishing in these sorts of conditions have already been described. Another virtue is that because of its very slight draft, it is affected much less than other craft by river currents. As James Hornell observed in southern India,[54] where a boat would cross a swift stream obliquely, often landing a long way downstream from its point of departure, the coracle in skilled hands goes straight across without any great exertion on the part of the ferryman. As well, it is easy to make and light to carry around.

From its development came the final type, the long skin boat. The southern Tibetan craft illustrate this process. When you enlarge a coracle, you do not just make a larger bowl-shape. That would merely become increasingly difficult to handle and board without capsizing. If instead you elongate the bowl shape, you solve these problems. This is what seems to have happened in Tibet when the pressure of traffic built up on the otherwise uncrossable rivers. If, however, you add an additional factor, the rough water of the open sea, an even more radical process is called for.

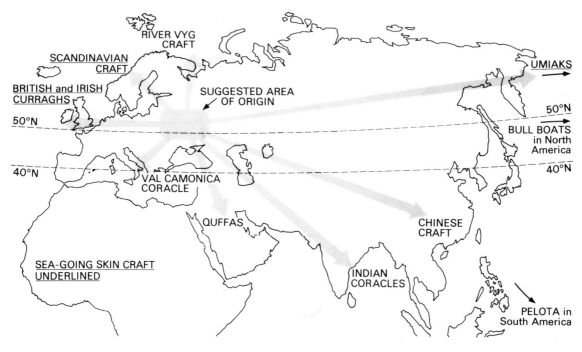

Map 4.1    *Distribution of skin boats – equal area projection (after Paul Johnstone)*

Borrowing Stuart Piggott's analytical assessment of early societies,[55] one would suggest that some group of wandering hunter-fishers, who were an innovating group rather than a conserving one, arrived on the shores of the ocean and there evolved the round river coracle into the long sea-going skin boat in response to the more difficult conditions facing them. This seems to have happened in at least three different areas – the British Isles, Scandinavia and Siberia.

What is more, in one of these areas, the same evolutionary process happened again at a later stage to produce the kayak from the umiak. In the Scandinavian prehistoric rock carvings, one can see seals and whales carved near skin boats that had already developed some fore and aft length as compared with a river coracle. Until recently the Eskimo and some of the Siberian peoples continued to hunt whales from umiaks. For seal-hunting, however, they evolved the most specialised of all skin craft, the kayak, the normally single-seated covered-in vessel of the hunter. This

spread from Siberia to Greenland, and if one takes into account unintentional wind-driven voyages, even on occasion reached Scotland.[56]

Thus a clear geographical situation emerges. The skin float and the coracle share a basic area, highly concentrated in central Asia and spreading out from there to the Atlantic coast of Europe and the American continent, though the skin float does not seem to have shared the spread north of 40° N. The skin raft appears to have developed from the skin float when settled living conditions, urban populations and markets produced a need for large loads to be carried regularly on certain rivers in the Middle East and Asia. The curragh, if the name can be used for convenience for all British long skin boats, the Scandinavian vessels, the *baidars* and the umiak all occur north of a line drawn somewhere between 45° and 50° N, the converse, as it were, of the skin float. There is an obvious explanation for this in one of the major differences between skin boats on the one hand and skin floats, rafts of all types, reed-bundle boats and dug-outs on the other. The skin boat is an extraordinarily dry craft at sea, as anyone who has been in a curragh or umiak will agree. They are so light, have such a shallow draught and rise so easily to a sea that they take remarkably little water aboard. As to the inflated float, one might put up with crossing a chilly mountain river on one, as the Baktiari did when crossing the Karam River in western Persia,[57] but this would hardly tempt a fisherman in northern waters.

In warm seas it would make little difference to have a certain amount of spray coming inboard or even washing around all the time. North of a certain line, however, it would start getting very uncomfortable and in the circumpolar regions it would be intolerable. This fits neatly with the known distribution of the dry, sea-going skin boat being in latitudes above 45° to 50°. It also fits in, incidentally, with the use of clothing. The skin trouser-suit has a very similar sort of distribution, as compared to the variations on the toga of more southerly areas, and requires the same sort of skills and techniques in its making.

If one looks at a map of the world now with this latitude in mind, a number of interesting points arise. South of the Equator none of the great land masses of the world stretches beyond 50° S except the tip of South America and the very southern-most part of New Zealand. One would not expect, therefore, to find long sea-going skin boats in the southern hemisphere except possibly in the very south of South America. Equally, one should not find sea-going rafts and dug-outs in higher latitudes in either hemisphere.

It is feasible, then, to suggest that until tools and evolving techniques of carpentry made planking available, any regular sea voyages in the pre-historic period which took place in latitudes above 45° to 50° were probably made in skin boats: this especially applies to the northern hemisphere. Exceptions are most likely in areas where there are particularly big trees available or the peoples concerned are inclined towards conserving rather than innovating methods. This could have useful implications in the study of situations where there is no *prima facie* evidence as to what type of craft were used.

## Origin of skin boats

The area where the skin boat originated was central Asia. This categoric statement by James Hornell was worked out almost entirely from the early-twentieth-century distribution of these craft.[58] Using additional archaeological evidence not then available to him, it would not be difficult to evolve a simple diffusionist model based on his proposition. For instance, working clockwise round the Eurasian land mass, one could see the British Isles, Scandinavian, Karelian and Siberian evolutions of the long skin boat as logical radiations from a central Asian starting-point. South of 40° N, other radiating lines seem to lead to a related type of craft, the inflated skin float, so still making sense of the same starting-point.

In the Middle East, the fact that the skin boat was in use in Mesopotamia in early times but not in Egypt, where the papyrus tradition prevailed, again suggests that any theoretical source would have been north of Mesopotamia. Equally, since the skin rafts referred to by Pliny and the *Periplus* are in the Red Sea, but not in the Mediterranean, where such sparse skin boat references as there are seem to be to river craft on the northern side,[59] this suggests that a source might have been east as well as north of Mesopotamia.

However, the once-fashionable practice of ascribing every innovation found by archaeologists to invasions and immigrations has now been challenged by a more rigorous examination of the evidence for such movements. As Colin Renfrew has said, we are now forced to go beyond the traditional diffusionist notions of cultural contact, and instead of the chess game of migrations, we have to look at cultures and peoples in their own right.[60] What should replace Hornell's statement, then, is a study of the general circumstances of climate, geography and technology that have led in known places to the appearance of skin boats. One essential is the presence of the right kind of leather-working tools, particularly bone needles or awls, since without these only the simplest of single-skin craft would be feasible. One would not look at areas with a warm climate and slow-moving waters or lakes, where reeds would be likely to grow and be an easier source of a usable craft. Areas with trees with suitable bark again would also provide an alternative to the skin boat. However, trees in themselves do not necessarily imply the possibility of dug-outs existing, since until the coming of polished stone tools and the food supplies necessary for a group to stay long enough in one place to make one, a skin boat could well be a quicker and simpler alternative. A cold climate and fast-moving or rough waters would strongly predispose a traveller towards the dry-riding and spray-avoiding qualities of the skin boat. Any craft which rode low in the water, was liable to get waterlogged or take spray aboard would be less attractive once an area of colder climate was reached. As we have seen, this is indeed borne out by both the past and present distribution of skin craft, with its strong northerly bias.

Looking at these points together, one might then say that, once appropriate bone tools were available, the fast-moving rivers north of 40° latitude in the bare plains of central Eurasia seem the most likely place for the skin boat to have evolved – so to that extent Hornell could well still be broadly correct, in geographical terms.

What then happened is speculation. Presumably these circumstances might have occurred in a number of places and inspired the sewing together of hides round a simple framework of withies. When this happened on the coast, more enterprising groups, as has been suggested, might have developed the coracle into the even more seaworthy curragh or umiak, the long skin boat.

There is, however, one exception to this rule. The southern Indian coracle suggests that the idea of the skin boat may have reached the sea on the south-east coast of the Indian peninsula, a geographically inappropriate area in the terms already defined, but was never developed there into a sea-going craft because there were other easier alternatives available on the warm waters of the Indian Ocean.

It is interesting that, while among the aboriginal population of India, represented by the Veddas and the Chenchu, the proto-Australoid physical type is dominant, among the equally hunting and gathering Munda-speaking peoples there are strong physical characteristics of Mongolian type and origin.[61] Their short skulls and slanting eyes are notably non-Veddoid. These Munda-speaking people are found in eastern central India and southwards from there. It is hard not to see here a possible link between the isolated appearance of coracles in south-eastern India and these people of central Asian type. The pattern it suggests (though of course more research would be needed to confirm it) is that the proto-Australoid aboriginal peoples of the sub-continent belonged to the early reed-bundle and raft-using groups, of whom some, as has already been suggested, eventually appeared in Australia and Tasmania. Subsequently, in one of the many infiltrations and invasions from the north that are characteristic of the later history of Pakistan and India, a hunter-fisher people from central Asia may have introduced the idea of the skin boat, being themselves in turn pushed on and isolated in south-eastern India by other later invasions. So this may be an example of what Gordon Childe called 'stimulus diffusion' or culture contact.

The next problem is to try and suggest a date or a period for the evolution of the skin boat. This is hardly likely to have happened on any scale before awls and needles were in general use. It might be possible, if difficult, to make a skin float by carefully flaying an animal hide through one opening and then lashing all the apertures, but it was sewing techniques that made the skin boat proper really feasible.

The latest time, on the other hand, must have been before the appearance of the Arctic Art which produced carvings of skin boats in Norway and Russia. These carvings are placed by Maringer and Bandi between the end of the sixth and the second millennium BC.[62] Marstrander suggests the transitional period between Late Glacial and Postglacial.[63] Grahame Clark and Stuart Piggott suggested the third to the second millennia BC,[64] though this was before the calibration of radiocarbon dates.

Thus the third millennium BC is the latest time the sea-going skin boat could have appeared. This suggests that either the immediate Postglacial period or the Late Pleistocene are the alternatives for its original development. Of the strong connection between sea travel and the circumstances of Postglacial times there can be little doubt. One of these was the rise in sea-levels caused by the melting of ice-sheets and the lifting of the weight of these from the earth's surface. Then the climatic changes and alteration of open landscapes into forests led to the disappearance of animals to hunt, and the way of life of many hunters had to change. This is reflected, for example, in the great shellfish middens on the coast of Finistère and the Tagus estuary, where the Mesolithic hunters eked out their diet with the products of the shore.[65]

At the other end of the Eurasian land mass, the north-eastern, we have as yet no recorded rock art to give us a glimmer of the antiquity there of the sea-going skin boat, though this is so much a basic part of Eskimo life that if one can date the early progenitors of these people back to Late Postglacial times, one would expect the umiak to have been in use then. In any case, it seems likely that as far as the north-eastern extremity of Asia is concerned, the same broad outline would apply. That is to say, a hunter-fisher origin, possibly Upper Palaeolithic, a sea-going development in Postglacial times at a Mesolithic stage of culture, and then the appearance to mingle with it of dugouts and simple planked craft developed by Neolithic peoples using polished stone tools, would probably have left the sort of evidence that is available to us today.

One answer then to the question when the skin boat evolved is that its total development occurred in Postglacial times and that this happened on, or reached, the northerly coasts of Eurasia, where the skin boat became a sea-going craft sufficiently quickly to take the Obanians to their living sites, the early Norwegian peoples up the west coast of that country, and the fishermen of both areas out to catch deep-sea fish.

A possible alternative, it seems, would be a central Asian beginning as an inflated float or crude bowl some time after the needle had come into general use in Late Pleistocene times in Upper Palaeolithic circumstances, spreading with the widening range of hunter-fisher groups until in Postglacial times the stimulus of changed living conditions caused certain groups on the more northerly coasts of Eurasia to evolve the sea-going long skin boat to take them fishing, to off-shore islands or to new sites on new shores.

The crudest form of coracle needs only very simple materials for its making – skins, fastenings of some sort and a framework which can be of withies, boughs or even driftwood, like the one Thorkils Orrabeinsstjup is described as making in the Floamanna Saga when he was wrecked on the barren east coast of Greenland shortly after Erik the Red had first colonised it in the tenth century AD.[66]

That the handling of skins was an early human skill is hardly in question: the abundance of scrapers on early sites makes that very clear. As well, this simple form of craft could be made quickly and a South American practice underlines another advantage – its portability. The Jesuit Martin Dobrizhoffer, describing in the late eighteenth century how the nomadic South American Abipones crossed the rivers of the Gran Chaco by a craft made from a bull's hide, illustrated this very well.[67]

A hairy, raw and entirely undressed hide is made almost square, by having the extremities of the feet and neck cut off. The four sides are raised like the upturned brim of a hat, to the height of about two spans, and each corner is tied with a thong, that they may remain erect, and preserve their squareness of form . . . Into a hole in the side of the pelota, they insert a thong instead of a rope, which a person, swimming, lays hold of with his teeth and with one hand, whilst he uses the other for an oar, and thus gently draws the pelota along . . . If many days' rain has wetted the hide and made it as soft as linen, boughs of trees are placed under the four sides and across the bottom of the pelota; these support the hide and strengthen it to cross the river in safety.

He also says that this hide was carried by the wife, suspended from the side of the saddle together with all her domestic chattels, to say nothing of infants as well. No Stone Age people, of course, could have matched the horse part of that description, but nothing else would seem to be out of place in Upper Palaeolithic Eurasia.

Bearing in mind this theoretical model, how

does it look set against what we know of the Upper Palaeolithic situation in central Asia? It would be appropriate here to quote what Grahame Clark and Stuart Piggott have to say about the Gravettian.[68] The main focus of this advanced Palaeolithic culture, which they say was in several ways more richly endowed technically than its predecessor, the Aurignacian, was in central and eastern Europe. The number of sites showing prolonged settlement in the zone of the southern USSR between the Rivers Don and Dniester and within latitudes 50° to 35° N also suggests that this, too, was a key area. This fits neatly with the suggested geographical area of origin for the skin boat. Then eyed needles from Gravettian sites at Gontsi and Mezin in the Desna basin give hints of the use of skin clothing, and spatulate tools of bone and ivory, recalling those of Morton in Fife, may have been employed in working leather or skin, while fish vertebrae necklaces again suggest an interest in water if not yet deep-water fishing.

Thus at a stage of man's history (c. 25,000 BC), marked by increased dynamism where along with many other tools of antler, bone, ivory and flint he evolved eyed needles and fish-hooks, one culture – the Gravettian, based in Russia and central Europe – apparently moved freely over large distances in areas where the skin boat survived subsequently on rivers and on whose oceanic fringes in Postglacial times the long skin boat was developed. Gravettian peoples must surely have crossed many rivers in the process of achieving their wide spread. The importance of rivers in any case at this stage is well marked for instance by the distribution of Upper Palaeolithic sites in the USSR, which are virtually all on the banks of rivers.[69] They had the technical means and materials to make simple skin boats and they existed in the area of the probable origin of the skin boat.

These arguments seem to suggest then that in central Asia, in the Upper Palaeolithic period, a simple form of river coracle or inflated skin float may have been evolved by makers of Gravettian tools. Whether this will ever become more than a theoretical argument is doubtful: it is almost certain that no direct evidence of a skin boat could survive from that period. There are, however, two cave paintings which may just possibly show skin boats of this early type. Cave paintings and engravings are notoriously difficult to date, and are often highly subjective in their interpretation. Therefore both these examples have to be considered very cautiously.

In the red, brown and black painting in the shelter at Minateda, Albacete, Spain, there is a drawing which, as published by Kuhn[70] and Maringer and Bandi,[71] could be construed as a boat. What inclines one to think it might be of skin is the proportion of height to length (which appears to be too deep for a dug-out) and, more important, the characteristic concave line beneath the bow and the stern. This curved line caused by the shrinking of the skin covering on its framework is unique to skin boats and can be seen on contemporary Eskimo umiaks (see Figure 4.4). On the other hand, the Minateda boat may be a horizontal bow from which the remains of the bowman who once held it have worn away. Bows like this are not uncommon.[72]

The broad bracket of dates put on these paintings is between 12,000 and 3000 BC.[73] As a type it may therefore take us back beyond the Scandinavian and Russian examples to the early river prototypes which started the skin boat on its progression over thousands of years to the umiak of today.

The other example, from the cave of Las Figuras in Andalusia, southern Spain, is much more definite in its outline but its interpretation as a boat is a good deal less certain (Figure 4.14a). If it is a boat, it is the most primitive skin-boat type of all, the basket bowl. This painting was described by the Abbé Breuil and M. C. Burkitt in 1929 as being 'a kind of "half-moon" having a number of small lines projecting from its diameter like a fringe'.[74] This has been taken to be a side view of a 'domed hut on piles'. An alternative, and more likely, possibility is that it could be a comb, since a number have been found (Figure 4.14b) of very similar shape to the painting.[75] Oddly enough, this dual interpretation as boat or comb is shared by another painting (Figure 4.14c) in the Portuguese Dolmen de Antelas near Aviero.[76]

4.14   (a) Painting of a skin boat (?) from Las Figuras rock shelter in Andalusia, Spain (after Breuil and Burkitt, Rock Paintings of Southern Andalusia, 1929)

(b) Ivory comb from the Iberian Bronze Age (after Renfrew, Antiquity, vol. 41, 1967)

(c) Boat or comb (?) from a painting in the Dolmen de Antelas, Visieu, Portugal (after Savory, Spain and Portugal, 1968)

The best argument for the Las Figuras painting being a boat is the exceptional number of waterfowl (geese, duck, flamingoes, swans, waders and one moorhen) painted near it. According to Breuil and Burkitt, more than one-third of the drawings in this cave are of birds,[77] though with the exception of one or two neighbouring caves, birds are normally rare in this art complex. The explanation of this comes from the near-by Laguna de la Janda, a large lake where many migrating birds stop on their way from Africa to Europe. It seems possible that the hunters might have used a basket-like framework of withies and a skin cover to pursue their prey; such a boat would have been very like the Las Figuras painting as well as being more secure than the chance reed bundle suggested for lake-margin hunting in chapter 1. The unique nature of this migration resting-place, as reflected in the avian emphasis in the cave paintings, might account for the unique nature of the half-moon object.

44

Map 4.2  *Britain and Ireland,
showing some of the places mentioned in
chapters 4, 5, 10, 11*

# 5 Dug-outs and the evolution of the plank-built boat

## Planked boat origins

The early forms of the craft considered in chapters 2 to 4 enabled man to exploit river, lake and sea for food, and to extend his activities to new continents. Various built-up forms were evolved from these early craft. As we saw in chapter 2, the simple log may be improved by linking several logs together to make a raft, or by increasing its freeboard to produce what may be called a raft-boat. But this form is capable of little further development, although it is thought to have influenced the form and structure of Chinese planked boats (see chapter 14). Similarly the reed bundle became the reed boat which, certainly in Egypt, influenced later plank-built boats. The variety of forms evolved in the skin tradition were described in chapter 4, where we saw how the skin boat became the dominant type in latitudes higher than about 50°, especially in the northern hemisphere where it undoubtedly influenced subsequent planked boats.

In chapter 3 it was suggested that in two isolated areas, Siberia and western South America, sewn plank boats possibly evolved from bark canoes. We may then ask whether we should look behind all primitive sewn planked craft to see if they might have evolved from the bark boat. For evidence one would have to look outside the settled temperate areas where the dominant dug-out superseded most other more primitive craft. But only in the case of the Chilean *dalca* and the Kuril Islands craft does there seem to be any surviving evidence,

and even then the case is not proved. It seems highly likely that of the primitive sewn planked craft we know (and they range from the archaic Mediterranean types reflected in the '*cumba sutilis*' (the sewn skiff in which Virgil (*Aeneid*, Book VI, 413–14) puts Charon), to the early Arab craft, the Baganda boats of Lake Victoria, the boats of the sixteenth-century Finns and Lapps, the many forms in India, the Ainu boats from the Kuril Islands, and the highly successful craft of the Polynesians),[1] nearly all were derived from the dug-out, either the ordinary dug-out or the expanded softwood version, with a washstrake on each side.

The extended dug-out, as well as the multiple dug-out, is indeed the most crucial type of craft. As we shall see in later chapters, it had a most important part to play in the Mediterranean and was a major influence in the peopling of the Pacific. We can reasonably assume that it was as relevant in the early periods in Indian and Indonesian waters and was certainly dominant in Central America and the West Indies, as far as aboriginal craft were concerned. Once the forest farmers of western Colombia and northern Ecuador acquired the dug-out all other aboriginal craft in that area disappeared.[2] Introduced by the Spaniards to areas further south, there, too, the dug-out in more recent times started to spread until replaced by modern planked craft.[3] In Thompson's study of Maya navigation,[4] as in McKusick's survey of the West Indies,[5] the dug-out is by far the most important craft. In Australia, the evidence is that the dug-out appears as a contribution from neighbouring more evolved societies, which the Aborigines, however much they admired and preferred it, could not achieve themselves without borrowed tools and the borrowed idea.[6]

## The simple dug-out

When considering the dug-out as a potential ancestor of more elaborate forms, it is important to remember three points. The first is that this was a craft for temperate regions. In the higher latitudes at sea it gave way to the skin boat, although there are exceptions, notably the north-west coast of the American continent and New Zealand, which are both noted for their plentiful supply of extremely large trees. The Indians of the British Columbian coast, who owed their affluence largely to the rich runs of salmon up their rivers,[7] produced the largest dug-outs in the world from Oregon pine. When occasional trunks of this huge tree drifted from the American west coast to Hawaii, they were highly prized there, since the dug-out-builders had no need to raise the sides additionally with planking.[8] In New Zealand the kauri trees provided almost as good a start, because the great size of the trunk allowed sufficient freeboard to make sea voyages possible.

The second point is that building a dug-out with a simple tool kit appropriate to the Mesolithic or Early Neolithic probably took a relatively long time. Du Tertre, for example, describing Carib canoes in the seventeenth century, says that before the Carib people had European tools they spent entire years making their boats;[9] while the Maoris, having chosen a suitable tree, planted a crop near by so that they could live off it the following year while hollowing out the felled trunk.[10] This meant that dug-outs were developed and used by settled communities. This does not restrict their use to agricultural communities, since there have been plenty of groups from Mesolithic times on, like those of Star Carr, Yorkshire, or the Danube fishermen of Lepenski Vir who had a secure enough existence to stay in one site long enough to make dug-outs. But, by and large, the greatest development followed the introduction of the more settled life of the agriculturalist.

The third point is that although Mesolithic and Neolithic tools could certainly work softwoods, it is doubtful whether hardwoods could be satisfactorily fashioned into a dug-out until metal tools became available. However, the effectiveness of stone tools on a timber such as oak needs to be investigated experimentally before we can be certain on this point. On the other hand, the workmanship exhibited on the mid-second millennium BC planked boats from North Ferriby, Humberside,[11] showed that Bronze Age woodworking techniques were more than adequate for building dug-outs of oak, and this has been confirmed by the recent radiocarbon dating of several oak dug-outs to the Bronze Age.

The evidence for the use of dug-outs is just about world-wide within the temperate zone. Unfortunately it has seldom been possible to obtain a reliable date,[12] although this situation will change as more radiocarbon analyses are undertaken and when it becomes possible to date dug-outs dendrochronologically. At the moment the earliest securely dated find in Europe is that from Pesse, Netherlands (Figure 5.1), which has a date of c. 6315 BC in radiocarbon years (Gro-486). How-

5.1    *The dug-out from Pesse, Netherlands, which has been dated to* c. *6315 BC (Biologisch-Archaeologisch Instituut, Groningen University)*

ever it is not certain whether this is in fact a boat rather than some other form of dug-out vessel.[13] Other published radiocarbon dates in Europe range from *c*. 3060 BC for the Praestelyngen 1 dug-out from Denmark (K-1473) to the thirteenth and fourteenth centuries AD (ST-27, T-1429, Pi-84, R-894α, D-71, Q-1245). The Praestelyngen boat is made from a log of lime; the earliest dug-outs known to be of oak are dated to the mid-second millennium BC (Q-288, BM-213, R-375). At the other end of the time-scale dug-outs are known to have been in use in Europe until the present century.[14] The wide use of dug-outs (mostly improvements on the simple dug-out) outside Europe in recent times is discussed in chapters 13 to 16, and their use in earlier times is also investigated.

## Making a dug-out

Sir Cyril Fox was able to examine a dug-out from Llyn Llangorse, Powys, soon after it was re-covered, and in his classic study published over fifty years ago[15] he was able to suggest how this boat had been made. There was no sign of fire being used, and thus Sir Cyril suggested that the process of hollowing out the log started with a broad and deep hole probably at the centre, followed by smaller holes cut with chisel or gorge and mallet at convenient points, so that by means of wedges the wood might be split off. The process would be repeated until the bottom was ap-proached. It is interesting that in the Llangorse

canoe the last set of holes had gone too deep so were still visible when the floor was levelled off. The sides were made to a uniform thickness by cutting grooves (some of which were still visible in 1926) down them and then chipping away the wood in between. This method deduced by Fox has several modern parallels from places where dug-outs were recently made.[16] It should be noted, however, that fire can be used to assist in the hollowing of a dug-out without leaving any traces in the archaeological sense.

A good account of one version of the fire-using method is that seen by Peter Kalm, the Swedish traveller, being used by the Delaware Indians in AD 1747. After burning down a tree, taking care by using wet rags not to let the fire spread up the trunk, they set about hollowing it out.[17]

They lay branches along the stem of the tree as far as it must be hollowed out, set them on fire, and replace them by others. While these parts are burning, they keep pouring water on those parts that are not to be burnt at the sides and ends. When the interior is sufficiently burnt out, they take their stone hatchets and shells and scoop out the burnt wood. These canoes are usually thirty or forty feet long.

It is likely that similar techniques were common over much of the world from early times until the present day.

## Developments of the simple dug-out

Because they are so narrow, the simple dug-outs have limited lateral stability and there is world-

5.2    *The dug-out from Llyn Llangorse, Powys. Sir Cyril Fox found gouge and chisel marks on the inner surface of the far side (National Museum of Wales, Cardiff)*

wide evidence of man's search for improved stability, principally by heat expansion of the beam of the boat, by the use of stabilisers and outriggers, and by joining two or more dug-outs together.[18]

## Multiple dug-outs

When Professor Atkinson devised his experiment in 1954 to find out how the bluestones had been brought to Stonehenge from their source 135 miles away in the Prescelly Mountains in Wales, he postulated for the river section of the journey a craft made up of three 'dug-outs' secured together with a platform on top.[19] The experiment showed that such a craft was entirely adequate for this purpose. It drew very little water and was simple to manoeuvre and to propel, either by hauling or punting. Prehistoric examples of such craft are known from a number of countries. Such is their efficiency that they have even survived in central Europe into the twentieth century. A most interesting example is the craft still found on the Dunajec, a tributary of Poland's main river, the Vistula, which consists of no less than five dug-outs lashed together. The advantages of such a craft are not difficult to see. The Dunajec has a stony bed, often with rocks projecting, the depth of the water changes rapidly, its course is winding and in places narrow, and the current strong. In such conditions a raft would be too unwieldy and difficult to manoeuvre, as well as being liable to ground in the shallows. A displacement craft, on the other hand, however skilfully handled, might always be liable to touch bottom or strike an underwater rock, and the speed of the current would make this both more likely and more disastrous. A multiple dug-out steered by paddle would, however, be more manoeuvrable than a raft, its flexible lashings letting any of its members ride over an obstacle, and even if one was holed, the buoyancy of the others would be sufficient to keep it afloat.[20]

The fascinating thing is that though the Dunajec dug-outs are gradually being replaced by craft made of wooden planks, such was the effectiveness of the multiple craft on this particular river that it preserved a tradition among the local

craftsmen that could well go back to the time when improved stone tools and living conditions first made the making of dug-outs feasible. As such, the practical details of its construction and use are an example of what could well have been prehistoric practice. Poplar is the wood normally used for these craft, which are just under 6 metres long, wider at the stern, and with a long sloping bow. Since they are usually carried back upstream on carts, and therefore need to be lifted out of the water, a rod is passed through a hole in each side near the bows, and at the stern a projecting ledge is cut out of the solid trunk. The dug-outs are joined together by another rod which goes across all five above the individual rods in the bows, to which it is secured by lashings. At the stern (Figure 5.3) the dug-outs are secured by a series of turns through holes in the sides with a cable of twisted hemp about 12 cm in diameter. These are the resilient arrangements which allow any one member of the craft to ride up, if its sloping bow strikes a rock,

5.3   *The after end of a multiple dug-out from the River Dunajec, Poland (National Maritime Museum)*

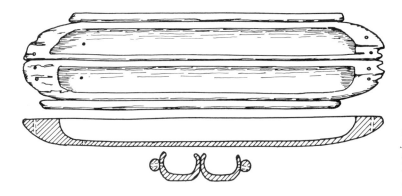

5.4 *Drawing of a double dug-out from Surnuinmäki, Finland, with stabilisers ( T. I. Itkonen,* Kansatcteellinen Arkisto, *Helsinki, 1941)*

without checking the progress of the others.[21]

The Dunajec craft may be a rarer and more elaborate version than most, but it still gives a very interesting picture of a technique which must have been common over much of prehistoric Europe. Paired dug-outs linked in a variety of ways are known to have been used in recent times in Oceania, India, Albania, Spain, Russia and Scandinavia; finds interpreted as pairs have been excavated from France and Germany, and some from England are possibly of this type.[22] As Grahame Clark[23] has pointed out, once draught animals came into use for transport, you needed something more stable than a single dug-out to ferry them across rivers, and a paired dug-out, with the animal's forelegs in one craft and its hind legs in the other, was a good answer.

In the Pacific area (see chapter 15) paired dug-outs of great size were evolved, ones that were fully capable of carrying great loads over long sea voyages.

## Expanded dug-outs

In north-west Europe, from Finland and Estonia eastwards to Siberia, and in India and the Americas, simple dug-outs have been expanded by various forms of heat treatment (Figures 5.5, 5.6) so that the boat is made broader, thus improving its stability.[24] At the same time this expansion reduces the freeboard amidships – this may subsequently be regained by adding a washstrake (see Figure 5.7) – and generally the ends of the boat will rise, giving it a characteristic sheerline.

5.5 *Heating an aspen dug-out in Satakunta, Finland, in 1940 (National Museum of Finland, Helsinki)*

5.6   *Forcing the sides of the Satakunta dug-out apart (National Museum of Finland, Helsinki)*

This technique is suitable for only certain species of timber, and even then great care is required as overheating or overstraining the boat when the sides are forced apart during this expansion process can result in a burst and ruined boat. Dugouts can thus have been expanded only where suitable timber species were available, and only when the necessary fineness of heat control had been acquired. Heat treatment is not necessarily by fire, for in Finland, Estonia, India and America in the recent past, dug-outs have been expanded after being heated in a warm sea or by the sun on a hot beach.

Crumlin-Pedersen[25] has argued strongly that the expanded softwood dug-out was the principal type from which the planked boat of northern Europe was developed. This point is considered further in chapter 9.

## Stabilisers and outriggers

An alternative way to improve stability, and thus enable dug-outs to be used on other than inland waterways and estuaries, is by the use of outriggers or similar stabilising devices (Figures 5.4, 5.8, 15.14). Grahame Clark[26] early recognised the importance of such timbers in the evolution of seagoing boats, and McGrail[27] has recently drawn attention to several examples in the European archaeological record of stabilising timbers similar to outriggers but fastened directly to the dug-out's sides. True outriggers are not known in European waters, but in other parts of the world they have been and are used extensively, especially in the Pacific (Figures 15.14, 15.15).

## The evolution of planked boats

The simple dug-out or one that has been expanded may be extended by the addition of strakes to give extra freeboard and additional load-bearing

5.7   *After the ribs have been fitted to the expanded Satakunta boat, washstrakes are added to the sides (National Museum of Finland, Helsinki)*

5.8   *A nineteenth-century dug-out with stabilisers in Manila harbour, Philippines (National Maritime Museum)*

capability (Figures 5.7, 5.9). It is generally agreed that many forms of planked boat evolved from this process. Such strakes were probably sewn or lashed on at first, and were subsequently fastened by trenails or mortise and tenon joints, and later by iron nails. This extension technique was widespread and examples are mentioned in almost every chapter that follows.

As we shall also see in later chapters, expansion and extension (and possibly the pairing) of dug-outs, and the use of stabilising timbers, enabled man to evolve planked boats which could be used for functions and in conditions never before thought possible. The dug-out may not have been used in the earliest times, but in its several forms it seems to have played a most important role in water transport since the Neolithic over a vast area of the inhabited world. Because it was so very widespread, it almost certainly was an ancestor of the majority of planked boats and ships.

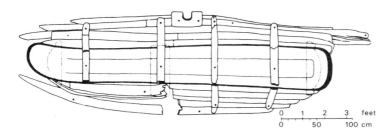

5.9   *A plan of the fourteenth-century AD Kentmere boat from Cumbria drawn by David Wilson during excavation in 1955. The dug-out base has ribs and washstrakes added to it (D. M. Wilson,* Medieval Archaeology, *vol. 10, 1966, Fig. 30a)*

# Part Two

# Europe

# 6 The earlier Mediterranean

## The obsidian trade

During the last few years our idea of early Mediterranean seafaring has been completely changed by a substance not immediately connected with the sea. Obsidian is a black volcanic glass whose sharp edges, when fractured, were highly prized by prehistoric man. It is also now one of the best indicators there is of early sea voyages.

In 1964 Cann and Renfrew[1] published in an elegant study a method, mainly dependent on measuring by spectrographic analysis the barium and zirconium content, through which the volcanic source of most obsidian could be determined. Since in an area like the Mediterranean there are relatively few sources of obsidian, this was an extremely valuable way of studying the movement of any specimen found in an archaeological context. In a later study, Renfrew, Durrani, Khan and Taj[2] refined the method by using analysis of fission tracks and uranium content as additional identification. This was useful because some obsidian, such as that from Hungary and the island of Melos in the Aegean, showed similar composition when examined only by optical spectroscopy. On the other hand, the types can be distinguished by study of their fission tracks which are made by the random disintegration of uranium molecules after the obsidian has been formed. By counting these and comparing their number with artificially-induced fission tracks, which can be distinguished optically, it is possible to discover both the age of the obsidian and its uranium content. The chances of obsidian from two different sources having the same age and uranium content as well as the same pattern of trace elements is fairly remote. Hence one can distinguish between the Hungarian obsidian which was formed between three and four million years ago and that from Melos which is either some five million years older or a million years younger, even though both have much the same trace elements.

Finally, in yet another study[3] a third technique, using neutron activation, was presented for distinguishing the sources of obsidian. This relied on measuring the relative concentrations of different elements in the obsidian after irradiation in an atomic reactor. So specific is this process that it is now possible to distinguish between the two sources on Melos at Adhamas and Dheheme-negaki, which are only to 10 kilometres apart.

The archaeological implications of these studies are many. The one that concerns us here is the picture that emerges of some of the earliest sea trade in the world for which there is positive evidence. In the words of Renfrew, Cann and Dixon,[4]

not only in the Aegean but in the western Mediterranean and the near East we are obtaining categorical evidence of sea travel over very great distances . . . Even more surprisingly perhaps the very voyages made by the mainlanders to Melos in the earliest neolithic times themselves presuppose a prior knowledge of the existence of the material. How they first learnt of it we cannot know but it must surely have been in the course of travel for other purposes or perhaps even through prospecting itself. This in turn hints at a very confident mastery of sea travel.

In some ways these studies were also deflatory. The 'liparite' previously thought to have reached Knossos from the island of Lipari, and the Melian obsidian thought to have been found in Malta, proved to have come from much nearer sources. But in every other way the picture of sea travel that emerged was remarkable. Obsidian from Melos has been identified in the very earliest pre-pottery Neolithic levels of Argissa, Sesklo and Soufli in Thessaly. Six blades of obsidian from the comparable stage at Khirokitia in Cyprus show that by perhaps 5690 BC there was already trade between that island and the Anatolian mainland. Even earlier dates come from levels with obsidian at Knossos (6100 ± 180 BC) and Nea Nikomedia (6220 ± 150 BC), while finds on the islands of Chios and Skyros confirm the maritime nature of this trade.[5]

This vigorous scene of commercial activity by sea was surprising enough, but it did at first seem to have a certain logic. The finds seemed to show that, while on land obsidian found in pre-Neolithic levels had travelled 300–400 kilometres from their sources, none reflected sea travel. Only with the emergence of settled farming conditions did trade by sea seem to develop. Then came the evidence from the Franchthi cave in the Greek Argolid near Porto Cheli. Excavations in this cave have produced two very important results. One is perhaps the most completely stratigraphic sequence in Greece from Late Glacial through Mesolithic to Late Neolithic times. The other is the earliest prehistoric context in the Aegean in which obsidian has been found.[6]

When tested by the fission track technique, this obsidian, from a level in Franchthi dated by radiocarbon to the middle of the seventh millennium BC (P-1522), was found to have come from the Melos source. Yet Melos is 120 kilometres by sea from the cave. Moreover, the voyage there and back must have been made a number of times because the Melian obsidian with its typical pearly lustre occurs in a number of successive layers. In fact Renfrew suggests that the Franchthi obsidian could well claim to be the earliest positive evidence for the transport of goods by sea from anywhere in the world.[7]

## What type of boat?

These conclusions face the nautical archaeologist fairly and squarely with a problem. In what sort of craft was the obsidian carried? The Mesolithic data from Franchthi are interesting because the obsidian is not the only evidence for sea-going. From the earlier sequences, it seems that the occupants of the cave were hunters, living mainly off red deer. Then there appear, in the obsidian layers, a large number of fish-bones. Evidently in the seventh millennium BC they had become fishermen and acquired at the same time the ability to voyage to Melos.

The problem of how to make a dug-out with a microlithic repertoire of tools is not one that seems to have yet been solved. Artefacts thought by some to be small dug-outs have been found in Mesolithic contexts: the pine one from Pesse in the Netherlands (Figure 5.1), dated to about 6315 BC, is one of the best known examples.[8] There is also the Scottish one found beneath the carse clays at Friarton near Perth, though in fairness it should be said that the distinguished archaeologists Gordon Childe and Lacaille who worked in Scotland both doubted its great age, a doubt which has recently been echoed by McGrail.[9] At Franchthi, the Mesolithic occupants burnt large numbers of bones, so possibly they produced dug-outs by burning and scraping, though the excavator reports no example of a shell or bone implement used in this way, and all the stone tools were very small.[10] Only in the later Neolithic levels do polished stone axes and adzes begin to appear.

## Skin or basketry?

One therefore has to consider the alternatives. Could the islands of the Mediterranean have been reached in the same sorts of skin boats as probably took the Mesolithic fishermen of Britain out to the Western Isles of Scotland? There is no doubt that these sorts of craft can be a crucial element in the process of discovery. Stefanson[11] makes the important point that the most likely craft in which to make chance discoveries of islands should combine a major disadvantage with a major virtue – namely, a tendency to make leeway with the ability to stay afloat. He goes on to quote the Eskimo sealskin boat, the umiak, as a nearly perfect example of this. It is hopeless to try and row such a craft against a strong wind. Since it is so light, it has very little momentum, and a headwind will blow it as far back each time as a heave on the oars has advanced it. He suggests that it must often have happened that when craft of this kind were crossing a bay or making a trip between islands, the wind would change or get up and, if this was accompanied by cloudy weather, the unfortunate boatmen might easily end by rowing in the wrong direction so that it would not be at all difficult to end up at an unknown island a hundred miles or more away.

Possibly one might think that skins were less easily preserved in hot climates, and there were less easy conditions around the Mediterranean for raising cattle.[12] Yet there is no lack of evidence for the early use of leather – among the Badarians, for instance, of Upper Egypt who in the Early Predynastic stage buried their dead in skin outer garments. Later, the sails of Athenian war-ships had leather corners, and hide coverings were used against spray, and we have from the *Odyssey* and from Sumerian texts excellent descriptions of quite different early methods of preparing leather:[13] 'As when a chief his people bids to stretch a huge bull's hide all drenched and soaked with grease, they in a circle ranged this way and that, pull the tough hide till entering in, the grease is all absorbed, and dragged by numerous hands the supple skin to the utmost length is stretched', is how Homer puts it. The Sumerian method of about 800 BC is rather more technical. 'This skin you will drench it in pure Masaba flour, in water, beer and first quality wine, with the best fat of a pure ox, the alum of the land of the Hittites and oak galls will you press it, and you will cover the bronze kettle-drum with it.'

On the other hand there is little doubt that the lack of a need comparable to that of northern peoples for protective clothing would not have encouraged the development of the technology involved in tanning, cutting and sewing the large pieces of hide needed for skin boats. The same climate which made trousers redundant also meant that being awash at sea was much less irksome. The fisherman whose craft was a half-submerged log or reed bundle would hardly have found the lack of freeboard much of an inconvenience.

A possible argument for the presence of skin boats in the early Mediterranean period is a rather odd model in whitish clay from Phylakopi on Melos with a pronounced cut-water bow, oculi ('eyes'), and vertical lines painted on the sides (Figure 6.1). The bulges between these lines have led some people to suggest that this is an attempt to represent ribs with a hide hull swelling out in between, but Marinatos, after studying the original carefully, is convinced that these undulations are simply fortuitous, and the fact that the ribs are shown is not enough on its own to suggest that this is a skin boat.[14] In any case, whatever it is, it is a solitary and odd example.

So, on the whole, it looks as though skin boats did not play a part in early Mediterranean sea travel and some support for this comes from the Canary Islands. When the Spaniards conquered these mountainous islands in the fifteenth century, they found there a virtually intact Mediterranean Neolithic culture. The islanders grew wheat, barley, beans and figs, reared sheep, goats and pig, and made coarse pottery. But they had one serious lack: the islands contained no stone suitable for

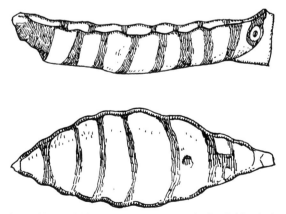

6.1   *Clay model boat from Phylakopi on the Greek island of Melos (after Landström,* The Ship, *1961)*

making the polished stone axes so characteristic of this stage of development. As a result, once the original craft that had brought them, their animals, their seeds and a few imported polished axes to the islands from North Africa wore out, they apparently could not replace them. So they remained isolated from each other on their seven islands, except for the occasional chance visit from the mainland.[15]

One would perhaps have expected them first to attempt some form of reed-bundle craft but there may not have been any suitable reeds available on the islands. What is certain is that they had the materials necessary to make skin boats, since they tanned goatskins for clothes and sewed capes with bone needles. What was lacking was the conception.

Other even less likely alternatives in the prehistoric Mediterranean one should at least consider are basket boats, log rafts and pot rafts. According to Strabo, 'paktons', small woven basket boats like those of Indochina and Japan, were used on the upper Nile. Rafts were far more widespread, and many classical sources describe them, from the charming one shown on a Contorniate coin (Figure 6.2) of the fourth century

AD to the more massive affairs used to transport elephants from Megara near Athens to Epidaurus in the Argolid in 316 BC, or the vast one described by Theophrastos which transported Corsican timber, driven by no less than fifty masts and sails. Most extraordinary of all are perhaps the rafts made of timbers lashed to pots. Hercules is shown on an Etruscan jewel, floating on one – suitably perhaps, since Metellus in 252 BC used these strange craft to carry elephants between Sicily and Italy.[16] There is no reason to suppose that their use did not go back to an earlier period, but they are unhandy craft in their simpler forms and it would seem unlikely that they would make the to-and-fro voyages implied by the Melian obsidian.

## Reed

Much the most likely answer for these early voyages would seem to be some form of reed-bundle craft. This is one of the most easily made of all primitive craft, needing only the simplest of equipment for its construction. Its widespread existence in ancient Egypt, where the papyrus plant was the source of building material, and Mesopotamia has already been mentioned. There is also the quotation from Isaiah 18: 1–2: 'Woe to the land shadowing with wings, which is beyond the rivers of Ethiopia; That sendeth ambassadors by the sea, even in vessels of bulrushes upon the waters'.

Nearer to Franchthi are two enigmatic craft published by Arthur Evans in his classic work *The*

6.2    *The sea-goddess Isis Pelagia on a raft on a Contorniate coin of the fourth century AD (after A. Evans,* The Palace of Minos at Knossos, *London, 1935, Fig. 148)*

6.3    *Craft on a gold signet ring from the island of Mochlos, Crete (after A. Evans,* The Palace of Minos at Knossos, *Fig. 919)*

*Palace of Minos*. One is on a gold signet ring from the island of Mochlos, off Crete (Figure 6.3), the other on a ring from Tiryns, Argolid. The former, with its rather shapeless hull, could be interpreted as a reed-bundle craft with a horse's head at one end and a knot with the reeds splaying out beyond it at the other. The craft on the Tiryns ring is rather more conventional and has a crescent-shape with vertical lines at intervals along the hull. It recalls a recently excavated engraving of the Roman period from the Israeli site of Bet She'arim (Figure 6.4). This has a deeper hull and a less pronounced crescent-shape, but otherwise, with its vertical lines, is not dissimilar. The significance of the vertical lines is that planking is normally horizontal, while reed-bundle lashings are often vertical and at intervals. So if an artist was at all accurate in his representations, these vertical lines could be taken as signs of a reed, rather than

planked, craft. This is rather similar in general outline to the graffito of a vessel observantly noted by Basch[17] in the '*Maison aux stucs*' ('House of the tiles') on Delos. There is little doubt that this also represents a reed boat because the bow shows clearly a lashing round the end of the reed bundles. The probable *ex-voto* nature of many Delos engravings, suggested by Basch, call to mind the engravings noted by Diana Woolner on a portal of the temple of Hal Tarxien in Malta, for which she suggested a similar reason.[18] And at least one of these might also represent a reed boat. So it is not impossible that reed boats once existed in the Mediterranean and survived, just as they did in Egypt, up to classical and indeed to modern times, and that more are waiting to be noted among engravings and so on from the Mediterranean's past.

Within recent memory there have in fact been

6.4   *Roman age graffito from Bet She'arim, Israel (Maritime Museum, Haifa)*

boats on Corfu made from the common reed (*Phragmites*). They normally carried a crew of two who used paddles to take them out to the lobster-baskets laid in deep water off the strong western cliffs of the island. In the view of the local fishermen these were unsinkable. They also described a method of fastening two craft stern to stern with long poles thrust through the bundles and firmly lashed, which produced a cigar-shaped craft that, it was said, would take you anywhere.[19]

The importance and significance of these craft is threefold. They show that an indigenous tradition of reed-boat building has existed on a Mediterranean island. They show that the materials were at hand on these islands to make this sort of craft. And the making of such craft would have been well within the technological capacity of a Mesolithic people. So if one has to speculate what craft were used by the collectors of obsidian, some form of reed-bundle craft seems much the most likely. The same goes for the Natufian fishermen of the Mesolithic Levant whose fish-hooks suggest some sort of sea-going and, even earlier, for any crossing of the Straits of Gibraltar.

There is, however, one reasonable objection that has to be considered. That is the sparseness of the evidence left behind of this tradition if it once existed across the breadth of the Mediterranean. Here the South American situation is quite enlightening. If one looks at Clinton Edward's maps of the distribution of aboriginal craft on the west coast there, one sees that dug-outs and reed floats are mutually exclusive.[19] The dug-out, according to Edwards, predominates over other craft in its aboriginal tropical home.[20] Moreover, whatever happened in pre-Conquest times, there is specific evidence that the dug-out replaced the reed-bundle craft after the coming of the Spaniards, until in fact the general use of the European planked boats in the nineteenth century in turn ousted the dug-out.[21] These parallels cannot of course be pushed too far. But at least this example shows that it is not unlikely that, where a reed-bundle tradition existed, it could very well be completely obliterated by a later dug-out tradition when polished stone axes and adzes become available.

## The dug-out

It is perhaps worth-while here to consider a Greek Macedonian site from the Neolithic period such as Nea Nikomedeia. This was a pottery-using farming settlement not far from the coast with a radiocarbon date of *c.* 6100 BC for its early levels. The houses had a timber framework whose biggest postholes were 30 cm in diameter and 65 cm deep. Oak was well represented in the charcoal samples, and the excavator, while unable to define always a clear difference between axes and adzes, considered some of the polished stone tools had features which suggested use as adzes. Fish-bones were common at all levels.[22] Thus, while there is no specific evidence for dug-outs here, the possibility of their being made and used is certainly more supported by the evidence than at Franchthi.

Dug-outs were in no way strange or out of place in the later Mediterranean scene. Pliny's description, for instance, of one example is 'arundines vero tantae proceritatis ut singula internodia alveo navigabili ternos interdum homines ferant',[23] while Torr records that among the places mentioned in classical writings as having mon-oxylons (dug-out canoes) in common use are the Elbe, the Guadalquivir, the north coast of Spain, the delta of the Nile, the Rhone, the Danube, the Dnieper and the west coast of India.[24]

When it comes to possible illustrations of early versions of such craft, these are sparse and not always easy to interpret. The best known are two models of what appear to be dug-outs, one apparently double-ended, the other with a high stern and a 'ram'. This latter appears to be much the same sort of craft as are shown on some Cycladic so-called 'frying-pan' vases from Skyros dated to the Early Bronze Age, which may have held water for use as mirrors. Landström[25] suggests that it is possible to see in these a development from a simple dug-out with a high stern into one in which the stem post is first bent up slightly and then grows into a virtually double-ended craft. This would be an advance on a pure dug-out and Landström adds a sewn-on washstrake to his reconstruction (Figure 6.5).

However, these early Mediterranean craft are

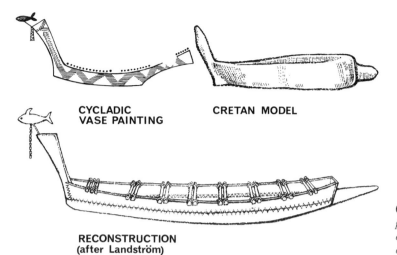

**CYCLADIC
VASE PAINTING**

**CRETAN MODEL**

**RECONSTRUCTION
(after Landström)**

6.5 *Painting on a Cycladic 'frying-
pan' vase; a model dug-out from Crete;
a conjectural drawing by Landström of
an Early Bronze Age boat*

not so simple as to avoid being the source of a
prolonged controversy: was the high extremity at
the bow or the stern? Disagreement about this
crucial point has been going on since Tsountas[26]
first published the vases in 1899. He and Arthur
Evans, the excavator of Knossos, believed that
these Cycladic craft had stem posts, not stern posts,

and that their 'rams' or horizontal projections
were aft. Evans was guided to this point of view by
the fish which were shown like wind-vanes on the
top of the high extremities. These, he believed,
were facing forward, so the high extremity would
have been at the bow. He thought that the
horizontal projections were 'fixed rudders'.[27]

Map 6.1 *Central and eastern Mediterranean*

Jacquetta Hawkes, Sinclair Hood, R. D. Barnett and other distinguished scholars also took Evans's view.[28] But there were others who thought differently. Köster, for instance, went so far as to write 'nul marin ni nul constructeur naval n'hésitera, fut-ce même un instant, à reconnaître la poupe dans la partie la plus élevée des bateaux.'[29]

Many ways have been used to try and settle this question, including studying the position of the oars, since it might be a convention, for instance, always to show them at the start of a stroke. Some fragments of clay tablets from Knossos show a design of oarsmen with enough detail to say that they are at the start of their stroke, thus revealing where the stern is, and in

6.6   *Face B of the disc from Phaistos, southern Crete (BBC)*

other cases, where both rowing and steering oars are shown, this practice is confirmed, since the steering oar being aft can be accepted as one of the few firm rules. Unfortunately this method does not work in the case of the Cycladic craft. The artists who decorated the vases obviously did not think the position of the oars was relevant, because in some the oars point one way, in some the other; and again in some examples the situation is a little perplexing because the oars on one side are at the start of their stroke and on the other at the finish – perhaps they were holding water and turning.

A more convincing test is the one applied by Marinatos in his classic work on Creto-Mycenaean shipping. This was to observe the direction of the various ship symbols used in the writings of the period. According to this method, in a hieroglyphic script such as that used on the Phaistos disc from southern Crete, all moving objects, including ships, are shown facing the opposite way to the script. On the other hand, in the Minoan scripts all living creatures, as well as objects, face in the same direction as the writing.[30]

On the Phaistos disc, the ship sign is usually fitted in at right angles to the line of writing, presumably to save space, but on face B, where towards the end the writer had more room, the ship is put in parallel to the writing, which thus settles which is its bow (Figure 6.6). From this, Marinatos evolved the rule that the higher extremity is always aft, so that if a Cycladic craft was travelling in the direction the fish-vane was looking, it would be going stern first.

The controversy continued, swaying this way and that,[31] until in the 1960s there were two developments. In 1965 C. Doumas published two newly discovered rock carvings from south-east Naxos which added a different form of illustration of these controversial craft.[32] One was particularly interesting because it showed an animal being driven aboard (Figure 6.7). Doumas subsequently supported the high stern point of view, basing this partly on Marinatos's argument that a rowed vessel would travel most of the time with a following sea, and therefore need protection aft, partly on analogies with dug-outs from New Zealand and Tahiti with high stern posts.[33]

In 1967 Colin Renfrew[34] published three lead

6.7   *Rock carving from south-east Naxos, Greece, showing an animal being driven on board a boat (Doumas,* Korphi t'Aroniou, *1965)*

boats from Naxos which had been given to the Ashmolean Museum by Professor Dawkins through Arthur Evans many years ago, but had never been previously published (Figure 6.8). This was probably because the material of which they were made, lead, was unusual and therefore their authenticity had been doubted. However, Renfrew's study of Cycladic metallurgy in the Aegean Early Bronze Age showed that, on the contrary, lead was quite a popular material then, and this led him to consider the lead boats authentic products of the Chios–Skyros culture. He also considered they solved the longstanding problem of the 'frying-pan' craft, corroborating that the higher end was the bow, since the stern of the lead models is indicated by a square folded-back extremity. However, further study does suggest that even these models do not settle the argument, and that an alternative interpretation is possible.

First, two of the models are broken or incomplete, and it is the most incomplete one that is the closest in appearance to the 'frying-pan' vessels. Second, if one measures the angle between the hull and extremities of the lead boats and the 'frying-pan' boats, there is a very considerable difference. The angle in the lead boats varies from 21 to 35 degrees, while in the 'frying-pan' boats it averages about 70 degrees. This at least raises the possibility that these are two different types of craft. This idea is further reinforced by measuring the hull size of the lead boats. In the most complete one, the main flat-bottomed hull is 24.5 cm long, the bow 8.95 and the stern 7.6 cm. In the second nearly complete one, the hull is 21.2, bow 6.2 and stern 5.2 cm. Moreover, in both cases, the volume of the stern is in fact greater than that of the bow, since the bow is much narrower, while the stern retains the flat bottom of the hull. Only the third model, which, as has been said, has one end broken off, is truly L-shaped. All this suggests that the lead models represent a different type of craft, probably double-ended, familiar in the ancient Aegean.

Finally, Lionel Casson has added his distin-

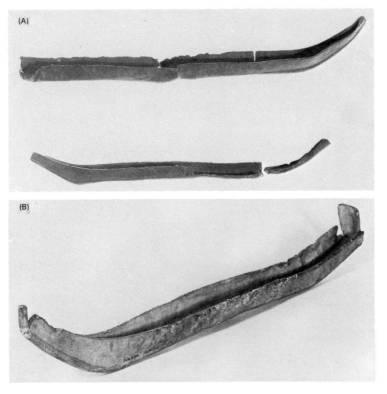

6.8 *Three lead model boats from Naxos, Greece, now in the Ashmolean Museum (Ashmolean Museum, Oxford)*

6.9   *A double-ended fishing boat on a Tunisian mosaic, now in the Musée du Bardo (Roger-Viollet)*

guished views to the controversy.[35] He supports the high bow theory, for three main reasons. The first is the lead boat models in the Ashmolean. The second is a vase painting on a Mycenaean clay box found at Pylos, in which the stern of a ship is clearly indicated by a steersman, and the bow has on it a fish facing forward, very like the Skyros ones. Third, he cites a ship graffito from Cyprus dated between 1100 and 1200 BC which has a high upright bow and a needle-like projection aft with a bellying sail amidships clearly indicating which is which. The horizontal projection, Casson says, still needs explaining, but it is not a ram for naval warfare because that does not appear until much later. Possibly the best explanation is that the projection was to take the shock of beaching, and this could well be done stern first.[36] Then the high bow would face the oncoming waves, as the Palaikastro model, for instance, seems well designed to do.

But though Casson considers the controversy settled, there are still arguments on the other side. The Pylos craft and the Cyprus graffito could, like the lead models, belong to a double-ended category of craft. As to the fish facing forward: on the so-called ring of Minos there is a craft whose stern is clearly indicated by the position of the steersman, but on the bow is a seahorse facing aft.[37]

Then it could be argued that the little craft shown on a stele from Terenouthis (Figure 6.10) of the fourth century AD, despite being even further removed in time than the Cyprus graffito, could be much closer in type to the original dug-outs, and

6.10   *Fourth century AD stele from Terenouthis (Kelsey Museum, University of Michigan)*

6.11    *Engraving from the* 'Maison aux stucs' *on the island of Delos, Greece (after Basch,* BCH, *supplement 1, 1973)*

this has a high stern. And there are Köster's and Marinatos's sea-keeping arguments which have been reinforced by another scholar of distinction, J. S. Morrison, in a review of Casson's book.[38] A high bow, unbalanced by any comparable weight aft, would surely weigh the craft down by the head and hold up its progress. On the other hand, in early seafaring, as St Paul for one so graphically described, anyone caught out in a blow ran before it. In this situation, a high stern would give the steersman useful protection. Morrison also makes the point that, in a rowed vessel, the steersman needs a high position to see over the rowers' heads.

Finally there is the intriguing craft noted by Basch also in the '*Maison aux stucs*' on Delos. This engraved craft strongly recalls in general shape the Skyros vase vessels, with three important variations. It has a cabin on which a goddess is standing; it has a horse's head instead of a fish on top of its high extremity; and, perhaps most important of all, it is clear that the high extremity is the stern and the horse's head is facing aft, because it has two large triangular-shaped steering oars, as opposed to the nine rowing oars which are very similar in composition to Cycladic ones. Basch's suggestion is that a representation of an early Cycladic craft must have survived on a ring perhaps, or in a temple, to provide a model for the sailor-engraver to copy many centuries later.[39] If this is indeed so, and he made his replica faithfully, then he may also have solved incidentally the stem or stern question of the Skyros vases for us.

# 7  The later Mediterranean

The reed boats and the dug-out derivatives described in the last chapter would have been quite capable of carrying the limited quantities of obsidian involved. Nor were there then any other goods which would have demanded bigger-capacity craft. Settlements in the early agricultural stage had to be self-sufficient as far as food was concerned because they could not rely on seaborne traffic to supplement their own resources: that would have been too uncertain.

**Metal tools and trade**

The introduction of metal changed this: it became much more feasible to build ships which were capable of carrying this new valuable commodity. It is possible to wedge and adze planks out of a tree-trunk with stone tools, bone or antler chisels, shells and even beechwood wedges, but it must have been an exceedingly laborious business. Metal tools made larger-scale production much easier.

Colin Renfrew has pointed out how profound the influence of metallurgy was in the eastern Mediterranean upon the cultures of the Early Bronze Age: 'The principal metal types have a wide and rapid distribution: double-spiral pins, awls in incised bone handles and tweezers, as well as tools, weapons and more precious objects are widely found.'

What is more, the implications of this metal trade seem to be borne out by a study of animal bones in archaeological contexts found in Cyprus.[1]

Schwartz's study of some 10,000 bones shows that while small domesticated animals like sheep, goat, pig and little Persian fallow deer had been taken to the island and were present at sites from the pre-pottery phase up to the Early Bronze Age, cattle (probably *Bos taurus*) appear in the Middle Bronze Age, to be followed by the horse in the Late Bronze Age. Schwartz suggests that the appearance of *Bos* may be linked with the copper trade. So some systematic exchange of goods in the Aegean in the latter part of the third millennium BC, in ships now large enough to carry cattle, seems virtually certain.

Renfrew has made the important point that another result would have been a widespread and more rapid exchange of information. One obvious candidate for this last category is the idea of the sail, 'one of the most easily diffused cultural traits of man', as Richard LeBaron Bowen has said.[2] Rowing might be another: according to R. C. Anderson and also C. Torr, oars replaced paddles on the Nile about 3000 BC.[3] A third trait might be the technique of joining planking by pegs or mortises and tenons. These then were the influences acting upon the ships of the Bronze Age in the Mediterranean. The result was that boats became ships, and the first great island state came into existence.

**Crete**

The evidence for the type of boat used in Crete is sparse and difficult to interpret, so much so that it

7.1    *Minoan seal with ship (Ashmolean Museum, Oxford)*

would not be impossible to dismiss it all and say the Minoans ruled an island empire without ships. However, the obsidian and metallurgy trade, as well as the geographical setting, do contradict this, so it is necessary to try and make what one can of the little information available.

We can see something of the achievements of the Minoan naval architects reflected in their talismatic seal-stones, on which the exceptional obsession with ships, as V. G. Kenna points out, in itself could be taken to indicate the nautical interests of their makers.[4] Very few other surviving seals from other Near Eastern areas show ships at all. However, these numerous ships on Cretan seals

are not very easy to understand. As F. Benoit has said, 'vases, seals and graffiti are silent about the nature and shape of the hull under the water-line'.[5] However, since the evolution of the sea-going sailing ship is one of the crucial moments in western maritime history, it is worth seeing what can be said about the considerable differences between the high-ended dug-outs of the Skyros 'frying-pans' and the ships on the earlier Minoan seal-stones. Fortunately we have other more or less contemporary ship representations which help to clear up one major difficulty. One source is the engravings made on one of the portal stones at the temple of Hal Tarxien on Malta. Maltese pre-historic chronology is a matter of some discussion. Renfrew has suggested that the finishing date for the Tarxien phase should be moved back to about 2300 BC in view of the tree-ring calibration of radiocarbon dates;[6] this means that the ships could have been carved about the middle of the third millennium BC. There are a good number of types of craft recorded at Tarxien, but none seems to show anything closely resembling the tubby noticeably crescent-shaped round ships of the Minoan seals (Figure 7.1). This suggests that this particular aspect may have been forced on the seal-carvers by the conventional shape of the surface on which they had to work, and this is borne out by the ships in the wall-painting from Thera (Santorini), where the vessels are notice-ably long and flattened (Figure 7.2), compared

7.2    *Marinatos's drawing of one of the ships on the wall painting from Thera (after S. Marinatos,* Excavations at Thera, *VI, Athens, 1974, Plate 9)*

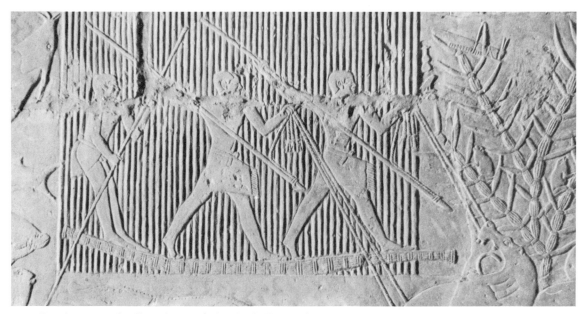

7.3   *Egyptian papyrus-bundle craft in use for hunting buffalo (author)*

with the abrupter crescent-shape of the seals. If one therefore, in the mind's eye, stretches out the ships on the Minoan seals at once one gets something which fits far more understandably with the other contemporary illustrations and is also more easily derived from the Cycladic dugouts.

## Egypt

The Egyptian aspect of boat evolution is certainly the best documented. Of the derivation of this particular tradition from papyrus craft there is little doubt. Papyrus-bundle craft stayed in use there, at least for hunting in the marshes (Figure 7.3), throughout the Old, Middle and New Kingdoms, a period from *c*. 2700 to *c*. 1000 BC. Edgerton has pointed out that the verb that seems most characteristic of ship-building in the minds of ancient Egyptian scribes is 'to bind', while the papyrus umbel design, the shape of the ends, and even, as Landström has suggested, the colour of many later Egyptian craft, were all derived from these humble predecessors.[7] The body of the vessel was usually green for papyrus, and the yellow bow

7.4   *The re-assembled Cheops ship; Ahmed Youssef, the restorer, in the foreground (Ahmed Youssef)*

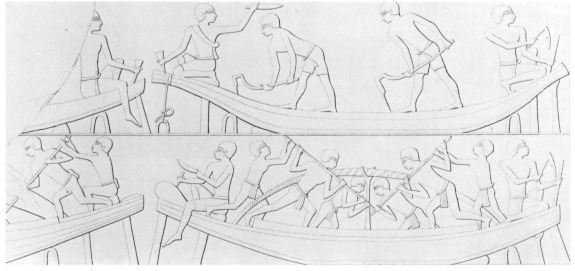

7.5 *Internal view of the re-assembled Cheops ship (Ahmed Youssef)*

and stern reflected the leather or canvas covering that was stitched on to keep the ends neat. Other inheritances were the bipod masts, which spread the strain on the papyrus hull, the many backstays from the mast, which again reduced the pull on any one attachment to the hull, and the athwart-ships trusses which helped to hold the feet of the masts.

However, Landström departs from tradition by arguing that apart from hunting and fishing craft, boats of papyrus did not exist from Old Kingdom

times on. What appear to be papyrus boats, he claims are in fact wooden boats built in a papyriform shape for religious reasons, from the Thinite period (3000–2770 BC) to that of Tutankhamun (*c.* 1352 BC). In his view, at the end of the Predynastic period, probably inspired by the appearance of copper tools, simple wooden boats came into use.[8] Basically these consisted of three thin planks, a bottom and two sides, sewn together.

It was the need to enlarge and strengthen this basic design which produced the characteristic

7.6 *Drawing of a painting from Zawyet el-Mdin, Egypt, showing boats being built, one with a hogging truss (British Museum)*

early Egyptian ship design. Hitherto, the slightly later stages of this design has been seen largely in terms of the Dahshur boats (Figure 7.7) which were excavated in 1893 near the pyramid of Sesostris III, and the well-known quotation from Herodotus which described Egyptian ships as being built of short lengths of acacia wood, brickwork fashion, with cross-beams but no ribs.[9] Now, however, with the publication of the details of the Cheops royal ship, which was found in 1952 dismantled in an almost completely air- and watertight grave to the south of the Pyramid of Cheops, the picture has changed. The reconstruction of this ship has revealed a vessel of some 40 tons displacement, 43.4 metres long and 5.9 metres wide. The wood, all 1,224 parts of it, is mostly cedar of Lebanon with some sycamore. The strakes, up to 22.72 metres long and 13–14 cm thick, are joined by hook-scarfs at their ends, with adjoining strakes being secured by innumerable yards of lashings and pegs in the thickness of the strakes. The ship is flat-bottomed and perhaps its most surprising features are its sixteen transverse floors and the central plank, held vertically by stanchions, into which the cross-beams slot. The

decks lay on these cross-beams between two further planks resting on stringers along each side. Battens ran along each of the seams on the inside under the stitching.[10]

This splendid craft, nearly 5,000 years old, towering 8 metres above its keel line, and information embodied in models and illustrations, give a sound idea of ancient Egyptian ship construction, as well as suggesting that decked ships go back well into the prehistoric period, as the Cheops ship must surely have been the product of a long-established tradition.

The well-known painting from Ti's mastaba (tomb) at Saqqara shows axes, adzes, saws and chisels in use, as well as the pegs which fit into the thickness of the strakes. Other paintings from Zawyet el-Mdin (Figure 7.6) and the tomb of Nefer show vessels under construction with a truss curved from bow to stern over a forked support.[11] Landström's interpretation of this is that the bottom planks were first bent to the required curve by the truss before the side strakes were attached by pegs and lashings, then the frames and central shelf would have been added in the case of large craft, and cross-beams and decking in all cases.[12]

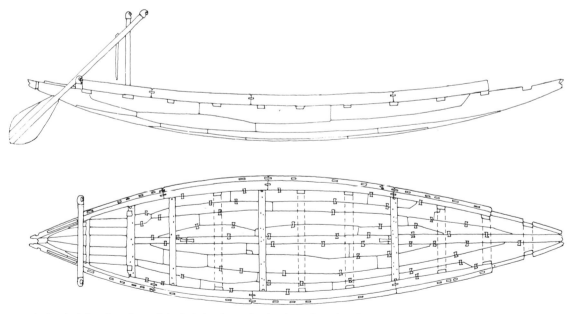

7.7  *A plan and elevation of one of the Dahshur boats showing hour-glass-shaped tenons joining the planks (after Landström, Ships of the Pharaohs, 1971)*

Thus would have been produced the 'taut bow' element, with the hogging trusses and swifters so familiar on later Egyptian vessels, and so necessary to give strength and keep the shape in the absence of a keel. Heavy cargo, too, even if it was stowed on deck where the weight would be absorbed by beams and sides as well as the deck itself, would tend to spread the sides unless countered by a swifter.

In the case of the Dahshur boats (Figure 7.7), the strakes have plain butt joins at each end and are attached to each other by pegs and by hour-glass-shaped tenons, without stitching or lashing, a much cruder technique than that of the Cheops ship. Landström suggests this may be because they were intended for the burial voyage of less important people than the Pharaoh, and anyway this simpler technique may have been used for a long time, but without a previous example surviving.[13]

Already in the Thinite period, and a little later during the reign of Sneferu in the Old Kingdom, there are mentions of Lebanon and cargoes of cedar wood,[14] and by the time of Sahure, 150 years or so later, there is no doubt about the overseas ventures of the Egyptians. On the Palermo stone, Sahure is recorded as importing myrrh and electrum from Punt in Somalia, a practice which Save-Söderbergh has argued was a regular one from the earliest times to the end of the New Kingdom.[15] Sahure's ships are well illustrated and almost certainly embodied the principles already listed: flat bottoms; pegged, scarfed and sewn strakes; hogging trusses and swifters; and probably frames or floor timbers.

Egypt gained its existence from the Nile and it would be astonishing if some of its many indigenous ships had not ventured on to the open sea. Among the plentiful evidence that this did indeed happen is one of the earliest sailors' yarns. 'I had ventured out on the Big Green in a ship 120 cubits long and 40 cubits broad. One hundred and twenty of Egypt's best sailors were on board. They looked to the sky, they looked to the land, and their heart was braver than the lion's. They foresaw a storm before it had come, and a tempest before it struck.'[16] And the disadvantages of a sailor's life were already very clear: 'For the sailor is worn out, the oar in his hand, the lash upon his back, and his belly empty of food.'[17]

## Ship-building techniques

The Cheops (Figure 7.5) and Dahshur (Figure 7.7) ships, as well as paintings like those at Zawyet el-Mdin (Figure 7.6) show that, in Egypt, strakes were joined both by lashings and pegs, or hour-glass-shaped cleats in the thickness of the wood, with cross-beams or floor timbers added later in the construction process. So evidently the 'shell' technique of ship-building goes back at least to 3000 BC. In this method, the hull was put up first and the internal strengthening structures were added later, unlike a skin boat, where the 'skeleton' was built first and the covering was added afterwards.

The evidence for sewn boats in the ancient Mediterranean has been summarised by Lionel Casson.[18] Its memory was still well alive in the Classical period as in Virgil's version of Charon's skiff – 'cumba sutilis' (mentioned in chapter 5); and Agamemnon told the Greeks that after nine years at Troy the planks of their ships were rotten and the cords had worked loose.[19] Lionel Casson has pointed out that both Aulus Gellius and Pliny later in the Classical period assumed that Homer was talking about the twine used to sew the planks together. Pacuvius, in one of his plays, decided that Homer's description (*Odyssey*, Book V, 244–8) of the craft Odysseus built to get away from Ogygia was not primitive enough so instead, like Virgil, he gave him one sewn with cords. So it seems reasonable enough to assume that sewn planks would have characterised many early Mediterranean craft.

Then it looks as if the Dahshur way of joining strakes by hour-glass-shaped clamps prevailed in other areas of the Middle East. Lionel Casson has recently re-interpreted some of the nautical vocabulary collected by Armas Salonen in the 1930s, when much less was known about ancient ship-building techniques, from the Sumerian, Akkadian and Assyrian languages. The two words in particular Casson concentrates on are '*dubbin*' and 'eme-sig'. The literal translations are 'finger-nail or claw' and 'lower tongue'. Rather than 'lower ribs' and 'floor timbers' as proposed by Salonen, Casson suggests that 'dove-tail clamp' and tongue-like 'tenon' of a mortise and tenon joint would be a much more likely translation, and these appear in the original inventories in the right sort of number. It therefore seems highly likely that the wooden craft used on the Tigris and Euphrates in the first two millennia BC were also built in a similar way, edged-joined with tenons and mortises, or some form thereof, as earlier Egyptian and later classical ships.[20]

There is independent confirmation of this in Stuart Piggott's fascinating study of early wheeled vehicles. He has shown that wheeled vehicles were known in Transcaucasia from the early third millennium BC, and in the ancient Near East from the time of Uruk IV, which should be dated at least a couple of centuries before 3000 BC.[21]

Piggott goes on to show that in the Near East some of the early wheels, like those from Susa and Ur, were held together by an external bar (Figure 7.8). Later this clumsy type disappears in favour of the more widely spread tripartite wheel in which mortises were bored in the thickness of the three planks and then dowels inserted. The techniques and tools required for this would be similar to those required for a planked ship.

Metal would have had an important part in all this, as joinery of any elaboration is dependent on the use of metal tools. In Aldred's view, the introduction of copper tools in Egypt towards the end of the fifth millennium BC did much for the technique of joining timber.[22] However, according to Piggott, the technique of dowelling a tripartite disc wheel demanded the skilled use of chisels and gouges,[23] and these do not become available until the later third millennium BC, when tanged chisels were in use from the Aegean to Trans-

7.8 *Relief from Mesopotamia of about 3000 BC, showing a cart with barred wheels drawn by onagers (Directorate General of Antiquities, Baghdad)*

caucasia and from Moravia to east of the Caspian Sea.[24] Piggott's description of mortises in these ancient wheels being cut with a narrow metal gouge, and finished by reaming out, compares interestingly with Casson's interpretation of 'tet-renen d'ara panta' ('he bored them all') in the *Odyssey* (247), when Odysseus is building a boat to escape from the island of Ogygia and bores 'all his planks to make slots for tenons'.[25] He then fits them to each other and 'hammered it [the craft] with dowels and joints'. Finally he set up decks by fastening them to close-set frames. Such a trans-lation, Casson suggests, makes sense only if applied to a shell-built, mortise-and-tenon-fastened craft. It is not clear, however, whether the famous Greek voyager was using the round pegs of the early techniques, or the later and more subtle flat mortise and tenon method of the Classical world for joining his strakes together.

A piece of wood found by Emory in Tomb 3504, the burial place of Uadji, third king of the First Dynasty in Egypt, with its tenons at either end pierced with holes for retaining dowels (Figure 7.9), strongly recalls Classical mortise and tenon ship-building practice.[26] Yet the Cheops ship does not embody the method, and Petrie long ago pointed out[27] that

the heavy strong chisel came in [to ancient Egypt] with the free supply of copper in the first Dynasty; it was set in a wooden handle and struck by a mallet to cut the mortise-holes in beams for boats and house building . . . The connection of boards was by slots and flat tongues down to the VIth Dynasty; in the decay of work which followed, the easier method of boring round holes and inserting pegs of wood was adopted. Slots and tongues were again revived and are found in coffins down to the Greek period.

So although the Egyptians had the capacity to make flat tenons from the fourth millennium on, they do not appear necessarily to have used it for ship-building, and indeed may have abandoned it for the simpler round peg after the sixth Dynasty (late third millennium BC). Since also the tri-partite wooden wheel with inserted pegs existed in a swathe from Lčašen and Trialeti in Trans-caucasia to Ur and on to Harappa (see chapter 13), one has therefore to be cautious about any

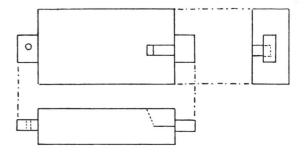

7.9   *Rectangular block of wood with tenons at either end pierced with holes for retaining dowels; from a First Dynasty tomb, Uadji, Egypt (after Flinders-Petrie,* Royal Tombs of the First Dynasty, *part 1, 1910)*

hypothesis as to where and when the Classical mortise and tenon method with dowels was first used in ship-building.

We can say, however, that Egyptian craft, Sumerian craft, Homeric craft, and of course the many later Classical ones we now know about, had strakes joined by pegs, hour-glass cleats or mortises and tenons. This form of 'shell' construction went on until the shortage of shipwrights skilled in joinery (after the fall of the Roman Empire) possibly worked against this powerful but tedious method of construction. The mortises got wider apart, then were confined to the strakes below the waterline, and probably vanished about the tenth century AD, though Casson has argued that Roman mass construction suggests that the use of moulds, which could be the precursors of pre-erected ribs or 'skeleton' construction, came in rather earlier.[28]

An interesting problem is the date when the technique of strengthening these mortise and tenon joints by hammering metal nails through the dowels securing them, and the fastening of inserted frames the same way, was introduced. This is where chariotry again provides a useful analogy with this practice, which is so generally seen in Roman wrecks.

In his careful study of the felloes (the equivalent of tyres) of ancient chariots, G. Kossack[29] points out that those on the four-wheeled wagon from the fifth kurgan (burial mound) at Pasyryk in Upper Altai consisted of two bend-round boards. These overlapped by some 30 to 40 cm and were attached through the overlap by pegs and lashings. These wheels seem to resemble the considerably older Shang and Chou ones of the late second millennium BC. They also recall, in general carpentry techniques, the methods used in the Cheops ship.

By the middle of the second millennium BC, chariots with spoked wheels had reached the Mycenaean and Aegean world, and the remains of a wheel and hub from the tomb of Amenophis III, with a suggested date of a quarter of a century before Tutankhamun, shows that these spoked wheels, though without any metal in them, could have elaborate mortise and tenon joints between nave and flange.[30] Then come the splendid cast-bronze wheels with four, five or six spokes of the Classical world, in which the felloes consisted of short lengths of wood set radially at right angles to the channelled rim of the bronze wheel and possibly nailed on.

The next advance is when the cast-bronze wheel is replaced by a multi-spoked one with a double layer of wooden felloes, secured by U-shaped metal clamps through them. Perhaps the most significant examples to us of this type are those found in very good condition in a necropolis at Salamis in Cyprus. Several of these particular wooden felloes have overlaps, or scarfs, fastened through by long iron bolts. Then the two layers of felloes are mortised and tenoned into each other with a metal clamp going round them both, an iron bolt joining the two parts of the clamp. In addition, the bodies of some of the waggons have a large quantity of nails hammered into them.[31] Kossack suspects these late seventh century BC wheels were similar to those shown in late Assyrian palace reliefs.[32]

This is not certain evidence that metal fastenings were used in ships in the Mediterranean by the seventh century BC. But the securing of a wooden mortise and tenon joint by a metal bolt through it is very close in conception to the techniques used in later Classical vessels. And the shipwrights and chariot- and wagon-wheel-makers must surely have discussed their respective methods in the wineshops at least. So if we have to look for the introduction of metal fastenings somewhere between the period of Homer, who does not seem to make Odysseus use them, and the recently-excavated fifth century BC Porticello ship from the Straits of Messina, which definitely had them, one would suspect it was not later than the seventh century BC.

## Evolution in the Mediterranean

Summing up, then, one might very cautiously suggest that the progression in the Mediterranean may have gone something like this. First there were reed boats, followed by dug-outs, to which extra strakes were added by sewing or lashing. It is possible to build a craft simply with lashed strakes and no internal strengthening or stiffening. Strabo describes the boats of India and Ceylon as 'made' on both sides, without bilge-spanning pieces (*metrai*),[33] and more recent examples are known. However if any considerable load-carrying was involved, it must soon have become clear that either a cross-member from gunwale to gunwale, as in the Dahshur boats, or a floor timber bent up at each end to follow the upward curve of the sides as in the Cheops ship, gave valuable added strength. Next some brilliant innovator, or perhaps in the case of the Minoans a clever copier of the Egyptians, saw the advantages of joining strakes by pegs, cleats, or mortises and tenons rather than by lashings, though the two methods may have existed in the same craft for a while.

Thus may have evolved the sailing merchant-men of Crete, whose crisp sturdiness of outline does suggest that they may well have had mortise-and-tenon-joined strakes and multiple floor timbers like the Kyrenia ship whose ancestor, in a sense, they were.

## Mast and sail

One problem this suggested evolution has left out so far is that of the mast. The sail, it seems very likely, was evolved on the River Nile. The conditions which led to this are not difficult to work out. Here was an early area of civilisation, clustered closely round a navigable river which was both a link and a focus for that civilisation. In addition, the River Nile flowed north, while for most of the year the prevailing winds blew south. These conditions positively demanded a craft to drift down the Nile and sail back up it.

Some authorities have said that the earliest illustration to show a craft capable of doing this was on a Naqada pot (Figure 7.10) in the British Museum dated to about 3100 BC. However in 1960 Richard LeBaron Bowen suggested that there was another pot some 100 years older which not only showed sail but also suggested how the sail might have come into use on the River Nile.[34]

Bowen noted that there were some even earlier vases which show a many-oared boat with two shrines or cabins amidships and what could be a shield on a pole between them (Figure 7.11). Many examples of these animal skin shields are known both from illustrations in antiquity and contemporary use among the Dinka, Bari and so on.[35] LeBaron Bowen suggested that if a shield made of animal skin was set up like a banner on a pole in a boat during religious ceremonies, it would only be a matter of time before someone observed that it was helping to move the boat before the wind. So the sail may well have been

7.10  *Vase from Naqada, Egypt, of about 3100 BC, showing a craft with sails (British Museum)*

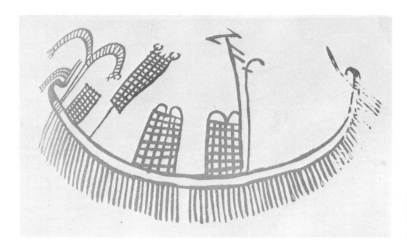

7.11 *Reconstruction drawing by Landström of craft with banners and shrines depicted on an Egyptian vase of about 3000 BC*

invented accidentally from this practice of using shields as ceremonial banners on board boats.[36]

The bipod mast with many backstays imposed by a papyrus hull was not replaced by the single mast until the Sixth Dynasty.[37] Landström has also made the interesting point that in the early periods, with the mast forward of the centre, the craft would sail only before the wind, and sails were high and narrow. When the mast moved nearer the centre and sails could be sheeted fore and aft, sailing with the wind abeam was possible and wider, lower sails became necessary, because the old high ones would have threatened stability.[38] Thus were derived the familiar sails of Hatshepsut's punt armada, craft which have been described as racing galleys because they needed to get past the navigationally dangerous and waterless shores of the Red Sea as quickly as possible.

In Babylonia very different conditions prevailed. Both the prevailing wind and the rivers moved more or less south, thus producing the practice described by Herodotus of rafting downstream and then breaking the raft down for the return up-river by land, with the skins on donkeys. A cuneiform text also describes the Babylonians sailing downstream,[39] but being towed upstream by men. Only when the wind shifted occasionally to the south was it possible to sail upstream. Not surprisingly, then, do we find the earlier evidence for the use of sails in Egypt, where the hieroglyph for 'sail upstream' was a boat with a sail, while that for 'fare downstream' was a boat with a steering oar but no sail.[40]

Both on the surviving Cretan seal-stones and at Tarxien on Malta there are sails which seem extremely Egyptian in style.

## The keel

The evidence that a different technique of shipbuilding from the flat-bottomed Egyptian one did develop in the Mediterranean, probably based originally on a dug-out, derives mostly from the ram or forefoot projection. A ram implies some sort of keel, which is hardly logical, or at least very difficult, to have in a flat-bottomed craft. On the other hand it is a natural feature on a built-up dug-out. Not till Necho's reign does Landström show any example of a ram from Egypt,[41] whereas it existed from the earliest times in the Aegean, even if only as beaching protection at bow or stern. The Egyptians had to use elaborate knees and trusses to support the foot of a mast, whereas in a dug-out-derived craft, the keel member provides a natural mast-step.

In a recent study of the ships of the Phoenicians, Lucien Basch sees a direct link with those of their predecessors, the Minoans. His evidence is a terracotta model from Byblos of a Bronze Age Phoenician merchantman, the ships of the Peoples of the Sea carved on a temple of Medinet Habu (Thebes) and the two ships shown on a Proto-

7.12   *Two views of a ship with amphora and an anchor stone on a vase from Cyprus (British Museum)*

geometric crater of about 850 BC from Fortetsa in Crete.[42] All these, Basch suggests, show a type of rounded double-ended merchantman which must have come into general use in the eastern Mediterranean in the Bronze Age and gone on being used well into the first millennium BC. Moreover a version considerably modified but still recognisably related appears on the bas-reliefs of Sennacherib's palace at Nineveh, which shows the fleet of King Luli of Tyre and Sidon fleeing from Tyre in 701 BC.[43] Other sources of illustrations of this same type are the fourteenth century BC ships shown in the tomb of Neb-Amun in Egypt, and the rather defaced craft from the tomb of Ken-Amun. From Cyprus come other examples: one is on a vase and is notable for its cargo of wine and round

stone anchors (Figure 7.12). Then there are a number of terracotta models of boats of the sixth century BC found at Amathous (Figure 7.13), some of which are beamy rounded double-ended craft with a mast-step amidships. These seem to be absolutely in the Minoan tradition.[44] Basch believes the first three examples have keels, since they have rams, or the vestigial remains of them.[45]

Certainly by the Homeric period, literary references show that the keel with its hard-sheathed forefoot to take the shock of beaching was long-established and familiar. The ship Odysseus built on Calypso's isle had no keel, as opposed to the ordinary craft in which he was wrecked off Scylla's rock, when he survived by lashing the mast and keel together.[46] This would tend to suggest

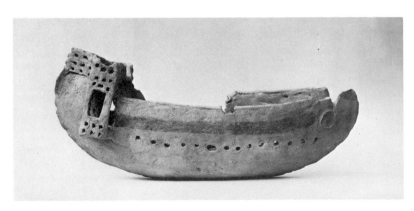

7.13   *Terracotta boat model from Amathous, Cyprus, sixth century BC (British Museum)*

7.14 *Eighth century BC Attic ship on a Late Geometric decorated vase from the Dipylon cemetery, Athens (Louvre, Paris)*

that the keel-less craft was the more primitive and unusual. On the other hand Calypso brought him cloth for his sail and he set up a mast on his makeshift keel-less craft, which might suggest that mast and keel did not necessarily go together. So both keeled and flat-bottomed craft could well have co-existed from the earliest times.

**The war-ship**

Meanwhile a quite different process had been going on. While the craft discussed so far in this chapter have been round ships, with the accent on sea-keeping and cargo capacity, the Skyros dugouts also had a potential for development as longships. It is not difficult to see a second coherent line of descent from them through the Bronze Age craft shown on a fragment of a vase from Volos in Thessaly, and the Mycenaean ship on a pyxis from Messenia, to the war-ships on the Dipylon group of vases of the eighth century BC (Figure 7.14).

Naval warfare started a good deal earlier than used to be thought. No longer does the engagement between the Peoples of the Sea and the Egyptian forces of Rameses III in 1190 BC have the doubtful honour of being the first recorded sea battle. That now passes to the battle when the Hittite ruler Suppiluliuma defeated the fleet of

Alašiya (Cyprus) in the thirteenth century BC prior to the conquest of that island.[47] Other Ugaritic texts of the same period mention a series of naval battles

7.15 *Reconstruction model of a round ship from Bet She'arim, Israel (Maritime Museum, Haifa)*

7.16    *Painting of a long-ship from the tomb of Jason, Jerusalem (Israel Department of Antiquities and Museums)*

in which many ships were involved: one fleet from Ugarit in the service of the Hittites had no less than 150 ships.[48]

The Linear B tablets found at Pylos in Greece also show that the war-ship was an important element in defence strategy in the Mycenaean period. This leads Linder to suggest that the common factor in Homer's 'Catalogue of Ships', the Linear B tablets and the Ugaritic administrative texts was a 'long-ship', a craft designed specifically for war.[49] So it seems that the two categories of vessel that dominated the Mediterranean for so many centuries, the long war-ship and the round merchantman, probably date back at least to the thirteenth century BC.

Thereafter the Aegean became the great centre of sea warfare as the Greeks developed the *pentekontor* and the *trieris* and the circling and

ramming tactics which went with them, the '*diekplous*' and the '*anastrophe*'. 'Straightway, at a signal, the oars fell as one and smote the deep water'; Aeschylus then goes on to describe[50] the battle of Salamis, in which the *diekplous* was used.

In spite of this early start, according to Basch the ram as an instrument of warfare did not appear in the eastern Mediterranean until about the eighth century BC, when one is shown on a damaged Assyrian fresco from Til Barsip. Later still, rams appear on the ships of King Luli, fleeing from Tyre in 701 BC. This was a case of Greek influence, which also extended westward, since the Etruscans, too, about the same time, modified their own craft to take a Greek ram.[51]

It is intriguing that recent findings of the National Physical Laboratory at Teddington have borne out the practical skill of the early Mediterranean shipwrights. Studies to improve the economy and sea-keeping ability of merchant ships have shown that an underwater 'ram' has a beneficial effect, especially when craft are heavily laden. The 'ram' under water generates a system of surface waves which cancels those formed by the bow, thus reducing the resistance to motion of the craft and improving its performance.[52]

Specialised war-ships were the product of special conditions like those that produced the *trieris*, the *pentekontor*, and the *liburnian*. The Phoenicians could not do without war-ships but showed their practical sense of economy by developing a craft that would to some extent double as either war-ship or merchantman: this was the '*kirkarah*', '*gurgurru*' to the Assyrians, '*kerkouros*' to the Greeks. Basch has pointed out that just as the Phoenician war-ships retained a rounded shape, so some at least of their merchantmen had a warlike fighting deck protected by shields, and two banks of oars.[53]

## Literary evidence

A certain amount can be deduced about the nature of these war-ships and merchantmen, and how they were handled, from later Greek literary sources. Although a great deal of change must have occurred between Minoan and Homeric and later times, there are some things it would seem reasonable to read back into the earlier period. According to Theophrastos in the fourth century BC, keels were made of oak to withstand the wear of beaching, while ribs were sometimes of pine for lightness.[54] Plato discusses the availability of different types of wood for ship-building in one district: 'There is no fir to speak of nor pine and not much cypress; nor could one find much larch or plane, which shipwrights are always obliged to use for the interior parts of ships.'[55] This contrasts, as one would expect, with the Cheops boat, some of the structure of which was of juniper and soapberry, while the oars were of cedar of Lebanon and hop hornbeam, and the wooden pegs used for joining planks were of acacia.[56]

Some of Homer's ropes were of 'well-twisted ox-leather', while Herodotus describes them as being made of papyrus and hemp, and Moschion seems to indicate that they were prevented from rotting by pitch, which was evidently also used for covering the hull and caulking the seams.[57] The ropes on the Cheops boat, of which there were a considerable number, were, on the other hand, of halfa grass and *Desmotachya bipinnata*.[58]

Some passages of the *Iliad* illuminate shipbuilding practices. Hector's heart is as hard as the shipwright's adze. The interlocking balance of a hard fight resembles the accuracy with which a cunning shipwright trims his planks and fits them closely together. The tholepins at which the oarsmen sit are hook-shaped, to which the oars are attached by leather grommets.[59]

Perhaps the most revealing descriptions are those of getting under way and mooring. When a ship is ready for sea, the captain clears out the channels which were cut to receive the keels when the ship was beached and removes the piles of stones which have shored up the hull. Then the crew go aboard with the gear and mast and sail, let go the mooring lines and row out to sea until a favourable breeze appears. Next the mast is set up, the forestays secured, the sail on its sailyard hoisted, and the lines running through the lead brail rings shaken so they run out and the sail unfurls.[60]

The wind blows full in the middle of the sail, and the surging wave sings about the keel as the ship goes. The ship runs, accomplishing her course with a wave that follows. So then the crew make the tackle fast through the swift black ship, and when they have finished they set up mixing bowls of wine, well-crowned, and pour libations to the immortal ships' gods, created for ever.[61]

The usual practice was to beach the ship at night. This is confirmed by the absence of any means of cooking aboard the fourth century BC Kyrenia merchant ship excavated from the sea-bed off Cyprus, in contrast to the similarly excavated Yassi Ada ship of the seventh century AD, which had a rather elaborate galley.[62]

A voyage from Crete to Egypt with a following wind is said to have taken four days, giving an average speed of about 4 knots, though Casson calculates $4\frac{1}{2}$ to 6 knots for the later Roman period, under favourable conditions.[63] On the way, as Odysseus did on his voyage from Calypso's island, the captain kept his eye on the Great Bear, 'which always wheels round in the same place and looks across at Orion the Hunter with a wary eye'.[64] On approaching his destination, the captain orders the sail to be furled and stowed and the mast lowered. As the craft approaches the beach, she is turned and rowed stern first until just before grounding, when anchor stones are dropped from the bows and lines, known as 'hold-fasts of swift ships', are run out to the shore and secured. On occasions, ships ride off-shore with anchors out fore and aft. Some harbours are so good that the anchor stones and shore lines needed off an unsheltered beach are not required, and ships can ride to a single cable.

Herodotus, but not Homer, mentions the use of the sounding lead and line, though it is shown on models from Meketre's tomb in the Middle Kingdom Period.[65] Professor Morrison suggests that a passage in the fourth century BC work *Mechanica*, attributed to Aristotle, describes tacking into the wind and that this practice is confirmed by Nicander and Virgil.[66]

## Anchors

Another source of evidence are Gerhard Kapitän's and Honor Frost's pioneering studies of ancient anchors. Many of these stone objects, pierced with tell-tale holes (see Figure 7.12), have been classified as 'loom-weights', 'cult objects' and so on. In due course when enough of them have been properly recognised, recorded and analysed, it may well be possible to derive something of the nature and date of the ship that dropped them.[67]

Already, the existence of anchors of half a ton weight in the temple of Baal at Ugarit shows that large ships and embryo harbours must have existed by the nineteenth century BC, and literary evidence confirms merchantmen of 450 tons burden were common by 1200 BC.[68] Miss Frost distinguishes between three types in ancient use: small flat stones with several holes pierced to take

sticks which gripped into sand; larger stones with a single hole which, on a rocky bottom, held a ship by weight alone; and last, a weight anchor combined with two wooden prongs that held on either sand or rock, which finally led on, via the single bent stick, to the traditional anchor as we know it today, said to have been invented by Anacharsis about 600 BC.[69]

## Evidence from wrecks

The Cape Gelidonya wreck, excavated by George Bass on the sea-bed off the southern coast of Turkey, is so far the oldest Mediterranean ship examined. Unfortunately its hull was so battered that not much structural information could be got from it. Even so, the few fragments do show that trenails fitted in bored holes were used in its construction, and it seems likely that sewing and metal fastenings were not.

This wreck gives a vivid picture of the last voyage of a sort of Phoenician tramp ship that had sailed from Syria to Cyprus about 1200 BC, and there collected the ingots of copper and tin and the scrap-metal which made up its cargo on its final trip westward. Only 11 metres long, with its oil lamp and cylinder seal for stamping documents, its sets of weights, the razorblade and knucklebone, this little ship seems in one way so small, homely and insignificant. Yet its ton of cargo is easily the largest hoard of pre-Classical copper and bronze implements ever found in the Aegean area and the information embodied in its content gives a new picture of trade in the Aegean and of the sea-going activities of the Phoenicians centuries before the conventional textbooks suggested they started their sea wanderings.[70]

Later ships, also excavated on the sea-bed, seem to confirm this picture. The Kyrenia ship, with its inkwell and cargo of almonds as well as millstones and amphorae, and the Straits of Messina or Porticello ship, with its wooden fishing-line reel and wood-handled iron-tipped awl, both, in David E. Owen's view, confirm that the carriage of mixed cargoes over long distances, was a common practice by the fifth century BC.[71]

## 'Hupozoma' or hogging truss?

Wrecks have not so far thrown much light on the vexed question of what was the 'hupozoma'. This Greek word, together with 'entonoi' which is often found with it, presents problems to translators and nautical historians. It seems to be a form of rope, used structurally, but how is not yet generally agreed. Plato likens 'hupozomata' and 'entonoi' to the nerves and tendons of a living creature, the preservation of whose tension is essential to the safety of the ship and the well-being of the body. Greek inscriptions show that they were difficult to fit, since this had to be done with a certain number of men; they were important, since they came at the top of the list of gear for ships; they were contraband of war; the normal number was four to each ship; and they were fitted to ships on the active list. Unfortunately no one has so far found a detailed description of the method of fitting them.[72]

J. S. Morrison, who has collected much literary evidence about them, thinks 'hupozomata' were swifters, horizontal cables going round the outside of the hull to stop it working under the stress of heavy weather or battle. They would have been secured, he thinks, to a strop or girdle round the stern, and tightened by twisting the 'entonos'. He is inclined towards this view in part by the meaning of the word 'hupoloiphe', which means paint for the outside of the hull, suggesting that 'hupo' might mean something connected with the outside of the hull. He is supported in this interpretation by several illustrations: a galley of the first century BC in a frieze now in the Naples Museum clearly shows swifters in use round the hull;[73] and a bronze lamp from the Erectheum in the shape of a ship. However, a second century BC carved relief of the stern of a ship half-way up the acropolis of Lindos (Figure 7.17) is clearly frapped by an intertwined band passing vertically around the hull, which makes Casson think that 'hupozomata' could also be used for 'frapping' lines, as when the sailors in St Paul's ship 'used helps to undergird the ship'.[74]

Benoit[75] has yet another point of view. He thinks they were 'hogging trusses' – cables derived from

7.17 *Drawing of a second century BC carved relief on the acropolis of Lindos, Rhodes, showing the stern of a ship with rope passing around the hull (after Casson,* Ships and Seamanship in the Ancient World, *1971)*

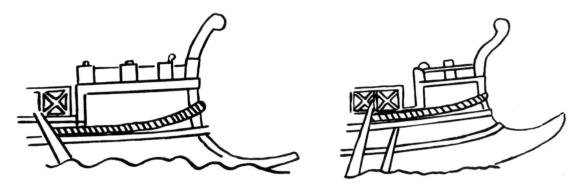

7.18   *Reconstruction drawings of ships with horizontal straps around one end: from Trajan's Column, Rome, and the Triumphal Arch, Orange, France (after A. Evans,* Palace of Minos*)*

Egyptian practice which ran fore and aft from stem to stern, usually over a forked stanchion and with a bar through the strands to twist them taut; these gave longitudinal strength to the hull.

Another possible explanation comes from Basch's observations that certain representations of Greek and Roman craft have horizontal strops or girdles shown round their bows and sterns, in particular on the ships carved on Trajan's Column in Rome and the Triumphal Arch at Orange in France.[76] Basch comments, quite rightly, that these ropes appear to be movable and they make sense only as the girdles or '*koruphaia*' to which the '*hupozomata*' would have been attached, since they seem to disappear inside the hull and have no other function.

One can safely say, therefore, that some rope to increase the structural strength of the hull was crucial in the Greek period, as swifter, undergird or hogging truss, or all three, so that, as Apollonius Rhodius put it, 'the planks should fit well with the dowels and withstand the opposing force of the sea'.[77] The Egyptians, from the period of Sahure (Old Kingdom) on, also used both fore-and-aft trusses and swifters, and one would expect it in the

Egyptian style of ship-building but it is more puzzling in the Minoan and Phoenician traditions. Such evidence as we have appears to show neat, handy craft whose high bow and stern suggests a good solid stout framework based on a keel, probably with closely-spaced tenons as well. There are two possible explanations why a hogging truss was necessary. First, war-ships had to be light (in order to be speedy) and long (to accommodate the necessary oarsmen), and this may have over-strained the available structural technique. The other reason may have been, with the increase in the number of ships being built, a shortage of suitable large timbers. It is interesting, for instance, that Procopius was surprised that a vessel which was kept as a monument of great antiquity in Rome had planks which were all of one piece instead of a number being scarfed together. Later, the Byzantines were so amazed at the lengthy strakes of the ships of the Vikings that they described long-ships or 'dragon ships' which had made the river journey across Russia to Miklagard (Constantinople) as '*monozell*', a word which means 'single pieces of timber'.[78]

# 8 The Atlantic

As the Admiralty Pilot makes clear, anyone who sails westward beyond the site where traditionally Hercules set up the 'pillars' to warn seamen to trespass no further into the outer ocean at once enters a very different and far less agreeable world. In place of the relatively steady breezes of the Mediterranean summer he may at any moment meet a gale or be becalmed in a thick fog. If he tries to hug the coast, he may be cast up on rocks by the onshore swell, or swept off course by the tides. If he strikes boldly out to sea he may be blown out far beyond his capability for returning and never make land again. As Don Pedro Nino said even as late as AD 1406, with the characteristic reaction of a Mediterranean sailor to a voyage from Spain to the English Channel: 'The Western Sea is not like the Mediterranean Sea, which has neither ebb nor flow nor great currents ... It is most evil, especially for galleys.' No wonder the Arabs called the Atlantic 'the Sea of Darkness' and in the Dark Ages it was associated with Satan.[1]

In the late Middle Ages, the challenge given by these conditions provoked one of the great advances of seafaring. Portugal, the meeting-point of Mediterranean and northern seamen, saw a revolution in nautical technology: northern and Mediterranean ship-building and handling techniques were fused to produce the many-masted craft which made possible the great explorations. The rough-weather lore and knowledge of tides and shallow-water sounding, such as that possessed by Chaucer's shipman who had no peer in his knowledge of tides and moon, 'streams' (currents)

and dangers, and of 'lodenmenage' (which is basically the use of lead and line and of leading marks[2]), were joined to the more sophisticated navigational skills of the Venetians, Majorcans and Arabs – the books of sailing directions, the charts drawn to a scale (of which the Carta Pisana of c. AD 1275 is the earliest surviving example) and tables to work out the course made good.[3] With compass and hour-glass, quadrant and astrolabe as well, the Portuguese mariners had the means at hand to begin discovering a wider world.

Many centuries before, according to Strabo, the Phoenician port of Gades (Cadiz) sent as many vessels to the outer sea as to the inner.[4] So the Atlantic coastal waters of Spain and Portugal must have presented a challenge to the Mediterranean seaman at an early period, and almost certainly evoked an answer, just as they were to do so spectacularly again in the late Middle Ages.

Those great stone tombs of prehistoric Europe, the megalithic monuments, were once believed to have originated in the eastern Mediterranean. A few years ago there would have been little doubt about their maritime distribution. As the distinguished prehistorian Gordon Childe saw it, the megaliths had spread mostly by sea, though also across France, from the '*tholoi*' tombs of Mycenae to the Orkneys, swept along on this lengthy journey by some evangelical urgency.[5] Now, however, radiocarbon dates calibrated by dendrochronology suggest that megalithic construction may have originated in a number of different places in Europe – Denmark, Britain,

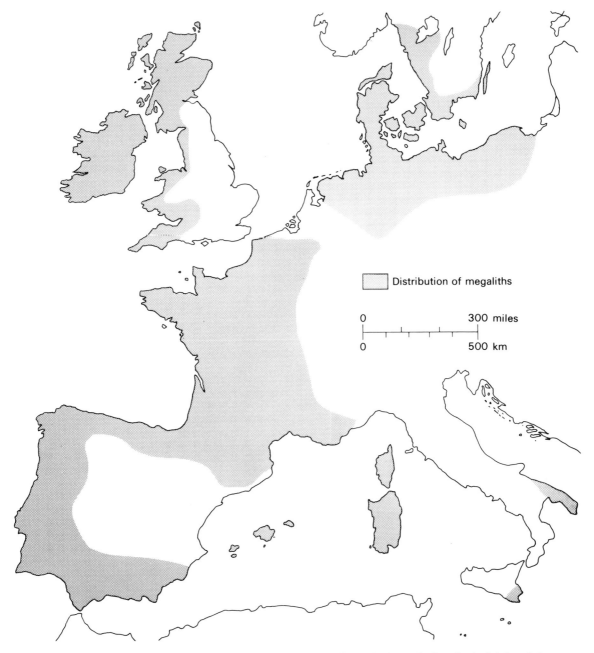

Map 8.1   *Distribution of megalithic monuments in Europe (after D. and R. Whitehouse,* Archaeological Atlas of the World, *London, 1975, p. 149)*

Brittany, Spain, and possibly Ireland as well – long before the Mycenaean tombs were built.[6] One cannot therefore argue with total confidence that their distribution necessarily implies that boats of some sort were the means for spreading this cult, however sea-orientated the sites of these remarkable stone constructions appear to be.

The same uncertainty goes for the maritime

part of other controversies. There certainly were Mesolithic peoples who scavenged along the sea-shore, like those whose middens and burials have been found at Muge, in southern Portugal.[7] Later, agriculture developed, with the settled conditions which would encourage dug-out-making, and in the Chalcolithic period even Colin Renfrew admits that there were certain imports by sea into Iberia from North Africa.[8] These may not have travelled great distances, as he argues, nevertheless there seems to be some evidence, such as the influence of Sicilian 'Diana' ware on passage-grave pottery of the Alemtejo region of Portugal or the eastern Mediterranean derivation of some of the artefacts associated with the later Tagus rock-cut tombs, that Mediterranean peoples may have reached the western sea-coast.[9]

When it comes to the craft used for this possible sea-going, the evidence is extremely scanty. The early skin-boat evidence from Spain, discussed in chapter 4, shows that their use could in theory go back at least to a period when they overlapped with the reed or papyrus-bundle craft which have already been identified as the most likely craft for the earliest Mediterranean voyages. Besides skin

boats, Strabo also referred condescendingly to dug-outs which in antiquity were the predecessors of built river craft on the Guadalquivir.[10] The only way to say anything constructive about how these basic types and their derivatives may have reacted to the challenge of the Atlantic seems to be to start at a later date and try to work backwards.

### The ships of the Veneti

The ships of the Veneti astonished Julius Caesar. His description of their exceptionally high bows and stems, flat bottoms, heavy oak strakes and cross-timbers, iron anchor chains and leather sails makes it quite understandable that these craft were more at home in the difficult seas of the coast of Brittany than were the Roman craft.[11] Since only literary descriptions of them exist, a good deal of speculation about how they looked has gone on. Stones from the sea-bottom off the Morbihan, for example, are said to have been ballast from which one can derive something of the keel shape of the Venetic ships.[12] Rather than this or speculation about possible similarities with later craft like the *sinagot* or *chasse-marée*,[13] it would seem more

8.1 *Drawing of a* ponto *from the mosaic at Althiburus, Tunisia*

profitable to accept the interpretation by Jal and by de la Roncière and Clerc-Rampel of the passage in Caesar's later works about the *ponto*, and see in this cargo-carrying vessel of the Gauls the name given to Venetic-type craft by the Romans.[14] There is a surviving illustration of a *ponto* in the mosaic of Althiburus in Tunisia and it provides an outline that fits pretty well, except for one detail: Caesar makes no mention of a ram, and the Althiburus *ponto* has one. One might suggest that this could be a decorative addition by a Mediterranean artist working a long way from Gaul, and this is supported to some extent by the story of Vatinius, one of Caesar's commanders, who in an emergency fitted rams to some *actuaria* –

light oared galleys – to add to his fleet (Caesar, *Bell. Alex.* 44.3) – yet the *actuaria* on the Althiburus mosaic is most definitely shown with a ram. On the other hand, this operation of Vatinius might just refer to the putting on of the bronze casings of rams, which were often salvaged and stockpiled by the Greeks, and indeed three such have been found in the Rhine.[15]

Ships on some coins of the Atrebates in the Cabinet des Médailles in Paris (Muret et Charbouillet nos 8611 and 8613), which rather resemble *ponti*, do have a sort of forefoot under the bows.[16] One of the bronze models of a Gallo-Roman river boat from Blessey (Côte d' Or) also has a ram (Figure 12.5). So one is left with a

8.2 *Peter Marsden examining the Blackfriars 1 ship during excavations in July 1963 (Peter Marsden)*

problem. Did Caesar think rams so common in war-ships that he did not mention that the Venetic ships had them? Or did they indeed not have them until the Gauls took to them in their cargo ships and river boats under Roman influence?

## The Blackfriars 1 ship

This perhaps is a minor detail, and much greater light was thrown on the ships of the Veneti of southern Brittany by a vessel found in the River Thames in 1958. This is the Blackfriars 1 ship, and Peter Marsden, its excavator, has the credit for instigating a new cast of thought about indigenous shipping in the West in the pre- and post-Roman periods (see Figure 8.2). In the mud of the Thames on 6 September 1962 under the shadow of Blackfriars Bridge, the wreck of a wooden ship was partially laid bare by mechanical grab. With the help of a temporary coffer dam and the London Fire Brigade, the difficulties of working on the bed of the river with the site clear only for about $2\frac{1}{2}$ hours each tide were overcome, to reveal the remains of a flat-bottomed, keel-less, iron-fastened craft of oak. Thanks largely to the pottery sherds in the layer of gravel trapped between the collapsed side of the vessel and its bottom, it was possible to date it to the second century AD.

In view of its cargo of Kentish ragstone and its flat bottom, beamy shape, and chine, Peter Marsden suggests that it was a Romano-British sailing barge accidentally sunk in the Thames while carrying to London a cargo of building stone quarried in the Maidstone area of Kent.[17] Its main interest is its method of construction, which it largely shares with the New Guy's House craft – a Roman river barge, part of which was found in 1958 on the site of a new surgical block of Guy's Hospital in Bermondsey in south London. The fascinating thing about these two craft is that although they belong to the Roman period, they were not built according to the usual Roman methods. A large number of wrecks of the Roman period have been found in or near the Mediterranean, ranging from the small boats which lay beside the big galleys in Lake Nemi, south-east of Rome, and the seven barges from the 'Portus' of Rome, to several merchantmen. Though only the most recent of these wrecks have been explored at all scientifically, they have led to a fairly general agreement about the techniques of Roman shipbuilding. This suggests that these craft were built first with a shell of planks, each joined to its neighbour by mortise and tenon joints in the thickness of wood with dowels at right angles through the tenons, and that any frames were subsequently inserted and attached to the planking by wooden trenails with copper nails often driven down the middle. It is true that this generalisation has been challenged,[18] but by and

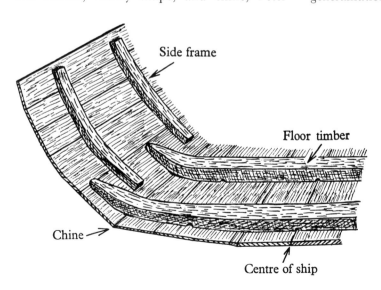

8.3  *Construction details of the Blackfriars 1 ship (Marsden, MM, vol. 51, 1965, p. 61)*

large this technique with its closely-joined un-caulked strakes seems to have been standard Roman practice;[19] it was certainly used in the County Hall ship found in London in 1910, even though its strakes were made from a species of oak that does not grow round the Mediterranean.[20]

The Blackfriars and New Guy's House craft, in contradistinction, did not have mortise-and-tenon-joined strakes but there was a caulking of hazel twigs in their seams, and in the Blackfriars 1 ship it was possible to deduce that the method of construction was as shown in Figure 8.3. The bottom strakes as far out as the chines were probably laid out first, then floor timbers were put on top and the strakes nailed to the floor timbers from outside the hull. The outer ends of the floor timbers curved upwards and to these were nailed

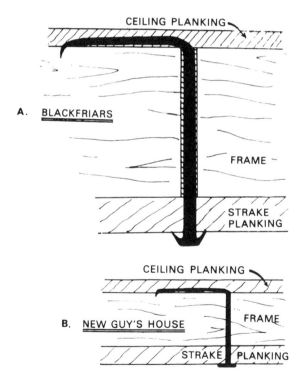

8.4 *Methods of fastening the planking to the frames of the Blackfriars 1 and the New Guy's House ships; note that in the Blackfriars 1 ship the nail goes through a* peg *in the floor timber (after Marsden,* A Roman Ship from Blackfriars, *1966)*

the first side strake. The lower ends of side frames were then probably fastened to these strakes, giving at this stage a semi-skeleton outline. Next the remaining side strakes would have been nailed to the side frames, with the conical hollow-headed copper nails being driven through pegs in the floor timbers and then clenched by turning the points towards the axis of the ship (Figure 8.4). Finally, the ceiling, the deck beams and decking would have been added.[21] Peter Marsden points out how closely the Blackfriars 1 ship matches Caesar's description of those of the Veneti. Both were made of oak, had flat bottoms, massive cross-beams fastened with nails, and were heavily built.[22]

## The Bruges boat

These characteristics then prompted a re-examination, by Ole Crumlin-Pedersen, among others, of the Bruges craft, particularly with regard to the similarities between its mast-step (Figure 8.5) and that of the Blackfriars 1 ship.[23]

The Bruges boat was found in 1899 5 metres down during the excavation of the Bruges–Zeebrugge canal. The remains are 7 metres long, with an estimated original length of about 15 metres, and they are now stored in the Musée de la Marine at Antwerp. None of the drawn reconstructions of this craft has been entirely happy, but Crumlin-Pedersen considers that it may be placed in the cog category, with possible links with the Blackfriars ship. Peter Marsden[24] also queried the fifth or sixth century AD date previously given to the Bruges craft, and a recent radiocarbon date of AD 180±80 (HAR-472) has confirmed his suggestion.[25] Marsden's recent investigations have also indicated that this ship was probably carvel-built like Blackfriars 1.

8.5 *The Bruges ship's mast-step in a transverse frame (National Scheepvaartmuseum, Antwerp)*

## 'Celtic' shipbuilding

In the late 1960s Detlev Ellmers postulated from documentary evidence, and from consideration of the characteristics of the Blackfriars 1 ship, the existence of an indigenous western European tradition of ancient ship-building which he christened 'Celtic'.[26] The main elements of this, he suggested, were a flat bottom and hard chine, with no mortise and tenon fastenings of strakes, but caulking, and nails hammered through the strakes into the floor members or side frames with the end of the nail then bent back and knocked into the wood. Subsequent boat finds along the Rhine (particularly at Zwammerdam in the Netherlands), as described in chapter 12, confirmed these characteristics, at least for river craft, and added two new features: a thwartships mast-step and massive floor timbers, often in pairs or in threes.

Ellmers pointed out that the origins of this indigenous tradition of western European shipbuilding, which was quite different from either the Roman or the Scandinavian, must go back well before the Roman period and be reflected in all sorts of craft.[27] He has also indicated one contributory stream of development in the form of the split dug-out (see chapter 12). This, however, does not throw any light on how far south this 'Celtic' tradition ran, or whether the Veneti represented its southernmost extension.

## The Portuguese *saveiro*

This is where it is perhaps worth looking at two interesting types of twentieth-century Iberian Atlantic coast craft, the *saveiro* or *xavega*, and its smaller southern brother, the *meia lua*. The *saveiro* is spectacular to look at, as well as interesting, and it is sad that, at the time of writing, there are said to be only three still in use in Portugal. However, one has been obtained by the Exeter Maritime Museum in England, where it will be preserved. As long ago as 1952, T. C. Lethbridge suggested that the unusual and archaic nature of their shape, as well as their primitive features – no keel, no rudder, no mast – might mean that *saveiros* were descendants of Tartessus (near Huelva in Seville)

8.6    Meia luas *on the Costa da Carparies, southern Portugal – notice the horizontal run of planking at the ends (author)*

8.7    *An internal view of a* meia lua *(author)*

and begetters of the ships of the Veneti.[28] He supported this thesis by pointing out the important difference between beach and estuary boats. Beach craft always face a specific situation – through the breakers from a flat shore. A suitable form for this, with a flat bottom and at least one high extremity

8.8　*A* saveiro *being launched from the beach. The wooden fork at the stern is being pushed by oxen (David Goddard, Exeter Maritime Museum)*

to face the breaking waves, could have been evolved many centuries ago and survive in a remarkably unvaried shape, except occasionally for the stern, from Gibraltar to Cape Wrath. No such conservatism was forced on the estuary boatman. He had no surf to worry about and no limitation on launching weight or depth of keel. Moreover, he had sheltered water in which to try out new ideas and these again might be stimulated by seeing strangers and visiting craft who would seek shelter on occasion in an estuary or inlet, whereas they would never except in an emergency run ashore on an open beach. *Saveiros* are launched from beaches into the open Atlantic (Figure 8.8) on wooden rollers by oxen pushing on a wooden fork against the stern post, and Lethbridge's theory of beach conservatism indicates that they may be an ancient design. Shortage of resources, isolation and the need to be absolutely certain of the performance of their craft in the open Atlantic would perpetuate this conservatism.

It is hard, seeing a *saveiro* being built, not to feel it would have been a perfectly familiar method to the 'Celtic' Rhine boat-builders.[29] The pine planks are first bent to the required curve by wetting them, putting them under tension and lighting a fire of pine shavings underneath. Pine trunks with a right-angle bend near the root end

are selected for the frames. A line of blocks is then laid, in the open air near the launching-place, to support the centre bottom plank with the rocker (longitudinal curve of keel) required and the positions for the frames are marked on it. Using a measuring rod marked with the half-breadths of the boat's bottom at each station, the outer bottom

8.9　*A* saveiro *under construction, with L-shaped part-frames fastened to the bottom planking (author)*

planks are next fitted, leaving a gap in the bottom at this stage. The frames, each consisting of an L-shaped section and a side timber, are then fashioned using an adjustable mould. The long arms of the frames are then fastened to the planking by trenails, and the top strake is fitted and fastened by trenails to the frames, to be followed by the short side frames and then the remaining side planks which are fitted horizontally, despite the great sheer at bow and stern: this latter is a distinctive feature of these Portuguese boats. Finally the boat is detached from the blocks and rolled on its side for the remaining bottom planks to be fastened in place, and the planking is then caulked with hemp.

The *saveiro* does not have a mast, but the far more numerous *moliceiro*, the seaweed-gathering craft of the Aveiro lagoons, which is built by the same shipwrights in the same yards, does; and it is set in a thwartship step like the 'Celtic' ones.

8.10 *Making trenails for a* saveiro *(author)*

One has, of course, to be very cautious when using a modern craft, however primitive and unusual, as a source of comparison with ancient vessels, without more archaeological evidence than the apparent similarity of *saveiros* to the craft of the Roman period carved on altars to the Deae Nehelenniae at Kalkleen in the Netherlands.[30] Nevertheless, if one accepts that there are great similarities between the way the *saveiro* is built and Ellmers's 'Celtic' vessels; and Lethbridge's point about the conservatism of beach boats and that these might hint at the survival in the *saveiro* of an ancient tradition, then a number of interesting points emerge.

One important one is the link to the south. There are two factors about the *saveiro* which are of some significance here. These are that even in its highest extremities, as with the *moliceiro*, its strakes are horizontal, and this is a characteristic that it shares with the Maltese *dghaisa* and the Venetian gondola.[31] Second, again like the *dghaisa* and the gondola, some of the oarsmen of the *saveiro* row facing forward and pushing. So this Portuguese fishing boat has Mediterranean as well as 'Celtic' elements.

## The *hippos*

This calls to mind an important craft of the ancient Mediterranean world, the *hippos*. This craft is the centrepiece of the well-known story, passed on by Strabo from Poseidonius, that Eudoxus, one of the most enterprising explorers of antiquity, during his second return voyage to India about 112 BC, had found on the shores of East Africa near Cape Guardafui the wooden prow of a ship with a horse's head carved on it which showed it originally came from Gades.[32] There is no need to take this sailor's yarn at its face value and assume that an Iberian *hippos* had circumnavigated the Cape of Good Hope, even though it might seem a logical way of trading with Somalia and Arabia without suffering the exactions of the Ptolemies.[33] What is important is the light the story throws on the *hippos*. These ships must have been seaworthy to fish regularly along the west coast of Africa, quite apart from being thought capable of

8.11  *A seventh century BC brooch with a* hippos *from Aliseda, Cáceres, Spain (author)*

8.12  *A gold coin with ship, from Gaul, dated to about 100 BC (Bibliothèque nationale, Paris)*

reaching East Africa, yet the sophisticated ship captains of Alexandria considered them vessels of the poorer sort; in other words, crude and primitive. A silver brooch of the seventh century BC, found at Aliseda in Spain, shows one of these horse-headed double-ended craft (Figure 8.11). So its geographical nearness in antiquity to the *saveiro* is not in doubt. Its likeness to the better known illustrations of *hippoi* from the eastern end of the Mediterranean, all of them mastless, needs little underlining either. These latter suggest that in Phoenicia *hippoi* were a sort of handy cargo lighter, normally without sails, probably flat bottomed. In this, as well as their appearance, they do in some ways recall *saveiros*. R. D. Barnett in fact sees a direct link between *hippoi* and the ships of the Veneti.[34] Though he did not quote them, four small gold coins from Gaul (Muret et Charbouillet nos 6926–6929), dated to about 100 BC, support this view of Barnett.[35] These coins, copied from staters of Philip of Macedon, have on their reverse side a horse with a chariot-driver who holds the reins in his left hand and in his right a model ship. Three of the coins are rather worn but the ship is very clear on the fourth. It has an upright stem and stern and a mast with a yard amidships (Figure 8.12). Below the gunwale are a row of dots, possibly shields or oarports, and below that a double curved pattern. On the stem and stern are horned animal heads facing outwards, certainly giving the craft a strong resemblance to the *hippos*. A rather similar type of vessel is represented by a clay model of a boat from Corneto, though in this case the upright bow and stern are decorated with bird rather than animal heads.[36]

Bearing these in mind, it seems necessary, in order to make any sense of the ramifications of the *hippos*, to go back to the last chapter. There it was argued that one of the developments after the Skyros dug-outs was most likely a flat-bottomed craft, the planks secured by cross-bars, and possibly at first sewn to each other. While the masted Minoan trading ship, the prototype of the round *gauloi*, was developing, and eventually inspiring, Phoenician craft such as those on Ken-Amun's tomb and the Fortetsa crater, presumably the older simpler flat-bottomed type must have gone on existing as an inshore vessel, cargo lighter, tender and so on. Barnett has also suggested that the horse's head on the *hippos* might have been inspired by the odd-looking Minoan craft with reversed horse's head shown on a seal from Mochlos[37] (see Figure 6.3). On the other hand, it may just have been their 'work-horse of the sea' function that suggested the analogy.

The illustrations we have of the Phoenician *hippos* on one of the bronze bands from the Balawat gates (Figure 8.13) of Shalmaneser III (859–824 BC) and on a wall relief from the palace of Sargon II (722–705 BC) at Khorsabad in Iraq (Figure 8.14) are a good deal earlier than the literary

8.13  *Bronze reliefs on the Balawat gates of the Assyrian King Shalmaneser III (mid-ninth century BC), with Phoenician* hippoi *on the upper strip carrying tribute from Tyre (British Museum)*

8.14  *Wall relief from the palace of Sargon II (722–705 BC) at Khorsabad, Iraq (Louvre, Paris)*

references in Sophocles, Pliny and Strabo.[38] Yet they too give a feeling of a humble hard-working type of craft, just what one would expect to be ferrying tribute from the island of Tyre to the mainland, as the Balawat craft is doing.

## The gondola and the *dghaisa*

A. F. Tilley has pointed out the very interesting similarity between the Balawat craft (Figure 8.13) and the Venetian gondola.[39] The lines of bow and stern with their overhangs, the decoration of each extremity and the action and stance of the rowers are very close, particularly when it is remembered that it was only after AD 1797, when the Venetian state collapsed in financial ruin, that it became standard practice for one gondolier rather than two to man these craft.[40] In his study of the evolution of the Venetian gondola, G. B. Rubin de Cervin says that while the earliest literary reference to a gondola dates from AD 1094, it is probable that these craft had their origin when the first Venetian settlers were fleeing from the dangerous mainland and seeking refuge in their flat-bottomed craft in the intricate waterways of the marshes, and that the modern Venetian *barchetta* or *mezza gondola*, a much humbler though seaworthy version of the gondola, is nearer to the prototype than the sophisticated one-man craft of today.[41] Tilley goes further back and sees links between the Venetians and the Phoenicians.[42] First he points out that the Romans called the inhabitants of Venetia an ancient people, and that between 1200 and 800 BC, when the Phoenicians played an important part in Mediterranean trade, the head of the Adriatic would be an excellent place to pick up goods from the amber route down through central Europe. Second, the trade routes of the Phoenicians have been traced by their practice of giving names like 'Phoenikous', 'Phoenix' and 'Finike' to their watering stops, and 'La

Fenice' could be one of these. Then Venice shared with the great port of Tyre the practice of having a 'sacred ship', the *bucintoro*, from which the Doge performed annually the rite of marriage with the sea. Finally, it has been suggested that the word 'gondola' may be derived from the Latin '*cumbula*', a diminutive of '*cumba*', a type of craft which Pliny says was invented by the Phoenicians.

Despite all the changes in ship-building technique that have taken place in the Mediterranean in the last 3,000 years, the gondola still has three fore-and-aft bottom planks (*colombe*) which are secured by frames, of which the middle frames alone are built up in three pieces, oak being used for the cross-piece traversing the planks, while the side pieces are made of elm.[43] It may also be worth saying that the elaborate metal bow pieces, which today seem almost an abstract design, in the double-ended eighteenth-century AD gondola illustrated by Jal (Figure 8.15) do look very like a horse's head. In fact, once one has seen this shape, even the modern ones start to look like degenerate versions.[44]

Moreover, the gondola is not the only example of the continuity of the *hippos*'s influence in the Mediterranean. Tilley has also pointed out the close similarity between the Khorsabad relief (Figure 8.14) and the Maltese *dghaisa*, especially the four-man racing version of the latter, known colloquially as 'fancy boats'. The *dghaisa* is a

8.15   *An eighteenth-century Venetian gondola (from Jal,* Glossaire nautique, *1848)*

8.16   *Four-man racing* dghaisas *in Grand Harbour, Valletta (Malta Government Tourist Board)*

double-ended craft with a flattish bottom amidships, a tholepin for each oar, and no rudder or other provision for steering.[45] Rather similar small craft also exist in the Lipari Islands, though many now have engines.

As Tilley says, the Khorsabad craft is being propelled essentially in what the Admiralty seamanship manual calls 'diso (*dghaisa*) fashion'.

It is an interesting thought that this technique of rowing standing and facing forward may be directly descended from the Phoenician practice, and that both the gondola and *dghaisa* may belong to a tradition of small simple working craft which goes back to the earliest Minoan period.

## Mediterranean and Atlantic seaboard developments

Reverting now to the western Mediterranean and the Atlantic seaboard, it is suggested that Strabo's *hippoi* from Gades which fished off the North African coast and the craft on the Aliseda brooch and Gallic coins were the western equivalent of the Khorsabad and Balawat versions, and that the differences between the *saveiro*, on the one hand, and the gondola and *dghaisa*, on the other, show the effect of different circumstances working on the same basic original type. All are mastless except for the much later Gallic ships, rudderless, with horizontal planks, more or less flat bottomed and double ended, but, as one would expect, the *saveiro* is altogether a larger and tougher craft with far more pronounced extremities to face the bigger seas of the Atlantic. This hypothesis then could be taken as a diffusionist's delight, since it suggests a link between Phoenicia, the Adriatic and the Mediterranean and the western coast of Iberia and western European ships of the Roman period. If this were so, then the *saveiro* would be a remarkable survival of a crucial link, with its Mediterranean elements of horizontal strakes and forward-facing oarsmen, and its 'Celtic' method of construction. An alternative possibility is simply that over the centuries the *saveiro* collected techniques and influences from both north and south to evolve into its present form.

Perhaps the most likely explanation is that the split dug-out technique is one that is so obvious that it could be very widespread, if not universal, and this flat-bottomed start provided the basis for strong simple craft over a wide area which survived particularly in isolated areas where they functioned effectively for the job in hand. Only if a ship of the Veneti or the 'Celtic' type was found with horizontal strakes high up in bow or stern would a really wide ramification of the *hippos* be confirmed.

Meanwhile, the similarity in the building method of the *saveiro*, the Blackfriars 1 ship and the Zwammerdam craft, all with flat bottoms, hard chines, U-frames, caulking, and using neither true shell nor skeleton construction techniques, cannot be denied. If one adds the Mediterranean elements in the *saveiro*, the horizontal strakes and the rowing facing forward, then this suggests the reasonable hypothesis that the Iberian coast was a likely place for Mediterranean and western European influences to have met and mixed.[46]

## Sail

Another aspect of the Venetic ships that impressed Caesar were their sails of leather. Presumably the sail first arrived in the west in the Minoan period and must certainly have been commonplace by the time the Phoenicians were traditionally replacing Tartessus with Gades in the twelfth century BC. How quickly it moved north, one cannot say.

According to Ellmers, a Roman tombstone from Bad Junkerath shows the upper parts of a cargo craft with a leather sail set. This sail is exceptional in having three battens across it, almost in the manner of a Chinese junk. He also claims that one can see the same type of partitioned sail being lowered on a craft portrayed on the 'Okeanos-Mosaik' from Bad Kreuznach. What is more, this suggested leather sail has a distinct greyish colour, as compared with the yellowy whiteness of a conventional linen sail on another craft in the same mosaic.[47]

If Lethbridge and Barnett are right about the links between the *saveiro* and the *hippos* and the Venetic fleet, and Caesar correct about the flat bottom of the latter, the implication is perhaps that while the sail arrived in the west on the

'round' ships of the Minoans and Phoenicians, the peoples of the Atlantic coast chose to borrow the idea of the sail, but put it in their own older well-tried flat-bottomed *hippos-saveiro* design.

## The evolution of planked craft

Another question is: when did the built-up planked craft first appear in the Atlantic? On this latter point there is certainly no answer at the moment, but there is one interesting piece of speculation inspired by a painting in the Dolmen de Antelas in Portugal (see Figure 4.14c). Beatrice Blance believes it may be a ship.[48] On the other hand it may well be a comb as Savory suggests;[49] but if it does represent a comb, it is still possible that the artist, or the comb-maker, might have made the article in question like a boat, and even Savory admits that the art here is quite realistic. If it does in any way represent a boat, or the memory of a boat, then it would indicate that the same sort of high roughly double-ended craft as the *saveiro* was in use off the West Iberian coast as early as the megalithic period in the west, say from 3000 to 2000 BC.

To sum up then: what this evidence, much of it very tentative, seems to suggest is that, either through direct influence or through similar problems producing a similar solution, the coastal fishermen and river boatmen who perhaps crept out of the Guadalquivir and other rivers occasionally into the Atlantic in their dug-outs followed one of the Mediterranean patterns of expanding a dug-out into a flat-bottomed craft strengthened by cross-pieces and with the high extremities which the Atlantic and the shore breakers made essential. Under the stimulus of open sea conditions, such craft would tend to become higher-sided and as strong as materials would permit. Neither would sea warfare have subsequently modified them in the way that Aegean circumstances produced the *trieris* and other long war-ships. In the Atlantic the first need was to stay afloat in rough seas and the second to be able to beach without damaging the hull. Hence the ultimate difference between Caesar's ships and those of the Veneti.

Nor was this evolutionary process confined to France and Iberia. In chapter 11 the evidence for its happening also in the British Isles will be discussed.

## Skin boats

But possibly from a very early period the high-ended craft of Iberia, even if they had outmoded reed- or papyrus-bundle craft and dug-outs for deep-sea voyaging, must have overlapped the other possible answer to the big seas of the ocean, the skin boat. The reasons for suggesting 45–50° N as a rough southern boundary to the skin-boat area have already been put in chapter 4. These parallels of latitude contain neatly enough the area of Ushant–Brittany where in the fifth century BC, according to the Massiliote *Periplus*, the trans-shipment of goods from planked to skin boats seems to have taken place.[50]

But by Caesar's time the southern planked craft had completely taken over there. So this might represent a later stage of a long process whereby planked Iberian craft of a *saveiro* type had gradually extended their influence northward. In that case skin boats might have operated off the Iberian Atlantic coast at an early period, subsequently leaving behind a legacy of technique with Strabo's Lusitanian mountaineers. This overlap problem is worth considering, even if there are no certain answers, because as radiocarbon dates for megalithic sites becomes earlier, the question whether there was any sea link between

the different sites of these great stone tombs becomes ever more difficult.

The richly intricate field of megalithic art, with its sparse adherence to realism, does not give much help here. It is not difficult to see in Co. Meath, if one wants to, a plan view of a curragh in one of the designs at Cairn T at Loughcrew, and 'Coffey's ship', carved on one of the stones inside the great burial mound of New Grange near the River Boyne in Ireland, has also been taken to represent a boat, though few authorities now accept this.[51] Instead, the carvings at Mané Lud in Brittany have grown in favour and are currently considered more likely to represent vessels.[52] Almost all one can say about these latter is that they seem to have the turned-down ends more characteristic of skin boats, with the effect of skin-shrinking on their shapes, than of the upswept bows of wooden *saveiro* types. So that merely gives a slight reinforcement to the idea, already suggested, that skin boats were in general use as far south as Brittany, if not Iberia as well, in the megalithic period, possibly manned by the more conservative groups of people who went on living largely by fishing alongside their formally 'Neolithic' agricultural neighbours. Descendants of these same sailor-fishermen were probably responsible for the carrying trade in the Bronze Age which produced the famous Huelva hoard of scrap metal and weapons from the estuary of the Odiel, as well as bringing to Spain such specifically Irish objects as the cauldrons found at Cabárceno (Santander) and Lois (Leon) and the 'flesh-hooks' at Hio (Pontevedra).[53]

8.17 *A curragh under way in the Irish Sea with the author in the bows (author)*

8.18  *A saveiro's 10-metre oar pivoted on a tholepin, as are the curragh oars in Figure 8.17 (author)*

There is a curious link between modern Irish curraghs and Portuguese *saveiros* in the unusual way in which the oars of both are attached to the hull by a pin through a bull, or block, on the loom of the oar. It seems certain that the early skin boats of the north were paddled and that rowing was evolved in the Mediterranean. So these two ancient and conservative maritime traditions, the Iberian and the Irish, still embody evidence of the moment when they came in contact and some enterprising Irish paddler, possibly with the sort of outbred gene-mixture Professor Darlington would consider likely to produce enterprise,[54] persuaded his companions to try the new technique and equipment from the south.

## Reed craft

It may surprise perhaps those who watch current developments of nautical archaeology in the world's press that nothing has been said so far in this chapter about any craft resembling the papyrus *Ra II* in which Thor Heyerdahl made a second and successful attempt to cross the Atlantic. His voyage showed that tightly-lashed papyrus would resist waterlogging longer than many people thought, long enough to cross the Atlantic, and thereby incidentally corroborated the likeli-hood of early Mediterranean voyages in reed-bundle craft. The contemporary reed boats on the River Lucus in Morocco also suggest that a tradition of this type may have stretched the length of the Mediterranean to the west coast of North Africa. But by making *Ra II* large and deep enough to stay afloat for more than two months, Heyer-dahl also made the vessel so heavy and clumsy that it was virtually impossible to paddle or row it against the wind. Without leeboards, too, a device for which there is very little ancient Mediter-ranean evidence, it would sail only a point or two each side of the wind. So would anyone in antiquity have built a craft in the neighbourhood of a prevailing wind and current which would be so difficult to return to its starting-point? As Heyerdahl himself has quite rightly emphasised, the sailors of the past were no fools.

Heyerdahl's thinking about the impact of ancient Egypt on central American civilisations by way of accidental drift voyages is a subject for diffusionists and non-diffusionists to argue. But there is one interesting reflection that has emerged from an entirely different subject. This is the increasingly general identification of Plato's Atlantis with the great period of Minoan civili-sation, and the suggestion that it was the explosion of the volcano on the island of Santorini which destroyed the main cities of the Minoans. The story of the destruction of a great metropolis in the 'far west' was handed on from the Egyptian scholar-priests of the goddess Neith by Solon, Critias and others to Plato. By the time Plato wrote it down in his later dialogues, the Greeks had become familiar with the western Mediterranean and the Phoenicians for many centuries had been trading with Gades. The author of the Psalms, too, seems to have thought that from Tartessus (Tharsis) to Arabia and Saba described a dominion from one sea to the other (72:8–10). So to Plato the 'far west' had to be beyond the Pillars of Hercules, and the idea of St Brandon's Isle, Hy Brasil, the Fortunate Isles and so on had already received their first impetus. But if the identification of Atlantis with Santorini and Crete is correct, and the vulcanologists' evidence is complicated and still controversial,[55] then to the Egyptian priests of 1500 BC who noted the great disaster, the 'far west' was still close enough to be in the Aegean.

So Heyerdahl's achievement does not perhaps prove very much beyond the durability of papyrus, even though it is certainly not impossible that a vessel of the past, particularly a Phoenician one, might well have survived an accidental crossing between the continents.

# 9 Scandinavia

## Stone Age skin boats

The farm known as Evenhus stands on the peninsula of Frosta where it juts furthest out into the Trondheim Fjord. To reach it involves a two-hour journey by train and bus from Trondheim on the west coast of Norway. Past the farm orchard, in a fringe of fir wood looking down a gentle slope to the fjord, is one of the great galleries of marine prehistoric art. Carved into a rock-face there are a curvetting whale and a whole series of boats, some of them decorated with symbols but all of them a very particular type (see Figure 4.2). The other two main sites where carvings like this can be seen,

9.1 *Rock carving of a skin boat from Evenhus, Norway* *(author)*

Skjomen in Ofoten and Rødøy in Helgeland, are not at all easy to get at but Evenhus, even without signposts, is not hard to find. No nautical archaeologist can look at these carvings unmoved. If not as beautiful as the Minoan seal-stones, they are much larger and easier to study and much clearer than the ship carvings at Hal Tarxien on Malta. One sees in bold outline the craft in which prehistoric man in the Postglacial period braved the often violent seas of the coasts and skerries of Norway and worked his way as far north as Finnmark.

Ever since G. Gjessing first appreciated the true significance of these carvings,[1] they have been accepted as skin boats. They are deep and rather tubby and mostly with abrupt turns at bow and stern. Moreover, in a considerable number what seem to be two pairs of ribs are shown. All these features point towards a skin boat, as Gjessing rightly saw. There is thus not much doubt about the craft except that recurring question: which is the bow and which is the stern? Professor Brøgger, joint author of the classic work on the origins of Viking ships, suggested that the higher end is the prow.[2] This higher end, however, in the vast majority of cases ends in a pair of short open parallel lines. If there were only one or two examples one might suspect that either wear of the rock or inattention on the part of the artist had resulted in that end of the boat not being finished off. Fortunately there is a perfectly good explanation which suggests that these parallel lines were deliberately drawn to represent handles for lifting the craft. Such handles are known to have been fitted to umiaks at the other end of the Eurasian land mass, in the Aleutians. A skin boat is most vulnerable when beaching, and these 'handles' could be used to raise either bow or stern clear of ripping the hull on shingle or rock.

For many years a distinction was made between the naturalistic 'Arctic Art' of Scandinavia and the later more symbolic 'farmers' art', and it was conventional to classify the 'Arctic Art' as Stone Age and the so-called 'farmers' art' as Bronze Age. However, Professor Hagen has pointed out that this sort of distinction can easily lead to incorrect over-simplification.[3] While the practice of carving ritual pictures on rock may date back to the Stone Age, we now know that the hunter-fishers who practised the 'Arctic Art' continued to flourish during the Bronze Age when the 'farmers' art' was at its peak, and the two may well have been influenced by each other, as indeed we can see at Evenhus where a Bronze Age concentric circle appears on a boat of an early type (see Figure 10.4), a craft which is also significant from another point of view, as will be seen in the next chapter.

Thus it is not surprising to find arguments about the date of these carvings. Some must certainly be early, since they were done when the sea-level was much higher than at present. For instance the carvings on the River Sag are on an inaccessible cliff-face and seem to have been done from a boat when the sea was perhaps 45 to 50 metres higher.[4] There is, however, no specific evidence to link these carvings directly to the earliest Norwegian inhabitants.

On the other hand it is possible to look at the problem the other way round. The Høgnipen sites south of Oslo, like those of the subsequent and better known Fosna and Komsa complexes, must have been based on sea travel. Though the three small Høgnipen sites are now some 20 kilometres inland, the local topography suggests that originally they hugged the shore where, amongst the islets and skerries, an arctic fauna thrived.[5] Professor Hagen sees the inhabitants of these sites as roving bands of huntsmen living close to the sea-shore, hunting big game on land as well as sea.[6] It is thus not at all unlikely that somewhere between 10,000 and 7000 BC these hunters, and the herds of reindeer they hunted, travelled north to follow the conditions they were used to, the treeless plains and shores where arctic conditions prevailed.

The later Fosna hunters are better known, since hundreds of their sites have been found. Radiocarbon analyses from these sites have produced dates between 7750 and 6060 BC,[7] and they seem to have divided into two groups: those who hunted reindeer and fished in rivers and lakes on the high mountain plateau of southern Norway, and those who stayed by the coast of western Norway. Leaving aside the question of whether the former used boats or ice to reach the few island sites which have been found, there is no doubt about the sea-going nature of the latter group. Their settlements avoid the inner, more temperate, fjords and starkly face the ocean, on headlands and islands, sounds and creeks, ready to tap the inexhaustibly rich yields of the hunting and fishing grounds. As Professor Hagen says, good boats must have been essential for travel along that stormy coast.[8]

The Komsa Culture, too, of which some hundred sites have been found in Finnmark and on the arctic coast of Russia, west of Murmansk, seems to have been entirely coastal. All the sites are either by the ancient coastline or near it, on islands or headlands, and they do not seem to have moved inland up the rivers.[9]

The third early hunting culture of Norway, named from the site of Nøstvet 20 kilometres south of Oslo, was also based on fishing, and their settlements too, for much the most part, were within easy reach of the coastline.[10] To this culture also belongs a site which underlines in a particularly dramatic way the crucial nature of sea travel to these people. This is the little island of Hespriholmen on the outer fringes of the Bømlo archipelago between Bergen and Stavanger. Here was the best supply of greenstone in western Norway, and the working of it in the prehistoric period has left a great cavity 30 metres broad and 11 metres high carved out of the rock-face. It has been calculated that as 11,000 cubic metres or nearly 3,000 tons must have been removed, at a maximum of 3 cwt a boatload, 20,000 boat journeys must have been made to this island across the treacherous 7-kilometre strait, much of it open to the ocean.[11]

The organisation of the quarrying and distribution of the half-finished artefacts over much of the coastal area of south-western Norway must have been a remarkable achievement, but it is the situation of the island that is particularly significant, facing the Atlantic and where landing was possible on only occasional days. The implications are clear. All these early Norwegian peoples depended on the sea and on sea-travel in conditions which could often be appallingly difficult. Their presence goes back, in the case of the Høgnipen groups, to a period before forests had spread north behind the retreating ice, and subsequent groups of hunter-fishers continued to live virtually the same sort of life until the period of the great migration.[12]

Since this way of life was so determined by ecological conditions, so long lasting and so conservative, it is not very rash to suggest that their boats did not change much either. While we cannot say specifically that these were exactly like the carvings of Evenhus, Rødøy and Skjomen, it seems probable that they were not very different. We can check this too by the differences between the western Norwegian carvings and those found on the River Vyg in Russia. On the banks of this river close to the White Sea and the little town of Soroka, more than 600 carved figures have been found, including some 50 boats.[13] The smaller boats, which are most like the Norwegian ones, only rarely show ribs or 'handles', mostly have a prominent reindeer head on the bows, and have a

small ram forefoot. Thus there are plenty of differences but, on the other hand, the basic shape seems to be very similar. Hallström, who has made a prolonged study of these northern carvings, does not think these Russian craft are skin boats.[14] However, he himself draws attention to features which seem to argue against his interpretation. For instance the protective forefoot 'ram' is far more necessary on a skin boat than on a dug-out or plank boat, and these projections are very conspicuous on the River Vyg carvings. He notes the rather rare craft for this area, on which ribs are visible. Again, ribs are a prominent feature of skin boats, brought out either by the transparency of the hide (see Figure 9.9), or as ridges standing proud where the skin has shrunk and tightened round the frame. Moreover, one of the larger Russian carvings has at the stern a sort of hoop, quite different from the crew figures, which one could well imagine giving lifting purchase in the same way as the 'handles' on the Evenhus craft.

If one then accepts these arguments for the Vyg carvings probably being skin boats, the carvings show that the shape of the smaller type is basically very similar to the Norwegian ones. It is when one comes to the development of these boats into larger craft that the differences start becoming more than decorative details. However, before seeing the different ways in which these two related types of craft evolved, one should perhaps first consider their relationship, because if Norwegian Arctic Art, and the boats carved by its practitioners, had an ultimate Russian origin, this might explain the very different later developments of the skin boat

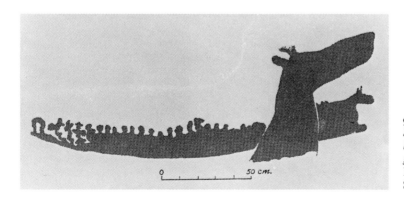

9.2  *Rock carving from Vyg, White Sea, northern Russia, of a long skin boat, crossed by another carving of a giant reindeer (Hallström,* Monumental Art from Northern Sweden, *1960)*

9.3 *Rock carving of a skin boat from Forselv, Norway
(after Marstrander, Østfolds Jordbruksristninger, 1963)*

tradition in the British Isles as opposed to its evolution in Scandinavia.

Attempts have been made to link the Komsa Culture with Upper Palaeolithic groups who lived on the plains of Russia and Poland and likenesses have been seen with the Ahrensburg, Swiderian and Pinneberg/Lyngby groups.[15] However, these somewhat romantic attempts to find a far distant origin have not yet acquired much evidence to support them, as neither the interior of Finnmark, northern Finland, northern Sweden nor the coast of the White Sea has yielded any traces of Komsa-type finds.[16] Cultures in Russo-Siberia of a similar period are by no means identical, and anyway in the vast distance between the two, finds are totally lacking. Certain features in the Askola Culture of southern Finland are similar to Komsa ones, but again there is a great gap between the two. It seems best therefore, for the moment, to assume that the Komsa peoples were simply the most northerly of the groups who in Postglacial times worked their way up the coast of Norway, following the game and the fish. What does seem very likely is that their travels were sea-based and took place in skin boats. If one also accepts Professor Hagen's arguments that these people had reached Finnmark by 7000 BC in the Pre-Boreal period and the archaic Palaeolithic character of their culture was determined by the arctic conditions there

which were similar to those experienced by the tundra hunters of more southern parts in Upper Palaeolithic times, this seems another indication that the simple skin boat may have evolved before the last glaciation.[17]

Agreeing then that the Norwegian and Russian carvings are probably not directly related, it becomes important to see what elements are common and might therefore delineate a possible Upper Palaeolithic forerunner. The 'handles' in the Norwegian and hoops in the Russian at the stern, and the Russian animal heads and forefeet seem to be individual local variations. This leaves the characteristic tubby deep hull with sharply turned ends. Many of the smaller Russian carvings seem to share a similar shape and proportion with the Evenhus and other carvings. The rare carvings where a man is shown apparently seated in the craft, as in Skjomen no. 1, Rødøy no. 3 and Evenhus no. 30, give some scale, and the number of ribs helps.[18] Possibly therefore the basic vessel was a rather squat coracle with little sheer to the gunwales, bluntish fore and aft, with considerable freeboard in proportion to the length, which might perhaps have been 4 metres long. This compares with the 3 metres of the smallest sea-going Irish curragh, the Donegal version.[19]

The similarity of these carvings to Eskimo ones of umiaks has been noted by a number of writers.[20] Of course, the umiak in most cases nowadays is considerably longer, but there seems to be no reason why one basic type should not have been ancestral to the umiak, the White Sea craft, the western Norwegian ones and the British Isles series.

What is more, it would be by no means hard to see in such a basic craft, to which the Evenhus and smaller Russian carvings are still fairly closely related, a source for the kayak. This is venturing on dangerous ground because there is remarkably

9.4 *Illustration of an Eskimo umiak
from Alaska (after Marstrander,
1963)*

little evidence about the origin of the kayak. However, if one accepts that Brøgger's Evenhus nos 30, 3 and 15 and Hallström's Vyg no. 2.II have the usually accepted naturalism of Arctic Art (and the accompanying animals suggest this very strongly), one sees, especially in the dramatic Russian carving, a strong suggestion of a use of the craft which approaches that of the kayak, namely one hunter in his craft pursuing his prey with a harpoon (Figure 9.5). Deck over with skin the bow and stern of the Evenhus and Vyg craft and you have something like a kayak. Once you deck in a craft, you can reduce its freeboard, as there is that much less need to rely on height above the surface to keep out spray. When this might have happened, or how, one cannot say, but these two carvings at least suggest a use of a similar hunting craft to the kayak, whose evolution would therefore post-date them technologically.

An alternative to decking in a craft to make it more seaworthy would be to give it a higher stem and stern, a process already observed in the Mediterranean. Certain carvings (Figure 9.6)

from Gåshopen on the island of Söröya in western Finnmark may show such a stage.[21] Another illustration of this process is in the Navestad group of carvings near Oslo, of which the most interesting one is no. 2 on Navestad Pyntelund V, which has seven diagonal ribs and a short, plain upright stem and stern a little longer than the height of the hull (Figure 9.7). The Vyg craft with ribs, on the other hand, has only four and a half. These rib markings of course are an inexact guide, but the increase does seem to be of the order one would expect from a craft which might have been an ancestor of the kayak to one which could take several men to sea (seven men, for instance, are shown in the left-hand Gåshopen boat on Figure 9.6), or carry the loads of stone axes from Hespriholmen. The Russian craft on the other hand developed lengthways. The largest Vyg carvings keep the same basic outline with reindeer head and forefoot but the boats become much longer (Figure 9.2), an indication perhaps that these did not have to face the open sea conditions imposed on the western Norwegian craft.

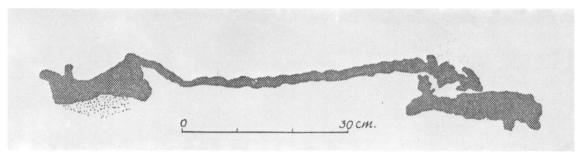

9.5   *Rock carving from Vyg, northern Russia, showing a hunter in a skin boat harpooning a marine animal (after Hallström, 1960)*

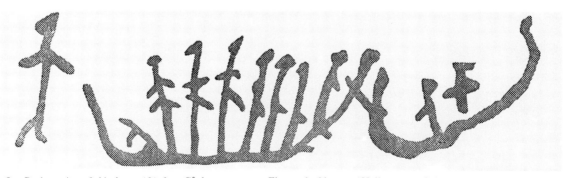

9.6   *Rock carving of skin boats ( ?) from Gåshopen, western Finnmark, Norway (Hallström, 1960)*

## The Bronze Age

The increase in size of the Scandinavian craft was presumably the prelude to the development of one of the most spectacular chapters in marine prehistory, the Bronze Age craft carved in their thousands over Scandinavia, ranging in size from the 4.4 metres of the huge one at Bjornstad in Norway (Figure 9.8), with its forty-eight crew strokes, to many only a few centimetres long. These elaborate and spectacular craft revealed to us by the so-called 'farmers' art' of the Bronze Age are also noted for the problems and arguments they have occasioned among archaeologists. Certainly they are not very easy to interpret, with

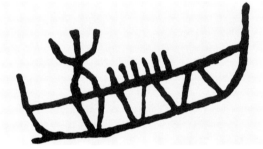

9.7   *Rock carving no. 2 from Navestad Pyntelund V, near Oslo (after Marstrander, 1963)*

their frequent complicated double bows, apparently deep hulls, and puzzling vertical strokes which sometimes seem to represent ribs, sometimes crew members.

The interpretative situation changed, however, with the publication of a masterly study by Sverre Marstrander of the carvings in the Skjeberg area of Ostfold near Oslo, the richest of all concentrations of this Bronze Age art form. Marstrander thinks the carvings can be divided into two main styles, the simple and the rich. The ships carved in the simple style are cautious and austere in outline and have undecorated prows. The ones carved in the rich style are much more elaborate and have heads of animals on their prows and other decorative effects. Marstrander considers the reason for the difference between these two styles to be the decisive chronological factor, the simple always being the earlier. Other differences merely reflect the six main types of craft, any of which can be done in the simple or rich style, according to whether they are earlier or later.[22] Marstrander then argues powerfully that these craft are skin boats. The curving of the hulls and the double bows, he suggests, are incompatible with dug-out or raft construction. Ribs and frames would not

9.8   *4.4 metre-long rock carving at Bjornstad, Skjeberg, Norway (Universitets Oldsaksamling, Oslo)*

have been shown if they had been covered by planks, whereas in a skin boat they do show. To support this argument, Marstrander shows a photograph of an Eskimo umiak with the sun shining through the hide hull (Figure 9.9) and giving a silhouette of its framework very like that shown in some of the carvings.[23]

An interesting and quite independent correlation of this transparent effect comes from James Hornell,[24] writing long before Marstrander applied it to the interpretation of the Scandinavian carving. Hornell quotes a description by Gabriel Beranger of a curragh in a book called *A Tour of Connaught* written in 1779. This craft was made of basket-work covered with the hide of a horse or cow and Beranger commented, 'as the members were six or eight inches apart and the sun was shining bright and the skin transparent, it seemed to me to be a vessel of glass, as I could see the water through it.'

Another interesting point Marstrander makes is about the closed loop which rounds off the stern of some craft. Quite rightly he points out that such a feature not only would have no point in a planked craft, but it would also be impossible to make it

with such materials.[25] On the other hand it is quite feasible to make this shape with a withy framework; in fact it is a logical thing to do rather than to leave a rod-end waving about in the water, and it is also very similar to the looped ends seen on Koryak and Chukchi sledges (Figure 9.11).

## An experimental skin boat

Since other elements among the carvings, such as animals and chariots, appear to be accurate and realistic, Marstrander believes these carvings represent ships which once existed, and are a reasonable likeness of them. He has therefore boldly ventured two reconstructions of such craft.[26]

In the summer of 1971, Marstrander and I carried out a plan to build and test a replica of one of his designs. The construction was done by Mr Odd Johnsen of Frederikstad, southern Norway, a builder of small clinker-built fishing and motor boats. He used eighteen trees, mostly alder with some lime, cut from the wood near his boat-shed, and many metres of rawhide thongs for lashings.[27] No metal was used, all joins being either pegged,

9.9 *Eskimo umiak with the sun shining through it showing the skeleton of the boat (after Marstrander, 1963)*

9.10  *Rock carving from Amoy, Norway, showing a boat with a looped end (author)*

or lashed, or both. Johnsen did the work almost entirely with an axe and knife, though an electric drill was used to speed up making the holes for the pegs.

The first stage was the laying down of the keelson, squared off from the largest tree, and the scarfing of a stem and stern piece to it. Onto this were pegged the nine U-shaped frames, which were each made of three round pieces of wood pegged together. This use of pegs was an arguable point: no evidence for their use, for instance, has been found in the Hjortspring boat from the island of Als, eastern Denmark. On the other hand, Chapelle reports that the Eskimo of the Alaskan coast pegged their floor timbers into the chines of their umiaks and the ends of the chines to their keelson, while in the big whaling umiaks trenails were used in scarfs with lashings on top,[28] which is in fact how Johnsen attached the figurehead piece and high stern. Pegging the frames to the keelson gave our craft considerable rigidity. Using only lashings would have made a more curved and flexible structure, which the carvings suggest did sometimes happen in the Bronze Age.

Next the chine members and gunwales were added, followed by an inner stringer each side, and three stringers each side of the keelson were attached to the underside of the frames. The most problematical part was the bottom, since the carvings give virtually no information about this. Marstrander's design specified a flat one without rocker or deadrise (longitudinal or transverse curve of bottom).

The hull cover was made of eight cow-skins. Since these were bought from an Oslo tannery, they had their hair still on, and this obscured the effect of the ribs showing through scraped skin. They were joined by glue and a double seam through an overlap, and warmed axle-grease was worked into them to improve their water-resistance. None of these points was considered to affect the craft's basic performance in any way, but we did not feel it to be worth while to test one of the crucial factors in skin boats – how long the skin hull

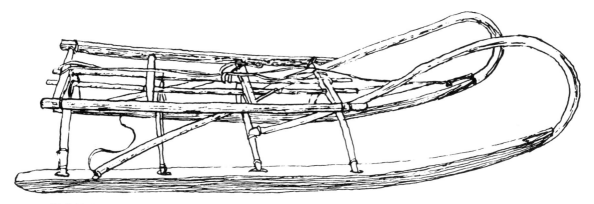

9.11  *Chukchi sledge with looped ends (after Marstrander, 1963)*

would remain waterproof – though the butter and pitch used in the construction of St Brendan's curragh seems to have been adequate for considerable voyages.[29] The cover was taken up over the gunwale and down a little way inside, from where continuous lacing was led around the top stringer. This again is an Eskimo practice and gives the umiak the valuable quality of being able to absorb and withstand the shock of impact with large masses of floating ice.[30] We found it useful, too, when bumping alongside a quay. The most difficult point was how to fit the skin covering round the bow and stern extensions. In the end Johnsen put it outside the keelson, with a hole at each end for the extensions, and then ran the keel completely along the outside. He also pegged the keel to the keelson through the skin covering; a doubtful move, as it did cause a small leak. Finally the high inner bow with its figurehead and the stern were added, the outer bow scarfed onto the keel, and thwarts inserted into three of the frames.

The overall length was 6.98 metres, greatest width at gunwale height 1.32 metres, and average height of side members of frames, 0.53 metres. The construction took Johnsen, virtually single-handed, 200 man-hours in an overall time of one month. Allowing for the time-saving of the power drill for making the peg holes (which are perhaps questionable anyway), and steel tools, a crude estimate of the time needed in the prehistoric period to build such a craft would be 250 man-hours, say five men for a week, excluding the preparation and sewing of the hull covering. This compares interestingly with Arima's account of a umiak built in 1960 at Ivugivik, Hudson Strait, for the National Museum of Canada.[31] This slightly larger craft took Henry Aunalik, the master umiak-builder, and his two helpers just under three weeks to complete. The umiak's covering required the skins of seven bearded seals, which had been buried for a month in a sandy beach, and the sewing services of fifteen women.

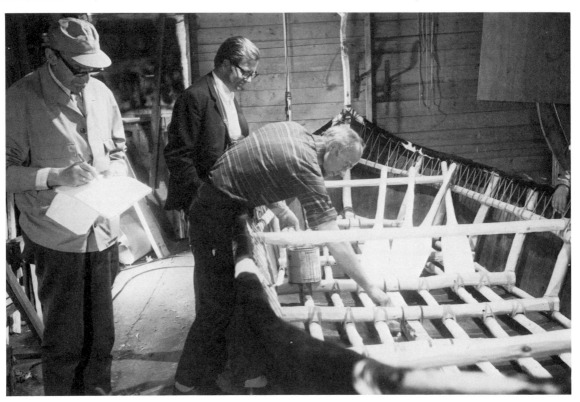

9.12   *The 'Kalnes' experimental skin boat nearing completion (author)*

9.13    *The 'Kalnes' boat afloat*
*(author)*

9.14    *The 'Kalnes' boat under way*
*(author)*

When our craft was launched, it proved to be handy, sturdy, stable and seaworthy, and certainly looked not unlike the carving at Kalnes near Høgnipen from which it was derived. The only drawback, apart from the need to place feet and loads carefully, proved to be a slight tendency to swing to starboard, possibly because of some small asymmetry, and the absolutely flat bottom.

Testing was done under two headings: those in which we could measure the results, and those in which we observed and recorded as best we could. The first measured test concerned its carrying capacity. Twelve 50-kilo sacks of sand and a crew of six reduced the freeboard from 50 centimetres to

9.15    *Rock carving from Kalnes, Norway (author)*

32.5. This was certainly adequate for most conditions – in fact the crew reported that the craft paddled more easily with the added momentum. This is considerably in excess of the load used by Professor Hagen in calculating the number of boat-trips necessary to remove the 11,000 cubic metres of greenstone quarried on Hespriholmen.[32]

The speed test was done over a measured kilometre, paddled both ways to cancel out any effect of tide or current. The conditions were good and the crew were told not to race but aim at a speed they could maintain for a good period. The result was just under 3 knots.

Beaching, which was an unmeasured test, showed the functional nature of the double bow very clearly. The crew paddled until the extended bow grounded on rock or sand. The momentum was checked, the bow lifted, the crew jumped out and carried the craft up the beach. The unladen weight was 180 kilos, easy for six men and possible for four to carry. So simple and easy was this operation that the test crew soon became very casual about it.

Another very interesting element turned out to be the lifting action of the extended bow when under way. Any bow heaviness was more than compensated for by the lifting effect when moving through the water. As a wave approached, it began to lift the bow-piece before its crest reached the hull, thereby helping to keep the boat dry and riding well. This is an effect that does not happen with a curragh or umiak; in fact it must be virtually peculiar to these Bronze Age craft, so it was all the more interesting to see it happening.

Throughout the trials the weather remained obstinately fine, so the most testing occasions, as far as seaworthiness was concerned, was when the craft was towed at speed (8 knots), or went through the wash of large tankers or fast ferries. Though this was not as satisfactory a test as we would have wished, it was clear that the craft was stable, very dry, and rose easily to the waves in a way highly reminiscent of a curragh. This would have been even more so if Johnsen had given the sides more flare in the manner of a umiak.

The most positive result was to show how adequate and normal such a craft was. Any

impression of the eccentric, exotic or cranky, which the rock carvings might possibly give, was entirely absent. The craft was quick and relatively simple to make (apart from the problem of putting the extension pieces through the hull covering), easy and light to land on an open beach or rock, and seaworthy. A comparable planked craft would have been far harder and more time-consuming to make with Bronze Age tools, heavier and more difficult to beach, and probably less seaworthy.

Of course this does not prove that the rock carvings do represent skin boats. But it does show the weakness of any alternative interpretation which argues against the skin boat because of its lack of seaworthiness, as Eskeröd has done.[33] Quite apart from these experiments, there is far too much evidence to the contrary throughout this book for there to be any need to re-argue this here, except that it is possible to suggest how this particular myth gained currency. Eskeröd, for instance, cites Nansen,[34] who certainly cannot be disregarded until one looks closely at the most likely quotation on the subject:

This boat [the umiak] is up to ten or twelve metres long, and is completely open. It has a wooden ribbing, which they make of driftwood, and is covered with sealskin. It is very narrow in proportion, and flat-bottomed. It is easy to row, but the form makes it an uncomfortable and bad sea-boat, and so the Greenlanders make for shore with it as soon as there is much wind. It has quite commonly a little sail to set up in the bow. Sailing, however, is not a thing the Eskimos have mastered, or been very keen on, in the past at any rate . . . In the women's boat the Greenlanders kept moving all summer through . . . In those days they could sometimes undertake long voyages, both on the west and east coast. For instance, on the east coast families might travel from the Angmagssalik area, $65\frac{1}{2}°$ N, all the way to the trading posts west of Cape Farewell and back again – which meant a distance of 500 miles each way.

So there are obviously bad sea-boats and bad sea-boats! One that could make a thousand-mile journey with a crew of women off the coast of Greenland would not perhaps come within most people's definition of this attribute. It well may be that Nansen was commenting on a characteristic of skin boats which is well established: the impossibility of driving them against the wind. This, combined with their less good qualities under sail, may have led him to compare them unfavourably with European craft, but immediately afterwards he was giving an unconscious tribute to their suitability to local conditions.

## Dug-outs

An important point to be emphasised is that if the rock carvings do represent skin boats, this does not mean that there were no dug-outs in use at the same time. Once the forests spread north, and reasonably settled conditions arose, it would be ridiculous to suggest that this was so in face of the evidence of the numerous finds.[35] What is in question is how they were used. Hallström, in his study of the rock carvings of Nämforsen in Sweden, believes that these do not represent skin boats since, among other things, skin boats could not support the weight of the elk heads at the bow.[36] He believes this is so of the River Vyg Russian carvings also, which he thinks are related to the Nämforsen ones, since the arrangement of

the crews, the shape of the men, and the elk heads are similar,[37] and he favours the raft as the most likely interpretation. Furthermore, he thinks the Gåshopen craft were a form of raft.[38] One might here quote Hornell's comment.[39]

Rafts may be and are widely used in tropic seas, for semi-naked men can there endure continuous soaking for days together as waves wash through their low-lying craft. In the bleak northern seas, the exposure entailed by raft voyaging, sometimes consequent upon the foundering of a ship at sea, is usually fatal within a comparatively short time to all but the most hardy, except during the short period of warm weather in the height of the summer. Hence raft voyaging has never been practised in the North and we cannot look to the raft as the prototype of the clinker-built boat.

Hornell was surely right about this. On the other hand, there are at Nämforsen certain carvings of a type of craft which has a long straight single-lined body and a pronounced animal's head at the bow. These contrast completely with any of the carvings like the Evenhus ones or those of Marstrander's Solberg, Hafslund or Navestad groups where the hull is shown as deep and full, and are a very different shape from Marstrander's 'simple style' examples, whose hull also consists

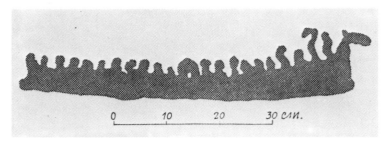

9.16 *Rock carving of a boat with an animal head at the bow, from Vyg, northern Russia (Hallström, 1960)*

9.17 *Rock carving from Nämforsen, Sweden, of a ship with an animal head bow (Hallström, 1960)*

9.18   *The Roos Carr model boat and crew – probably Bronze Age (Hull Museum)*

only of a single line. These straight-lined craft with their animal heads inevitably recall certain surviving examples of animal-headed dug-outs from the British Isles, namely the model found at Roos Carr in Yorkshire (Figure 9.18), and the dug-out from Loch Arthur or Lotus, south-west of Dumfries in Scotland (Figure 9.19). Scandinavian connections of the Roos Carr model are discussed in chapter 11. Nämforsen is by sheltered waters of the Baltic, where perhaps an animal-headed dug-out was in use and inspired some of the rock art. This would not be surprising, since it is only the theorists' generalisations, not actual practice, that make categories neatly exclusive.

9.19   *The bow end of the dug-out from Loch Arthur (or Lotus), Dumfries and Galloway, Scotland (National Museum of Antiquities of Scotland, Edinburgh)*

9.20    *A model of the Hjortspring boat from Als, Denmark (National Museum, Copenhagen)*

## Planked craft

The next stage of development in Scandinavia is the appearance of, first, lashed-plank craft such as the Hjortspring boat, and then, later in the Iron Age, clinker-built rowing vessels like the Nydam boat, a precursor of the Viking ship. The Hjortspring boat, which has been dated to about 300 BC, was found in a bog on the island of Als together with paddles, weapons and various other objects, where presumably it had been thrown as an offering after a victory. It was about 18 metres long, and its basic structure consisted of five broad strakes of lime wood sewn together with wide stitches caulked with resin and attached by lashings through cleats to frames of hazel twigs.[40] It has been reconstructed in the National Museum in Copenhagen, with the double projecting bow and stern of the skin boat; certainly it shares with these craft, and many subsequent craft of the Viking period, an outstanding lightness and flexibility.

On the other hand, this craft embodies a major change of structural technique from skin boats. These latter have their skeleton built first – the '*nomeis*' Herodotus noted in his account of coracle-building[41] – which is then covered with the treated skin. The Hjortspring boat, however, is of shell construction with the frames inserted afterwards. So significant does this seem to Arne Emil Christensen, for instance,[42] that he rejects the possibility of the Scandinavian rock carvings representing skin boats, and believes Scandinavian craft through the ages were the product of a continuous wood-working tradition.

Ole Crumlin-Pedersen holds a less extreme position. He agrees with Marstrander that the Hjortspring boat is a wooden-planked version of a skin boat, made possible probably by the appearance of iron tools, which made it much easier to produce thin flexible planks.[43] But he disagrees with Marstrander about the evolutionary process that led to craft such as the Nydam boat.

This clinker-built craft (Figure 9.21), dated to AD 350–400, was found in the Nydam bog in south Jutland in 1863. It has iron fastenings and a keel, though the latter has not yet achieved either the strength or depth of the later Norse examples.[44] The lashed frames also hark back to the Hjortspring boat as do the single unscarfed oak strakes,

9.21    *The Nydam boat excavated in 1863 (Schleswig-Holsteinisches Landesmuseum)*

27 metres long and 50 cm broad.[45] It is now in the Schloss Gottorp Museum in Schleswig. Despite the lack of a mast, this long rowing vessel, with maximum beam of *c.* 3 metres, its fifteen oars a side and large steering oar anticipates in many ways the classic northern ship of the Viking age, which, in its various forms, long-ship, knarr, coastal craft and fishing boat, was to range from Constantinople to Newfoundland and from North Cape to Sicily.

Crumlin-Pedersen's hypothesis, which is well demonstrated in the splendid Viking Ship Museum at Roskilde, is that this crucial change was inspired by and derived from the expanded soft-wood dug-out.[46] This is made by using almost all the circumference of a tree trunk, which is hollowed out through a narrow strip until the walls are sufficiently thin. Then, with each end encircled by a band of withies to prevent cracking, the shell is heated by fire (Figure 5.5) until it can be forced open and the sides held out by cross-bars (Figure 5.6). This same process also lifts the ends, thereby giving the typical northern ship profile and shape. One-piece ribs are then inserted and held in place by trenails near the top. Finally a washstrake is added at each side (Figure 5.7). The resultant 'esping' or 'aspen' is a remarkably light and handy craft, virtually another wooden version of a skin boat. In fact the Finns still propel a contemporary version with a kayak-type double paddle.

Crumlin-Pedersen, as well as describing a contemporary expanded and extended logboat from Satakunta in Finland, describes a number of historic examples. The oldest are from fourth century AD boat graves at Slusegärd on the island of Bornholm excavated between 1958 and 1966 by Ole Klindt-Jensen.[47] Crumlin-Pedersen also cites two craft dredged from the bottom of the sea south-east of Bornholm near Gotland by Polish trawlers, which are now in the Museum Morskie at Danzig.[48] Then there is the Vaaler-Moor craft, excavated in 1870 and now reconstructed and on display with the Nydam boat in the museum at Gottorp Castle.[49] This undated craft is some 12 metres long with twelve inserted single-piece ribs and ten thwarts.

9.22   *The four-oared* faering *or ship's boat from the Gokstad Viking age ship (author)*

Another significant point about the 'aspen' is its continued use as a ship's boat in the Baltic. Both the ninth-century Gokstad ship from the Viking burial mound on the west side of Oslo Fjord and the seventeenth-century *Wasa* (now in the museum at Stockholm) had 'aspens' as tenders, so indeed a very considerable period is involved.[50]

This interesting thesis has led Marstrander to comment in turn, very sensibly, that perhaps one should not look for a unilinear development.[51] One should expect inheritances from both skin boats and dug-outs to appear in later, more evolved, craft and the Hjortspring boat could be an example of this, with the double bow coming from the skin boat and the inserted frames from the expanded dug-out. He also puts forward the rather intriguing suggestion that the idea of overlapping the edges of strakes to produce the characteristic clinker design of Viking craft might have been inspired by the overlapping joining of skins in the hull of a skin boat (Figure 9.23). This practice of joining skins by a blind seam so that the needle and stitch never goes right through the skin is still used by the Eskimo.

Perhaps the best thing about this latest theory

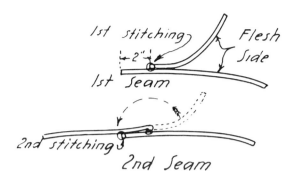

9.23 *Eskimo method of joining together two skins in a blind seam (Adney and Chapelle,* The Bark Canoes and Skin Boats of North America, *1964)*

of Marstrander's is that it would suggest a great variety of intermingling types, and this variety is in fact reflected in the development of early medieval craft in northern Europe.

## Sail

Though we know the sail was used by the Veneti and the Irish before the Roman period, it is not until the Åskekarr boat from Sweden of the early Viking period (*c.* AD 800) that there is definite evidence of the sail in Scandinavia. It has been argued that the steering oar of the Kvalsund craft, of a century or so earlier, was designed for sailing as well as rowing, but there is not much other evidence to support this argument.[52] So it is probable that it was not until the eighth century AD that true keels, securely attached steering oars and strong mast-partners mark the coming of the sail to the north, and the Vikings acquired the technical capacity to make the raids which so terrified the inhabitants of coastal Europe.

Tacitus reported that the Scandinavians had no sails on their boats in his time, and Professor Falk has pointed out that the fact the Old Norse word for 'mast' (*vida*) is quite different from the west German word 'mast' is a strong argument against the antiquity of the mast in the north, and he goes on to suggest that the practice of sailing and the word 'sail' itself (Old Norse *sigla*) must have come

to the northern peoples from the Frisians, who would have learnt this skill from the Romans or the Gauls.[53]

There are two possible reasons why such an apparently seamanlike and skilled race as the early Scandinavians should not have used the sail. One is simply the nature of the Baltic. The fact that galleys were still an important element there until virtually the coming of steam[54] at least suggests that it was something more practical than sheer conservatism which valued the rowed craft. The Hjortspring boat, the Ladby ship from Denmark and the Finnish archipelago fleet of Henry Chapman were all very much in the same tradition.[55]

Another reason, which has not to my knowledge been argued before, is the wind-borne nature of skin boats; this might also apply to expanded dug-outs that have no keel and are of light structure. This is a severe disadvantage when trying to row against a strong wind, and it is virtually impossible to do so because of the lack of momentum. On the other hand, with a following wind a skin boat rides so much on the surface and is so light that it is virtually blown along. Quite remarkable speeds over a distance are obtained in curraghs for this reason. This then may be why there was no great necessity to develop the sail in these early skin craft and possibly in expanded dug-outs, and why the aboriginal use of the sail by the Eskimo in umiaks is scarcely ever reported, and then not always in circumstances where European influence can be completely ruled out.[56]

It has sometimes been suggested that some of the decorative elements in the Bronze Age carvings and razor engravings (Figure 9.24) of Scandinavia may represent a branch of a tree that was held up in the bow to perform the function of a sail, and it is interesting that Chapelle suggests that an old Nova Scotia expression, 'carrying too much bush' – meaning over-canvassing a boat – may refer to a Micmac Indian practice, noted by early settlers, of putting a leafy bush in the bow of their canoes.[57] If this practice existed, it would fit in with the lack of any driving need to develop the sail, as a branch or the windage of the craft itself would already sufficiently ease the labour of rowing.

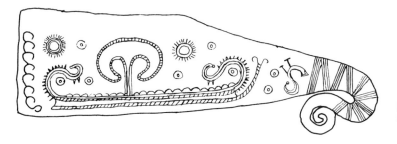

9.24   *Bronze Age engraving which may represent a boat with a tree branch (after Marstrander, 1963)*

## Medieval developments in northern Europe

The skin boat in its many forms, the expanded dug-out and the ordinary dug-out at least hint at the rich complexity which probably existed in prehistoric Scandinavia and which it is so difficult to try and categorise because the surviving evidence is so inadequate. This same complexity is also evident in the subsequent development of early medieval craft in northern Europe. The cog is one of the most important of these. In the course of deepening the River Weser at Bremen in 1962, almost the complete hull of a cog was found, and its subsequent excavation and restoration (Figure 9.25) have complemented the information given

about this type of craft by the many seals that show it (Figure 9.26).[58] The Bremen cog, which dates from the fourteenth century, had a straight stem, flat carvel bottom, clinker-built sides and a castle aft. It was 25 metres long and 8 metres in width and height, reflecting both the cargo capacity and height of freeboard – which were its great advantages over the northern type – and the depth of water it drew and its slow speed – which were its drawbacks. Perhaps the most surprising element was the presence of a keel, suggesting Scandinavian influence. It has been suggested that the cog was essentially a German development of the thirteenth century onwards, but Crumlin-Pedersen has assembled a good deal of evidence to

9.25   *The fourteenth-century Bremen cog found in the River Weser in 1962 (Focke-Museum, Bremen)*

9.26 *A late thirteenth century seal of Harderwijk, Netherlands, showing a cog (Roger-Viollet)*

9.27 *A seal of New Shoreham, Sussex, dated to 1295. The ship depicted is probably a hulk (National Maritime Museum)*

contradict this. As well as the influence suggested above, there is the existence of the 'Kugghaan' or cog harbour at the trading centre of Birka in Sweden, which vanished about AD 1000.[59] This suggests that cogs could well have been trading to the Baltic by way of the Limfjorden, thus avoiding the dangerous route round the Skaw, from the Zuider Zee and the Frisian waters where conditions suited their flat bottoms. The twelfth-century wreck Q75 excavated in the early 1960s by van der Heide in the Zuider Zee would support this thesis, since its flat bottom and clinker-built sides suggest it is a cog.[60] Even earlier, in the tenth century there is the reference to 'cog-sculd' in a statement of dues from Utrecht.[61]

While the cog was essentially flat bottomed, another quite different round-bottomed craft with which the cog was eventually to merge was the hulk. By a lucky chance we have some idea of what this craft looked like, since the ship modelled on the seal of New Shoreham (Sussex) in AD 1295 (Figure 9.27) can be positively identified as a 'hulk'. According to Crumlin-Pedersen, this town was formerly known as 'Hulkesmouth' and round the seal are these words: 'Hoc hulci signo vocor o's

sic nomine digno', which he translates as: 'By this picture of a hulk, I am called Mouth, which is a worthy name.'[62] The characteristics of this type of craft seem to be a strongly curved shape, strakes converging at each end and often lashed round there, and no keel or stem. Besides the New Shoreham seal, coins struck near the mouth of the Rhine at Dorestadt (Figure 9.28) and Quentovik in about the eighth century AD show this craft. But the best-known example is the boat (Figure 9.29) which was found in 1930, 2.3 metres below the present sea-level by a gang of navvies digging a new canal near Utrecht.[63] The wear on the bottom and the absence of any gear or loose parts

9.28 *Eighth-century coin from Dorestadt, near the mouth of the Rhine (Koninklijk Penningkabinet, The Hague)*

9.29 *The Utrecht ship (Centraal Museum, Utrecht)*

suggested that it had been abandoned after a long hard-working life. Estimates of its date varied from the second to the fourteenth century AD, until the matter was settled in 1959 by a radiocarbon date of AD 790±45.[64] It is now in the Utrecht Museum.

The craft was built of oak, moss caulked and fastened with willow trenails, though a few iron nails had also been used. It was 17.8 metres long and 4 metres wide amidships. The main structural features were a heavy bottom plank, three strakes a side, of which the middle one was half an oak trunk used as a sort of rounded wale, two gunwale pieces, and thirty-eight heavy frames sometimes only extending across the bottom, sometimes reaching half-way up the bilge strake. There were no stem or stern pieces, only extensions of the bottom plank. In the eleventh floor-timber there was a small rectangular socket for a mast. If one accepts this was for a towing rather than sailing mast, then Dr J. P. W. Philipsen's argument that this craft was too strongly built just to be a canal barge might suggest that the hulk was evolving from a river to a sea-going craft on the lower reaches of the Rhine about the end of the eighth century.[65]

Last there are the craft of the Slavs, or the Wends – as the Norsemen called these occupants of the southern and eastern shores of the Baltic. Crumlin-Pedersen has shown that their war-ships

were like those of the Scandinavians with a few local variants, but in their river and off-shore transports they produced a truly indigenous type, the 'pram', or '*prammu*' in Old Slav. An example of one of these craft with its flat bottom, transverse floors and square stern is the craft dating from about AD 1300 found in 1934 at Falsterbo in Sweden.[66]

All in all, that gives at least four major categories of craft in the north in the Viking period: the classic northern type, inside which there existed a minimum of the five varieties found at Roskilde; the cog; the hulk; and the pram. We have seen cogs influencing northern ships, and northern ships influencing cogs. The *barco rabelo* of Portugal may even be an example of northern clinker-building moving south, just as the cog, with its possible southern origin, moved north into the Baltic.[67] And the interesting thing is that, as the earliest known craft are all well-evolved examples, these four types could have been in existence some centuries before these known craft were built. Add the expanded dug-out, the ordinary dug-out and possible lingering skin-boat traditions in the more northerly parts, and one begins to get some idea of the multiplicity and variety of craft in the north in the late Iron Age period.

# 10 The British Isles: skin boats

Though the Atlantic side of the British Isles presents almost as sea-dominated an environment as western Scandinavia, we have unfortunately no comparable series of rock carvings to tell us in what sort of craft the lively maritime activity of the prehistoric period was carried on. This activity must have received a further stimulus with the appearance in the fourth millennium BC of crop- and cattle-raising agriculturists.

This emergence of agriculture in the British Isles was a maritime event for two reasons. There was the need to transport animals across water, which had not occurred among hunter-fishers, and the subsequent growth of larger communities gave a stimulus to trade.

## Stone axe trade

Fortunately for us, one of the main objects involved in this trade, the stone axe or adze blade, is both durable and susceptible to analysis capable of establishing its origins. Petrological analysis of thin sections of stone and, more recently, trace element analysis by atomic absorption spectroscopy similar to that used with obsidian,[1] have made it possible to follow the augite/granophyre of Graig Llwyd (Gwynedd), the porcellanite of Tievebulliagh and Rathlin Island (Co. Antrim), the greenstone of Great Langdale (Cumbria) and the chalcedony of Cissbury (Sussex) in their travels from the so-called axe factories. After the blades had been fashioned and polished, they were traded around the British Isles to the farmers clearing forests for their crops and building sheds for their stock. As with the more recent study of obsidian sources in the Mediterranean, this is an invaluable measure of maritime activity. To quote Grahame Clark's study of this trade, 'water presented no barrier, but on the contrary a ready medium for transport and it may well be significant that all known factories are near the coast.'[2] This evidence that soon after the middle of the fourth millennium BC axes from Ulster reached the Mersey, Scotland and the Hebrides, that Great Langdale axes reached Arran and the Isle of Man, and Graig Llwyd products travelled as far as the Channel Isles, makes it all the more extraordinary that as recently as forty years ago it was seriously argued that the first cattle to reach Britain must have been driven there dry-shod before the Channel was breached because no craft existed that would have brought them there across water.[3]

What is more, radiocarbon dates, even uncalibrated ones, show that this axe and adze trade was flourishing very early, possibly even in the Mesolithic period, as has been mentioned in chapter 4. The farmers of Hembury Hill (Devon), for instance, which has a date of c. 3330 BC (BM-136), were already using axes from Cornwall, while the Great Langdale chipping floor has a date of c. 2730 BC (BM-281).[4] Whoever carried on this trade, a point which will be discussed later, evidently did so very soon after crops and cattle raising became widespread in Britain, if not before.

Then there is the question of the distribution of

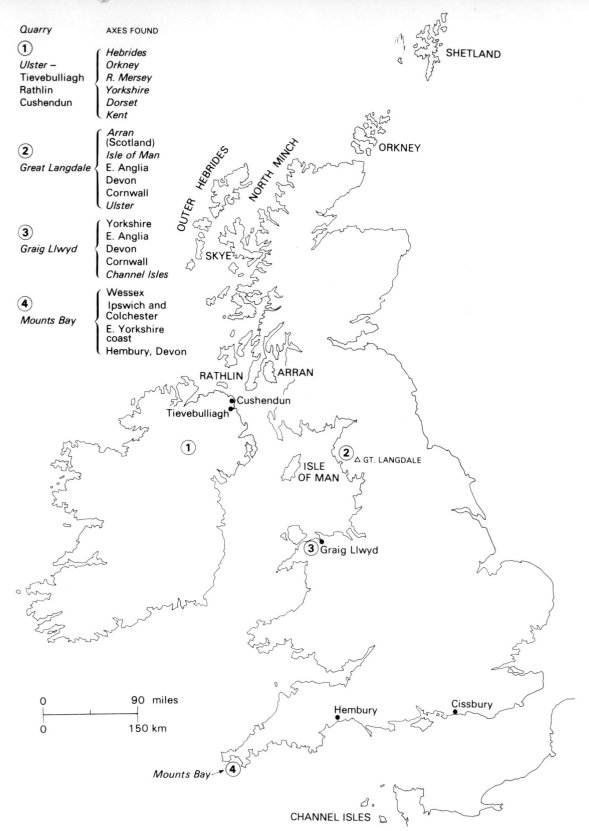

**Quarry**     AXES FOUND

**①**
Ulster –
Tievebulliagh
Rathlin
Cushendun

{ *Hebrides*
*Orkney*
*R. Mersey*
*Yorkshire*
*Dorset*
*Kent* }

**②**
*Great Langdale*

{ *Arran*
*(Scotland)*
*Isle of Man*
E. Anglia
Devon
Cornwall
*Ulster* }

**③**
*Graig Llwyd*

{ Yorkshire
E. Anglia
Devon
Cornwall
*Channel Isles* }

**④**
*Mounts Bay*

{ Wessex
Ipswich and
Colchester
E. Yorkshire
coast
Hembury, Devon }

SHETLAND

OUTER HEBRIDES

NORTH MINCH

ORKNEY

SKYE

RATHLIN    ARRAN

●Cushendun

Tievebulliagh●

**①**

ISLE
OF MAN

**②** △ GT. LANGDALE

**③**●Graig Llwyd

0     90 miles

0     150 km

Hembury●     Cissbury●

Mounts Bay → **④**

CHANNEL ISLES

Map 10.1    *Sites of origin and of use of stone axe and adze blades in Britain and Ireland*

megaliths in the British Isles. As has been argued in chapter 8, these are now much less an indicator of maritime contact than they were once thought to be. However, it cannot be denied that in the British Isles, their distribution – for whatever its reason (soil, climate, tribal divisions, geological appropriateness) – has also a maritime character (Map 8.1). This is hardly surprising since without debating any question of to what extent there were separate and independent developments of megaliths in different areas, easy travel in the megalithic period was broadly confined to the uplands like those that carried the Ridgeway and Icknield Way, or to the sea. This is well borne out by, for instance, Clough and Green's finding that stone axes from Cornwall found in East Anglia are concentrated either near the Icknield Way or along the coast and the lower reaches of rivers.[5] Coastal trade from Cornwall as an alternative to the overland route is also suggested by Keen and Radley's study of Yorkshire axes.[6] So if axes could be traded round the coast from Cornwall to the Ipswich and Colchester area and even to the East Yorkshire coast, it is hard to imagine that there would have been no seaborne contact between the megalithic areas each side of the Irish Sea and up the west coast to Orkney. Whether in the process the boatmen concerned shared any common religious attitude to the great stone tombs is perhaps as irrelevant as whether today all Hull trawler crews are Church of England.

The next problem is whether, from the usual sparse evidence, we can obtain any idea of the craft that carried on this seaborne trade. It has already been argued in chapter 4 that the Mesolithic people of the Western Isles and Ireland most likely used skin boats, since the separation of Ireland from Britain left a considerable sea-crossing from an early date, which accounts among other things for the absence of the common hare in that island and the poorer and more sub-Arctic flora there.[7]

## Classical times

We then apparently have a gap until we come to the skin boats described by Rufus Festus Avienus as being used by the proud seamen of the Oestrymnides, the first progenitors perhaps of the shopkeeping reputation of our island.

Laxe jacentes, et metallo divites
Stanni atque plumbi, multa vis his gentis est,
Superbus animus, efficax solertia,
Negociandi cura iugis omnibus:
Notisque cumbis turbidum late fretum,
Et beluosi gurgitem Oceani secant.
Non hi carinas quippe pinu texere,
Facere norunt, non abiete, ut usus est
Curuant faselos; sed rei ad miraculum.
Navigia junctis semper aptant pellibus
Vorioque vastom saepe percurrunt salum.

[Lying far off and rich in metals
Of tin and lead. Great the strength of this nation,
Proud their mind, powerful their skill,
Trading the constant care of all.

They know not to fit with pine
Their keels, nor with fir, as use is,
They shape their boats; but strange to say,
They fit their vessels with united skins,
And often traverse the deep in a hide.]

This important passage from the *Ora Maritima*, whose preservation we owe to the publication of a solitary manuscript of it by V. Pisanus in Venice in 1488, is generally held to embody parts of the Massiliote Greek *Periplus* or coastal pilot. While various authors have suggested dates round about the sixth century BC for this, Berthelot (the editor) went much further and decided that Avienus's use of the name Oestrymnis for the cape in Brittany (probably Penmarche, the southern tip) which Eratosthenes called Kabaion and Ptolemy Gabaion) implied a tradition going back beyond the Greeks and Phoenicians to the period before these reached Tartessus at the mouth of the Gualalquivir and Gades.[8] This would imply that the Britons who disdained to make their hulls of pine and fir, but used sewn-together skins and braved the vast ocean on a hide, had caught the attention of the Mediterranean world before 1000 BC, although this was more probably because of their rich supply of tin and lead rather than their eccentricity in naval architecture.

## The Caergwrle bowl

Skin boats were certainly flourishing in the Roman period and in the Dark Age, and one can hardly visualise them evolving out of planked craft or dug-outs. Skin boats are by and large the product of hunter-fisher groups, and their evolution, like reed-bundle, bark and dug-out craft, and probably rafts as well, has, as far as we know, been into planked craft, rather than the reverse. Unfortunately the earliest piece of evidence which might tell us something about these earlier skin boats is in itself full of queries. This is the Caergwrle bowl (Figures 10.1, 10.2), a small oval vessel which was found near Hope in Clwyd more than a century ago and is now in the National Museum, Cardiff. It is generally agreed to be a model of a boat because of its shape, the ornament, and the gold sheet decoration round its rim. The chief motif on this gold sheet is a series of concentric circles, and these have been responsible for much argument as to whether they represent shields, or sun discs, or some such symbol. Since this is virtually the only informative impression of a craft we have from the British Bronze Age, to which period most people assign the bowl, it is essential to try and get as much information as possible from it.

There is the general point that shields are far more likely to have been fastened to a planked boat than a skin boat and the most obvious parallel for carrying shields along the gunwale comes from the Viking long-ships, although it is generally agreed that this was done only in harbour,[9] the scene on the Bayeux Tapestry showing shields on

10.1 *A view under the 'bows' of the Caergwrle bowl (National Museum of Wales, Cardiff)*

ships under way being considered to be an artistic convention derived from the appearance of a loaded invasion ship at anchor.

There is, however, the difficulty that Viking practice seems to have left about half of the shield above the line of the gunwale. The Caergwrle

10.2 *The Bronze Age bowl from Caergwrle, Clwyd (National Museum of Wales, Cardiff)*

artist must then be accepted as not reproducing this effect accurately, or the shields must have been carried differently from the Scandinavian fashion, with their full diameter below the gunwale. The average diameter of known Bronze Age shields from the British Isles (and certainly those from Brumby, near Scunthorpe, and the River Trent (Figure 10.3) are very similar to the Caergwrle discs) is 60 cm,[10] which would surely bring the shields very near immersion in any sort of a sea. This seems a disadvantage from both the warriors' point of view and probably the sea-keeping capability of the craft as well. Furthermore it would require either some sort of extruding rack or a regular series of holes in the hull to secure the shields by lashings through the hand-grips. Either of these alternatives seems impractical and highly unlikely.

If the shield theory is not practical, then one has to take seriously the alternative possibility that the discs are some sort of symbol, possibly solar, and that the Caergwrle bowl craft may not represent a planked boat but a hide one or a coracle. Though this is disputed by one distinguished prehistorian, Professor C. C. F. Hawkes, who sees a likeness between the Caergwrle craft and the similarly-

shaped Phoenician craft of King Luli of Tyre and Sidon,[11] other writers, notably H. N. Savory and J. X. W. P. Corcoran, have preferred not to make the long leap to the eighth century BC eastern Mediterranean, but to support the skin-boat interpretation.[12]

The interpretation of the motifs on the gold sheet as symbolic discs of some sort reinforces the idea that what we are considering is a skin boat. There are at least three examples from Scandinavia which seem to support this theory. One is in the group of carvings, already discussed, from Evenhus where among the umiak-type skin boats carved on the main rock-face is one which has a disc of concentric circles very similar indeed to the Caergwrle ones, allowing for the cruder carving dictated by the rock surface, in an identical position below the gunwale (Figure 10.4).

Among the later group of carvings of ships on the island of Amoy near Stavanger there is one showing four discs along its hull (Figure 10.5). While these are not as similar to the Caergwrle ones as the Evenhus example, nor in as similar a position, they do follow the Caergwrle bowl in being in a row along the side of the craft.

The third, and perhaps best known, example

10.4 *Rock carving from Evenhus, Norway, showing a skin boat with a disc of concentric circles (author)*

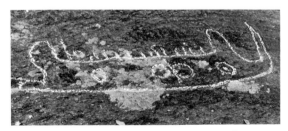

10.5 *Rock carving from the island of Amoy near Stavanger, Norway, showing a boat with discs (author)*

10.3 *Bronze Age shield from the River Trent (City Museum, Sheffield)*

comes from the group of small gold boat models found at Nors, near Thy in north-western Denmark, and now in the National Museum at Copenhagen. These small and battered votive boats (Figure 10.6) have patterns of concentric circles along their hulls, and their fineness of entry and the pointed V-shape of their sections suggest a skin boat more strongly than a dug-out. The ribs, the framework on which the gold sheet is placed and the parallel with the Evenhus carvings also argue in favour of a skin-boat interpretation.

To sum up, we have four examples of craft which seem to be decorated with circular symbols. The Evenhus one has always been accepted as a skin boat. Since Marstrander's analysis and experiment, there is a strong case for thinking the Amoy carving is one too. The Nors gold boats also appear more likely to be skin than wood. The

Caergwrle craft would fit neatly into this group especially as it is unlikely, structurally and nautically, that shields would be carried on the hull, and in the only other example we have, the Roos Carr boat (Figure 9.18), the shields are shown on the crew's arms. Symbols, on the other hand, could be put on skin boats without any structural problem. While it might still be argued that the Caergwrle bowl could be a wooden craft, with solar symbols on it, there is further evidence which reinforces the skin-boat interpretation. The most likely explanation for the lines across the bottom of the bowl is that they represent ribs.[13] This again, as in the case of the Nors boats, suggests a hide hull. There would be little point in showing the ribs of a wooden boat because they are covered by strakes. If an artist records any detail of a contemporary boat, it is nearly always the strakes

10.6 *Gold boat models with concentric circle decorations, from Nors, near Thy, Denmark (National Museum, Copenhagen)*

if they are present[14] (see for example Figure 10.7). On the other hand, ribs are a prominent feature in skin boats because not only are they made conspicuous by the skin covering shrinking and clinging to them, but in certain circumstances the skin can become transparent as well (Figure 9.9). If the lines across the base of the Caergwrle bowl are the only constructional details of the craft the artist chose to record, it is surely likely that they would be of something very noticeable, and the ribs of a skin boat certainly seem much the most likely answer.

The Caergwrle bowl also has oculi on the bows. Possibly because this particular concept, in so far as it existed in Scandinavia and the circum-Polar zone, seems to have been embodied in the animals' heads which often surmounted the prows, oculi on the hull are scarcely known in this area. On the other hand they are a conspicuous part of the Mediterranean tradition. T. C. Lethbridge's ob-servation[15] of the link between curraghs and *saveiros* in the way their oars are attached to the hull has already been discussed in chapter 8. This may well be evidence of a Bronze Age contact between Iberia and the British Isles. The *meia luas* of the Costa de Caparica, south of the Tagus estuary, a smaller version of their northern *saveiro* counterparts, are still today conspicuous for their oculi (Figure 10.8). Perhaps the oculi on the Caergwrle bowl represent another Iberian in-fluence which never got as far as Scandinavia, but which arrived in Britain because of the tin trade. If these arguments are accepted, we have then at least a Bronze Age element in the line of British skin boats which the various Roman writers commented on later.

## The Broighter boat

The next example is the delightful Broighter

10.7   *Noah boat-building scene from the west end of Lincoln Cathedral (Courtauld Institute)*

10.8   *Oculus emblem on the bows of a Portuguese* meia lua *(author)*

10.9 *The gold model boat which formed part of a first century BC hoard found at Broighter near Limavady, Co. Derry (National Museum of Ireland, Dublin)*

boat model from Co. Derry (Figure 10.9). This superbly delicate piece of goldwork was found together with a gold collar, two twisted torques, two chain necklaces and a hanging bowl by a ploughman in 1891. This hoard is generally dated to the first century BC. For a time the mast and oars were thought to be later additions, but analysis of the gold has shown that they are contemporary with the hull. This could well be a representation of a skin boat, although Farrell and Penny do not entirely rule out other craft.[16]

### The Bantry pillar

Then there is a gap of several centuries till the eighth century AD carving of a ship on the Bantry pillar in Co. Cork, south-west Ireland. This pillar is over 2 metres tall and 26 cm wide and stands on top of a rounded grassy hill overlooking Bantry Bay, where Wolfe Tone once landed and the British Atlantic fleet had a base. Both faces are carved in low relief but the details are not easy to see, and it was not until 1964 that a photograph,

taken with strong artificial sidelighting, was published (Figure 10.10), showing the craft being rowed heavenward up the pillar.[17]

The other side is clearer and better known, and on stylistic grounds Dr Françoise Henry ascribes the carving on it to the eighth century AD.[18] This date is crucial because the first Viking raid on Ireland took place in AD 795. Thereafter, such was the impact of the Scandinavian raiders in their long-ships that when in the ninth and tenth centuries the monastic sculptors carved such unwarlike scenes as Noah in his ark, they used Viking long-ships as models. A surviving example is the charming scene carved on the cross-shaft at Killary, Co. Meath. The dove is sitting on the masthead of a perfectly good Viking long-ship.

The Bantry boat in contrast is quite un-Viking in character. There is not a sign of the high prow and stern and, far from being double-ended, the proportion of bow to stern is something like $2\frac{1}{4}$ to 1. Furthermore the craft seems to be riding high on the water, as all curraghs do, and, most interesting of all, it has the sweetly-curved sheer and the long

10.11 *A modern curragh being walked to the sea in Co. Kerry (author)*

10.10 *The boat carving on the eighth century AD stone pillar near Bantry, Co. Kerry (author)*

heaving on one oar or two. If they are sculling, then their craft would be virtually similar to a Kerry curragh, whose 8-metre length normally accommodates four oarsmen. On the other hand if there were eight rowing, plus the steersman and a figure in the bow of which a hint seems to remain, then the size of the crew and the craft would match Columba's, while nine would match Bran's crew on his voyage to the Island of Joy and the Land of Women.

Finally, one rather charming detail confirms that the Bantry boat was indeed part of a long-

10.12 *A Kerry curragh or navog under way with four pairs of oars (author)*

lifting bow, so well seen in the modern Kerry version, which would enable it to rise to and ride over almost any sea. We are fortunate that whoever carved this boat did so with great skill and realism. This is no primitive work, or the stylised achievement of a landlubberly monk. The attitude of the helmsman leaning exhortingly forward, the angle of the steering oar, the position of the crew with stroke pulling a little harder than everyone else, the bend and heave of the oars, are all remarkably vivid and convincing.

Of course not all points about this craft are clear. There is no way of telling if the crew are

10.13 *Captain Phillips's late seventeenth century drawing of a curragh under sail (Pepys Library, Magdalene College, Cambridge)*

lived Irish curragh tradition. Captain Thomas Phillips made a drawing for Samuel Pepys in 1670 of the 'Portable Vessel of Wicker ordinarily used by the Wild Irish' (Figure 10.13). If one looks at it closely, there can be seen on the stern a small cross virtually identical with the one on the stern of the Bantry boat. There can be little doubt there of the continuity of boat-building tradition over nine centuries at least.

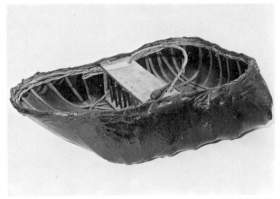

10.14 *Coracle from the River Teifi, now in the Welsh Folk Museum, St Fagan (National Museum of Wales, Cardiff)*

## From the Mesolithic to the medieval

The surprising and informative thing about this sequence is how consistent and coherent it is. The Caergwrle bowl and the Broighter boat are similar in hull form. The Broighter boat and the Phillips drawing, as has been noted by a number of authorities including Laird Clowes,[19] are closely related, while the Bantry boat's outline is virtually indistinguishable from that of a modern Kerry curragh. All have a noticeable straight run of gunwale with little sheer and a short curved stern. The only development, first noticeable in the Bantry boat, is the lengthening out of the rise of the bow to give the characteristic line of the modern large curragh.

It is also worth noting that if one accepts the Mané-Lud megalithic carvings of the Morbihan as possible early skin boats, their shape would also fit quite easily into this suggested sequence.

It looks, then, as though there are elements which can fill the gap in the British Isles skin-boat tradition between the Mesolithic and the Classical period, and carry it on to medieval times. This is helpful since one would suppose that for any type of craft to attract as much notice among Roman writers it would have had to exist in good numbers over a considerable period. Had this literary tradition been all there was to go on, one would have been left to speculate on the antiquity of the skin boat. As it is, it seems possible to suggest with some confidence that this continuing tradition could well have lasted perhaps five thousand years. Though the British Isles version had flatter lines and much less exaggerated extremities than the Scandinavian later types, it would still have been part of the great continent-wide northern hemisphere occurrence suggested by Marstrander.[20] Furthermore, it would explain and make feasible sea travel round the British Isles from a time before the development of agriculture up to the Roman period, and in the case of the west coast of Ireland until the present day.

## Neolithic migrants

What is not so clear is the relationship between the early cattle- and crop-using peoples of the British Isles and this skin-boat tradition. The starting-point for their first crossing to Britain is much argued, usually on the basis of matching pottery styles on both sides of the Channel. Professor Piggott suggests they may well have come in part from western and northern France, in part from the northern European plain.[21] Humphrey Case is more specific. He rejects the usual reliance on the evidence of pottery and large collective tombs as being inappropriate to the hazardous and hungry early stages of maintaining a farming cycle in a strange new land. Cutting and piercing tools, on the other hand, would be essential from the start, and parallel traits in arrowheads to those of the early British Neolithic lead him to the Chasséen culture of the Paris basin. Later pottery elements imply some influence from Late Danubian groups on the Channel coast, so his starting point would be a Chasséen group of ultimately southern French origin settled on the north-east French or Belgian coast and in contact through seasonal movements with a Late Danubian group.[22]

Both of these, of course, had come a long way

overland before they reached the Channel and the North Sea, the former across France from the western Mediterranean, the latter by great rivers and loess soils of central Europe. At the most they could have had a remembered tradition of the craft which had traded obsidian over the Mediterranean sea-ways, or of river dug-outs.[23] What happened when they first faced the much more difficult conditions of the North Sea?

Sites of an agricultural people in the southern Netherlands have been given uncalibrated radiocarbon dates of 4470–4060 BC,[24] as compared with the date for Hembury Hill, and other British Neolithic sites with fourth millennium BC dates. This suggests that it may have taken several centuries for some innovating group to respond to the new challenge of the open sea, and make their way across the Channel.

The query is: did they evolve an answer to the demands of sea-going themselves, or did they simply recruit the boats and boatmen they found there? The latter seems more probable, even though it is only inference which suggests this. Grahame Clark,[25] for instance, has pointed out that after the introduction of farming to southern Scandinavia, the trade in stone axes based on the island of Bømlo off the south-west coast of Norway was carried on by hunter-fishers, probably in 'very little boats, and very light', and carried overland as the Finns did in the time of Ohthere. So was that of objects made from Olonetz green slate, whose distribution ranges from the Arctic Circle to Estonia. The fluency of the axe and adze trade in third millennium BC Britain has already been mentioned, as has Ritchie's case for taking this back to the Mesolithic in some cases.[26] It seems logical then that where movement to or round islands was involved the traditional nautical expertise of hunter-fishers would be an obvious and relevant quality on which to depend. The subsequent stages of achieving a settlement over the sea have been made the subject of a most interesting study by Humphrey Case of the Ashmolean Museum, Oxford.[27] To start with, he limits the time when a prehistoric community would have moved to the months August to November, when the crop was harvested, grass good and adequate, and leaf-fodder green. One might add that if a cross-Channel move was involved, October would almost certainly have been the latest date for sea travel. This communal move would have been preceded by small exploratory groups, living by hunting and collecting, during the early summer months. The whole process might well have taken several years, in these stages:

(1) Exploration of the foreign coast and hinterland. This could follow an accidental discovery by a wind-blown fishing vessel on the lines discussed in chapter 6.
(2) Despatch of stock for summer grazing with small groups of herdsmen, and return to the parent community for the winter ('booleying' as practised in Ireland in the recent past).
(3) Booleying continued combined with sowing and harvesting of crops (and return to the parent community for the winter).
(4) Despatch of a group for permanent settlement.

Even then, Case points out, there might be frequent recourse to the parent community for such things as service of stock, to avoid the problem of catching, roping, throwing and carrying a bull weighing half a ton into a skin boat.

All this presupposes fluent and frequent sea voyages, of which only the skin boat seems capable at such an early stage. Further north, when one reaches Neolithic sites such as Skara Brae and Rinyo in Orkney, this becomes even more so. The strong circum-Polar element in many of these sites confirms what one would expect from their situation.[28] Surrounded by seas as difficult as those of the Pentland Firth, where a 1914–18 destroyer is reported once simply to have sailed under the confused seas to her end, the islands are not very likely to have produced planked vessels stout enough to have survived. It must therefore have been skin boats in the circum-Polar tradition which brought settlers and their unique breed of cattle to Skail Bay and Rousay in Orkney and took them fishing for cod and coal-fish.

Could the skin-boat-using hunter-fishers have become the traders and sailors of the early farmers of Britain and in turn taken the newly-acquired habits of pottery-making and cattle-breeding out to islands which only assured seamen would have a chance of reaching? This is no new idea. As Stuart Piggott puts it, a dual pattern of life must have persisted for many centuries in many regions, with a give-and-take of techniques between the two economies.[29] As Paul Mellars says, the small copies of late Neolithic arrowheads, made with a typical microlithic technique, found apparently associated with Mesolithic industries at Shewalton Moor in Ayrshire, Risby Warren in Lincolnshire and a number of sites in the Tweed valley, clearly allow the possibility of groups practising an essentially Mesolithic technology and economy surviving for a considerable time alongside the early farmers.[30] The traditional antipathy in Britain between sailors and farmers may then even date back to the fourth millennium BC.

There is another possibility – that the first farmers came over in fine weather in improved dug-outs, leaving the hunter-fisher peoples to be more daring, such as trading axes to the Northern Isles and round the Irish Sea. If Robert Raikes[31] is right and the climatic optimum, prolonged spells of easterly weather, and other postulates for getting dug-outs onto the northern seas cannot be justified, then this perhaps is not very likely.

## The building and the use of skin boats

If we accept that the modern curragh is a descendant and outcome of a skin-boat tradition extending back to the Mesolithic, as argued above, then it is important both because it gives us a yardstick to measure the capability of the ancient version and because we have in the Irish monastic literature a lively source of information and description of these craft and their voyages. The *Odyssey* is often quoted as the earliest detailed literary account of a long sea-voyage. Yet in a sense Adamnan's account of St Cormac being driven into the Arctic on one of his journeys in search of solitude represents an even earlier tradition of sea-going. Odysseus after all had a planked vessel which represented some thousands of years of development from those of the first obsidian merchants. Cormac's, on the other hand, if possibly larger, would hardly have seemed very strange to the Mesolithic sandloopers beachcombing on Oronsay.

The building of one of these craft is well described in the *Life of St Brendan*:[32]

Sanctus Brendanus et qui cum eo erant, acceptis feramentis, fecerunt naviculam levissimam, costatam et columnatam ex vimine, sicut mos est in illis partibus [near Mount Brandon in Kerry] et cooperuerunt eam corii bovinis ac rubruatis in cortice robovina linieruntque foris omnes juncturas navis, et expendit quadraginta dierum et butirum ad pellis preparandas assumpserunt ad cooperimentum navis, et cetera utensilia quae ad usum vitae humanae pertinent. Aborem posuerunt in medio navis fixum, et velum, et cetera quae ad gubernationem navis pertinent.

This account with its details of the iron tools used, the wickerwork sides and ribs covered with cow-hide, the tanning of the hide and the covering of the seams with pitch, and the stocking of the vessel with provisions for forty days and butter to dress the hides may be compared with the early seventeenth century description of how the Irishman Dermot O'Sullivan made a craft to cross the Shannon when all hope of escape from the troops of the Earl of Thomond seemed gone.[33]

Next day, which was the seventh of January, on the instructions of Dermot, they betook themselves to Brosnach wood, very dense and therefore a safe refuge, and surrounded themselves with a rampart constructed of tree trunks with a small ditch on the outer side. In two days they built two boats of osier and timber; twelve horses were killed and their hides used to cover the boats . . . The boat which Dermot designed was built in the following way: osiers fixed in the earth by their thicker ends and bent back to the centre towards one another, were bound in place with cords and these formed the hull of the vessel. To this stout wooden gunwales and thwarts inside were added. The exterior was covered with the hides of eleven horses; oars and thole-pins were also fitted. The bottom, because of the nature of the material and for the purpose of avoiding rocks and jagged points, was flat. The length was 26 feet, the width six and the height five except at the prow which was raised a little higher to throw off the waves.

The construction of the second boat was in the hands of O'Malley's horseman. It was made of osiers without crosspieces; the bottom was shaped like a circular shield and the sides were much deeper than the bottom required. A single horse-hide was sufficient to cover the bottom.

These boats were carried by night on the soldiers' backs to the Shannon at Port-a-Tulchain and in them O'Sullivan began secretly to transport his men across. Ten of O'Malley's soldiers boarded their boat. But the vessel being both small and overweighted by its useless superstructure, foundered with the men in midstream. Dermot's boat, which would hold 30 men at a time, carried the others across in safety, the horses swimming behind at the ends of halters tied to the stern.

This account is interesting for a number of reasons. The dimensions of the big vessel suggest that, while the length and rising bow recall a Kerry curragh, the greater width and depth would produce more the hull-shape of the Broighter boat. The capacity of the eleven-hide boat, which was thirty men, agrees with Hornell's rule of thumb that a 'three-hide' craft would carry nine men.[34] But perhaps the most interesting detail of all is that the curragh was built upside down. In his great survey of curragh types and building techniques which Hornell made just before they started seriously going out of use, he recorded that Irish curraghs, including even the Boyne River ones which are the most primitive, are built bottom up.[35] This is in contrast to the Welsh coracles, whose construction, in the case of the Teifi ones, Hornell describes in this way.[36]

Before using, the laths (of split and trimmed willow branches) are soaked in hot water or wrapped around with cloth dipped in boiling water, in order to render them more pliable. When ready, seven are laid parallel upon a floor or on a level piece of ground, spaced apart from 4 to 5 inches. Ten short laths are interlaced with these at right angles, forming, however, only seven transverse frames, as the first three are each formed of two laths in order to give local strength. Lastly two extra long ones are arranged sattire fashion, likewise interlaced with the others. Adjustments by eye having been made, weights are placed at the principal points of intersection to keep the laths in position while being bent up. The next proceeding is to insert the seat and its supports by bending up the ends of the second and third transverse laths, counting from the after end, and passing them through slots made near each end of the seat plank. The ends of two of the main longitudinal laths are next bent up and secured in the appropriate curve by cords stretched between; these serve as guides. The lowermost unit of the wattled gunwale is now begun. Usually it is started below the seat on the left side;

then working forwards it is woven round the ends of the frames which are bent up successively as work proceeds. This plait makes a half circuit of the gunwale, ending a little in front of the seat on the right side. A similar semicircular plait is worked on around the after end of the framework, but instead of forming the under side of the gunwale it is bent down to form a semicircular strengthening band round the after end of the bottom. A second plait of withies succeeds, which is carried continuously the whole way around the tops of the upturned ends of the frames; this plait passes below the seat. In the same way the third plait is wattled on; its withies are stronger than those in the other two, as this plait forms the margin of the gunwale and has to stand heavy usage. It passes over the ends of the seat which are thus sunk about $1\frac{1}{2}$ inches below the top of the gunwale. Two men are needed during these operations, one to bend up and hold the laths, the other to do the wattling.

Only when this process is complete is the framework turned bottom up for a coat of preservative to be put on, followed in due course by the cover.

The Boyne River coracle on the other hand is begun by the insertion of thirty-two hazel rods, about 3 metres long, in an elliptical oval marked out on the ground.[37] The gunwale is formed by weaving strong withies in and out of the upright rods. Then the rods are bent down to overlap their opposite members and secured together at each point of intersection. When this basic hull is complete, it is eased out of the ground and covered with hide. This is tautened by hammering down the projecting bases of the hazel rods, which finally are cut off almost flush with the gunwale and covered with a protective ring of withies.

The more elaborate construction of a Kerry curragh reflects the refinements that have developed in the course of time, though the general process is still related. The double gunwales are made and fastened first, their shape being determined by a plan drawn out on the ground. Then the ribs are inserted in the slots which have previously been cut in the lower gunwale, and the stringers and the keelson planks added to those to complete the framework. The use of different wood for the different parts also reflects the complicated traditions that lie behind this method of construction.

Hornell declared that the Eskimo umiak, like the southern Indian coracle and the Mesopotamian *quffa*, was built the right way up.[38] However, he gives no source for this statement and it is possible that some confusion has arisen in descriptive accounts, since, according to the record made by the National Museum of Canada of the building of a umiak (illustrated in Figures 4.11 and 4.12), the structure is turned right way up

10.15  *(a, b) Two stages in the building of the frame for a River Boyne coracle (National Museum of Ireland, Dublin)*

at different stages in the operation. Basically, however, the start of the building occurs with the gunwale face down to the ground. Then stern and bow blocks supported by stern and bow posts and pairs of ribs are put in, followed by the keel and bottom stringers and remaining ribs. So in this the umiak resembles the curragh and suggests that the innovation which turned the coracle into a sea-going craft may have been a common element right across Europe and Asia.

Unfortunately the *Navigatio* of St Brendan makes no comment on this point, but its detail is the earliest full account we have of the making and the use of one of these craft.[39] Since the *Navigatio* descriptions of the column of crystal and of the island of smiths' forges might reasonably be taken to reflect some knowledge of icebergs and vol-canoes, one would be inclined to agree with Hornell[40] that Brendan certainly reached Shet-land and probably Iceland, although other auth-ors have seen the saint reaching North America, the Bahamas and the Azores.[41]

Adamnan's Life of St Columba also refers to skin boats, and is remarkable for the way, among the miracles and the details of the saint's mis-sionary work amongst the Picts, it illustrates the essential part curraghs played in sixth and seventh century AD life in the Western Isles. They sail to and fro between Scotland and Ireland, meet adverse winds, storms and sea-monsters – includ-ing, coincidentally, one in Loch Ness – haul barges loaded with timber and are used upside down as temporary shelter by a thief who has fled to an uninhabited island.[42] The biography also gives in many phrases a strong feeling of the nautical cast of this life. The monks undertake the 'hard labour' of a sea voyage, as it must have been when rowing was necessary much of the time; face great danger in the rolling tides of the whirlpool of Breccan; or during a storm bail out the bitter bilge water (*amaram aquam*).[43] A number of interesting techni-cal details are also revealed, such as the existence of a keel; the mast being stepped and lowered according to the wind, rather than being left in position all the time (in which it resembles the umiak); and that liquids were carried on board in skin bags which were left to soak in the sea to clean them after use.[44]

But it was to a particular characteristic of the Irish monastic church that we owe the most vivid account of skin-boat ocean voyaging. This was the impulse to go and search for solitude in the pathless sea. Columba's had been a missionary exile.[45]

How rapid the speed of my coracle
And its stern turned upon Derry.
I grieve at my errand o'er the noble sea,
Travelling to Alba of the ravens.

Cormac, by contrast, simply desired to find solitude. The account of his third attempt to do so has been called the most remarkable glimpse of geographical adventure since the days of Pytheas the Greek, in the fourth century BC.[46]

When this said Cormac was toiling over the ocean waters for the third time he began to be in peril well-nigh to death. For when his ship in full-sail during fourteen summer days and as many nights, held on a course straight from the land, before a southerly wind, towards the region of the north, his voyage seemed to go beyond the limit of human experience, and return to be impossible. Whence it happened that after the tenth hour of the same fourteenth day certain awful terrors, almost too great to be borne, arose on every side; for certain loathsome and very dangerous creatures, which up to that time had never been seen, came into sight, covering the sea; and with a terrible rush they smote the bottom and sides, the stern and prow so heavily that it seemed as though in the end they would break through the leather sheathing of the boat. And as those who were there afterwards related, they were about the size of frogs with very terrible stings and more like swimming than flying creatures, and they also swarmed over the blades of the oars.

Fortunately for Cormac, Columba at that moment called on the brethren at Iona to pray with all fervour for him, since by voyaging too far, 'he had ventured beyond the bounds of human discovery and now suffers horrible alarms from monsters never before seen and almost indescrib-able'. That very instant the south wind veered to the north, and after many more days Cormac returned safely.[47]

This surely is an authentic account of a voyage under conditions which must have been familiar to many of our prehistoric ancestors. There are so

10.16 *(a–e) A curragh or navog under construction in Co. Kerry (National Museum of Ireland, Dublin)*

many details which ring true. The characteristic quality, already discussed, of the curragh being carried by the wind and the impossibility of rowing against it. The seaworthiness in standing up to fourteen days of driving across the north Atlantic. The meeting with the school of Portuguese men-o'-war (*Physalia physalis*) carried with the Gulf Stream to the latitude of Iceland, as still sometimes happens. The searing pain caused by the neuro-toxin in their tentacles which can be brought into a boat by the very oars which may rashly have been used to fend off these sinister creatures, so well described as frog-like and more swimming than flying.

One detail in particular would convince anyone who has travelled much in a curragh. One of the unique characteristics of that craft is the feeling it transmits of the sea around it. There is none of the even solidity a planked craft conveys. The water becomes a much more broken-up turbulent body, tapping, probing, gurgling all over the place, so that it seems to knock against different parts of the hull in a quite random way. It is very easy to understand that in a sea apparently full of the unaccustomed horror of Portuguese men-o'-war one might well imagine these *bestiolae* were actively banging against the hull and threatening to break through the thin hide covering.

As Mrs Chadwick has pointed out,[48] St Columba lived in the period when the oral traditions of Irish literature were gradually giving place to the written records of Latin learning. Adamnan, his biographer, was elected to the abbey of Iona in AD 679. He was thus in a favourable position to record the tradition of events handed down less than a century after they happened by brethren of Columba's own church. He was as near as it was possible for a writer to be to the conditions of this particular kind of prehistoric sea travel which had been going on for many centuries.

### Irish voyages to Iceland

Adamnan's account of Cormac's voyage also inevitably raises the question of whether the Celtic monks reached Iceland in their curraghs. Even if we reduce the fourteen days of northward sailing by half to compensate for the customary exaggeration, that would still have brought Cormac, at the ninety or so miles a day which T. C. Lethbridge reckons is a cautious average for a day's sail at that period, well within reach of Iceland.[49] However, none of the finds in the National Museum of Iceland in Reykjavik could be described as Celtic. Acceptance of Irish monks reaching Iceland depends therefore on two things, literary evidence and place names.

The later Norse occupants of Iceland themselves described their predecessors. A passage in the Book of Icelanders written by Ari the Learned, Iceland's first historian in the vernacular, some 250 years after the discovery of the island by the Norsemen in the ninth century AD, says: 'There were Christian men here then, whom the Norsemen called "Papar"; but they went away, for they did not want to live amongst heathen men; and behind them they left bells, books, and croziers.'

This is confirmed by two other writers, Dicuil (an Irish monk) and Bede. In his *De Mensura Orbis Terrae*, written about AD 825, Dicuil says: 'It is now thirty years since some Irish monks who lived on that island [Thule] from 1 February to 1 August told me that not only during the summer solstice but for several days on either side of it, the setting sun hides itself as if behind a small hill, so that there is no darkness for even a very short time, and a man can do whatever he wishes, even pick the lice from his shirt, as if it were broad daylight.'[50] The casual detail of the lice is particularly convincing. About a hundred years earlier, Bede had written in his *De Temporum Ratione* that the voyage between Britain and Thule took six days.[51]

In support of these literary references, we have a considerable amount of place-name evidence. Off the south-east coast of Iceland lies Papey, 'the island of the Papar' (the Norse word for Irish monks). On this island is Irskishollur, 'the Irishmen's hillock'. On the south-east coast of Iceland is Papafjord, and the mouth of the fjord is called 'Papós'. This fjord, just north of the modern port of Höfn, contains perhaps the most intriguing name of all, Papataettur, because this means 'the ruins of the Papar', and there are indeed some grass-covered foundations there, but they are not at all accessible and have never been excavated. They may be no more than an abandoned stone hut or fisherman's shelter which some romantic antiquary christened with more imagination than reason. Yet their position has some significance. Most of the original Norse sites lie under the scattered modern farmhouses, like the dramatically burnt remains of Njal's barn, one of the few to be excavated. The reasons for this are obvious – shelter, fresh water, grass, communication with the next valley were as apparent and attractive then as now. Papataettur has none of these. It is set in a square of turf surrounded by rocks, and its only raison d'être seems to be that it is a sheltered site near the water's edge on the south-east corner of Iceland, which is the part nearest the British Isles.

The foundations appear to be those of two or three small round buildings and one oblong one with an entrance facing the sea. The building materials, as far as one can tell without excavation, were rough blocks of stone. The layout does not seem to recall any Celtic monastic plan. On the other hand it seems highly unlikely that these structures, whatever they were, were part of any Norse farm. But to castaways landing in the sheltered fjord this place might, with its square of turf surrounded by sheltering rocks, have offered a welcome site for a rough hermit cell or two. Only excavation can take this suggestion further.

## Skin boat survivals

By two centuries after Cormac's voyage, the superb creations of the Norse shipwrights had all but swept the curragh off the sea. The craft which once, according to a seventeenth-century translation of Gildas, the sixth-century monk, had enabled the dreadful groups of Picts and Scots 'to swarm like brownish bands of worms and eamots over the Scithian Vale [St George's Channel]'[52] and of which fifty at one time had been swallowed up in the whirlpool of Breccan,[53] came to be used only by fishermen like those described by Gerald of Wales in the late twelfth century.[54]

Some sailors told me that having once been driven by a violent storm during Lent to the northern islands and the unexplored expanse of the Sea of Connaught, they lay for shelter off a small island. Soon after the storm abated, they noticed a small skiff rowing towards them. It was narrow and oblong and made of wattled boughs, covered with the hide of beasts. In it were two men without any clothing except broad belts round their waists. They had long yellow hair, like the Irish, falling below their shoulders. Finding that the men were from some part of Connaught and could speak the Irish language, the sailors took them on board. They said that they had never before seen a ship built of timber.

Yet, as we have seen, such are the virtues of these craft that they still exist, many nowadays fitted with outboard engines. Two cows or twenty-one sheep is reckoned a good load to take out to one of the small island pastures in a Kerry curragh, recalling that the first British agriculturalists may have brought their stock over in much the same way.

To make the easiest and closest approximation in Europe to a Neolithic sea voyage, the place to go is Dunquin in south-west Ireland. For a pound or two you can be rowed out to Great Blasket, the biggest island in that group, in one of the curraghs that stand like black beetles upside down at the foot of the steep cliff-face. With the wind in the west the Blaskets more or less shelter you during the journey across, but if the wind is north or south of that you are virtually experiencing the open Atlantic. The modern curragh has a tarred canvas hull instead of sealskin or ox-hide, and its framework is fastened with copper nails, but that affects the speed and simplicity of its construction and its durability rather than its behaviour at sea.

Hornell thought that it was isolation, poverty and lack of timber that were responsible for its survival.[55] Though the Aran Islands and some other localities are barren, the last reason does not seem universally applicable to the west coast of Ireland. One might substitute for shortage of timber the great seaworthiness of these craft. The tactile sensation of having the sea only the thinness of a sheet of canvas away, the susceptibility of its balance and the need to place one's feet and anything else with care certainly make travel in a curragh quite unlike that in any other craft. Soon, though, one comes more and more to appreciate the reassurance of its sea-keeping quality, the extraordinary liveliness and vigour with which it rises to and surmounts the seas. It is only when one has had some experience of these craft in the open sea that its long history of usage becomes readily understandable.

The evidence for early voyages in the rough north Atlantic, even as far as Iceland, is there. Though in no way as lengthy as the journeys by canoe or raft in the Pacific, which were perhaps the most remarkable achievements of prehistoric sailors, they are still the dramatic climax of a very ancient and important type of prehistoric craft.

# 11 The British Isles: wooden craft

## Dug-outs

As discussed in chapter 5, dug-out canoes are not at the present time an entirely satisfactory subject for investigation, as, although many have survived in the British Isles, few have been securely dated, and they are known to have been in use from at least the early second millennium BC to the seventeenth century AD and later. A systematic examination of the evidence for the dug-outs of England and Wales recently carried out by Seán McGrail[1] revealed that dug-outs had been in use on the lakes and tarns of the highland zone as well as on the rivers and estuaries of the lowlands. The surviving evidence for boat-building techniques, however, is often difficult to interpret because the excavated material has fragmented, distorted and shrunk over the years, and because in the past only infrequently were adequate drawings made at the time of finding. Nevertheless it is possible to suggest that many of these boats were developments from the simple logboat, having added washstrakes and stabilising timbers, and possibly being paired. A few may have had fitted ribs, but there is more evidence for this in Ireland and Scotland where there are also indications that some dug-outs were propelled by oar rather than paddled or poled. When this Irish and Scottish material and the corresponding evidence from continental Europe has been systematically investigated, a more comprehensive picture should be obtained of the methods used to build and operate this ubiquitous craft. A programme of radiocarbon dating, which is now under way, and future dendrochronological work should throw further light on the development of techniques over time.

An intriguing variant of the dug-out scene is the model craft known as the Roos Carr boat now in Hull Museum. Whether this animal-headed craft (Figure 9.18) represents a dug-out or some other craft has been discussed ever since it was found in 1836 near Withernsea in Yorkshire about 2 metres below the surface in a bed of blue clay by labourers clearing a dyke. In 1851 the Reverend George Dodds, DD, in a lengthy paper, suggested that its inmates were the Noetic Ogdaod, or family of Nosh, who had been adopted as gods by the Phoenicians and thus brought to England.[2] Unfortunately for this theory, half of Nosh's family were female, whereas the Roos Carr crew were almost aggressively male until doctored by Victorian decency.

However, by 1881, a Danish amateur archaeologist had made a comparison with a number of other wooden figures found in Scandinavia and Scotland, which were very like those in the Roos Carr boat, to make the much more convincing suggestion that the period was earlier.[3] As Sune Lundquist says, 'every Nordic archeologist should no doubt agree with Mr. Feddersen in referring the figures from Roos Carr to the Bronze Age.' Lundquist then goes on to make a number of comparisons between Swedish Bronze Age rock carvings and the Roos Carr model, drawing especial attention to the way the calf muscles of the

11.1    *Craft on a third or fourth century BC vase from Liria, Spain (Arribas, The Iberians, 1963)*

men in both are stressed. Nor can one deny that some of the rock-carved ships of Bohuslän are very reminiscent of the Roos Carr boat. The animal head on the prow with its quartz eyes, too, has a strong hunter-fisher affinity. If the British skin-boat tradition had a flat gunwale and lacked the double bow of the Scandinavians as discussed in the last chapter, could not this Roos Carr model be another example to go between the Caergwrle bowl and Broighter boat, with its prow expressing a closer link to the Scandinavian element than the Iberian-influenced oculi of the Caergwrle bowl, just as the geography of their sites would suggest? It is tempting to think so. One remembers too the Hjortspring boat where a skin-boat type seems to have evolved into a planked version. But, on the whole, the shape of the Roos Carr craft is so close to that of a dug-out that it seems this latter must be the most likely answer.

This in turn suggests a parallel much further to the south. This is the craft shown on a vase from Liria in Spain of about the third or fourth century BC.[4] This, too, is full of warriors armed with shields and spears and has an animal head for its bow, and the vase enables us to see it is involved in a river battle (Figure 11.1). What is more, there is an even stranger parallel between the Liria and the Roos Carr craft. In the British Museum, in the Greenwell Collection, there is a barbed bronze spearhead which was turned up in the last century by some workmen while digging for brick clay at North Ferriby, not all that far from Withernsea where the Roos Carr boat was found. In an interesting piece of deduction, Christopher Hawkes and John Bartlett have suggested that this spearhead with its very short socket-tube and pegs behind the blade was designed to be lashed to a

long shaft by rawhide, with the object of allowing the shaft to fall on impact but still remain attached to the spearhead.[5] If the target was an enemy soldier's shield, this encumbrance might uncover him for a second spear or a hand-weapon attack (Figure 11.2). This harpoon principle is well known from many ethnological examples, as well as the Roman legionary's *pilum*. Professor Hawkes also suggests that this device may have been evolved to counter the leather-covered wooden shields of the Bronze Age and he quotes the red-deer-antler harpoon heads found at Skipsea, Withow and Hornsea Gasworks, not far from North Ferriby, as possibly suggesting the existence of a hunter-fisher tradition of harpoon-making which lasted on into the late Bronze Age to give weapon-smiths the idea for this new retiarius-like weapon.

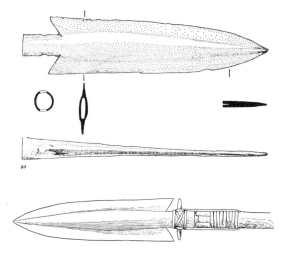

11.2    *A bronze spearhead from North Ferriby, Yorkshire, and a conjectural method of its use as a 'harpoon' (Hawkes and Bartlett,* PPS, *vol. 31, 1965, pp. 370, 372)*

The interesting thing about the Liria vase is that it shows both a vessel like the Roos Carr one and men in it with shields on their arms; and in those shields are sticking what seems to be dangling portions of hurled spears.

From Iberia one might then move eastward to Sardinia. Here, following on the development of the castle-like *nuraghi*, the copper deposits encouraged in the early first millennium BC a flourishing group of bronze-smiths,[6] whose attractive handiwork, very popular among Etruscans and Romans, included large numbers of boats. According to Zervos, these were not reproductions of contemporary craft, with the possible exception of two from Vetulonia and Scala di Boes which are more realistic and bear some resemblance to later small craft on Roman mosaics.[7] The others were rather Boats of the Dead and embodied sacred memories of ancient vessels: hence the holy symbols carved on some of them (Figure 11.3). From our point of view the significant points are the animal heads on the bows and whether they were dug-outs. If they are too ancient in concept to be planked craft, their rounded elliptical shape could be derived from skin or bark craft, but on the whole a dug-out basis seems the most likely. The absence of sheer supports this, as does the sort of built-up balustrade on each side which some of them have, and the length in proportion to the width just about comes within a dug-out range. The absence of skin and bark boats in other Mediterranean contexts would also favour the dug-out solution, especially if these craft, as Zervos suggests, represent an archaic tradition, which sacred craft, as has been said, so often do.

Remembering then that there is a Scottish example from Loch Arthur in Dumfries and Galloway (Figure 9.19) of an animal-headed dug-out,[8] and the Nämforsen and Russian rock carvings discussed in chapter 9 which may be of dug-outs, we then seem to have evidence of this type of craft from Britain to Spain, and possibly from the north of Europe to the central Mediterranean, over a period from the middle of the second millennium BC to the third century BC. The idea of putting an animal head on a boat is a fairly obvious one, oculi being a more sophisticated expression of the same thought. Yet it is rather extraordinary to think of this practice existing the length of Europe in a swathe more extensive in distance than that of the megaliths.

It does not seem to be linked exclusively to dug-outs, since the Scandinavian-evolved skin boats appear to have had animal heads on the bows, and the hull of Pepys's 'Wild Irish' craft (Figure 10.13) could almost be taken from a Sardinian bronze model. Yet when it comes to small light craft, an ox-skull with good horns weighs quite an amount, and a dug-out must have been a better support for one than a skin or bark craft. Does this suggest, then, that for two millennia across Europe, boatmen in a hunter-fisher tradition gave animal heads to their dug-outs and hurled harpoons at their enemies' shields? The evidence at the

11.3  *Bronze boat model from Sardinia, early first millennium BC, with 'animal' head bow (British Museum)*

moment is hardly strong enough for that, but the similarity between the Roos Carr and Liria craft is nevertheless striking.

## Planked boats

One might well have been left with little more than such speculations to advance the account of wooden craft in Bronze Age Britain had it not been for the sharp eyes of E. V. Wright. In the early spring of 1938, on the northern bank of the Humber estuary, he noticed the ends of three wooden planks sticking out of a bed of clay which has the fortunate quality of preserving organic materials remarkably well. At the time these planks were thought to be the remains of a Viking ship. In fact subsequent work over the next twenty-five years revealed the remains of no less than three examples of what proved to be Bronze Age boats (Figures 11.4, 11.5, 11.6).

11.4    *One end of Ferriby boat 1 while being excavated from the inter-tidal zone at North Ferriby in 1946 (E. V. Wright)*

11.5    *The scarf in the keel plank of Ferriby boat 2 (E. V. Wright)*

11.6    *Ferriby boat 3 during excavation in 1963 (E. V. Wright)*

Excavation of these craft was extremely difficult, because of the tides, the glue-like clay in which they lay, and the interval in excavation caused by the Second World War, when the tides eroded the covering clay and washed away parts of the boats. However, they do give an extraordinarily interesting picture of an unusual type of craft from a period where little other maritime evidence exists (Figure 11.7).[9]

Boats 2 and 3, and possibly 1 as well, had been deliberately dismantled and have the appearance of being discarded portions of used boats. Their bottoms were made up of three planks, some of which were composite with scarf joints, or re-paired. All planks were shaped out of great oak trunks, each log having been split down the middle longitudinally and one plank hewn from each half log, the keel plank being nearly twice as thick as the others. The estimated original length of boat 1 is 51.70 feet (14.35 metres) with a maximum beam of 8.55 feet (2.60 metres). The two outer planks of the bottom, which in boat 1 were some 35 feet (10 metres) long and 3 to 4 inches (8–11 cm) thick, were sewn to the keel plank by separate stitches of yew withies, twisted and cracked like wicker for flexibility. The probable sequence of assembly was to caulk the seams with dry moss, insert the covering laths of oak, and then stitch up the planks

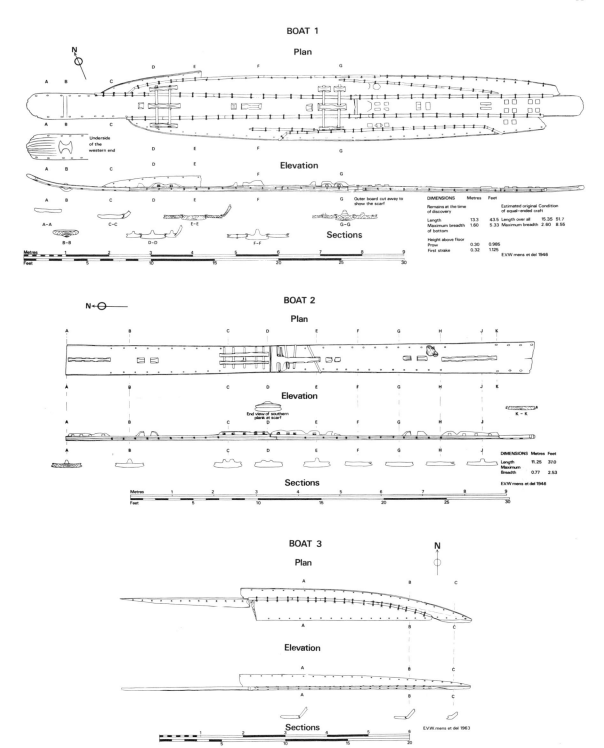

11.7  *(a, b, c) Measured drawings of the three Ferriby boats (E. V. Wright)*

and wedge the holes. In this way the joints would have been tightened, a process which would have been continued by the swelling of the materials when the craft was put in the water.

The bottom structure was stiffened by a series of transverse bars made of ash in boat 1, oak in boat 2. These passed through mortised holes in the large ridges or cleats which had been left standing when the bottom planks were adzed down. The transverse bars were jammed in these holes by wedges. In boat 1, there were four pairs of these, and in addition a number of other blocks and ridges were left standing on the keel plank.

The most important discovery, perhaps, was pieces of the first side strake of boats 1 and 3. This had been carved with great accuracy from solid wood and was a most remarkable example of boat-builders' skill. A further proof of the builders' elaborate technique lies in the change in the type of seam between the side strake and the outer bottom plank, and between the side strake and the keel, where they join at the end of the craft.

The smoothness of the general finish is also remarkable. When excavated it was still possible to see the long parallel strokes of an adze, which, from the shallowness of the shaving, most likely had a single-side cutting edge 2.5 cm wide, and of an adze with a cutting edge of approximately 7.5 cm across. The transverse bars, particularly those from boat 1, showed patterns which could have been made by a heavy knife or draw-shave. The holes for the stitches, either square or oval, were remarkably uniform in size. The holes running virtually up to each end of the keel plank of boat 1 suggest that there were two or three planks a side, and this in turn made feasible E. V. Wright's first reconstruction of the probable appearance of the original craft (Figure 11.8). No frames or thwarts were found in the excavation, but the suggested arrangement in the reconstruction makes use of the additional slots in the keel-plank cleats. In recent years E. V. Wright has developed his earlier ideas to produce different tentative reconstructions (Figure 11.9). Some of his ideas have been turned into measured drawings by naval architect John Coats, and models of these reconstructions are now on display at the National Maritime Museum, Greenwich. Further research on this aspect of the Ferriby boats continues.

The radiocarbon dating of these craft has not proved a simple matter, because many parts of the early finds were preserved in solutions containing glycerine before Libby had evolved his technique. However, some yew stitches and a small slat from directly beneath boat 2, which had been preserved dry since 1941, gave a date of $1483 \pm 210$ BC and $1596 \pm 110$ (Q-837). A small *Alnus* branch from under boat 3 produced $1170 \pm 105$ BC (Q-715). An oak sealing slat, thought originally to have been associated with boat 1 but proved subsequently to have lain above boat 3, produced $750 \pm 150$ BC (BM-58). Further samples from the boat remains at Greenwich have recently been dated[10] at the Radiocarbon Laboratory at Cambridge and these confirm a mid-second millennium BC date in radiocarbon years for these three boats. Dendrochronological research is now in progress on the surviving timbers, and it may prove possible to give a more precise date, and also add to our knowledge about the timber from which these great boats were made.

These finds then give a unique picture of a Bronze Age craft, clumsy in some ways, but made to an elaborate and sophisticated design which was clearly not a chance one, since all three craft were closely similar. As always, such a find raises many

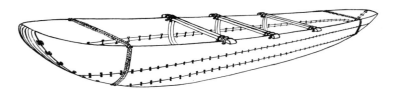

11.8   *An early conjectural reconstruction drawing of Ferriby boat 1 (E. V. Wright)*

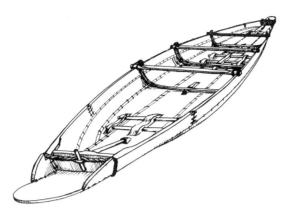

11.9   *A later reconstruction drawing of Ferriby boat 1*
*(E. V. Wright and John Coates)*

problems. One is the function of the furrowed grooves on the underside of the bow, and the adjacent winged cleat. Possibly they may have had something to do with the beaching technique, since an associated find was a piece of forked timber which has been identified by E. V. Wright as part of a windlass.[11]

## The Brigg 'raft'

The closest parallel to the Ferriby boats is the remarkable craft found in a brickyard near Brigg in Lincolnshire in 1888 by some workmen removing clay for brick-making (Figure 11.10). The surviving bottom part was reported to consist of five planks tapered at the ends with cleats similar to the Ferriby ones on the top cut out of the solid wood, through which were fitted transverse bars held in place by small wedges. Caulking, possibly of moss, had been put in the joints between the planks and this apparently was held in place by hazel slats fastened in position by fibres passing through holes 1 cm in diameter and on average 5 cm apart on each side. This so-called 'raft' was c. 40 ft (12.19 metres) long with a widest beam of c. 9 feet (2.74 metres).[12] There has long been discussion as to whether this was a 'raft' or a boat, and about the precise details of the features recorded in the nineteenth century. As it was known that at least part of the 'raft' had been left in the ground, the National Maritime Museum carried out a survey in 1973 and succeeded in re-locating its position between the old River Ancholme and the New Cut north-west of Brigg. The site was re-excavated in 1974 with the aims of lifting remaining timbers for further research and dating, and to find out more about the ecological surroundings in which the 'raft' had been abandoned.[13]

Seán McGrail, heading the excavation team from the National Maritime Museum, found the remains of six planks, rather than the five reported in the nineteenth century, and indications that the Victorians had extracted almost half of the timbers they had uncovered. The first and sixth planks had

11.10   *The Brigg 'raft' when it was first uncovered in 1888 (National Maritime Museum)*

sewing holes along their outer edges (Figure 11.11), indicating that further planks – possibly the side planking – had been fastened here when the boat was in use. Unfortunately neither end of the 'raft' was recovered and thus the full form of the hull remains in doubt. The presence of caulking designed to make the structure watertight, and the relatively complicated cleat and transverse timbers system make it unlikely that this was simply a raft but rather a boat, most probably of the flat-bottomed punt or barge shape.

Radiocarbon dates obtained by Roy Switsur of the Cambridge dating laboratory show that this boat was in use in the first millennium BC – c. 600 BC in radiocarbon years (Q-1199, Q-1200).

Preliminary interpretation of the environmental evidence recovered during the 1974 excavation shows that, at this time, the Ancholme region was a shallow creek open to the Humber estuary.

Research continues on this interesting find, and its relationship to the Ferriby boats – which are 1,000 years or so older – remains to be determined. Together these four boats give us unique glimpses at planked boat construction in prehistoric Britain.

## Two Lincolnshire dug-outs

Other related finds from the Humber region remain to be considered. The first of these also comes from Brigg but this is a large dug-out, 15

11.11    *The Brigg 'raft' re-excavated in 1974; the white spots mark sewing holes (National Maritime Museum)*

metres long, found close to the River Ancholme in 1886 during excavation at the Brigg Gasworks (Figure 11.12). The boat was made of a single huge oak tree and had a separate transom stern slotted into its after end. Another feature was the transverse ridges left standing on the floor; but what was exceptional was the way a crack in the starboard bilge of the hull had been repaired. As well as being caulked with moss, this had been covered with wooden patches, which had been fastened or sewn in position by holes through the patches and the hull in what one might call a Ferriby or Brigg manner. In addition, the largest patch had three cleats standing up on the inside, through which a bar could have been driven to strengthen the whole repair. Wood from the boat has been given a radiocarbon age of about 830 BC (Q-78).[14]

A number of holes also existed near the gunwale, which it has been suggested could have been used to give extra freeboard by attaching a washstrake, or extra stability by attaching longitudinal timbers externally. Unfortunately this craft, with the repair details so reminiscent of Ferriby techniques, was destroyed by fire in the Second World War.

Finally there is the dug-out which was removed from the bed of the old River Ancholme at Appleby in 1943. Only some 7 metres survived, but as well as a groove for a transom stern, the remaining part contained a crack about 6 metres long which had been repaired in a workmanlike way by making 2-cm-diameter holes in staggered rows each side through which a twisted fibre 'rope' had been laced. As well, thin wedge-shaped slips of wood had been found which were driven into the holes to secure the stitches. Similar cracks had been clamped tightly together by the flat double-headed cleats of oak recessed into the timber surface of the boat on each side of the crack.[15] This boat has been dated to about 1100 BC (Q-80).

## Boat-building techniques

This group of boats from the Humber area shows some of the techniques of boat-building which were available in the west from the middle of the second millennium BC to the middle of the first, a period when there is virtually no other evidence about plank-built craft available in this area. The boats also reveal how these techniques were expressed and modified by actual use in various stages of complexity. For all its apparent technological coherence, such a group of craft in-

11.12   *The Brigg dug-out excavated from near the River Ancholme in 1886 (Hull Museum)*

evitably raises many questions. Was it just the chances of survival and discovery that centred it in such a small area? Was it some intrusive element which came to shore just in this part of Britain, or did some brilliant local innovator happen to work here? Or were these methods far more widely spread, leaving us waiting for chance and improved archaeological techniques to give us a clearer picture of their distribution? The very uniqueness of the Ferriby and Brigg craft in Europe makes it all the more difficult to set them in any sort of context at present.

Perhaps the split dug-out technique (already mentioned in chapters 7 and 8, and later in chapter 12) seen by Ellmers as the origin of the later Rhine river-boats[16] could also lie behind the evolution of the Ferriby and Brigg craft. Next there is their use of laths sewn over moss caulking or luting to make the seams between strakes watertight. This is also a common and widespread practice from the Neolithic stage on, so any deductions from it should be used cautiously. But the significance of its presence in the 'Celtic' craft of Zwammerdan in the Netherlands, and of Bevaix and Yverdon by Lake Neuchâtel, Switzerland, in the Roman period is underlined by the almost universal absence of it in the classical mortise-and-tenon-fastened craft of the Mediterranean world. It does not seem impossible that this method of caulking the Ferriby and Brigg flat-bottomed craft might anticipate the existence of a widespread class of river or lake craft of which the Rhine 'Celtic' barges were later examples. This assumes that Bronze Age cross-bars through cleats were

replaced by 'Celtic' U-frames, and stitching replaced by nails. But in the absence of any evidence either way it is also possible that all were different local answers to an obvious need, and that resemblances are due to no more than an origin from split dug-outs and the available technical resources of a particular geographic area.

A rather more complicated hypothesis can be derived from the central plank of the Ferriby boats. This is marked by a distinct upward curve and rounding off at its forward end. It is not at all unlike the central plank of the representation of a barge whose shape we know about from a Roman lamp from Weissenburg in Bavaria (Figure 11.13). This has been modelled on the outlines of a classical river vessel, as was first observantly noticed by Ellmers.[17] He considers the craft to be like descriptions of a vessel found in the old Roman levels in Mainz in 1887 but then unfortunately burnt as firewood, and also like the Rhenish barges. This lamp is also very similar to E. V. Wright's first reconstruction of the Ferriby boat (see Figure 11.8), particularly as regards the bent-up central plank of the flat bottom. This might again mean no more than evidence for a wider spread in time and geography for the sheer-less flat-bottomed craft derived from the split dug-out.

There is, however, another possibility. If one looks at the underside of a Portuguese *saveiro*, one sees that this craft also has a central plank in a flat bottom which is bent up at its forward end (Figure 11.14). In fact if one takes E. V. Wright's point that the garboard strakes of the Ferriby boats are a

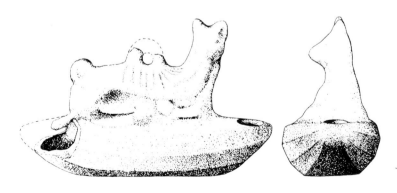

11.13    *Roman lamp from Weissenburg, Bavaria, modelled in the form of a boat (Deutsches Schiffahrtsmuseum, Bremerhaven)*

skilled exercise in three-dimensional mass handling of wood,[18] and then looks at the underside of the *saveiro* bow (Figure 11.14), an interesting comparison emerges. Taking the short-angled strake that butts up against the central plank, and the lowest strake of the side which is at right-angles to it, it is not hard to see that it would be quite easy for these two separate members once to have been one three-dimensionally-curved member joined to the centre plank of the bottom, just as in Ferriby. The links in building techniques between the *saveiro* and the 'Celtic' types have already been discussed in chapter 8. If, then, the Ferriby boats had had high bows and stern, rather than E. V. Wright's early sheerless reconstruction, then the Ferriby craft could be early fore-runners of sea-going 'Celtic' types like the Blackfriars ship, those of the Veneti, and so on.

11.14 *Underside of the bow of a Portuguese* saveiro (*author*)

## Coins and carvings

If this argument in favour of possible high bows and sterns is considered a possible hypothesis, it is worth considering here other rather unusual craft. One is shown on two Romano-British coins from the quinarius issue of Allectus (late third century AD) with '*virtus*' inscriptions. Ships on coins, as has been said constantly, have to be treated cautiously. The size, the limited area, and the ignorance of the artist often make them an unreliable source of information. On the other hand the coins of Marcus Aurelius Carausius and Allectus are artistically better than many, and Allectus, facing the likelihood of an invasion by Constantius Chlorus, had some reason not to be entirely ignorant of naval matters.[19] Most of the Allectus coin ships are reasonably conventional Roman war-ships with masts, oars, rams and stern shelters. The exceptions are on two coins (nos 1314 and 1316, Tray 32, in the T. G. Barnett Bequest in the British Museum) which show a relatively small double-ended rowing boat with a steersman, four crew and no mast (Figure 11.15). No. 1314 has a Victory figure in it as well and is not so clear as no. 1316. The craft they show are quite different from

11.15 *Coin (no. 1316) from the quinarius issue of Allectus* (*British Museum*)

11.16   *Carving of a boat on the Pictish symbol stone of St Orland's at Cossans, near Glamis (author)*

the other Allectus ones, or indeed from most Roman small craft, as for instance shown on the Thuburbo Majus mosaic. On the other hand they are not at all unlike a modern *saveiro* in form. It could therefore well be a local British craft pressed into service as a tender or messenger craft for the larger craft of the Roman galley fleet.

Then there is the boat carved on the Pictish symbol stone of St Orland's at Cossans, near Glamis in Scotland (Figure 11.16). This too is mastless, double-ended, and shown without oars, but no steering oar is shown and there seem to be more than four crew. Since the rest of the stone is

undeniably Pictish, and is dated by both Feachem and Allen to the ninth century AD, the craft is not likely to be Viking.[20] In some ways it recalls the Kvalsund boat of the sixth century AD,[21] but its likeness to the Allectus coin boat is a good deal closer.

Next one has to consider the craft carved in Jonathan's cave at East Wemyss, Fife, Scotland (Figure 11.17). This too is mastless and double-ended but lacks a crew, having oars shown instead. In view of the Pictish symbols also carved in the cave and its site within a Pictish area, it might seem logical to think these indicate its probable

11.17   *Rock carving of a boat in Jonathan's cave, East Wemyss, Fife (National Museum of Antiquities of Scotland, Edinburgh)*

11.18    *Second to third century AD sandstone disc from Jarlshof with an incised 'boat' (County Museum, Lerwick, Shetland)*

makers.[22] On the other hand, T. C. Lethbridge has suggested it is Bronze Age in date.[23] Either way, it does not help very much to settle the question as to what sort of ships the Picts used. The only other possible illustration of a Pictish craft seems to be on a sandstone disc from Jarlshof, Shetland (Figure 11.18). This was found in the course of the first excavations at Jarlshof by Robert H. W. Bruce between 1897 and 1905 and seems to be of the post-Broch, wheelhouse period. These discs, it is thought, may have been used as pieces in some form of game.[24] The craft has a square sail on a mast set forward of centre. Otherwise it is difficult to say more, since the overlapping lines give two different interpretations. One, if one follows the lighting of the photograph in the museum catalogue, shows a high, roughly double-ended craft. This could indicate a vessel that was not too far removed in type from the St Orland's and Jonathan's cave boats, though with a mast rather than oars. On the other hand there is a line running across from bow to stern just under the sail, and if one gives this equal emphasis, the craft becomes recognisably related to the Broighter boat and Pepys's 'Wild Irish' boat, with a flat run of

gunwale, virtually no sheer, and riding high on the water as skin boats do. Since either tradition could perfectly well have reached the Shetlands, there is little to go on to decide between the two interpretations.

So the nature of the Picts' boats remains a problem, along with many other aspects of their history. It would be pleasing if one could suggest that the well-known passage in Vegetius' *De Re Militari* about *scafae quas Britanni picatas* [or *picatos, pictas* or *pictos*] *vocant* might possibly mean that the Romans had pressed into service the local British craft of the type shown on the Allectus coins for inshore scouting, and that as these broadly resemble the St Orland's and Jonathan's cave carvings, a pun on Pictish and painted, or covered with pitch, according to which reading is preferred, would not be out of place when referring to the British description of them. Unfortunately, Vegetius goes on to talk about sails and ropes and is specific that they had twenty rowers '*in singulis partibus*', whatever that may mean.[25] They can hardly therefore have been very much like the small rowing boat of the Allectus coins. Nevertheless, both the Cossans and Jonathan's cave craft, with their raised bows and sterns, do fit more closely with a *saveiro*, Venetic, Allectus rowing-boat group, as far as one can see, than any Roman, Viking or other series.

## Distribution of skin and planked boats

The most satisfactory approach can perhaps be made if, omitting dug-outs, one plots geographically the craft mentioned in the last two chapters. The skin group, that is the Caergwrle bowl, the Broighter boat, the Bantry boat and Pepys's 'Wild Irish' boat, all come from the west of the British Isles. On the other hand, the *saveiro* and *meia lua*, the Venetic ships, the Gallic coin craft, the Blackfriars 1 ship, the Allectus coin boat, the Ferriby and Brigg boats, the Jonathan's cave boat, and the St Orland's boat all come from the Atlantic seaboard of Europe and the east side of the British Isles (Map 11.1). The skin group is short on numbers, and since one does not know if the Ferriby and Blackfriars 1 craft had raised ends,

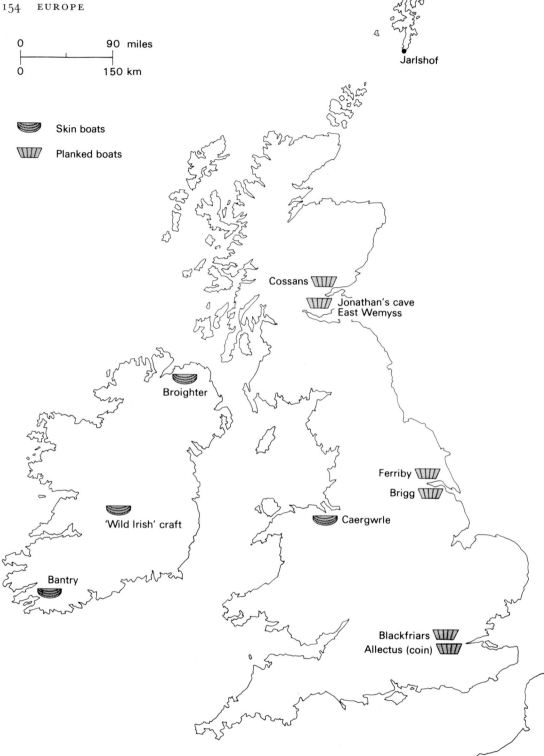

Map 11.1   *Distribution of skin and planked boats in Britain and Ireland*

or the Allectus, St Orland's and Jonathan's cave craft had flat bottoms with either transverse timbers or U-frames, the second group can be only a tentative one. Yet the groups do make a good deal of sense. In the west, one would expect a poorer area, more removed from civilisation, with rough seas, to see the survival of an old conservative tradition of skin-boat building. On the other hand, a more technologically advanced tradition of wooden ship-building might be more likely to develop on the Iberian, French and Low Countries coasts and then cross the Channel and North Sea to the eastern coasts of the British Isles, until both evolved into the sea-going and inland waters versions of Ellmers's 'Celtic' craft. When metal fastenings replaced stitching, or U-frames took over from bars through cleats, one cannot yet tell, though the Hallstatt and Le Tène periods, during which iron tools nourished what Christopher Hawkes has called 'the passion and tradition' of Celtic smiths,[26] would be possibilities.

## The development of planked boats

What emerges then is that in British waters in the early prehistoric period the skin boat and the improved dug-out were the available craft for sea voyagers, with the skin boat being more prominent in the rougher seas and more primitive areas of the north and west, and very probably in any open-sea journeys of any length. However, at some stage, presumably after the apperance of metal tools, the double dug-out evolved into the split dug-out boat. The evidence we have so far suggests that this happened particularly in the east, and may have been due to continental influence, either spreading up the coast from Iberia or possibly developing locally in a western European area from Iberia to Germany. In Britain at least, the Ferriby and Brigg evidence suggests that by the middle of the second millennium BC, and on up to the middle of the first, this built-boat construction had strakes joined by sewing and cross-bars running athwart-

ships through cleats left standing proud in the thickness of the strakes. The Ancholme dug-out repairs also show that wooden dovetail cleats were known and could in theory sometimes have been used to join strakes. Caulking was of moss between the strakes and covered with battens sewn into position.

By the Roman period, as demonstrated by the Blackfriars 1 ship, nails with their ends turned over and hammered back into strakes or frames on the inside had replaced sewing, and cross-bars through cleats had given way to U-frames and floor timbers. From the continental evidence, it seems that these frames were often in multiple groups. Caulking remained the same. Vessels of this 'Celtic' type were built in neither true skeleton- nor shell-fashion, and did not use the mortise-and-tenon fastening of strakes favoured by the Romans. It appears possible that this 'Celtic' type had both an inland-water version with little sheer, and an open-sea version with high bow and stern. If on the evidence of the caulking and the *saveiro*'s centre plank, the Ferriby boats are considered to have belonged to an early stage of this 'Celtic' type, then the geographical area of 'Celtic' boat-building on present evidence is bounded by the Iberian coast, Lake Neuchâtel, the Rhine and the Humber estuary.

Undecided questions are whether there was any influence on this type from the Mediterranean *hippos*, other than in its southern extremities, and when sails and oars, again presumably from the Mediterranean, arrived in the area. Sails were certainly used by the first century BC, but the fact that they were of leather could tie in with a possible earlier link with skin boats. On the other hand, since there is still a controversy as to how much the Anglo-Saxons used sails,[27] and that none seems to have been used further north in Scandinavia till the sixth century AD at least (see chapter 9), it is not impossible that Pytheas's canvas[28] was a seven-day's wonder in much of the northern seas he crossed in the fourth century BC.

# 12 European river craft

While in the past the technological capacity of prehistoric man to cope with sea-going conditions has often been underrated, it is important not to become so concerned with this that one neglects the great importance in early periods of inland water traffic. As Grahame Clark has pointed out, travel and transport in prehistoric times occurred very largely on water,[1] and indeed this remained the case up to the nineteenth century. It is easy to forget that in the seventeenth century it was quicker and more comfortable to go to London from Newcastle by sea than it was by road and how much more would this principle have applied in all earlier times, except perhaps the Roman. Rivers were crucial: it is a commonplace that the first centres of civilisation in Egypt, Mesopotamia, the Indian sub-continent and China grew up around them. In less developed parts of the world, the importance of river traffic in the past is reflected in the amber routes, the distribution of *Spondylus* shell ornaments and the Grand Pressigny flint trade.[2] So great was the use and importance of this river traffic, in fact, that some authorities have suggested that higher water levels existed in the past. For instance, St Sturm, in the eighth century AD, rowed well above present-day limits for boat navigation on the River Fulda when searching for a site in Germany to found a new abbey. Of Gaul in the Roman period, Strabo says: 'the course of the rivers is so happily disposed in relation to each other that you may travel from one sea to the other, carrying the merchandise only a short distance and that easily across the plains, but for

the most part by the rivers, ascending some and descending others.' This was helped even more because in Roman times rivers were regarded as public property.[3]

Yet the barge, the servant of this traffic, is one of the most neglected of all early craft. Fortunately, a considerable amount of evidence, including some specific examples, does survive from the Classical world, for example, and this gives a hint of the sort of situation which probably existed in other areas where rivers and inland waters were also important. Not surprisingly, some of the most elaborate come from Rome itself, whose position on the Tiber called for special measures as its population increased.

## Roman river craft

By the early second century BC, grain had begun its build-up into the city's chief import, reaching a figure of 500,000 tons annually by Nero's time. Wine and oil were other important cargoes, and timber which had been brought in as early as 192 BC was followed by building-stone, especially after Augustus introduced the fashion of using marble instead of the local tufa and travertine. As Casson says, heavy sacks and jars, unwieldy poles and ponderous blocks called for a special class of vessel to transport them up the Tiber after they had been trans-shipped from sea-going merchantmen in the open roadstead of Ostia.[4]

Excavations in 1958 of the harbour which the Emperor Claudius built to give better protection

12.1 *(a, b) Two sections of a relief on the statue of Father Tiber in the Louvre (Giraudon)*

to Rome-bound ships revealed among other things the remains of three flat-bottomed barges, presumably lighters[5] like those shown in relief on the famous statue of Father Tiber in the Louvre (Figure 12.1). This relief gives an informative and entertaining picture of barge life on Rome's river. One craft is simply being hauled upstream, the towing rope presumably attached to a low and no longer visible towing mast, since the high bow is clearly unsuited for that purpose. The second craft is being poled off from a possible collision with the third which is tied up alongside. This one reflects the other side of a Roman bargee's life. One man is

feeding a small fire under a pot, brewing up the Classical equivalent of the modern cup of tea, while a tally-clerk records the cargo coming aboard. Part of this is being carried up a gangplank on the shoulders of a porter, while another waits on board to stow it in the hold, revealed by the open hatch.

A more mysterious craft was the one called the *codicaria*. The literary references make it clear that this craft, operated by the guild of the Codicarii, was something out of the ordinary and it was B. Nogara in 1907 who first recognised one in a fresco (Figure 12.2) from the Vatican.[6] As well as a

12.2 *Portion of a fresco in the Vatican Museum showing a* codicaria *(Mansell Collection)*

12.3    *Gallo-Roman relief from Cabrières d'Aygues, now in the Lapidarium, Musée Calvet, Avignon (Roger-Viollet)*

rounded hull, and a special shape to the bow and stern, this vessel had an unusual mast: a bare pole with no sign of a yard, sail, rigging or stays. On the other hand it was set in the correct position forward for taking a towing line through a block at its top. This practice, which lasted many centuries, grew out of the need to keep the towline clear of the water and stop it rubbing along the bank. In 1953 Joel La Gall published two further illustrations of *codicariae*, including one carved on a cippus found near the Ponte Rotto in Rome, which revealed another characteristic of the *codicaria*'s mast, that it had cleats each side to enable it to be climbed without recourse to rigging or ladders.[7]

Casson subsequently found four more illustrations which added further details.[8] One of these, on a sarcophagus from Ostia, showed that the *codicaria* could be sailed, but that with its mast so far forward, the sail had to be a fore-and-aft one. The resultant spritsail is well shown on the Ostia carving. This sail must also have enabled the vessel to be used on the open sea, which explains why inscriptions record the use of *codicariae* at Salonae (Split) in Jugoslavia, Merobriga in Spain, and the Isle of Isbia, in none of which places are there rivers.[9] Another feature was that the mast could be lowered, as is shown in a relief in Salerno cathedral. Casson makes the point that this would account for the cleats, since the standing rigging

would be too light to be used for climbing and a ladder impractical with a mast which could be raised and lowered.[10]

Finally a mosaic of about AD 200 from Ostia shows another important piece of equipment, a capstan. Casson rightly derides attempts to see a use for this in weighing anchor or controlling double steering paddles.[11] A much more likely function was to heave in the towing line, or, in the absence of towing oxen or men, to haul the craft upriver or to its berth by the sweat of its own crew.

The *codicaria* shows how a highly specialised product could develop in the late Roman period. One interesting point it raises is how far back some of its elements go. The towing mast for instance also appears in a famous carving of the Gallo-Roman period from Cabrières d'Aygues (Var) now in the Lapidarium at Avignon (Figure 12.3) and has been claimed to have once existed in painted form on another well-known carving of a river craft (Figure 12.4) from Neumagen, Trier.[12] So it seems to have been well distributed in the Roman world at least.

The Avignon carving (Figure 12.3) is even more explicit than the Louvre relief. Three men, with lines over their shoulder and sticks in their hands, are hauling a barge loaded with wine-casks up a river, probably the Durance. The lead of the three towing lines to the mast is clearly visible. The

12.4　*Carving from Neumagen of Roman boat with wine-casks on the Moselle (Landesmuseum, Trier)*

vessel seems to be a widespread and important type, one of the *'lintres'* that Caesar refers to on the Saône and Seine, Livy on the Rhône, and Ovid on the Tiber.[13] What well may be remains of these craft have been found at Marseille and Narbonne, and a further idea of their probable shape comes from two bronze Blessey models (Figure 12.5) found in Côte d'Or near the source of the Seine, one in 1763, the other in 1873. These were almost certainly religious offerings from boatmen or entrepreneurs, and there seems little reason to disagree with Bonnard that they represent typical river boats.[14] Boats on coins can be enigmatic, but two coins of the Menapii in the Cabinet des Médailles in Paris[15] seem to show the same general shape of hull (Figure 12.6), as does the intriguing pottery vase found in 1816 at Nogent-les-Vierges.[16] Nor does their usefulness seem to have

12.5　*Two bronze vessels from Blessey, near the source of the River Seine (Musée Archéologique de Dijon)*

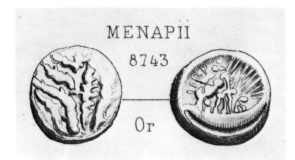

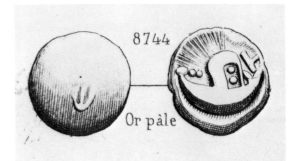

12.6   *Two coins of the Menapii (Bibliothèque nationale, Paris)*

stopped in the Roman period. Boats with bird-headed bows are shown in the Eadwine Psalter (Figure 12.7), on the altar front at Mas d'Aire, and in the porch of Amiens Cathedral (Figure 12.8), which gives an idea of the length of time they stayed in use as a good stout and useful everyday river craft.

12.7   *A detail from the Eadwine Psalter, MS. Harl.603, fo. 51, Psalm 103 (British Museum)*

12.8   *Carving in the porch of Amiens Cathedral (author)*

## Roman guilds

Records of the Roman guilds for watermen shed further light on aspects of river traffic. One of the most powerful guilds was the Nautae, who were closely associated with the wine merchants and usually described themselves as the Nautae of a particular river. For instance, the Nautae Druentici were the boatmen of the River Durance.[17] The most powerful seems to have been that based on Lyons working the Rhône and Saône, though they also handled overland work.[18] Doubtless they operated the raft of the Roman period excavated near Strasbourg. This was almost 14 metres long and was, Ellmers suggests, probably used for the transport of heavy building-stone.[19] It consisted of three beams fashioned at the bow like a ship and fastened together by metal chains with wedges at each end driven into wooden beams, strakes or logs and the chains twisted or tautened to hold them together. A set of three such metal raft-ties were also found at Heilbronn-Böckingen on the River Neckar, and Ellmers reports that very similar ones were still in use in this century on the Rhine.[20]

Another guild was the Ratiarii, who were originally loggers moving rafts of timber downstream. In the famous fresco of Althiburus, the craft used by this guild is shown as an odd little skiff with a sloping transom stern. Even more intriguing perhaps than the loggers were the Utricularii, whose badge (Figure 12.9) showed an inflated goatskin.[21] So job delineation was old already in the river trade by the Gallo-Roman period. The inflated-goatskin-raft men were obviously not to be confused with the log-rollers. Were they blacklegs from the former who helped Hannibal's army to cross the Rhône on goatskins and from the latter to get his elephants across on turf-covered log rafts? These last two guilds represent a direct derivation from two of the earliest river craft in the west, the floating log and the skin boat. In addition there must have been the raft and the dug-out in its various forms.

## 'Celtic' boats

One interesting feature that the Avignon (Figure 12.3) and Moselle (Figure 12.4) barges have in common is their cargo of barrels and there may well have been a link between the development of coopering and the evolution of the river barge in western Europe from the single or paired dug-out. The traditional liquid container of the Mediterranean world was an amphora: the wooden cask, in contrast, seems to have reached Rome from the peoples of central Europe. It was developed in Swiss localities from the Late Bronze Age onwards and the introduction of iron tools must have brought added speed of manufacture and great efficiency in the shape of dowelled staves and metal hoops (Figure 12.10). Strabo describes the Celts as fine coopers, 'for their casks are larger than houses and the excellent supply of pitch helps them to smear these pithoi.'[22] The size of the great crater of Vix, which was brought from Italy to France, proves that large loads could be carried on land.

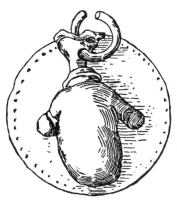

12.9 *Badge of the Roman guild of Utricularii (Grenier,* Manuel d'archéologie, *1934, p. 539)*

12.10   *Remains of an excavated Iron Age wooden cask (Mittelrheinisches Landesmuseum, Mainz)*

Nevertheless the notorious thirst of the Celts, the existence of casks to carry the wherewithal to quench it, and the stimulus to carpentry skills of the resultant trade must surely have had an effect on barge-building as well.

This type of skill may even have a relationship to the absence of mortise-and-tenon construction in the so-called 'Celtic' school of shipbuilding. The examples of mortise-and-tenon construction from the Classical period in western Europe known to date are all in what could be intrusive Roman contexts. They are some decking, a steering oar and one of the barges from Zwammerdam in the Netherlands;[23] the vessel found at Vechten near Utrecht in 1892;[24] the County Hall ship found by the Thames in 1910;[25] and an interesting description dating back to 1809 of a vessel found on the banks of the Somme surrounded by Roman weapons and pottery, and with a peach-stone in it.[26] Indigenous western craft do not have these mortises and tenons and this absence is reflected in chariot wheels from the same area and may indeed help to explain why this happened. In van der Waals's study of early wooden disc wheels from the Netherlands,[27] he describes the tripartite wheels from Ezinge which date from about 400 BC (Figure 12.11). These show several missing or broken pegs or mortises which must have caused the wheels to collapse.[28] So apparently the local technology was not capable of making this method work as well as it had done a good deal earlier in Transcaucasia or the Middle East. Local conditions may also have had something to do with

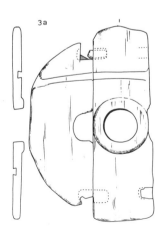

12.11   *Iron Age tripartite disc wheels from Ezinge, Netherlands (after van der Waals, Palaeohistoria, vol. 10, 1964, p. 122)*

this, especially as far as ship-building was concerned, because of the much rougher seas. In such a situation, the simpler but strong techniques of the cooper may have been of greater value to the builders of the Blackfriars and Veneti's ships than the more elaborate mortise-and-tenon methods of the Mediterranean shipwright.

In 1969 Detlev Ellmers, from a consideration of the Blackfriars 1 and New Guy's House finds described in chapter 8, literary evidence and iconographic representations, postulated a non-Roman type of shipbuilding which he called 'Celtic'.[29] His theory was confirmed dramatically within a few years. First at Zwammerdam, where the Roman frontier fort of Nigrum Pullum ('black chicken') in its marshy remoteness once overlooked a branch of the Rhine, no less than seven different craft were found.[30] Though no radiocar-

bon dates are yet available and dating is based on finds of Samian sherds and other Roman objects which could have been washed into the vessels, it looks likely that these craft date to the second century AD. Some of them are huge: one is no less than 35 metres long, with one of its oak strakes being nearly 23 metres in length.

The diversity of building techniques found at Zwammerdam is perhaps not surprising in a frontier situation. Here examples of the so-called 'Celtic' techniques of caulking with reeds and moss and fastening by nails with bent-over ends, familiar from Blackfriars 1, lay close to other examples fastened in a perfectly good Mediterranean mortise-and-tenon fashion. And the variety of craft reminds one once again how reality nearly always outdoes simple classification. Besides the great towing barges (Figure 12.12) with

12.12  *One of the great 'Celtic' barges during excavation at Zwammerdam in 1973 (Albert Egges van Giffen Instituut voor Prae- en Protohistorie, Amsterdam University, photo G. Verkuil)*

the keel-less, flat-bottomed floor planks secured by cross-members in ones, twos or threes, there are shorter squarer-ended craft, dug-outs and dug-outs with inserted frames and single strakes attached clinker-fashion each side (Figure 12.13).

The reed caulking in the 'Celtic' craft is noteworthy because of Pliny's comment that the peoples of the Low Countries pounded and inserted reeds in the seams of their ships, and that this filling was more tenacious than glue and more reliable than pitch.[31] Caulking must also have been used on some Classical ships because there was a guild of Stuppatores – caulkers – in Rome.[32] But, by and large, most finds show that the tightness of the mortise-and-tenon method made it unnecessary.

Other related 'Celtic' finds come from Switzerland. As long ago as 1911, a 10-metre steering-oar was dragged up from the bottom of Lake Neuchâtel by fishermen of Cortaillod. This had a hole in it for a tiller to reach down to the steersman from above his head, presumably in the manner of Blussus's craft (see Figure 12.16). The oar has given a radiocarbon date of AD 220 ± 100 (LV-269).[33] Further finds were not made until 1970. On 22 December of that year, in the course of a flight over the lake, Monsieur Egloff, cantonal archaeologist for Neuchâtel, saw on the lake bottom at Bevaix a craft about 20 metres long with numerous frames. The wreck was lying in only 2 metres of water and, after being photographically recorded, was lifted for conservation in 1972. It has given a radiocarbon date of AD 90 ± 70.

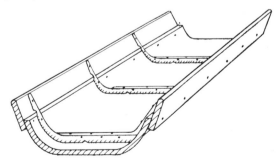

12.13  *The construction of Zwammerdam boat 3, an extended dug-out with inserted frames (de Weerd and Haalebos,* Spiegel Historiael, *nos 7–8, 1973, p. 396)*

The oak vessel was flat-bottomed without keel or even a central plank. Most unusually, the four main bottom planks were placed at an angle to the axis of the craft and stepped in relation to each other fore and aft (Figure 12.14). These were crossed by twenty-two pairs of L-shaped frames. There was also a mast-step well forward, presumably for a towing mast. Unlike the usual Roman or Scandinavian ones which lie fore and aft, this step was athwartships, thereby spreading the strain of the pull over the whole of the keel-less flat bottom. Four thousand iron nails were used in the vessel's construction, the main structural ones being driven from outside with the ends then turned and hammered back in. The seams were caulked, a row of small nails being hammered through a strip of willow underneath which was moss, and at the bottom a two-stranded thread.[34] The vessel thus was another addition to Ellmers's 'Celtic' classification.

As well as the unusual angling of its bottom planking, this Bevaix barge had an intriguing sequence of construction. According to Arnold, the planks were first fastened tautly to each other by cords passed round trenails standing up from holes made in transverse rows in the planks. Then more cords were taken at right angles round the now-adjoining planks. When the whole structure was rigid, the frames were nailed in place, the cordage removed and the holes filled in with hammered-home trenails.[35] If Arnold's interpretation is right, as seems likely, then the Roman Swiss were committing on a large scale the shipwrights' heresy of making many additional holes through the craft's skin.

In the 1960s a large river barge dated to the second century AD, and with some of the features of the 'Celtic' Zwammerdam barges, was unearthed at Kapel Avazaath near Zwammerdam. And a similar type of vessel was found at Yverdon (Figure 12.15), at the other end of Lake Neuchâtel from Bevaix, in 1971.[36] A recent find from Pommeroeul in Belgium[37] has similar features to these other finds, and together they suggest that to Ellmers's original 'Celtic' features of flat bottom, hard chine, and characteristic strake fastening and caulking method may be added an athwartship

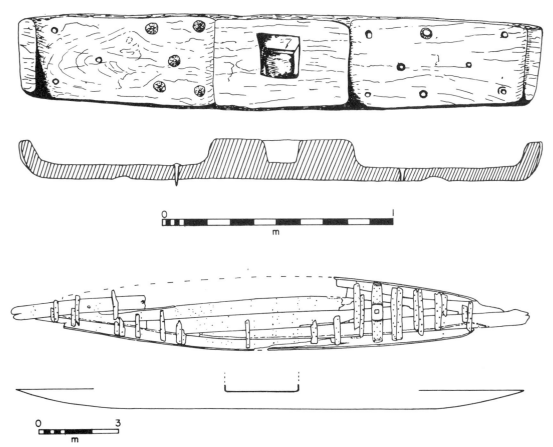

12.14 *A plan of the Bevaix boat, and details of the mast-step (after Arnold,* Cahiers d'archéologie subaquatique, *no. 3, 1974)*

12.15 *The Yverdon boat during excavation in 1971 (D. Weidmann,* Helvetia Archaeologica, *5, 1974)*

mast-stem and massive floor timbers which are often in pairs or even in threes.

## Types of river craft

Taking these Rhine finds and that of a later date from Krefeld in Germany,[38] which seem to be of the planked flat-bottomed type with sloping bows to push into the banks of the Rhine, and other archaeological evidence, Ellmers has suggested three main categories of European river craft.[39] One he derives from the dug-out, an early example being from the Untersberger Moor near Salzburg dated to the ninth century BC, which was wider and heavier at the stern, with a cross-beam inserted forward.[40] More attractive is a little gold model from Hallein, also near Salzburg, dated to the fifth century BC. This too is broader at the stern but perhaps its most significant features are the two large triangular-shaped rudders, at bow and stern, both on the starboard side.[41] Ellmers sees these dug-outs as ancestors of the boats shown on the Roman-period tombstone of a boatman called Blussus from Mainz (Figure 12.16) and the flat-bottomed craft from Yverdon, Bevaix, Zwammerdam and Krefeld. These craft, he believes, originated from split dug-outs with planking inserted between the two halves, thereby produc-

ing their flat bottoms and upright sides. Certainly Blussus's craft has the rudders at bow and stern so necessary for easing one's way round shoals and away from banks, and a towing mast. A rudder at bow and stern is also on the Rhine craft called *Oberlander* and *Nachen* which stayed in use till the twentieth century and which Ellmers considers are directly descended from such Roman-period craft as Blussus's.[42]

The second category comprises round-sectioned craft, with turned-inward bow and stern like the one shown on a Roman relief from Igel, Trier. Only the partial remains of a basalt lava millstone-carrying vessel sunk in the third century AD near Wanzenau in Alsace give a central European example of this type, which was very probably closely related to the *lintres*, or Roman barges.[43] With these latter remains were found a characteristic piece of gear, the iron fork which tipped a punt pole. Other surviving examples of this useful object range from Le Tène sites to the three gold ones found with the Broighter boat.[44]

Finally there are the incontestably Mediterranean Roman types like the Zwammerdam finds with mortise-and-tenon joints built probably by shipwrights imported for the purpose. Ellmers has suggested that the remains of a vessel some 12 metres long with close-set rowing benches, dis-

12.16    *A detail on the Roman-period tombstone of the boatman Blussus (Mittelrheinisches Landesmuseum, Mainz)*

covered in 1892 at Vechten near Utrecht, which had the Mediterranean characteristics, was one of the small supply ships which attended the large biremes or triremes of the Roman fleet.[45] These latter are well represented by the tombstone from Neumagen (Figure 12.4) which shows one of these war-ships with its ram.[46]

So our picture of the Rhine and its tributaries in the Roman period is now an infinitely more lively and varied one than it was in the 1960s, but it will probably take several more finds before we understand its full complexities.

## Canals and rivers

An interesting question is how far the banks of the Rhine were suitable for use by human towing power, either before or during the Roman period, and whether the banks were artificially improved in any way. The answer seems to be at the moment that the waterways generally used were natural, although a few canals were made by the Romans in Gaul for naval and military reasons. Perhaps the most pretentious of all Roman projects was the Emperor Nero's scheme to have a canal cut through the Isthmus of Corinth. As Suetonius describes, the Emperor, having urged on a group of Praetorian guards to the task, 'took a mattock

himself, and, at a trumpet blast, broke the ground and carried off the first basket of earth'. Hardly surprisingly, the scheme was abortive.[47] So was the Roman plan to join the Saône and the Moselle, which would have meant a canal 67 kilometres long climbing some 40 metres and then descending another 100.[48]

On the other hand, a lot was done to help travel on inland waterways by building quays and warehouses, removing navigational obstructions and even, as excavations at Orleans have shown, putting up lighthouses.[49] The harbour works at such places at Trier and Anreppen confirm that the same sorts of facilities were probably available on the Rhine.[50]

## Propulsion

Doubtless all the great river centres of ancient civilisation had roughly comparable stages of evolution to that of western Europe, with their own variations and emphases added. The huge barge carved at the Egyptian temple of Deir el-Bahari in which one of Queen Hatshepsut's 350-ton obelisks is presumed to have been carried down the Nile from Assuan to Karnak, or the strange craft 73 metres long found on the bed of Lake Nemi near Rome (Figure 12.17), possibly once the

12.17    *The second Nemi ship – destroyed in the 1940s (Accademia Americana, Rome)*

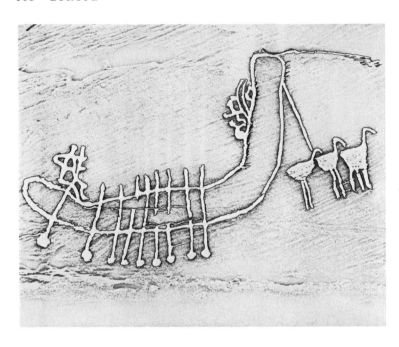

12.18 *Rock carving from Sayala, Nubia, showing ostriches towing a boat on the Nile (after Engelmayer,* Die Felsgravierungen von Sayala, *1965, Plate XLV)*

scene of the Emperor Caligula's orgies,[51] and the remarkable Chinese canal craft, studied in such detail by Needham, are examples.[52] But by and large, until the coming of the railways, the ordinary freight barge was the craft that mattered, a crucial element in travel and communication. These, as we have seen, were sometimes sailed or rowed and sometimes pulled by humans or animals. These latter could even be ostriches, to judge by the rather charming rock carving from Sayala in Nubia (Figure 12.18), though perhaps another carving near by in which a boatman has a towing rope in one hand and the tail of an ox in the other is more characteristic.[53]

In the vast majority of cases, though, it must have been manpower which moved the barges. A cuneiform receipt of the third millennium BC from Mesopotamia, given in return for oil rations, lists the crew of a river boat: '2 boat-towing men, 2 men at the outside rope, 1 man watching the depth, 3 able-bodied workers, 1 scribe'. These were the men who moved the cargoes of grain and oil, fruit and vegetables, cattle and wool, fish and milk, stone and bricks over a highly organised and elaborate canal system.[54]

The barges they used might vary in size from 1 to 11 tons, and the crew from two to eighteen men. An average-sized craft of 6 tons could cover 10 kilometres in a day, while a big team might double that distance. Downstream, when the river helped the haulers, the day's travel could go up to as much as 35 kilometres.[55] Only many centuries later, in the seventh century AD, did water-buffalo start taking over from men on the Tiber, eight being necessary for a 38-ton boat and twelve for one over 100 tons, and men were only finally banned from hauling on the Tiber by Cardinal Alessandro Lanti in 1800.[56] So, even if the massive iron hoops of the largest Zwammerdam craft's mast-fitting suggest a sailing mast, and the Blussus and Neumagen carvings confirm the contribution of oarsmen, the almost universal presence of a towing-mast-step shows that, upstream, men hauling were the prime means of propulsion. So what Sidonius Apollinaris called the 'curvorum chorus helicarionum',[57] the sad chorus of the haulers, with the lines over their left shoulders and sticks in their right hands, must have been a clear sign to most citizens of the past that a barge was making its essential way near by.

# Part Three

# Outside Europe

# 13 The Indian Ocean and Arabian Gulf

Fortunately for posterity, the Indo-Pakistan sub-continent was the main setting for the work of James Hornell. Up and down its coasts, over its inland waterways, he observed and recorded the extraordinary variety of primitive craft which until recently, and in some cases still, have survived there – the wooden blocks of the fishermen of the River Kaveri, the slightly more advanced pottery jars of their equivalents on the lower Indus, the 'chatty' rafts of Bengal, the inflated bullock skins of the Punjab, the rafts of Hardwar, in which a number of inflated skins were fastened together to make one craft, the coracles of the Tungabhadra and Kistna Rivers, the aloe-bundle floats of Kamalapuram, the reed rafts called *bindi* of the United Provinces, the log rafts or 'catamarans' of the east coast, the palm-tree dug-outs of Bengal, and the fishing canoes of Tinnevelly, in which a washstrake and inserted U-frames make the first step towards converting a dug-out into a built ship.[1] For some of these categories, evidence such as the carvings on the western gateway of the Buddhist stupa at Sanchi show that log-floats, inflated skins and craft with sewn planks were in use specifically in the first millennium AD.[2] But there is little likelihood that use of most of these primitive types does not date back much further than this.

## Early Indus craft

It would therefore be reasonable to suggest that the third great civilisation of the ancient world, the Harappan with its two great capital cities of Harappa and Mohenjo-Daro dominating the Indus valley, was as well provided with varieties of boats as those on the Nile and Tigris and Euphrates. Moreover, recent research has turned up evidence for coastal travel and trade between Sumeria and the Harappan dominions. Yet the information about the craft which sailed the Indus between 2500 and 1500 BC is disappointingly meagre. It amounts, by and large, to an impression on a seal, a piece of terracotta, graffiti on a potsherd, and some crude clay models.[3] The impression on the seal (Figure 13.1) and the terracotta object (Figure 13.2) seem to represent reed or papyrus boats. The lashings round the hull and the similarity to equivalent ancient Egyptian craft, with the cabin amidships and double steering oars, are the evidence for this. The graffiti on the potsherd (Figure 13.3) also recalls the Egyptian ships carved at Deir el-Gebrawi.

13.1 *Reed craft on a seal of the early Indus civilisation (after LeBaron Bowen, MM, vol. 42, 1956, p. 280)*

13.2 *Baked clay amulet from Mohenjo-Daro (University of Pennsylvania Museum, Philadelphia)*

13.3 *Graffito on an Indus potsherd (after LeBaron Bowen, MM, vol. 42, 1956)*

There is also another parallel with Egyptian ship-building practice, as now revealed by the Cheops ship, in the indirect evidence for the possible joining of strakes by pegs in the thickness of adjoining ones. Tripartite chariot wheels with their timbers fastened by pegs or dowels in holes in the adjacent parts have already been discussed in chapter 7. A small clay model of such a wheel, painted to appear tripartite, was excavated at Chanhu-Daro. So if wheelwrights had the skills and tools to do this, it is possible that Harappan shipwrights did also. Then it is worth noting that F. E. Paris reports that a nineteenth-century AD vessel on the Ganges called a *manche* was built in this same way. There are also other apparently Egyptian elements in recent or contemporary Indian craft, like the wide narrow sails of some Indus craft, spoon-shaped hulls, transverse beams projecting through each side of the hull, bipod masts, booms at the foot of sails, and so on. So the Indus valley civilisation may have had the same combination of vessel-types as the early Egyptian, planked with peg-joining, and reed or papyriform.[4]

In the days when Elliott Smith's views still had currency, all these things could be taken as evidence of direct Egyptian influence on the ships of ancient India. Even Hornell said, referring to various aspects of Ganges craft, 'the fundamental identity of these characteristics with those possessed by the boats of dynastic Egypt is too striking and comprehensive to be accepted as the results of coincidence or parallel development'.[5] However, today, such simple diffusionism is rarely accepted and it seems more likely that the Harappan civilisation and surviving primitive craft reflect some of the same tendencies and technical capabilities as the Egyptian without any direct influence.

The third category of craft from the Indus period is represented by clay models from Lothal. Some of these, it has been suggested, represent flat-bottomed barges for unloading craft berthed offshore. Others, more controversially, have recently been rigged with a mast inserted in a socket in the stern and tilted over the hull. In any case, the crudeness of their clay construction stops much in the way of deduction from them.[6]

### Indus/Sumeria trade

However, the excavations at Lothal are more satisfactory in the evidence they provide for other maritime elements of the Harappan civilisation. Setting aside the controversial structure which has been claimed to be a dock of a sophistication in

13.4 *Model boat excavated at Lothal, India – the fittings are modern additions (Archaeological Survey of India)*

hydraulic engineering not to be matched until late historic times, there still remains sufficient evidence to show that Lothal was an active deep-water port, one of several that studded the coastline of Kutch, Kathiawar and south Gujarat with Harappan ports in the late third and second millennia BC.[7] Dr George Dales, who has surveyed the westernmost Pakistan coast for Harappan sites, goes so far as to say:[8]

it is now quite clear that the Harappans engaged in highly organised sea-trading ventures to the west, and that it is at least possible that as well as Mesopotamia and the Arabian Gulf area, the southern coasts of Iran, Arabia and possibly even the east coast of Africa could have been involved in the sea trading activities of the Harappan period.

These recent surveys complement such classic studies as that by A. L. Oppenheim of the seafaring merchants of Ur. This showed from the Larsa tablets of about 1950 BC that merchants from Ur bartered their Mesopotamian staple goods at Telmun or Dilmun, which probably embraced the island of Bahrain and its hinterland, for copper, wood, ivory, stone beads and 'fish-eyes'

(which may have been pearls) from Makkan and Meluhha.[9] There has been a good deal of argument as to where exactly these latter two are, but there does seem now to be a reasonable consensus of opinion that 'Meluhha' may well have included the Harappan cities.[10]

Therefore when Sargon of Agade, in the second half of the third millennium BC, proclaimed proudly that ships from, or destined for, Telmun, Makkan and Meluhha were moored in the harbour outside his capital, one has to visualise craft capable of voyaging the length of the Arabian Gulf and on into the Indian Ocean.[11] These voyages would have been helped by winds there that are seasonal and reliable both as to direction and character, a fact reflected also in the *Puranas*, if not in the *Rig Veda* as well.[12] So to the dissatisfaction of knowing so little about the river craft of the Harappan civilisation is added the problem of what sort of ships carried on this monsoon-guided trade between Sumeria and the Indus valley. Fortunately some recently excavated seals from the Arabian Gulf do give a partial answer at least. These were found by a Danish archaeological

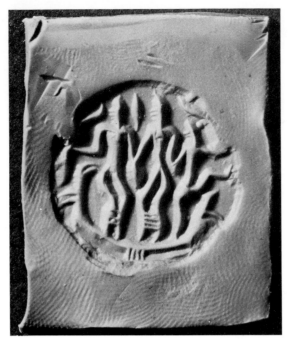

13.5   *Seal excavated from the reputed site of 'Dilmun' near Bahrain and dated to the end of the third millennium BC (Michael Rice)*

expedition in the 'Dilmun' layers, dated to the end of the third millennium BC, of sites on the islands of Bahrain and Falaika.[13] Like much else of the 'Dilmun' material, they seem to be intermediate between those of Ur and the Harappan sites, and

three of them show boats, all different though related, and all are fairly clear.

## Reed craft

The apparently earliest type (Figure 13.5) has an upright bow and stern, an animal figurehead, and lashings round the hull which suggest this was a reed-bundle craft. This is not surprising since the use of these craft continued from early Sumerian times, as discussed in chapter 2, to the contemporary period.

A modern type, for example, is the *huwayriyah* used by the Awazim fishermen of Kuwait for line-fishing off shore. This is made from date palm boughs which first have their leaves removed and are then buried in the beach sand at about the high-tide mark for some forty days to dampen them and make them pliable. These treated stalks are then tied together at the thick end in small bundles and fitted together in two layers to make a double bottom. To increase the craft's buoyancy, *harabs* (butts of palm boughs which are yearly trimmed off the tree) are placed between the two layers. The sides are built up last of all, when bamboo uprights and cross-pieces are fitted in and more bundles added. All lashings are of rope made from the beaten-out date palm-fruit stalk. The anchor is a flat coral stone with a peg in it, and a flat board with a hole in it supports a light mast.[14] It is not difficult to see that roughly identical

13.6   *A twentieth century reed boat in Bahrain (author)*

methods could well have been used to build the craft on the seal, with an animal head forward and a double tail aft added to the higher bow and stern. What is more unexpected is the strong resemblance this craft on the seal bears to some of the ancient rock-carved ships of Egypt's eastern desert (Figure 13.7). These, too, have pronounced upright bows and sterns and animal heads. Contrary to Winkler, who declared firmly that these craft of the 'eastern invaders' were not of reed, because no bindings were shown round their hulls, Landström believes the carvings portray papyrus craft, citing the line that appears to hold down the bent bow on some.[15] In his reconstruction he allows no built-up sides, possibly a doubtful interpretation since adding them, as in modern Arabian Gulf palm-frond craft, is no problem and their value in confining fishing catches and cargo is quite obvious. However, if their building material was indeed papyrus, this does seem to suggest they may indeed have been very similar to the Arabian Gulf seal craft.

## Egypt and the Persian Gulf

Links, of course, have previously been noticed between Predynastic Egypt and the Middle East. Many of the shells used by the Badarians for personal ornament came from the Red Sea or the Arabian Gulf, while some of the motifs of Naqada pottery are known on Western Asian pottery.[16] Both Petrie and more recently Elise Baumgartel have suggested a possible arrival route up the Wadi Hammamat to Upper Egypt:[17] 'Since the civilization of Naqada ... seems to have had its roots to the south of Egypt, whence people with kindred cultures entered Egypt again and again far into historical times, it seems likely that these influences came by way of the Persian Gulf'.[18] Modern opinion, however, has tended to turn more to the land route as the likely source of these parallels.[19] The Bahrain seal craft might therefore help to reverse this thinking a little.

One weak point in the 'Wadi Hammamat route' argument, if one can call it that, is Winkler's objection that none of the carvings is of reed boats. This can be countered in two ways. First, that the

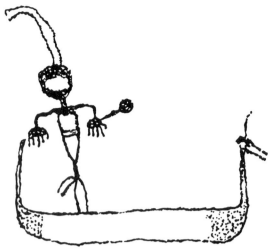

13.7 *Drawing of a rock carving from Egypt's eastern desert* (*Winkler*, Rock Carvings of Southern Upper Egypt, *1939*)

reed boat seems to become translated into a comparable wooden form with the appearance of metal tools, as indeed happened with the standard ancient Egyptian hull form. Second, the upright-ended craft on the Gebel el-Arak knife, which has long been noted for its similarities to Mesopotamian craft,[20] has lashing at one end which must surely imply a reed origin, if not an actual reed construction. Another objection to this attempt to link Egypt and the Arabian Gulf is the nature of much of the coast between, barren, hostile, lacking harbours and shelters, with tricky shoals off-shore, and frequented by pirates. This is what makes both Bowen and Hourani doubt the possibility.[21] Yet even today reed craft are in use along 670 kilometres of Arabian coast and the *shashah*, an apparently frail wicker fishing-boat of Oman, makes voyages of 85 to 170 kilometres.[22] It is not suggested that there were direct voyages from Bahrain or Falaika to the Red Sea in the Predynastic period or great invasion fleets passing the Straits of Bab el-Mandeb. What seems more likely is that reed craft were widespread then on all the Arabian and Red Sea coasts and that therefore either these, or their wooden successors, would have been prominent in the mind's eye of observers on the land route from the Red Sea to the Nile.

The question is then whether the long distance trade to the Indian continent was carried on in reed boats. Besides the foregoing information, one might cite in favour of this Pliny's report, probably derived from Eratosthenes, that vessels made of reeds, and with the type of rigging in use on the Nile, once used to take twenty days to sail from the Ganges to Ceylon, a time reduced to seven days by Roman ships.[23] So indeed it might have been possible.

**Wooden boats**

The next seal (Figure 13.8) shows a craft which must be related to the first, since the overall outline is similar and the animal heads on the bows identical, but now we have a double-ended craft with much greater freeboard, a mast amidships, and a steering oar aft. The absence of lashings, the general shape and the presence of a large mast all suggest that the construction must now be of wood rather than reeds.

The animal head on the bow, presumably that of a goat, is an interesting link in time, both backwards – to the earlier reed craft – and forwards. Zwemer, writing in AD 1900, describes an important stage in the building of an Arab craft in Bahrain like this.[24] 'Each boat has a sort of figurehead called the "kubait", generally covered with the skin of a sheep or goat, which was sacrificed when the boat was first launched. This blood sacrifice Islam has never uprooted.' Figureheads have a long continuity of tradition in European ship-building, but not perhaps as strikingly specific as this instance of a goat's head being used in the same way for three and a half thousand years.

The presence of a mast, however puzzling its appearance, also suggests that sails were in use east of Suez by the second millennium BC. If the preceding argument about the similarity between the first seal and the eastern Egyptian ships be accepted, then perhaps this latter country is the more likely source for this new device. However, since there also seem to have been links eastward to the Harappan area, it is not impossible, though perhaps less likely, that a sail evolved in the southeast Asian area could have been the operative influence.

The third seal (Figure 13.9) continues the story. The hull is still much the same, with plenty of freeboard, high double-ended bow and stern, and a mast amidships, but the animal head and the tails after have been replaced by two birds, and the

13.8  *A second seal from 'Dilmun' (Michael Rice)*

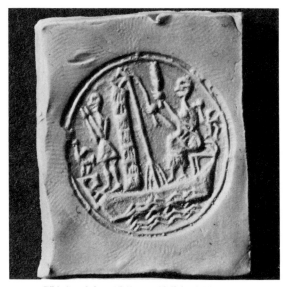

13.9  *Third seal from 'Dilmun' (Michael Rice)*

aftermost figure is seated and holds a line running up to the mast-head. But the extraordinary thing about this seal is the close resemblance the craft on it bears to the well-known picture in a manuscript now in the Bibliothèque Nationale by the scribe of a man of Wasit in Mesopotamia in AD 1237, the *Maqamat (Assemblies)* of al-Hariri (Figure 13.10). It is almost as if the seal-artist had made a copy, indifferent perhaps but still a copy. Of course there are additional details in the medieval craft: two masts, the extra deck with the arched ports, and no animals or birds on the extremities, but the overall shape and the man sitting aft holding the line are very close. Another less important but still interesting point is the oculi at each end of the later craft, a feature shared by the splendid ninth

century AD carved ship of Borobodur in Java (Figure 15.14), and the modern *mtepe* of Lamu in Kenya. These last also, incidentally, sometimes have a bird on the decorated trail-board of the bows, just in front of the oculus, though it has been argued that this is a fairly recent innovation.[25] Are these double oculi in some way the lineal descendants of the two birds on the extremities of the earlier boat? If they were, it would imply that the oculi aft should be looking forward like the bird, an amusing possibility not hitherto very generally canvassed.

LeBaron Bowen asserts firmly that the modern Arabian Gulf *bhum* is a lineal descendant of the medieval craft. 'The lines of this ship [the al-Hariri one] show that it is the prototype of the modern

13.10 *Illustrations from a Mesopotamian manuscript, al-Hariri's* Maqamat *(MS. Arabe 5847 fo. 119v), dated to AD 1237 (Bibliothèque nationale, Paris)*

*bhum* and show that the sewn boat of South Arabia is closely related to it.'[26] This seems a reasonable claim since the lines of the *bhum* are indeed similar, except that the modern craft have a greater forward rake of the stem.

So these three seals link up with modern and medieval craft to give us an apparently coherent succession of types from the early reed craft to contemporary dhows. Another very interesting thing about this line of development is that in many ways it matches that of the Mediterranean, the primitive craft elaborated with the appearance of metal tools into the double-ended masted merchantmen. Yet the eastern craft have a recognisably different style all the way through, a style that is still reflected in some of the contemporary craft from that area. The later two seals also go some way towards answering the question put earlier as to what craft carried on the trade between Mesopotamia, Bahrain and the Harappan civilisation.

## Sewn boats

But there are still a number of interesting problems to be settled, even if we know the outward shape of these craft. One point that does seem virtually certain is that they were sewn-planked. Historical accounts of this practice, which survived until recently in these waters, have been summarised by Hornell.[27] The *Periplus* of the Erythraean Sea of the first century AD mentions it, as well as vessels called *madarata* being built at Ommana on the south coast of the Arabian Gulf. As Hornell points out, this seems to be related to the Arabic word '*maddarr'at*', meaning 'fastened with palm fibre'. Then early in the tenth century AD, Abu Sayd reports that sewn-plank ships are a speciality of the shipwrights of Siraf, as opposed to the nailed vessels of the Mediterranean, and that the holes for the stitches were filled by oil mixed with various materials.

Shortly after this, accounts by European travellers to the East begin to appear, with duly patronising comment on the method of fastening ships' timbers. Marco Polo described the local craft as wretched affairs of which many were lost

because they had no iron fastenings and were stitched together only with twine made from the husk of the Indian nut. Then Friar Odoric, who died in AD 1331, sailed to Bombay from Ormuz in a 'bark compact together only with hempe', and the same technique was noted by Vasco da Gama, Ralph Fitch, John Eldred and many others in succeeding centuries.

A number of primitive craft continue, or did until recently, to use this method, notably the *mtepe* and the *mtepe-dau* of the Lamu archipelago on the East African coast.[28] Alan Villiers reported seeing sewn fishing boats on the Hadramaut coast of South Arabia just before the Second World War,[29] and further east, perhaps the most famous example are the *masula* surf boats (Figure 13.11) of India's east coast. Thomas Bowrey, who was a pepper trader in India from 1669 to 1679, has left a good description of these:[30]

> The boats they [of the Coromandel coast] doe lade and unlade ships or vessels with are built very sleight, haveinge no timbers in them, save the thafts [thwarts] to hold their sides together. Their planks are very broad and thinne, sowed together with cayre [coir], being flatt bottomed and every way much deformed . . . They are so sleightly built for convenciences sake, and realy are most proper for this Coast.

No iron at all is used in their construction, and Bowrey's drawing (Figure 13.12) does not quite get right the stapling effect of the stitches on the

13.11   *A masula (sewn boat) from the east coast of India (E. V. Wright)*

13.12    *Thomas Bowrey's late seventeenth century drawing of a* masula *boat (after Hill,* MM, *vol. 44, 1958, p. 207)*

outside, which recalls yet again the carvings at Sanchi, which include a craft of the second century BC fastened in precisely this way.[31] But perhaps more significant is the parallel observed by E. V. Wright between the construction techniques of the sewn *mahadalpuras* of Ceylon (Figure 13.13) and the Ferriby boats.[32] Evidently sewn planks with moss caulking held in place by oversewn battens is a characteristic technique of early metal technologies.

An interesting sidelight on the use of sewn planks in these eastern waters is the widespread myth, first recorded by the ancient Sanskrit author Bhoja, that iron nails would be drawn out of any ship that passed near a certain magnetic mountain, or, as the Portuguese who reached Calicut in AD 1500 put it, 'some of these vessels are built without any nails or iron for they have to pass over

the lodestone',[33] a case of a myth being provided to justify a conservationist technology. What finally imposed iron fastenings on the Arabs was the impossibility of mounting heavy guns on a sewn craft. For all their speed and seaworthiness, these craft were unable to dispute the mastery of the sea with the Portuguese, and so they had to adopt the practices of their victors. Hence the attractive decorated square sterns of some modern Arab dhows, which derive directly from the sixteenth-century iron-fastened European ships that had so forcefully advocated their technology. T. M. Johnstone and J. Muir have made the point that when a technique is borrowed from a people speaking a different language, the foreign term is usually taken over with the object or method adopted, since no other suitable word is available. So in Arabic today, '*kawiya*' expresses its debt to the Portuguese term for iron clenches, '*cavilha*', and '*kashtil*' describe the '*castelo*' that this fitting made possible to add to a vessel fore and aft.[34]

## Boat-building techniques

Reverting to the Harappan period, the fact that craft had almost certainly sewn planks leads on to three related problems. First, did any ancient shipbuilder in the Indian Ocean and Arabian Gulf follow Egyptian practice and use tenons and dowels to keep planks in place? Second, were

13.13    *Sewing on the inside of a* mahadalpura *boat from Ceylon (E. V. Wright)*

inserted frames used? And third, were the craft flat-bottomed or built up on a dug-out base as a keel? R. LeBaron Bowen believes that they did use edge-joining.[35] He has recorded that certain primitive boats of South Arabia have obliquely driven trenails made of bamboo for holding the plank edges in line, and that he thinks this practice, which was of ancient Egyptian origin, reached Arabia from India. Certainly some contemporary craft from the Indus also have their planking secured edge-to-edge with wooden pins,[36] and there is indirect evidence from the Harappan period that their chariot wheels may have been fastened in the same way. In his report on the excavations at Chanhu-Daro, E. J. H. Mackay describes the finding of a pottery model of a chariot wheel painted on both sides to indicate a three-piece wooden construction.[37] Since there was no sign of a transverse bar, presumably these wheels would be made with tenons and dowels. Mackay also says of the same site that metal-working was a craft which was widely practised there, so again there seems no reason to doubt their capacity to make this type of wheel.[38]

On the other hand, LeBaron Bowen feels that inserted frames were not introduced into the Indian Ocean until Classical times, when the Romans became involved in the Indian trade.[39] A matter of feeling this has to remain, because there

is little evidence either way. According to Basil Greenhill, edge-joining with inserted frames is almost universal in the river and sea boats of East Pakistan, and the same goes for many of the Indus river boats.[40] So the practice is liable to be ancient, but how ancient is another matter. Some of the Sanchi craft, the vessels on coins from Andra, India (Figure 13.14) and the two later Bahrain seal craft all have the crisp shape one associates with internal framing, as compared with the sloppier outline, for example, of the *masula* surf boats. On the other hand Hourani says there is no mention in any of the literary sources of any ribs or framework.[41] So again this is a matter that has to be left undecided.

## Development of planked boats

The final problem of construction is similar to the Mediterranean one. When the transition to a built-up planked craft took place, was it from a flat-bottomed type, like third millennium BC Egyptian craft, the *saveiro*, the Ferriby boats and *mahadalpuras* (Figure 13.13), or was it from a dug-out base? Modern Arabian practice would certainly favour the latter. When a modern dhow is built, the keel is laid first, and then the stem and stern pieces are set up. Next the garboard strakes are fitted into grooves which have been cut in the top of the keel and the sides of the stem and stern post, and these are followed by four more strakes a side, each being temporarily attached to its neighbour by staples. Templates are then attached outside the hull to hold the remaining strakes in position. Only then is a keelson laid down to clamp the inner edge of the garboard strakes more firmly and this is followed by the frames, consisting alternately of floor timbers scarfed to futtocks, and futtocks ending on the keelson without a floor. This clearly is an elaboration of a primitive technique of building up a dug-out canoe with sewn planks, with the advance of adding a keelson to strengthen the point of weakness at the edge of the garboard strake.[42]

On the other hand, F. E. Paris reported in 1841 the existence of an Arabian craft called a *beden-seyed* (Figure 13.15). This was 10 metres long, had

13.14 *Reconstruction drawing of a ship shown on a second century AD coin from Andra, India (after LeBaron Bowen,* American Neptune, *vol. 13, 1953, p. 202)*

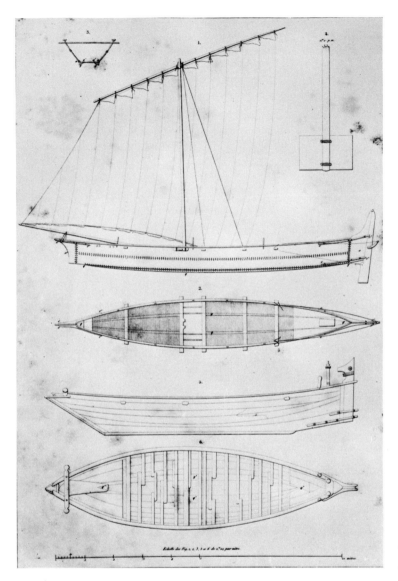

13.15 *Nineteenth-century Arabian* beden-seyed *(National Maritime Museum)*

no ribs, and a flat bottom consisting of a single plank from which the sides, made of two planks, rose at an angle of 45 degrees.[43] At much the same date, Haines reported that sewn boats used by the fishermen of Qishu had almost a flat floor and passed through the surf easily.[44] Then Bowen has said that sewn craft, i.e. the most primitive, are the only Arab craft to his knowledge to have a chine line.[45]

This is where the building material of these craft becomes relevant and starts to make some sort of sense of the situation. Local wood suitable for ship-building is virtually non-existent in Mesopotamia and the Arabian Gulf. Hence the dependence on reed craft or inflated skin rafts. The traditional remedy for this has been the import of teak from the Indian sub-continent. The tenth century AD Arab writers al-Masudi and Ibn Jubayr both say plainly that Indian Ocean ships were built of teak. Theophrastus, about 300 BC, describes the wood used to build ships in Bahrain, and says it lasts more than 200 years if kept under water. So this was almost certainly teak too.[46]

Earlier still, Ur-Nanshe, who founded a dynasty in Lagash about 2450 BC, recorded that the ships of Dilmun brought him wood as a tribute, and three centuries later the same practice was noted there by Gudea.[47] Then among the texts excavated by Sir Leonard Woolley at Ur was one on a tablet with this line (in Professor Kramer's translation): 'May the land Meluhha [bring] you tempting [?] previous cornelian, mes-shagan wood, fine sea-wood, sailors.'[48] No wonder Hourani could say that all timber for hulls built anywhere east or south of Suez nearly always came from India and its islands, the only exceptions being the fleets of Sennacherib and Alexander, who used their exceptional circumstances to bring timber from Upper Lebanon.[49]

The timber trade between the Indian sub-continent and the Arabian Gulf therefore seems to have been well established for some thousands of years. But a problem arises if one projects backward in time the situation to the period when, as the seals seem to show, the Arabian Gulf ship-builders were first turning their reed construction into strakes. How did they get the wood for this? Was there a supply then that no longer exists, from fossil sources in the desert, or better climatic conditions? There is certainly evidence for this from the little-explored archaeological sites in Saudi Arabia, where much of the surviving evidence suggests a wetter climate in the past.[50] Or did the reed craft travel far enough east to meet the wooden craft of the Harappans coming west at some intermediate place where cargoes of wood could be exchanged, just as the planked ships of the Mediterranean met the skin boats of the British at the Oestrymnides? It is an intriguing question, and aspects of it recur in later periods. The *huri* is a teak dug-out from the Indian sub-continent which was widely imported into Arabia, where the fishermen added washstrakes and stem- and stern-pieces, to make a five-piece canoe out of it.[51]

The catamaran too seems to have been impor-ted from Indian waters. So primitive types of craft seemingly could make the journey. But that does not mean they necessarily did so at an early period. It would seem therefore a hypothesis at least worth considering that when a certain amount of timber from the Harappan area became available, the reed-boat-builders of the Arabian Gulf translated their traditional craft into planked versions, retaining the old flat-bottomed shape and using the strakes as economically as possible. The *beden-sayed* could be a survival of this approach. Then when trade became more prolific, timber more easily imported and Harappan craft more in evidence, the changeover to using a whole tree as a dug-out base may have happened particularly in view of its additional strength when the stresses of mast and sail had to be faced. Going by the two later seals, with the firm strong line along the bottom of the hull, this could have happened by the second millennium BC.

To sum up then, early Harappan and Arabian Gulf craft seem to have been reed-bundle types. With the appearance of metal tools, some of these would have been converted into sewn planked craft. Some of the Harappan examples would have had dug-out keel bases and their planking may have been edge joined with dowels and tenons. The Arabian Gulf craft, on the other hand, were most likely flat-bottomed at first, and only through Harappan influence and timber did they convert in some cases to the dug-out keel principle to give the added strength needed by mast and sail. Possibly none of these types had inserted frames until a fairly late period, though there is no evidence at the moment as to when this additional hull strengthening may have happened.

But while the craft that linked these two great ancient civilisations are of dominating interest, one has to remember the danger of over-simplification. If climatic conditions had worsened, there could have been an evolution from local dug-outs to reed craft as the timber supply decreased, anticipating in reverse the change that seems to have happened later.

Then there were at least two other important elements present. One was the raft. It has even been suggested that the sailing rafts shown in the

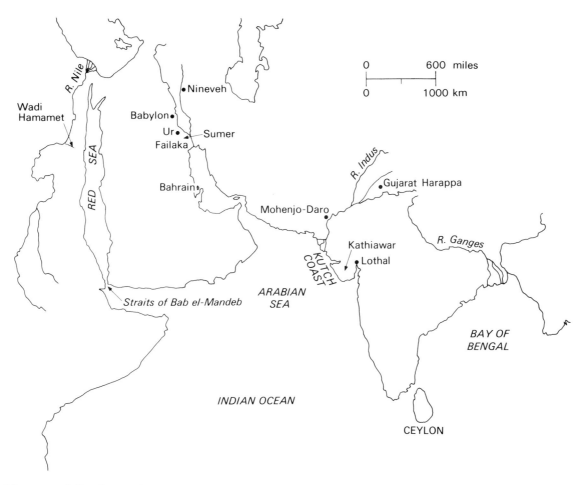

Map 13.1 *Indian Ocean and Arabian Gulf*

tomb of Amenophis II (*c.* 1500 BC) carrying goods from Punt in the Red Sea (Figure 13.16) represent an extension westward of the great Pacific sailing raft tradition,[52] about which a good deal will be said in later chapters. Since the Punt rafts appear to be steered by steering oars rather than centreboards, this is perhaps doubtful. From their shape it would seem more likely that these craft of

13.16 *Drawing of the sailing rafts shown on the tomb of Amenophis II carrying goods from Punt to Egypt (after T. Säve-Söderbergh,* The Navy of the Eighteenth Dynasty, *Uppsala, 1946, p. 24)*

13.17  *Bowrey's late seventeenth century drawing of an Indian 'cattamaran' raft (Hill,* MM, *vol. 44, 1958, p. 209)*

the inhabitants of Punt were related to the inflated skin rafts Herodotus mentions. Nevertheless it is interesting as showing both the sail in use on rafts and also the existence of yet another type of craft in the area. In the warm waters of the Indian Ocean, particularly on the eastern coast of the sub-continent, the continued and useful existence of the many forms of raft to this day recalls a situation that was probably much the same thousands of years ago. As Bowrey said of his 'cattamaran' (Figure 13.17), 'they will boldly venture out of sight of the shore, but indeed they Swimme (in generall) as naturaly as Spanyall dogs.'[53]

Finally, boldly venturing also out of sight of the shore came quite another type of craft, this time from the East, with all the confident originality of one of the other great traditions of early ship-building.

# 14 China and Japan

## CHINA

The ships came 'sailing like mountains with the wings of the winds on the surface of the water'. So the Arab writer Wassaf described his impression of the great Chinese junks he saw in the early fourteenth century.[1] Marco Polo, too, described the ships he saw in Indian waters, double-planked, caulked with oakum within and without, fastened with iron nails and their bottoms smeared with a mixture of quicklime, hemp and oil. They had, he declared, a crew of 300, small boats slung from the side, sixty small cabins below decks, one for each merchant, four masts, four sails, thirteen bulk-heads, and where the hull had been repaired, up to thirteen layers of wood sheathing.[2] Both these quotations come from a period shortly before Chinese maritime affairs reached their peak, when a great Chinese fleet of vessels larger and more advanced than any in Europe, under the direction of Chang Ho, eunuch, ambassador, admiral and explorer, was to range from Zanzibar to Kamchatka in what Needham calls 'the well-disciplined operation of an enormous feudal bureaucratic state'.[3]

Eight centuries before this, the well-known painting of a junk at Ajanta (Figure 14.1), so like a modern Pechili trading junk, shows that already some elements of the Chinese style of ship had impressed itself on watchers in the Indian sub-continent.[4] Then the *chhien Han Shu* has a passage describing Han trade with the South Seas, where the longest voyage took over twelve months, which

has led some scholars to suggest that Chinese ships were already reaching the western limits of the Indian ocean in the first century BC.[5] If the place name 'Huang-Chih' is interpreted as Massawa rather than Conjeeveram in Madras, then the Chinese sailors were reaching even the Red Sea at this time.[6] Thus it is clear that the unique school of Chinese ship-building has had a long, widespread and influential expression.

14.1   *Wall painting of eighth century AD junk in the caves at Ajanta, Hyderabad, India, in the Victoria and Albert Museum, London (after G. A. Horridge,* The Design of Planked Boats of the Moluccas, *National Maritime Museum, monograph no. 38, Greenwich, 1979)*

## Reed and skin

Originally the ship-building potential of the
Chinese geographical area was probably not very
different from the other parts of the world where
civilisation developed. According to Nishimura,
the ancient Chinese sometimes called a boat '*i-
wei*', 'a reed', and he quoted a line of an old poem:
'We crossed the stream on a reed.'[7] There is also a
word for bulrush raft, *pu-fa* or *phu-fa*, so it seems
reasonable to assume that there was some use of
reed-bundle craft in early China.[8] Then the upper
reaches of the Yangtze, Yalung and the Mekong
Rivers have seen coracles until recent times, and as
far back as the Warring States period (*c.* 300 to 400
BC), a boat one man could carry, presumably a
coracle, was described.[9] Rafts of inflated skins used
to bring cargoes of water-melons down the Yellow
River, were broken up at the end of their voyage
downstream on the Huang-Ho, and the lot sold, as
well as the cargo. In Sung and Ming periods, single
inflated goatskins (Figure 4.5) were used by
travellers to cross the same river.[10]

On the other hand, there was no shortage of
suitable timber, and the coastline was south of the
crucial 45°–50° parallel north of which the skin
boats' advantages in the open sea might have
applied; so, as one would expect, the *pi-chuans* –
skin boats, with their bamboo framework, which
are said to have been used by Chu-ko Liang for
scouting purposes in rivers with shallow rapids –
seem to have been less prominent in prehistoric
China than the dug-out and the raft.[11]

## Rafts and dug-outs

Archaeological thought in the Far East is currently
being revised, and a picture of the early stages of
the agricultural revolution there has emerged
which is becoming ever more detailed. According
to pollen profiles from Formosa, Manchuria and
Siberia, a warmer climatic period set in from
12,000 to 10,000 BC which was marked by higher
temperatures, thicker vegetation and rising sea-
levels.[12] The culture that seems to be related to this
changing ecological context from about 8000 BC
on is the late Hoabinhian. The subsistence basis of

this was evidently shellfish-gathering, fishing,
small-game hunting, plant-gathering and a certain amount of cultivation. Ground, or edge-
ground, stone tools were in use, as well as cord-
marked pottery. According to Kwang-chih
Chang, most inhabitants of tropical and sub-
tropical south-east Asia lived on estuaries or the
low terraces near by and depended mainly on
fishing.[13] They had a settled stable life which
enabled them to progress gradually from using the
abundant plant resources round them to deliberate control and cultivation of these. In fact he
suggests that among the first domesticated plants
were those that were used to provide containers
(bamboo trunks and bottle gourds) or cordage for
use in fishing.

The maritime emphasis here is clear. The settled
conditions and ground stone tools would have
made the use of dug-outs feasible, as well as the
raft. The dependence on fish and shellfish for food
and the siting of settlements near water would
have encouraged their use. Chang also suggests
that the small bamboo (*Phyllostachy* spp.) was
probably first cultivated in southern China and
the great bamboo (*Dandrocalamus asper*) in south-
east Asia and the islands.[14] The maritime significance of these particular plants will become
apparent in a moment. Then his inclusion of the
bottle gourd (*Lagenaris vulgaris*) among the early
cultivated plants of this area, since it figures
prominently in creation myths throughout south-
east Asia, is a warning against over-simplification.[15] The gourd raft is widespread in the
old world from Africa to Japan,[16] as well as in
possibly pre-Columbian contexts in Mexico,[17] so is
at least one possible variation on the dug-outs and
log rafts so far suggested.

In the crucial north China area, where, during
the succeeding Yang-Shao and Lung-Shan cultures the closely-knit agricultural villages grew up
round the rivers which cut through the rich loess
soil, it would be reasonable to expect that the
villagers had also already forms of water-borne
transport to suit their particular needs. Besides
remains of livestock and game, fish-bones and
molluscs have been found in excavations of sites
like Ch'eng-Tzu-Yai in Shantung, where an earth

wall 9 metres wide and 6 metres high encircled a large village site 450 by 390 metres. Here there was evidently what Robert Suggs calls a well-developed river-going technology with boats, nets and fishing tackle.[18]

Worcester (an authority on junks) and Needham have argued that both the sampan and junk developed from the raft and that one consequence of this is that there are no dug-outs in contemporary China.[19] However, there is a certain amount of recent archaeological evidence which contradicts this exclusion of the dug-out. A pollen profile from a core taken in 1969 from the bottom of a lake in the centre of Formosa shows that about 12,000 years ago there was a gradual but decisive growth of secondary forests near the edge of the lake and a steady accumulation at the lake bottom of the charred fragments of trees. These are interpreted by Matsua Takada, who took the core, as signs of human activity that persistently disturbed the primary vegetation of the area. According to Chang, if this is correct, the human groups responsible must be those represented by the cord-marked pottery culture, whose cultivating may have been responsible for the de-

forestation.[20] It is also reported by Worcester that, until recently, the aboriginal tribes who occupied the shores of this Formosan lake used a crude form of dug-out for shrimp fishing, with squared-off slightly overhanging bow and stern.[21] The head-hunting reputation of these tribes had kept them isolated until very recent times. The possibilities remain therefore that the cord-marked-pottery-users who lived near this Lake of the Sun and Moon some 12,000 years ago built similar dug-outs, thereby producing some of the recently recovered charred wood at the bottom of the lake.

In succeeding periods, one is on a good deal surer ground. In northern Szechwan, in the later Bronze Age period, a number of burials have been found where the bodies were in coffins which had been put inside dug-outs (Figure 14.2). The significant thing about these craft, which were some 5 metres long by 1 metre wide, is that they are square ended, and that the bow and stern (which have been left solid) have considerable overhang.[22] In fact they are highly reminiscent of the familiar punts of the Cam and Isis. They are in fact intermediate between a Formosan-type dug-out and the sampan.

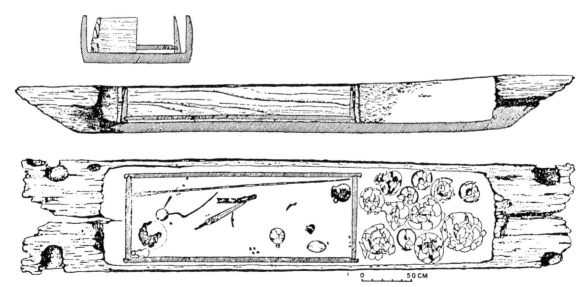

14.2 *A boat coffin from Pao-lun-yüan, Chao-hua Hsien, northern Szechwan, China (after Needham, Clerks and Craftsmen in China and the West, 1970)*

## The sampan

Next there is the existence in the second millennium BC on the famous Shang oracle bones of a pictograph for boat (*chou*), which looks like a small curved ladder, in other words a shape reminiscent of the sampan with its broad beam, flat bottom and open horned stern (Figure 14.3). In Needham's view, no other Shang pictograph enshrines so completely such a fundamentally distinctive characteristic of a great branch of Chinese technology. He also points out that the bamboo, the plant so familiar to every Chinese from a thousand uses, has, when sliced lengthways, transverse septs or partitions. This, he suggests, may have been the model for the sampan, with its blunt wedge shape, flat bottom and transverse partitions at each end.[23]

14.3   *Pictogram for* chou *(boat) on oracle bones from the Shang dynasty (1766–1122 BC) (Worcester,* Sail and Sweep in China, *Science Museum, London, 1966)*

14.4   *Model of a typical modern sampan (National Maritime Museum)*

The word 'sampan' ('three-plank') may reflect the simplest form of evolution from a plain dug-out. Or there may very well have been a process whereby a dug-out had even longer overhanging bow and stern until somebody cut a piece out, leaving the two horns. Certainly by the Bronze Age the tools and the technology were available to make planks and, if one needed confirmation, there is another Shang pictograph which refers to caulking the seams of boats. According to Worcester, the earliest actual representation of a sampan is in some stone carvings of the Han dynasty (AD 25–221).[24] These craft are decidedly similar in outline, with their two-man crew, to the Formosan dug-out, but by the time one reaches the craft carved in a tomb in Shantung about AD 147, it is definitely a sampan, not a dug-out, with the separate strakes shown, and much longer overhangs at bow and stern. This progression, marked by squared extremities, from the simple dug-out of the early agricultural period to the sampan of early historical times, is hypothetical, but the significance of the shape of the Szechwan dug-out and its relation to the Shang pictograph is undeniable, and considerably more informative than the legendary observation of the Emperor Huang Ti of *c.* 2967 BC that 'boats were made by hollowing out logs'.[25]

## The junk

As far as the junk is concerned there is more unanimity. Needham, Hornell and Worcester all agree that its origin lies in the raft.[26] As well as the river rafts common from Mesopotamia to China, sea-going versions still exist in considerable numbers, or did until recently, on the east coast of India and off the Chinese, Vietnam and Formosan shores. Hornell described in detail the construction of the well-known version from Formosa (Figure 14.5).

The raft platform is composed of many lengths of long bamboos of the greatest girth obtainable, and these are so bound together and secured by curved poles lashed athwart at intervals that the whole structure has a considerable sheer at each end. As bamboos taper gradually towards the

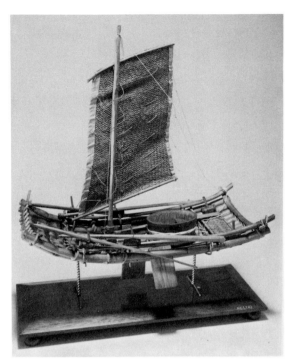

14.5  *Model of a Formosan raft or* tek-pai *(National Maritime Museum)*

upper end, the builders of Formosan rafts, by lashing them side by side with the upper ends directed towards the same point, are able to give a decided taper to the structure; the fore end, though wide, being distinctly narrower than the stern. Head and stern are truncate, the bamboos cut off flush, except that it is usual for the outermost one on each side to project, curving a considerable distance beyond the stern.

To see in the design of this sailing raft the rudiments of that on which the junk is constructed entails little strain upon the imagination. Substitute planks for bamboos, curve in the sides to form a half-cylinder or peg on side-strakes as in some Madras catamarans, close the open ends with transverse planking, add a deck, and the characteristics of a junk's hull are obtained.[27] These are: a flat or slightly rounded bottom without keel, stem, or sternpost; a transom stem and stern; no ribs or internal frames, but solid transverse bulkheads.[28]

Various other features of the traditional junk support this origin in the sailing raft. One of the most primitive of contemporary types is the Shantung trading junk. This has a flat bottom and very low deck, which is awash amidships when the craft is loaded. Only the hatch coamings stop the holds being flooded, and the resultant silhouette is quite close to a raft with a tub or case amidships. The great strength of the timbers of the hull also contribute to the impression of a raft, particularly as each plank is practically a squared-off tree running from stem to stern.[29]

## Plank fastenings

An unanswered question is when the strakes of sampans and junks became metal fastened. Presumably, like most craft in Neolithic conditions, the strakes were attached at first by lashing or sewing. Much later, in the Wu Ching Tsung Yao (Collection of the Most Important Military Techniques) of the middle of the eleventh century AD, there is a description of a type of a ship called a sea-falcon, or sea-hawk (*hai-ku*), which has planks attached each side. In possibly dubious sixteenth- or eighteenth-century drawings of this craft, these attachments are shown as lashings.[30] However, one suspects that the great metal nails, reminiscent of those of the Veneti, which were noticed by the Arab traveller Ibn Battutah and by Marco Polo in junks, go back a considerable way.[31] What may be the first mention of iron occurs in about 776 BC in a reference to a team of four 'iron-grey' horses.[32] By the beginning of the fifth century swordsmiths are recorded as using iron, and by the third century BC it was said that every cartwright needs his axe, saw, awl and chisel.[33] Presumably the same thing applied to the shipwright, and the list matches rather neatly Worcester's modern description of the junk-builder pinning and spiking strakes with double-ended nails, and leaving plenty of gaps for the caulker to fill.[34]

There is also an interesting passage in the dictionary of Huei-lin of perhaps the eighth century AD which quotes a third century AD description by Chang I of ocean-going ships called *po*. Christie infers from this and other passages that these ships were large non-Chinese sailing merchantmen crewed by south-east Asian peoples and engaged in the trade between East and West.[35] Huei-lin gives some details of these *po*, including the comment: 'they build the boats by binding together planks of wood, for the thin planks are likely to break. They use cords made from coconut fibre for lashings and they caulk them with the resin of canarium to make them watertight.'[36] The close way this fits descriptions of Arabian Gulf and Indian craft, as quoted in the last chapter, needs little underlining. But then there is the curious comment about the binding being used because the thin planks are likely to break. Christie suggests that the writer was most unlikely to have seen *po* under construction and therefore misunderstood the technique of sewing strakes and added a quite erroneous explanation for it.[37] In that case, one might assume that the conventional Chinese method by the eighth century AD, when Huei-lin wrote, or possibly even the third century AD of Chang I's *po*, was metal fastening. However, it is possible that the dictionary-writer knew nothing at all about ship construction, either Chinese or foreign, so perhaps not much weight should be given to this assumption, and any date for a change from sewing to metal fastening left open, as the two methods must have overlapped for many centuries.

## Masts

Setting aside then the question of how the strakes were joined, various other features of the traditional junk support its origin in the sailing raft, in particular the placing of the masts and rudders. Both the staggering of the masts athwartships, in order to avoid the blanketing of one sail by another (instead of having them all on a central fore-and-aft line) and raking them like the spines of a fan are characteristics unique to the Chinese.[38] In accounts by French ethnographers of Vietnamese sailing rafts, a cross-piece is mentioned with several holes, by means of which the masts can be shifted from one position to the other, a characteristic shared also by the 'flying fish catamaran' of the Coromandel coast and the *jangada* sailing raft

of Brazil, which between them pretty well encompass the distribution area of the sailing raft[39] (see also chapter 2). It is not difficult to see how a flat bottom of fore-and-aft logs or planks would encourage this moving of the mast-foot, just as a keel would limit its position to the central line, and presumably anyone evolving a junk from a raft would seek to retain the advantage of non-blanketing mast positions.

## Leeboards and rudders

In the same way, this structure must have encouraged the use of leeboards, thin planks thrust down through the gaps in the bottom to reduce sideways drift. The technique of steering by lowering some leeboards and raising others was still in use in the eighteenth century in the sailing rafts of the west coast of South America and was well described by the Spanish naval officers Juan and Ullos. Needham claims the invention of leeboards in China antedates anywhere else in the world.[40] On a more general basis Ling-shun Sheng concludes that sailing rafts were in use in China in the fifth century BC and that legendary materials exist which could imply that they existed as early as the thirty-third century BC.[41] So this means of both steering a raft and reducing its leeway, which is still practised in various differing combinations off the Coromandel coast, Vietnam, Formosa and Brazil, clearly has considerable antiquity.

From this practice there seems to have evolved, shortly before the first century BC, a logical development, the vertical axial rudder. It must have occurred to someone that in addition to steering by thrusting a leeboard down between the bottom boards you could gain additional control by rotating the board on its axis one way or the other. This suggestion is supported both by the characteristic position of the Chinese rudder, hung vertically without a stern post, either in a trunk through the hull, or in the after compartment or gallery, surely a direct derivation from the placing of a vertical leeboard in a sailing raft, and by a quotation from AD 1124 in which Hsu Ching describes a voyage to Korea.[42] 'At the stern, there is the rudder (cheng tho), of which there are two kinds, the larger and the smaller ... Abaft the deck-house, two oars are stuck down into the water from above, and these are called "Third-Assistant rudders" (sen fu tho).' Again this points to a derivation of the vertical rudder from the lee-board.

Needham has summarised the literary evidence about the appearance of the rudder.[43] In a late fifth century AD book there is a statement that a certain river is called the 'Downcoming rudder stream', which suggests there was already a difference between steering oar and rudder. By about AD 940, there is virtually certain evidence in a book by Than Chhiao. 'The control of a ship carrying ten thousand bushels of freight is assured by means of a piece of wood no longer than one fathom.' This must imply a rudder, since a steering oar or sweep would be much longer. In any case the archaeological evidence antedates these quotations by several centuries. In 1957 the excavations by the Kuangtung Provincial Museum and the Academia Sinica of some tombs in Canton of the Hou Han period, first and second centuries AD, produced a series of pottery ship models, which certainly so far embody the earliest example of a vertical rudder. One of these models, now in the Canton Museum, has a grapnel anchor at the bow, a series of deckhouses surrounded by a poling gallery, but most important of all, from the criss-cross of timbers in the after gallery hangs the trapeziform rudder, with a hole in the shoulder for the suspending tackle. So the first illustration of a Chinese rudder, median, vertical and axial, without stern post eyes or pintles but held by tackles, antedates by about a millennium the carvings in the West of ships with rudders on the fonts of Zedelghem and Winchester.

Whether the Chinese practice was responsible in any way for the European development is an open question. The al-Hariri ship of AD 1237, already discussed in chapter 13, has an axial rudder (Figure 13.10), but of course, contrary to Chinese practice, it is attached to the stern post, reflecting perhaps an adaption of the Chinese idea to Arab craft. Earlier, in AD 985, al-Muqaddasi, describing a difficult voyage in the Red Sea, speaks of lanyards or ropes operated by the helmsman.[44]

This certainly sounds rather more like a reference to tackle-controlled rudders than anything to do with steering oars. On the other hand it has been pointed out that another version of the *Maqamat* of al-Hariri, now in the National Library of Vienna and dated about a century later, shows the same ship but with an unmistakable steering oar, so it is possible that the artist of the earlier version may have been using knowledge of Chinese practice, and that John of Montecorvino's description of 'a frail and flimsy rudder' may not necessarily confirm an early Arab use of the hinged rudder.[45] Therefore it is still an open question whether some innovating Crusader transport captain took the idea from the East to the West.

Two further refinements to the axial rudder were made by the Chinese. That on the Han model already appears to be balanced. This technique for easing the work of the quartermaster was also practised by the Norsemen, and, earlier still, it could be argued that the high-fastened sloping steering oars of Blussus and from Cortaillod on Lake Neuchâtel (described in chapter 12) with their vertical tillers, as well as those of the ancient Egyptians, could possibly be turned axially with a balanced effect, rather than angled, even if Needham doubts the efficiency of this technique.[46] Nevertheless in the West the idea then went out of use until the period when Brunel boldly adapted it for his revolutionary ship, the *Great Britain*.

The other refinement was the fenestration of rudders. This eased the helmsman's work, reduced turbulence, yet left the efficiency of the rudder unimpaired.[47]

## Sail

For the origin of the special nature of the Chinese sail, with its battens and multiple sheets, we must, according to Poujade, turn again to the bamboo. 'The lattice sail is a product of the brilliant technology of the Chinese. It arose out of the logical development of surfaces made out of a local material (matting) fixed to another native material (bamboo), and its lightness, flexibility and resistance made it so useful on board a boat.'[48] While mat and batten sails with their multiple sheeting certainly meant that the Chinese had the aerodynamically best equipment for working to windward from the Han period onwards, it seems likely that the sail itself came to them from Indonesia. R. LeBaron Bowen, Jr has postulated that the sail evolved independently in Indonesia and Egypt, and that in the former it was a squaresail slung between two masts.[49] If this is correct the Chinese probably acquired their sails from Indonesia. The evidence again is a Shang pictograph of the second millennium BC for sail (*fan*),[50] which shows a trapezoidal almost square sail of matting or cloth set between two upright spars, suggesting that the acquisition took place before the two spars had converged to make the triangle of the familiar Pacific spritsail.

## *Yuloh* and paddlewheel

But if the Chinese did not invent the sail and only stamped their particular genius on its later shape, there were other devices they were completely responsible for. There was the *yuloh*, the self-feathering sculling oar, a most ingenious labour-saving device, whose invention Needham says is not later than the first century BC; copper sheathing of the hull long before its use in Europe; and articulated vessels.[51] Even more intriguing perhaps is the paddlewheel. Centuries before Roberto Valtorio included a picture of manually-operated paddleboat in his *De Re Militari* of AD 1472, Prince Tshao is reported in the official history of the Thang dynasty as giving orders, somewhere between AD 782 and 785, that 'warships should be made carrying two wheels worked by a treadmill, which stirred the water and caused the boat to move as rapidly as the wind.'[52]

Again, in about AD 1130, there is a rather delightful description of revolutionary enterprise when the leader of a peasant rebellion, Yang Yao, 'launched ships in the lake that were moved by wheels which stirred the water. A ram was attached to their bows, so that vessels carrying government officers were destroyed when they met these ships.' Evidently there were occasions when the 'well-disciplined operation of a feudal bureaucratic state' was threatened by its own technological ingenuities.[53]

## The magnetic compass

Of course the most famous Chinese maritime contribution is the magnetic compass. It is as early as the first century BC that the Lucretius of China, Wang Chhung, says, 'when the south-controlling spoon is thrown upon the ground, it comes to rest pointing to the south'. This seems to refer to an awareness of the properties of a magnetic spoon on a pivoting board.[54] Then after AD 450 the references change from 'lodestones attracting iron' to 'lodestones attracting needles'. After various implicit references to an awareness of declination, in about AD 1080, more than a century before the first mention in Europe by Alexander Neckam, Shen Kua in his *Dream Pool Essays* says that 'magicians rub the point of a needle with the lodestone, after which it is able to point to the south. But it always inclines slightly to the east and does not point directly to the south.'[55] No wonder that by the thirteenth century it was commonplace to read of Chinese sea-travel that 'at times of storm or darkness the pilots of the merchant-ships travel trusting to the compass alone. They dare not make the slightest error, since the lives of all in the ship depend on it.'[56]

As Needham observes, it is ironic that the technological advances which took the Portuguese in the fifteenth and early sixteenth centuries from the shores of Iberia to the fringes of China should be the magnetic compass, the hinged sternpost rudder, and multiple masts. The Chinese had clear priority over the West in all three respects, to say nothing of watertight bulkheads and free-flooding compartments. Their junks of the same period were much larger and probably a good deal handier than the *Santa Maria*, and, as Poujade says, they had more ships and more seafaring experience than the rest of the world put together.[57]

## Development of sampan and junk

To sum up, it seems that the dug-out and the raft, two of man's earliest craft, provided the source of a

14.6 *Model of a Foochow junk (National Maritime Museum)*

converging development in China from the Neolithic period onwards which eventually produced the sampan and the junk. An interesting point Needham makes is the similarity in approach of Chinese architecture and Chinese shipbuilding.[58] Both depended on transverse partitions or frameworks. This permitted the classical curves

of roofs, and in ships the watertight bulkheads and bluff stern and bow. Within the basis of this fundamental approach, as Needham has suggested in his impressive studies of Chinese nautical achievements, innumerable variations eventually appeared, sometimes embodying Indian, Arab and European features, to provide the extraordinary variety of recent Chinese and southeast Asian craft.

## The dragon boat

An exception that was right outside this tradition was the 'dragon boat' (*lung chhuan*), which was used for ritual races during the Fifth Month Festival. This was a long narrow craft driven by thirty-six or more paddlers.[59] While this still did have rudimentary bulkheads, its chief member was a keel or keelson. In order to prevent the hogging such a long thin craft might suffer, a strong bamboo cable sometimes ran from bow to stern. This is comparable with the Egyptian hogging truss, or, perhaps, the *hupozomata* of the Greeks. It is possible that shipwrights, faced with a similar technological problem and armed with much the same resources, came up with parallel solutions.

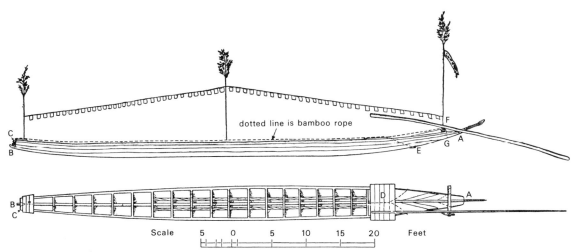

14.7 *Measured drawings of a typical Yangtze dragon boat. A, the dragon's tail; B, stump to carry dragon's head; C, wooden chock; D, platform; E, chock; F, transom. The bamboo rope or hogging truss passes from the bow (B) over chock (C) to the platform (D), where it divides: one portion being secured to the chock (E) while the main rope continued over the transom (F) to the counter at (G) (after Worcester, MM, vol. 42, 1956)*

Setting aside the occasional hogging truss, this type of craft (Figure 14.7) has parallels in Japan and more particularly in south-east Asia, nearly all with the great length, low freeboard, tumble-home amidships, long overhangs and detachable dragon or animal head which are their distinguishing features.[60] Whether these craft are part of a coherent and widespread culture associated also with long-houses will be more fully discussed in chapter 15. It is perhaps enough here to remark that they seem to be derived from the dug-out and represent at least one major tradition of boat-building in China that was entirely different from that of the junk.

## JAPAN

As with so many other aspects, early Japanese craft have basic similarities with the Chinese but with strong local variations superimposed. The finding in 1949 of worked stone tools at Iwajuka, Gumma, in a stratum believed to be lower than that containing the earliest pottery, set off the current pursuit of the Palaeolithic in Japan.[61] Since then, a considerable body of evidence has appeared in which parallels have been seen both with the stone industries from Choukoutien on the mainland and the Patjitanian of Java.[62] It is generally agreed that the makers of these tools reached the islands during Late Glacial times, along with the arctic hairy mammoth, at a period of low sea-levels. By the time the Jomon period started, however, the seas had risen. This culture lasted, as far as it is possible to tell from a spattering of radiocarbon dates, from about 4500 BC to about 250 BC.[63] It developed from a broadly Mesolithic stage into a pottery-producing and primitive agricultural one, which has been described as 'retarded Neolithic', until the metal- and rice-using Yayoi Culture gradually ousted it.[64] Besides cord-impressed pottery, its other dominating features are the mounds now partly or wholly buried, varying in size from a few square yards to 2 acres or more, which grew up close to its villages. These mounds contain a good deal of other refuse besides mussel

and oyster shells. Fish-bones, for instance, show that the vast majority of fish came from species which could be caught in the inlets near the mounds, especially at high tide.[65] But the occasional remains of deep-sea fish such as tunny, shark, stingray and even whale suggest more venturesome fishing, while a number of shells which come from depths of 10 to 40 metres confirm that it was not just strandings which supplied the deep-sea percentage. Fish-hooks and harpoons complement this picture. The former are rare in early Jomon mounds and the latter do not appear at all until the middle Jomon.[66] By the late period, however, harpoons have become long and multi-barbed, some having as many as five pairs of barbs.

### Dug-outs

Kidder links this more distant fishing with the appearance of polished axes.[67] The axes would have been used mainly for the extensive house-building of the time, but would also have made the production of dug-outs easier. As early as the first decade of this century Munro had noted two early examples of these which were kept in shrines, and many more, with both square and rounded ends, have been found in Neolithic contexts.[68] By the late 1950s, sixty whole or fragmentary dug-outs from early periods had been found. Kidder, like Matsuomotu, divides these into two types, one sleek with tapered bow and stern, not unlike those of the Ainu, the other with squarish ends and more vertical lines.[69]

### Rafts

That is fine as far as it goes, but it leaves one or two questions unanswered. If the dug-out developed with polished tools in the early to middle Jomon period, what happened before? Is it more likely that there was a blank period between the Palaeolithic tool-makers and the early Jomon shell-gatherers, due to violent volcanic activity, or was there some sort of continuity? If not, how did the shell-gatherers get there? It seems likely anyway, from the nature of their sites, that they frequently changed them, and the densely wooded terrain then suggests that these migratory movements probably took place on water as much as on land.[70] So it is at least possible that Nishimura was right in saying that the raft was the most likely original craft used to reach Japan.[71] He also emphasises the dominant place the raft once had in an area from Formosa to Australia, which is supported by the similarity of recent rafts of Babelthusp and Yap to south-east Asian ones.[72]

Some corroboration of the raft theory comes from the study of two shellfish, the *Anadara granosa*, a warm-water shell, and the *Pecten yesoensis*, a cold-water marine shell. Their distribution in the mounds, with both moving south as time passes, seems to indicate that Jomon man lived in a warmer climate, sub-tropical at least in south Japan.[73] This would strengthen any hypothesis about use of rafts or bundles of bamboos.

## Skin boats

According to Jochelson, the Ainu also came to Japan on rafts.[74] This seems hardly likely, as they are more connected with the northern part of the Japanese islands. This is not the place to go into the controversy as to whether the hairy and fair-skinned aborigines of Japan, the Ainu, are descended from the Jomon people or not.[75] What is more appropriate is to consider whether the Ainu or the Jomon people might have been makers and users of a now extinct skin-boat tradition, the equivalent of the one that existed in comparable

latitudes on the other side of the Eurasian land mass in the British Isles and Scandinavia.

One possible place of evidence for this is the finding in Hokkaido of some of a curious type of stone core characteristic of an Upper Palaeolithic-Mesolithic small tool complex which was widely disseminated in north-east Asia from Alaska to the Gobi Desert and Siberia to northern Japan.[76] This suggests that there may have been links between the early inhabitants of Japan and proto-Eskimo groups.

Then from at least the middle Jomon period on, scrapers for skin, usually tanged, often of obsidian, and needles made from bone, horn or stingray spikes are found.[77] Later still, there is the distribution of what Bandi calls 'prong harpoon heads', as opposed to the typical toggle harpoon heads of the Eskimo. These 'prong harpoon heads' have been found in Japan, Kamchatka, the Aleutians, Kodiak Island, and central southern Alaska.[78] In the Aleutians, where some Palaeo-Aleut sites have been dated to not later than 2000 BC, the harpoons are strongly linked with whaling and skin boats, which were possibly responsible for any cultural connections with the mainland.

Yet despite this suggestive evidence and his diligent searching, Nishimura could find, besides legendary and Chinese material, only one convincing example of the skin boat in the Japanese archaeological record. That was a carving of a whale-hunting scene on an eagle bone (Figure 14.8), which Professor Shogoro Tsuboi had found in 1907 while excavating a shell mound near the

14.8 *Whale-hunting scene carved on an eagle bone excavated from a shell mound near the mouth of the River Susuya in Sakhalin, Japan (National Maritime Museum)*

14.9  *Japanese picture of a skin boat from the Kamchatka Peninsula, eastern Russia (National Maritime Museum)*

mouth of the River Susuya in Sakhalin.[79] Nishimura later found a whale vertebra in the same mound. So it certainly seems reasonable to agree that the carved scene probably shows a skin boat of umiak type in a whale hunt.

Nishimura's other evidence for the 'ancient existence' of skin boats is a boat excavated on the banks of the Agauna River in Echigo Province which had planks sewn together with whale sinews.[80] This could be derived from a skin-boat type, but a more cautious and plausible explanation is that this was a craft at the sewn-strake stage of development, which might as a type date anywhere from a millennium or two BC to the nineteenth century. Finally there is the use of the word '*sappa*' for small boat, which Nishimura says is the same as the Manchurian word for hide boat.[81]

In summary, while one could expect there had been a Japanese skin-boat tradition, the case for it remains unproved and more evidence is needed to confirm the Ainu tradition that when their ancestors came to the land of Shamo (Japan), there were living there a group of dwarfs called Koro-pok-huru who sometimes used boats made of skin which were so light that they could be carried on the back.[82] Certainly when in the Yedo period a Japanese artist portrayed a Kamchatka skin boat (Figure 14.9), only total ignorance of the

type could have produced such a delightfully incongruous result.[83]

## Bark canoes

One explanation for this possible absence of skin boats is that the Ainu, or Jomon people, in the warmer well-wooded surroundings of the early period, used birch-bark canoes instead. Such a tradition existed, until recently at least, among the Tungus, and was described as far back as the Ming period by a Chinese traveller, Fang-Kuan Chang, who described how the Tungusu tribes of the lower Amur sewed the bark of birch trees to make ferry boats.[84] The Ainu used birch bark for many purposes – utensils, clothing, roofs, torches and so on – and in the Sapporo Museum there was a model of an Ainu canoe made of a single piece of birch bark, with gores cut into its four corners, sewn together, caulked with bog-moss and stiffened with osiers interlaced at right angles.[85]

## Sewn boats

The next evolutionary stage after the dug-out one would expect would be a craft with strakes sewn on to increase its freeboard. Here Nishimura has a most intriguing example (Figure 14.11). This is the traditional craft called *morota-bune* which used

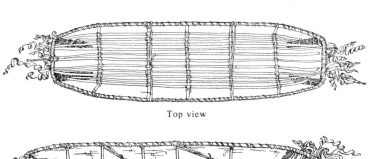

Top view

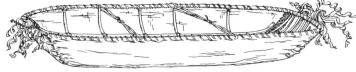

Side view

Front view

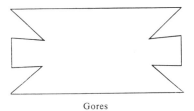

Gores

14.10 *Japanese Ainu bark boat (after Nishimura*, A Study of Ancient Ships of Japan, *part IV, 1931, p. 205)*

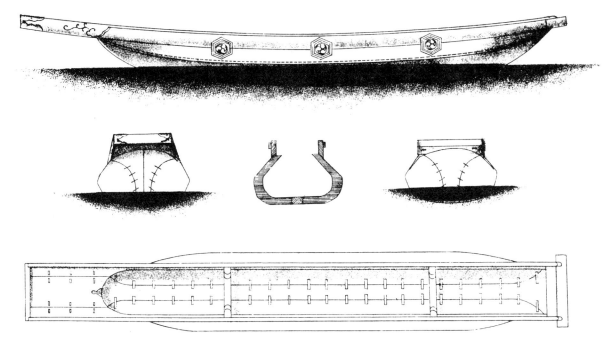

14.11 *A traditional Japanese craft*, morota-bune *(after Nishimura*, A Study of Ancient Ships of Japan, *part I, 1920)*

14.12   *Boat engraving on a third century BC bronze bell from Oishi, Japan (after Nishimura,* Ancient Rafts of Japan, *1925, p. 115)*

to be kept in the Mio shrine at Idzumo where it was used in a festival which, according to Nishimura, was linked to ancient types of ships.[86] This craft resembles Ainu fishing boats of recent times and is interesting from a number of points of view. Its stem, stern and sides are stitched to a dug-out base and it has a considerable overhang at one end and a slight one at the other. In fact if one wanted a craft intermediate between the Szech-wan dug-out and the 'three-plank' sampan of Han dynasty type, one could hardly have a more

specific case. That is not to say that, in ancient China and Japan, dug-outs universally evolved in this way into sampans, but at least the *morota-bune* shows one way they might have done so.

## Dragon boats

Another interesting craft is that shown on a bronze bell of about the third century BC which was dug up at Oishi village in 1868 (Figure 14.12). According to Nishimura, this is a reed boat.[87] Certainly it has the fluid curve these craft possess and recalls ancient Egyptian examples. Yet there do not appear to be any lashings round the hull, which is the surest sign of this type of craft. An alternative explanation is that it might be a dragon boat. The split line at the bow could be the horns of a dragon or other animal and its general shape is certainly right. There are traces of these craft later in Japan. For instance, there are the 'many handed' boats of Kumano, and C. W. Bishop says

14.13   *Japanese boats going out to meet two ships from Commodore Perry's squadron at Kurihama, Tokyo Bay, in July 1853 (Yokosuka City Museum)*

14.14    *A Haniwa pottery model of a junk from Saitobaru tomb, Saito, Mijazaki (National Museum, Tokyo)*

that the great war galleys of medieval Japan developed from dragon boats.[88] So these long thin crescent-shaped craft may well have been an early development of the dug-out alternative to the sheer-less *morota-bune*, and the upright stem and stern types to be described in a moment.

## Later developments

One of the valuable things about Nishimura's great work is that it recalls the complexity of craft that must have existed. Though the period when he wrote forced him to lean heavily on legendary material in the absence of the archaeological evidence that has appeared since, the list of types he described is impressive: rafts, dug-outs, bark canoes, reed floats, inflated deerskins, basket boats, calabash craft, and rafts made from pots and spear shafts.[89] It is surely likely that in due course archaeological work will eventually verify a complex picture like this, rather than any over-simplified reduction, say, to a few types of dug-outs.

By the time the largely Chinese-inspired Yayoi and proto-historical periods are reached, the basic dug-out seems to have evolved into either a craft with an upright stem and stern or one that approximates rather more to later types of junk. The former is well represented by a wall painting in the Meshurashi tomb, in which the two-legged bird standing on the bow will delight diffusionists with its similarity to the bird on the craft on one of the Bahrain seals.[90] On the other hand the two-masted craft in the Onizuka tomb seems easily visualised as a form of junk.[91] Somewhere between these two are the craft carved in positive fleets in the Midorikawa tomb.[92] With their heavy angled bows, these recall the craft (Figure 14.13) that went out to greet Commodore Perry in Tokyo Bay in 1853. A Haniwa pottery model (Figure 14.14) of the pre-Buddhist period (*c.* AD 300–600) reveals that at this time the ships of the Japanese were indeed anticipating the later junks which conservatism kept so similar for so long.

But while the Japanese shared with the Chinese the achievement of developing this highly successful type with its tremendously strong indigenous character, perhaps almost as important was the evolution in the south Chinese and south-east Asian area of the form of craft which was to carry out perhaps the most remarkable of all early maritime feats.

# 15 The Pacific

## Colonisation of the Pacific

Above 'marae-roa', the vast ocean expanse, the stars in the constellation of Te Waka o Tama-rereti, the Canoe of Tama-rereti, are placed so that they protect each other from the jostling of their two elders, the Sun and Moon, and so do not fall from the breast of Rangi, the Sky Parent. Beneath their friendly gaze, the broad sea-roads led from the motherland to the red sunrise.[1]

So the Maoris recorded in their ancestral legends some of the mystical elements they see in what more prosaic anthropologists and archaeologists have called one of the greatest achievements of the human species, spanning the entire Pacific Ocean and four millenia of time. To voyage the thousands of miles involved, in craft produced by a Neolithic technology, to people the last remaining habitable but unoccupied part of the globe was a quite remarkable feat.

To comprehend, chart and date this achievement scholars from Captain Cook onwards relied almost entirely on the impressive oral treasury of the Pacific islanders' genealogies, prayers and legends. The detailed nature of these tribal memories, local disapproval of any interference with the dead or the sacred temple areas, and the lack of antiquarian or fashionable appeal in the native artefacts all combined to channel the early study of the past in this area away from excavation towards compilation and study of traditional oral material.

It was not until the 1920s and 1930s that field studies of temples, house platforms, forts and so on began in various of the islands, such as Tonga, Hawaii, the Marquesas and Easter Island. Since the Second World War, the situation has changed considerably. The work of excavators like Gifford, Emory, Golson and Spoehr has at last given Pacific prehistory a firm and proper basis, and, more recently still, spectrographic analysis is adding sharper detail by showing, for instance, that obsidian had been carried some 2,000 kilometres from New Britain to sites in the Solomon Islands by about 1000 BC.[2]

## Marquesas Islands

To take another specific example, the excavations by R. C. Suggs in the valley of Ha'atuatua on Mika Hiva has given a very detailed picture of the earliest arrivals on this island in the Marquesas, even though it has been suggested that his radiocarbon date for this of 130 BC ($2080 \pm 120$ BP) should be modified to some five centuries later.[3] Here a tidal wave had exposed in the sandhills behind the beach in this deserted valley remains of ancient buildings, a burial area and numerous broken tools and other débris. Among these artefacts were some made from materials found not in the Marquesas or indeed anywhere in eastern Polynesia but in western Polynesia. So presumably they were brought from their original home by the expedition that occupied the island.

According to Suggs's interpretation of the evidence, the main group split on arrival into smaller ones, possibly the occupants of one or two canoes, to settle here and there on the east coast of the islands. At Ha'atuatua they first built a group of small, low boat-shaped thatch houses near the mouth of a stream at the north end of the beach. A little way away was a small sacred area, an oblong enclosure marked out by small stones a few centimetres high with two basalt columns standing inside it. These formed the altar, which the gods would occupy, if properly invoked, and round it in due course the dead were buried. Skeletons from these graves yielded evidence of probably ceremonial cannibalism, of ancestral preservation of male skulls, and, perhaps most important, of the undoubted Polynesian character of the bodies laid there.

From the remains scattered round the relics of the frequently-moved houses and the fires lit beside them, it was possible to tell a good deal about both what these voyagers had brought to support life in their new land, and their daily life. The standard domestic animals of the Pacific islands, the pig and the dog, had come with them and rats had presumably stowed away on their canoes, since the bones of all three were found. The bird-bones have not yet been identified, so it is not possible to say whether they also brought the jungle cock, used for its bright feathers, though this was definitely present by AD 1100. Coconuts, taro, yams and breadfruit were evidently also in their cargo, since the tools found include mother-of-pearl coconut-graters and rind-peeling knives of tonna shell. Thus archaeological evidence confirms some of the rather charming legends from other parts of the Pacific. One told by Sir Peter Buck describes how the sweet potato got its honorific Maori name.[4] According to Aotea legend, when in the fourteenth century AD chief Turi sailed from central Polynesia to the colder climate of New Zealand, his wife Rongorongo kept some sweet-potato tubers in a double belt round her waist to keep them warm against her body – hence their name, 'the Belt of Rongorongo'.

The more matter-of-fact archaeological record in the Marquesas also reveals the strongly maritime nature of the first settlers with their dependence on shellfish and fish, since fish-bones of all shapes and sizes, and the broken shells of edible shellfish littered the site. They also left their fish-hooks there, one-piece ones of mother-of-pearl which had been rough-cut with sharp basalt flakes and then finished off with blade-like files made of polished coral.[5] These early Marquesans also brought pottery with them – red, unpainted and of varying quality. Nevertheless, these sherds and a disc type of ornament in mother-of-pearl and some of their stone adzes all show strong Melanesian links. This fits well into a broad overall picture of a gradual occupation of the Pacific islands from the west over a period of perhaps four millennia (Map 15.1).

## Heyerdahl's theory

Since this contradicts Heyerdahl's well-popularised hypothesis that American Indians were responsible in a series of voyages in the other direction, it might be as well to outline briefly, without getting too enmeshed in the controversy, some of the reasons why the majority of scholars do not agree with Heyerdahl. Dr Spoehr points out that the Polynesian languages belong to the Malayo-Polynesian family which stretches from Malaysia and the south-eastern Asian archipelago right across the Pacific.[6] The botanical evidence is complicated and is discussed in more detail in the next chapter, but here it is perhaps enough to say that the Oceanic food plants, taro, bananas, breadfruit, and coconuts, as well as their domesticated animals, the pig, fowl and dog, all point more towards the old world rather than the new. On archaeological grounds Suggs sees great importance in the finding in a Late Neolithic context in south China of considerable numbers of stepped shouldered stone adzes which, he says, 'are distinctly Polynesian in type and do not appear elsewhere in Asia'.[7] Other Polynesian traits are the so-called 'patu', a flat-bladed chopping club found in the various forms throughout Polynesia and New Zealand, and some blade-like awls or files very close to the Polynesian equivalents in coral. Suggs points out that these Late Neolithic people of south China and similar groups in south-east Asia had a maritime bent, fish and shellfish

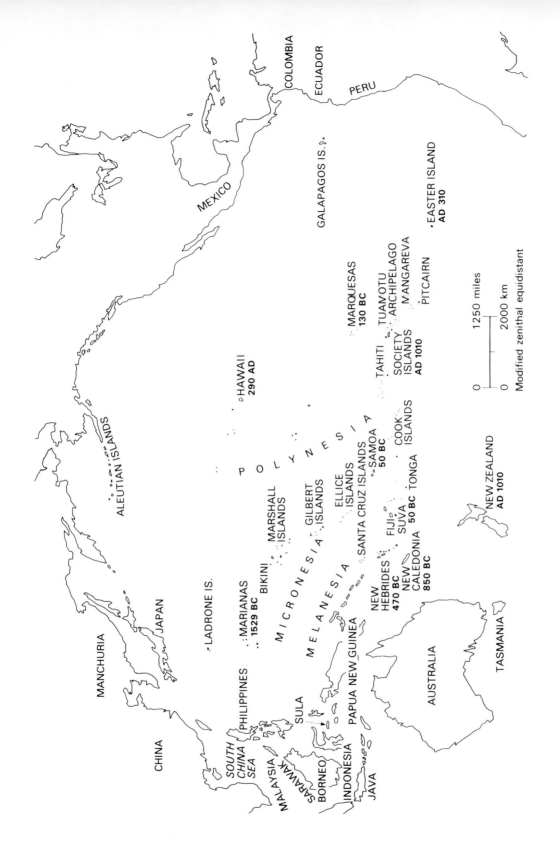

Map 15.1 *Pacific area, with radiocarbon dates for certain sites (after Grahame Clark, World Prehistory, 1977, p. 488)*

COLOMBIA
ECUADOR
PERU

MEXICO

GALAPAGOS IS.

EASTER ISLAND
AD 310

MARQUESAS
130 BC

TUAMOTU
ARCHIPELAGO
MANGAREVA

TAHITI
SOCIETY
ISLANDS
AD 1010

PITCAIRN

1250 miles

2000 km

0

0

Modified zenithal equidistant

CHINA

MANCHURIA

JAPAN

ALEUTIAN ISLANDS

HAWAII
290 AD

P O L Y N E S I A

LADRONE IS.

MARIANAS
1529 BC

BIKINI

MARSHALL
ISLANDS

GILBERT
ISLANDS

M I C R O N E S I A

ELLICE
ISLANDS

SANTA CRUZ ISLANDS

SAMOA
50 BC

COOK
ISLANDS

SOUTH
CHINA
SEA

PHILIPPINES

SULA

PAPUA NEW GUINEA

M E L A N E S I A

NEW
HEBRIDES
470 BC

NEW
CALEDONIA
850 BC

FIJI
SUVA
50 BC  TONGA

NEW ZEALAND
AD 1010

MALAYSIA

SARAWAK

BORNEO

INDONESIA

JAVA

AUSTRALIA

TASMANIA

forming a large part of their diet,[8] and that they were horticulturists and kept domestic animals. Suggs suggests that pressure from the more advanced Shang societies in north China, somewhere from about 2000 BC onwards, set off a chain reaction, pushing the marginal groups outward into the Pacific, not in large-scale one-way voyages but in a series of short movements, island-hopping and coasting, sometimes returning, with the season for travel carefully chosen. From the south China coast and south-east Asia, the archaeological record finds a trail of shouldered and tanged adzes, stone tapa-beaters, pig- and chicken-bones, fish-hooks and pottery, leading through Melanesia, New Guinea, the Philippines and Indonesia, eventually to the main Pacific islands.

Heyerdahl's strongest counter-argument perhaps is that winds and currents on the whole are against voyages from Asia eastward, while they would assist westward passages, a fact reflected in the two westward routes north and south of the equator named respectively after two Spanish sailors, Saavedra and Mendaña, who pioneered them.[9] On the other hand one has to remember that the trade winds reverse themselves for a part of the year, and the eastward-flowing equatorial counter-current exists, even if it is weaker. There is also the comment quoted by Elsdon Best that prevalent easterly winds would not have much effect on 'canoes built so as to sail closer to the wind than any other craft built by man'.[10] Admittedly that was written in 1909, but the point about the Pacific islanders' craft being able to work so well to windward remains valid.

A middle stance is that of Joseph Garanger. After pointing out how much work still remains to be done and how many areas still remain untouched by excavation, with the ever more complex additions to the overall picture they will provide, he goes on to argue:[11]

We should in future be less concerned to locate in the east or the west, the origin of a huge migration (which never existed as far as one can tell) so that hypothetical syntheses may be constructed for endless consideration: but rather we should be concerned to find and analyse the signs, influences, and traces of a

world in perpetual movement, of a world which for the first time in the history of human civilisation dared no longer to consider the ocean as an impassable obstacle.

## Pacific craft

Of the means by which this great maritime achievement was carried out we have a pretty good idea, at least in its later stages.

One of the principal craft, the outrigger canoe, was noted during Magellan's stay in the Ladrones in 1521 (Figure 15.1):[12]

Their canoes had lateen sails (in shape resembling a shoulder of mutton) and each had an outrigger – i.e. a light boom or pole running in the water parallel to the canoe – with which it is connected and preserved in its parallel position by transverse small poles securely fastened to each. The outrigger, by its weight and buoyancy, keeps steady the canoe, which, being a vessel of light and narrow construction, would, without such support, be in constant danger of oversetting. The canoes of these islanders were built alike at both ends, which enabled them to go with either foremost; and they sailed with great swiftness.

Normally the ocean-going outrigger had a dug-out body with a washstrake attached each side to give greater freeboard, but there were more elaborately built-up types, as Dampier reported, also from the Ladrones, in 1686.[13]

The natives are very ingenious beyond any people in making Boats, or, 'Proes', as they are called in the East Indies, and therein they take great delight. These are built sharp at both ends; the bottom is of one piece, made like the bottom of a little canoa, very neatly dug, and left of a good substance. This bottom part is instead of a keel . . . From hence both sides of the Boat are carried up to about five foot high with narrow plank, not above four or five inches broad, and each end of the Boat turns up round very prettily . . . The mast stands exactly in the middle, with a long Yard that peeps up and down like a Mizen-yard . . . Along the belly side of the boat, parallel with it, at about six or seven foot distance, lies another small Boat or Canoa, being a Log of very light Wood almost as long as the great Boat, but not so wide . . . And there are two Bamboos of about eight or ten foot long, and as big as one's leg, placed over the great Boat's side . . . by help of which the little Boat is made firm and contiguous to the other . . . The use of them is to keep the great Boat upright and from oversetting. . . .

I have been the more particular in describing these Boats, because I do believe they sail the best of any Boats in the World. I did here for my own satisfaction try the swiftness of one of them; sailing by our Log, we had twelve knots on our reel, and she run it all out before the half-minute glass was half out; which, if it had been no more, is after the rate of twelve mile an hour; but I do believe she would have run twenty-four mile an hour . . . I was told one of these Boats was sent Express to Manila, which is above 400 leagues and performed the voyage in four days' time.

There are many of these 'Proes', or Boats, used in many places of the East Indies, but with . . . a little Boat on each side.

An adequate testimonial, even if the twenty-four miles an hour was perhaps optimistic. As well as these reports of single and double outriggers, there were accounts of the other principal craft, the double canoe, like that by Mendaña of the one he saw in the Santa Cruz group of islands in AD 1595: 'They possess large handsome canoes, capable of carrying above thirty persons with their luggage, in which they navigate to distant parts.

The sail was of matting, wide at the upper part and narrow below. They sailed swiftly, and turned well to windward.'[14]

In AD 1616 Le Maire and Schouten gave a rather more detailed description of a double canoe met out of sight of land west of the Tuamotu group (Figure 15.2).[15]

The vessel navigated by these islanders was formed of two large and handsome canoes, which were placed parallel and at a convenient distance from each other. In the middle of each canoe a very broad, thick plank of a red-coloured wood, and very light, was placed lengthways upon its edge; across the two planks were laid some small beams, and upon the beams a platform of thin planks  The whole was compact and well-fastened together. Over one part of the platform was a small shed of matting, under which the women and children remained. There was but one mast and one sail. The mast was fixed in a step toward the fore part of the starboard canoe; the sail was of triangular form and attached to a yard which rested on the upper end of the mast, which was forked for that purpose. The vessel was steered with oars abaft. The sail was of matting, and towards the upper part of it

15.1   *Illustration from the account of Magellan's visit to the Ladrone Islands on Saturday 16 March 1521, showing a canoe with a single outrigger (Bibliothèque nationale, Paris)*

15.2 *Seventeenth-century drawing of a double canoe seen by LeMaire and Schouten off the Tuamotu Islands (Pepys Library, Magdalene College, Cambridge)*

there was marked a figure representing a cock . . . Their cordage was well made. They were provided with hooks for fishing, the back part of which were of stone, and the back or bearded part of bone, tortoise-shell, or mother-of-pearl. Everything appertaining to the vessel was neat and well-fitted for sea.

A mid-nineteenth-century account of a trip in a Tongan double canoe gives some idea of the speed, excitement and seamanship generated by these vessels, which could carry up to 150 people:[16]

Up went the huge sail, down went the great steer-oars, splashing into the sea, and away we shot like a racehorse. The breeze was strong. Every timber of the canoe creaked again, while the mast bent like a reed and cracked in its socket as if it would split the deck in two . . . Owing to the great rate at which we were going, the sea was like a hissing cauldron on either side of our course, and the vessel, instead of having

time to mount over the smaller waves, cut its way right through them . . . There cannot be a doubt that the peculiar shape of the Tongan 'kalia', or double canoe, and the arrangement of its large and single sail, are conducive to the attainment of great speed in ordinary weather . . . They have been known to live through severe and long-continued storms, chiefly owing to the fact that, so long as they hold together and do not upset, they cannot possibly sink, owing to the strong platform joining the hulls together.

**Maori war canoes**

These three types of craft, then, the simple outrigger canoe, the built-up outrigger canoe and the double canoe, and the raft of which more will be said later, were the vessels the first Europeans found ranging the Pacific. There is not much doubt either that they were the craft which made the great voyages which Suggs has described as genuine feats of navigation and survival of the highest rank.[17] Both legends and the tools found in archaeological contexts suggest that there was not much change in the technological capacities of the first settlers of many islands and their descendants encountered by Europeans. Of course circumstances could make their mark. When somewhere before AD 1125 ± 50, which is the earliest radiocarbon date we have so far from a moa-hunter site,[18] a group of voyagers from eastern Polynesia reached the shores of New Zealand, a very different environment greeted them. As well as the long-necked wingless moas, whose flesh was so crucial to the diet of the first arrivals, they saw great forests of tall trees, magnificent material for canoe-building. Over a period of time this caused the outrigger and double canoe to go out of use, their place taken by the great Maori single war canoe with its high stern and elaborate carving, propelled by perhaps a hundred paddlers. When the British occupied the country in the nineteenth century, these remarkable craft attracted a good deal of attention, and eventually a full study was made of practically every aspect of their construction and use. There must have been variations since the time of the early moa-hunters, and considerable differences from other Pacific areas. Nevertheless these canoes do give a very good idea of the approach, methods, time-scale and ingenuity of a Neolithic people's ship-builders. As an early settler put it: 'with rude and blunt stones they felled the giant kauri, toughest of pines, and from it in process of time, at an expense of labour, perseverance and ingenuity perfectly astounding in those who knew what it really was, produced . . . a masterpiece of art and an object of beauty, the war canoe capable of carrying a hundred men.'[19]

Two years was about the time taken to produce one of these craft.[20] The totara or the kauri were the most favoured trees, and the first part of the operation was to choose a suitable one. As with every stage of Maori, and indeed Polynesian, canoe-building, this was done with suitable ritual, in which everything was done to avoid ill-luck and placate the gods. A straight sound trunk of the right size and a good hauling route, possibly of

some miles, to the nearest water were the other factors. The chosen tree then had the brush and small trees round it cleared away, which indicated to all comers that it was reserved and not to be interfered with. A strip of bark might then be taken off one side in such a way that the exposed part would decay and make easier the task of hollowing. An indication of the lengthy nature of this operation was the practice, reported by a member of the Ngati-Porou tribe, of clearing ground and planting a crop near by in the spring before the tree was felled. Then in the autumn people would lift the crop, build huts and live there while the canoe was made.

The tree might be felled by a number of methods – from the simple peg-top, scarfs back and front, and burning the exposed roots – to elaborate and ingenious methods such as the ballista-powered or swing battering-ram devices (Figure 15.3) of the Tuhoe and Ngati-Porou. All the tools used in any of these ways were of stone or more occasionally shell. After the top of the tree had been removed, by fire or adze or both, the vast log 20 to 30 metres long and up to 3 metres wide might have to be rolled to its hollowing-out position. Levers, handspikes, parbuckles and even Spanish windlass techniques might be used for this (Figure 15.4).

The hollowing-out process which followed was long and laborious. As one old Maori said: 'The adze employed was a stone one. The other adze was fire.' Stone tools could not be used satisfactorily for cutting across the grain of timber. Instead a surface was first scored across the grain, then hewed off in line with it, in a sort of splitting or chipping technique. Fires were lit in a row and controlled by damping the wood with water. When they were extinguished, the charred wood would be chipped away, and the process repeated. Little was done in the way of measuring, the practised eye of an expert being relied on, with at most a charcoal mark on some slightly protruding piece of wood which had to be removed.

The rough-shapen canoe would be prepared for haulage by securing long poles longitudinally along its tops, with the ends protruding. Men stationed there were then able to give much help in

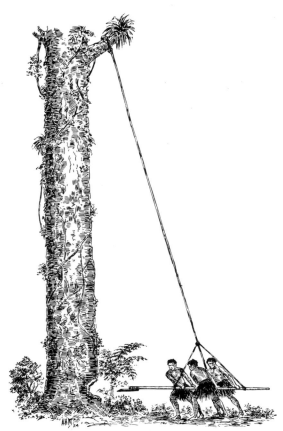

15.3 *Maori device for felling trees (after Best,* The Maori Canoe, *1925, p. 50)*

keeping the canoe from turning. Holes were bored in projections left during the hollowing-out, and through these hauling ropes were passed, two to four at each end. The ropes were carefully plaited in five strands from the dried leaves of 'ti torere' (*Cordyline banksii*) or 'ti kauka' (*C. australis*). The skids over which the craft slid were about 2 metres long, 15 cm in thickness, with one end smaller to ease moving them, and made from the 'houhou' (*Panax arboreum*) with its bark knocked off, which gave a satisfactorily smooth and shiny surface. Six men would lay down skids in front of the vessel and another six pick up the ones over which the hull had passed. The hauling was done to rhythmic songs, the leader beating time from the bows of the canoe. Going down a steep slope required special care. The two stern ropes were led out side by side straight astern and taken round a tree. The two bow ropes meanwhile were led back each side at an angle and also secured round trees. All ropes were then carefully payed out as the hull glided downhill. When the bow lines were fully extended, the stern lines were belayed round their tree and the canoe held, while the bow lines were taken further down the slope to new snubbing posts. In turn, the canoe would be held by the belayed bow lines, while the two stern lines were moved down.

15.4 *Maori log-rolling device (after Best, 1925, p. 55)*

In this way control was kept over the mass even on a steep slope.

When the canoe had travelled this way even as far as 30 kilometres, as was reported in one case, and the launching-site had been reached, a roof was built over the hull, while the final and most delicate stage took place, as a Maori of Te Kuiti described.

Then the master mechanics approach to shape and trim, leaving proper projections to be bored for the gunnel-strake lashings, and the inside is finished. The shell is now turned over and the outside rough hewn to approximate form, and four posts, two at each end and side, equidistant from the central or keel line, are firmly fixed in the ground. From post to post, at each side, a fine strong cord is stretched, from which all final measurements are set off, which, assisted by the expert eye of the master, ensures that both sides are to be exactly alike in outline of curve . . . During these labours no food must be brought near the work, no chips hewn therefrom burnt at the mess-fire; all is done in fear of the gods . . . For from the day in midwinter when the sap is low and the tree is felled, two, nay three years may subtend until the master says 'Toia te waka kia manu' (launch the canoe that it may float).

The outside of the hull was grooved with a double-shouldered adze, leaving a narrow intervening ridge. This the Maoris considered prevented the water clinging to the hull, broke it up, and stopped it impeding the hull's progress. The polishing of the inside was done by holystoning, a number of men rubbing the surfaces with pieces of sandstone.

Many canoes were of one piece, but some of the larger ones had bow and stern pieces added, the 'kaumi'. These were shaped so that they fitted the main part of the hull like a huge tenon and mortise. They were joined by lashings of three-stranded cord made from *Phormium* or *Cordyline*, which were taken through holes drilled in pairs through each side of the join by a stone-pointed drill. Grooves were made on both sides so that the lashings could be countersunk. Battens were sometimes put over the joins, except at the end of the tongue, and strips of dried 'raupo' leaves were used as caulking.

In this way, first the 'kaumi' were added to the hull, then the topsides, the thwarts, the figurehead, the high stern-piece and finally the flooring. The topside was as long a plank as possible, shaped to fit the sheer of the craft in carvel fashion. If the length made more than one plank necessary, the join was made towards the end of the vessel, the parts being butted together. These long planks were made by heating one end of a log until it began to crack. Wedges of hardwood were then hammered in to split it along its length. The pieces were adzed down to the right thickness, and then fitted to the hull at its centre. Then lashings from a post in the ground were taken round each end of the plank and tightened by twisting, tourniquet fashion, pulling it in to fit the ends of the canoe. The same sort of ingenuity was shown in the way the running lashing was tightened (Figure 15.5).

An alternative to the Maori technique of fastening the parts of the canoe together was the Fijian one (Figure 15.6) in which raised rims were left on the edges of planks that were to be joined, and the lashings passed through holes drilled in these. This method meant there were no lashings,

15.5 *Maori method of tightening lashings using a 'tanekaha' or 'mimiro' (after Best, 1925, p. 79)*

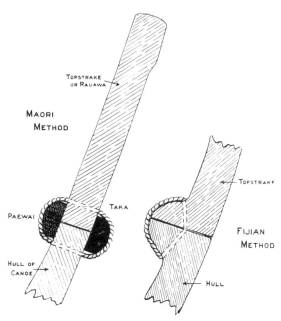

15.6 *Maori and Fijian methods of lashing a washstrake to the hull of a dug-out (after Best, 1925, p. 84)*

between each might be occupied by a man, his family and his baggage.

The flooring usually consisted of fore-and-aft battens laid on cross-pieces which, in turn, were laid on fore-and-aft rods along the canoe's sides held by a false rib of vine running up to the thwarts. In large canoes, two bailing-places might be left in the floor. The flooring was usually placed below the level of the junction of top-strake and hull so that the lashings there could be easily reached. Mats or bracken would be put on the flooring for long voyages. A hole for draining the bilge was normally put in the middle or slightly forward of the vessel: at sea it was closed with a wooden plug. Repairs were made by drilling holes each side of a crack, caulking it, and then lashing a batten over it. The lashings on the outside of the hull were usually countersunk.

## Other boat-building techniques

These procedures naturally varied over the Pacific area. Particularly sharp differences arose on coral atolls, and a Maori like Peter Buck was struck by the skilful frugality with which the inhabitants made use of their resources, which were so much more limited than those of the volcanic islands of central Polynesia or New Zealand itself.[21] Such trees as were available were carefully split into planks, so as not to waste the material chipped out in the process of hollowing a whole tree into a dug-out. Tools were made from *Tridacna* shells, instead

grooves or battens on the outside of the hull, which therefore had a much smoother overall finish.

Thwarts might be fitted to the Maori canoe by shaping them so that the shoulders rested against the inner edge of the top strake, or they might simply rest on the top strake and be lashed to it, again in countersunk grooves. Each thwart had its own name, and on colonising voyages the space

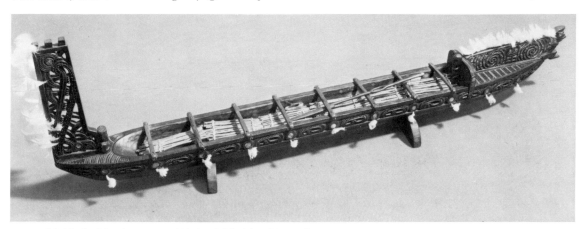

15.7 *Model of a Maori war canoe (National Maritime Museum)*

of stone. In place of the 'raupo' or bulrush-leaf sails, in the familiar 'triangular figure' observed by Captain Cook, the multi-purpose pandanus had to be used.

The Easter Islanders were even worse off for wood. One of the earlier visitors there, Roggeveen, in AD 1722 described their canoes as 'fitted together of small boards and light frames, which they skilfully lace together with very fine-laid twine' (Figure 15.8). In 1774, Forster amplified this by saying the size of the pieces was no more than 4 or 5 inches wide, and 2 or 3 feet long.[22]

Yet the basic similarities remain. The outline of a Marquesan canoe could hardly be more different from that of a Maori one. But there still is the dug-out body and the lashed battens covering the join with the top strake.[23]

Some of the techniques described above are similar to those used in the River Humber group of sewn vessels described in chapter 11, and the sewn boats of the Arabian Gulf, India and South America. If these practices, separated by thousands of miles and hundreds of years, could be so similar over matters like the technique of repairing cracks in hulls, or the lashing of battens over joins, then it encourages one to think that at an earlier technological stage, the reed-bundle craft might be an equally widespread reflection of the means and capacity of man to take to the water then.

## Seamanship and navigation

One element that was unique to the Pacific area was the vast distances to be travelled. Tahiti to Hawaii was for instance 2,400 miles, and Tahiti to New Zealand not much less. The seamanship and

15.8 *An eighteenth-century Easter Island outrigger canoe showing the short lengths of timber used (after Haddon and Hornell,* The Canoes of Oceania, *1936, p. 99)*

navigational skills required were undoubtedly of high standard. In Maori phraseology, coral rock, sea-monster, Long-wave and Short-wave, all could be encountered, and overcome by seamanship and holy invocations in a mixture which would surely have been quite familiar to St Columba.[24]

When a storm was in the offing, all gear was lashed and the awning tautly rigged. Splash-boards were attached each side, and also 'water-guards', an ingenious form of horizontal openwork platform which weakened the force of upward-surging waves. Two of the most skilful seamen would man the steering oars aft and another two the lifting-oars at the bow to keep the bow up into the seas at a slight angle. Another two would assist amidships. The anchor, usually of stone, might also be lowered at the bow to keep her head up, in which case some of the crew might move aft to counteract the downward pull of the anchor.[25]

Food on board did not present much of a problem even on long expeditions. In voyages from atoll areas, pandanus fruit, grated into coarse flour, cooked, dried and packed into bundles wrapped in leaves, was the main stand-by.[26] On volcanic islands, pounded breadfruit or taro had the useful quality of not spoiling easily once it had begun to ferment.[27] It too was stored in large leaf packages slung inside hull or deckhouse, or in a silo on deck. Dried shellfish such as the *Tridacna* kept indefinitely. Fowls on board were fed on dried coconut meat and could be killed when required and cooked on a fire lit on a specially-prepared bed of sand.[28] Fishing was a constant additional source of food, as was rain to the drinking-water supply. This was carried in large bottle gourds with wooden stoppers, coconut water-bottles or lengths of bamboo.[29] The deep-sea fishermen of Hawaii even went so far as to chill their drink supply by trailing the gourds in the water.

A more controversial aspect is the navigation during these long voyages. Unfortunately no European made a really deep study of this on first contact with the Polynesians, but of the effectiveness of the 'sea eaters', the great navigators there can be little doubt. During Cook's stay at Tahiti in 1784, the high priest, Tupaea, was able to give sailing directions for various distant islands, including some not then known to Europeans.[30] He also stated that long voyages were made only with great difficulty, thereby instigating one of the great controversies of Pacific history. Cook himself might be said to have first put forward the theory that accidental voyages were responsible for the settling of the islands. He thought the story of an accidental one-way voyage from Tahiti to Atiu Island in the Cook Archipelago would 'serve to explain better than a thousand conjectures of speculative reasons how the detached parts of the earth, and in particular, how the South Seas may have been peopled'.[31] The main champion of this view is Andrew Sharp,[32] who maintains that navigation techniques in the Pacific did not permit accuracy over long distances, and that therefore deliberate voyages of much over 300 miles did not occur, and the various islands were settled by fishermen blown off course and so on. On the other hand Buck has made the point that Polynesian women did not go out fishing in canoes with their menfolk, therefore no fishing crew could people an uninhabited island beyond their own life-span.[33] There is also the recent archaeological evidence that both Hawaii and the Marquesas were settled by well-equipped and so presumably purposeful expeditions.[34] It would therefore not be difficult to accept Katherine Luomala's view that the 'accidental voyage' thesis is more a stimulating notion than a proved case.[35]

It also seems apparent that, until recently, archaeologists have been inclined to under-rate the awareness of primitive people of the night sky. If some of the astronomical observance currently being credited to the Neolithic megalith-builders in western Europe is confirmed, then it would be reasonable to expect comparable achievements at sea.[36]

'The explorers followed a star over a new horizon, but ever they looked back at the stars over the homeland . . .' So Buck puts it,[37] and observations of 'guiding stars' as well as 'on top stars' must have been crucial. The Vikings seem to have sailed along the coast of Norway and then westward along the latitude of 61° or so on the ocean route to Greenland. The Pacific navigators do not seem to have done this so much as aimed at a point to windward and up-current of their desired distant target, then checked they were on the right latitude by zenith stars and turned directly towards the desired landfall. For shorter voyages, sailing by dead reckoning down a memorised star path indicated by a horizon star seems to have been the usual practice. Winds, currents, the run of the sea, land swell, water colour, deep phosphorescence, clouds above land, the loom – even the smell – of land, the flight of birds, 'sea marks' like the appearance of certain kinds of fish, drift objects, stone marker-pillars and beacons, might all be used. Light stones on ropes might be lowered from bow and stern to discover the set of the ocean current at different depths, and these in turn might indicate the winds to be expected.[38]

**The evolution of Pacific craft**

It is, overall, an impressive picture of ship-building and sea-keeping. Yet a number of questions inevitably arise. Where and how did the outrigger and double canoe evolve? What was the place of the raft in all this voyaging? And is it conceivable that larger more elaborate craft once existed in the Pacific area, of which no obvious evidence remained by the time the Europeans got there?

The first place to look for any prototypes of craft, if one accepts the basic Asian mainland origin of the Pacific peoples, is south-east Asia and the Indonesian Archipelago. Part of this area, the Sulu Archipelago, was described by the seventeenth-century Spanish historian of the area, Francisco Combés, as 'the most placid and rich sea that could ever have been discovered'.[39] In Malaysian waters an outstanding feature is the virtual lack of storms. Typhoons and cyclones occur occasionally in the north Sulu and South China Seas, but elsewhere in these seas, according to the Sailing Directions of the Hydrographic Office of the US Navy, gales have never been recorded in ships' observations.[40] Another characteristic is the high surface temperature here. And on much of the shores grows the tropical rainforest, including the *Dipterocarpacae* family of trees, many reaching 40 metres in height, an excellent source of timber of large size.[41]

Such conditions were obviously ideal for primitive man to take to the water, and he must have done so in three ways, on rafts, bark boats and dug-outs. An interesting intermediate form between the dug-out and the bark boat is the woodskin or expanded dug-out, which has been claimed in Europe to be so crucial in the development of the classic northern ship of the Viking Age (chapter 9). This type exists today, and has done at least as far back as 1840, in the *kabang* of the Mawkem, a so-called 'sea-nomad' people from the Mergui Archipelago off the west coast of Malaysia.[42] Though they do not seem to use as much of the circumference of the logs as the Finns, the Mawkem do widen the dug-out base of their craft considerably by a process of alternative soaking in water and heating, and then inserting transverse wooden thwarts to maintain the spread shape.[43] This produces a wide shallow trough amidships and high pointed ends.

## Dug-outs and long-boats

As far as dug-outs and rafts are concerned, historical evidence and modern survivals suggest rafts were largely used on the Indian and Chinese coasts while dug-outs prevailed in south-east Asia. Nevertheless dug-outs do seem to have played some part in early Chinese seafaring, as described

in the last chapter, and were certainly in widespread use in south-east Asia from the Neolithic period onwards. At least two authorities have seen a link between the next stage of boat development and the communal houses of the people who used them. This was the 'long-boat' of the 'long-house'-builders. These 'long-boats' were narrow dug-outs, with considerable overhangs and detachable animal or dragon head and tail, and they were associated over a wide area of south-east Asia with ritual and war. The Chinese 'dragon boats' have already been mentioned (Figure 14.7). In the third century AD they were described as coming from Cambodia and Cochin-China.[44] In the seventeenth century Diego da Couto mentions their presence in Siamese festivals and Burmese river races held before the king. In the nineteenth century, 'Chinese' Gordon's British soldiers called them 'centipedes', and other British soldiers met some of their stoutest opponents in them during the first Burmese war.[45] But much earlier than this, according to C. W. Bishop, the people of Wu and Yueh, who were accomplished seamen, and regarded boats as sacred, spread from China to Indo-China, south Korea, Japan, probably Formosa, south-east Asia and Indonesia, taking with them the 'long-house' and the 'long-boat'.[46] These then acquired a cult significance, perhaps from ancestral memory of the migration they had once made possible, among the Neolithic cultivators of Indonesia, and this was sometimes reflected, among other things, in the shape of the roof of their 'long-houses'.[47]

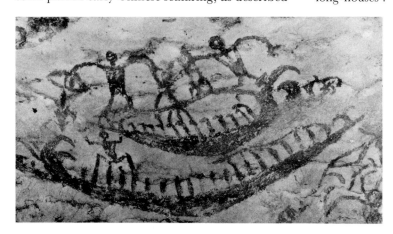

15.9   *Wall painting of built-up dug-outs in the Niah caves, Sarawak (Sarawak Museum)*

Whatever may be thought of these two theories, there are at least two other sources of ancient illustrations of 'long-boats' in this area to confirm their early presence there. One comes from the paintings on the walls of the Niah caves in Sarawak (Figure 15.9). Though an extremely lengthy chronology has been established for the occupation strata on the cave floor, it is of course difficult to associate the paintings with any particular one. Nevertheless, with the flat dug-outs also found there (Figure 15.10), they perhaps encompass the two main types of craft in ancient use: the small dug-out for fishing and inshore work, and the larger built-up dug-out for longer voyages. Tom Harrisson has pointed out that the well-recognised Dong S'on Culture of the Asian mainland tends to fade out in the islands but reappears with some remarkable parallels in the

15.10  *Small dug-outs recovered during excavations in the Niah caves, Sarawak (Sarawak Museum)*

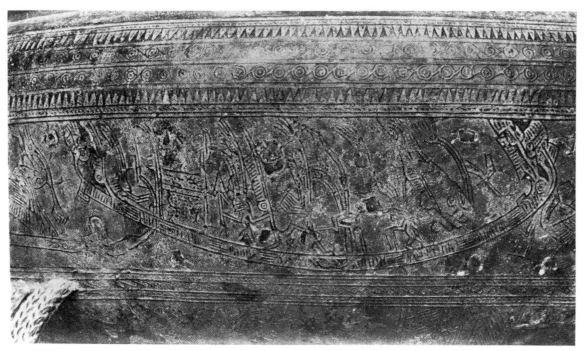

15.11    *Boat representations on a Dong S'on bronze drum from Ngoc-lu, Vietnam, dated to the second half of the first millennium BC (British Museum)*

contemporary life of the Ngadju Dyaks in the interior of south-east Borneo,[48] and it is the famous Vietnamese Dong S'on bronze drums of the second half of the first millennium BC that provide the other source of illustrations of a 'long-boat' (Figure 15.11).

## Outriggers

But however right Bishop may be in saying that considerably more sea-travel took place in these built-up dug-outs than was once supposed,[49] a subsequent development made such voyages more certain: this was the use of outriggers. Hornell has suggested that the evolution of the outrigger occurred on the great rivers of south-east Asia, the Irrawaddy, Salween and Mekong. He noted that the large native craft used there until recently were all based on the dug-out. But he singled out the outboard poling platform or gangway that runs along each side of the square-rigged Burmese 'rice-boat' as particularly significant. In the upper

reaches of these rivers, smaller and more primitive craft have, instead of the elaborate platforms of the 'rice-boats', only one or two bamboo stabilisers lashed upon the projecting ends of poles laid athwart the hull. Hornell believed the 'rice-boat' platforms also acted as stabilisers, and when they were adopted by sea-going vessels, their size was gradually reduced until they became the double outrigger.[50]

He also considered he saw the same process beginning to happen in embryo in South America, where on the River Iscuande in Colombia some dug-outs had balsa logs lashed on each side (Figure 15.13). In the larger dug-outs these balsa logs were even attached to transverse beams, so even though they did not touch the water unless the craft heeled, and were only a few centimetres from the sides, Hornell considered them to be an undeveloped form of double outrigger.[51]

Later on, back in Indonesian waters, the double outrigger was superseded, in his view, by the single, because the latter is far more efficient in the

15.12   *A small dug-out fitted with double outriggers, drawn by Admiral Paris in Banyou-Wangui, Java (National Maritime Museum)*

15.13   *Chocó dug-out fitted with balsa wood stabilisers, in Limones, Ecuador (Clinton R. Edwards)*

open ocean.[52] Moreover this change from double to single had taken place fairly recently in Madagascar and the Comoro Islands. When Houtman and Boothby described the craft there in the late sixteenth and early seventeenth centuries, they had double outriggers. In recent times they have single ones and only a vestigial float on the other side recalls the craft that once made the long journey from the Indonesian Archipelago to East Africa.[53]

Hornell's views about the origin of the outrigger have been challenged by Sopher and Mat-suomotu. Sopher thinks the absence of the outrigger from the coasts of continental south-east Asia, the eastern coast of Sumatra and the coasts of Borneo points to the conclusion that the outrigger was an island invention; whereas Matsuomotu favours an origin from double canoes in south-east China.[54] The places where it has been found in historical times tend to support Sopher.

The outrigger, whether island or mainland bred, still had its drawbacks in one respect. There was a limit to the amount of cargo and passengers it could carry. The remedy was to build a platform over the outrigger booms. Put walls of wooden lattice and a roof of 'nipa' thatch to shelter the occupants on the platform, enlarge the outriggers and you have virtually the famous craft carved on the great ninth century AD Buddhist frieze of Borobodur on Java (Figure 15.14). Boats like this are found in the Moluccas, Celebes and southern Philippines, if smaller and less elaborate.[55]

## Double canoes and rafts

But in spite of these modern survivals, in a form as large as the Borobodur version, it seems to have been a cul-de-sac. Instead, some unknown innovator thought of replacing the single-outrigger float with another canoe. The double canoe,

15.14   *Ninth century AD ship carving on a frieze in the Buddhist stupa or temple at Borobodur, Java (David Attenborough)*

according to Suggs, is recorded in Chinese historical documents as long ago as the eighth to fifth centuries BC.[56] So these massive vessels, up to 30 metres long, with considerable carrying capacity and unequalled seaworthiness, were available for perhaps two and a half millennia to reach the distant islands of the Pacific. There, however, they met a difficulty. One of the problems of isolated island societies is the loss of capabilities once freely exercised. For example, Dr Thomas Barthel has been led by his study of the 'rongo-rongo' script of Easter Island to suggest that this was part of an original Polynesian writing heritage, lost elsewhere in eastern Polynesia, but to which cryptic references still exist in the Marquesas and Tahiti.[57]

So it is not surprising that the skilled caste of canoe-makers should have disappeared for one reason or another in some islands. According to Peter Buck, if the measure of time given to genealogies is approximately accurate, in the Mangarevan Archipelago rafts had superseded outrigger canoes by the fifteenth century AD, and double canoes by the eighteenth century.[58] The question then has to be considered whether the rafts that are found in many parts of the Pacific were degenerative alternatives to the former outriggers and double canoes, or whether they preceded them, or were a valid contemporary alternative. Hornell had little doubts on this point: 'Everywhere throughout Oceania we come across evidence of the present or past use of rafts.'[59] Mangareva, Tonga and Samoa he cited as examples of islands where rafts figure largely in traditional legends. With Haddon, in their great work *The Canoes of Oceania*, he maintained that 'rafts were utilised freely in some at least of the movements from island to island of the first migrants into Oceania.'[60]

However, this double-layer thesis of the occupation of the islands, first wave on rafts, second in outriggers and double canoes, has been challenged by Nooteboom: 'The types of craft and the navigation of a people are not exclusively determined by the history of their diffusion. It must be said again, ships and shipping belong to the most living part of material culture. Shape and construction of boats always depend on their purpose, peculiarities of water, and availability of material'.[61] This is a good and fair point. Nevertheless it goes no way to answering the question what craft were used by the Palaeolithic Australoids, Veddoids and others from Indonesia, when more advanced peoples came from the north and pushed them out to sea. The Australian evidence would suggest reed and bark floats, but simple rafts might well be possible too, especially for those who reached Melanesia. This would explain legends like that of the Solomon Islanders who thought the stones for their megaliths were brought on a raft from some place a long way off in the days when they had not yet learned to make canoes;[62] and those about a dwarfish people called 'Manahune' whom the Polynesians believed were their predecessors in some of the islands.[63]

Then there is a third element, the shaped raft like the *konga* from Eddystone Island in the Solomons. There are a considerable number of these recorded in Melanesia. Their very positive shape with an exaggeratedly long centre log (Figure 15.15) hardly suggests the work of a ship-builder who could no longer build a canoe, or that of a pre-agricultural aboriginal. If these shaped rafts are indeed late survivals of ancient migrations from a raft-rich area, as has been suggested, then they might point to an even more impressive possibility, which will be discussed in chapter 16.[64]

A fourth tradition is the sailing raft, which certainly existed in the Pacific, but there is evidence neither of leeboards nor of long voyages by such craft.

## Chronology

To try and date all these elements is extremely difficult. The use of reed- and bark-bundle floats, and possibly the simplest raft, could go back at least to 20,000 BC. Edwards has suggested that the use of dug-outs by non-farming peoples like the sea-nomad 'Orang Laut' may imply that their ancestors used such craft before agriculture was practised in this area.[65] On the other hand, one has to remember that the primitive Negritos of the Andaman Islands use a dug-out with a single outrigger.[66] So even the most primitive of peoples can acquire more advanced craft from outside sources at a later period.

According to Christie there is some evidence that at the time the early Hoa-binhian, Guha Lawa and a contemporary flake and blade industry were present in Indonesia, crude canoes were in use.[67] Later the Round Axe people may have introduced the plank-built boat, and at some stage before the Shang period the sail was evolved, to be adopted after thousands of years of paddling by the raft-users as well. The next step was not so difficult, perhaps – to put a paddle between the logs of the raft and turn it into a leeboard. Finally someone had to evolve the technique of steering a course by positioning a number of leeboards.

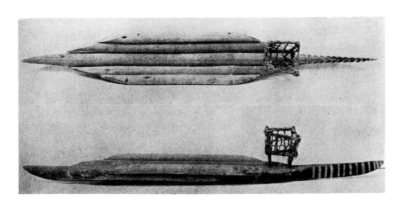

15.15   *Log raft or* konga *from Eddystone Island in the Solomons (National Maritime Museum)*

Edwards has suggested[68] that the odd second paddle at the bow of the Dong S'on bronze drum craft (see Figure 15.11) might be a leeboard. The craft itself is probably a built up dug-out, but if Edwards is correct, it suggests that the evolution of the sail-paddle-leeboard would stretch back well before 300 BC, perhaps even, speculates Edwards, to the third millennium BC.[69] That they existed by the ninth century AD there is no doubt, because they are seen being placed in position in the engraving at Borobodur (Figure 15.14).

As to the outrigger, one can perhaps take the earliest radiocarbon date for an island too distant to be reached by simple raft, say 50 BC ± 500 in Fiji,[70] and estimate how long before this the evolution of the outrigger started.

## Polynesia to America?

If the outrigger canoe had reached all the way from Indonesia to Easter Island between, say, 2000 BC and AD 850, then one has at least to consider a further possibility. Did the Polynesians take one more step and reach the American continent? There is certainly no technical reason why they should not have done so, though their reception there, re-victualling and return to starting-point are rather more questionable.

There is a Marquesan legend which describes a canoe of very great size called *Kaahua* which made a voyage in ancient times in search of lands. It was a double canoe with a number of houses on it, and carried a great quantity of breadfruit paste. So large was it that bailers had to climb up the sides from the bottom to pour the bilge water out. First they went to Nukuhiva; then they sailed east until they reached a large land called Jefiti. After remaining a while, they left some of the crew there and the rest returned to the Marquesas.[71] Since the only large land to the east of the Marquesas is South America, this legend does suggest that the Polynesians reached that continent. There is also a Raratongan story about a similar voyage to the east to a 'land of ridges'.

However, none of the Polynesian artefacts so far found in South America, such as Easter Island obsidian spear-heads or Polynesian stone adzes, has been recorded by archaeologists in proper archaeological contexts.[72] More promising perhaps is George Carter's study of a somewhat unlikely subject, the chicken.[73] This bird was present in the Indus valley civilisation in the third millennium BC and, as Rekmire's tomb near the Valley of the Kings shows, had reached Egypt by about 1500 BC as part of the tribute brought to the Pharaoh Tutmose III from a country in Asia.

In the New World, the first recorded landing of Europeans, presumably with chickens, was near Bahia in Brazil on 22 April 1500. Yet by 1540 the chicken was recorded as being established from the Atlantic to the Pacific and from north-west Brazil to Argentina. Carter uses the comparison between this implied speed of diffusion in the New World, and the far slower spread in the Old World, together with linguistic evidence which suggests an Asian origin, to argue that the chicken was present in pre-Columbian South America and had come there from Asia. Jose de Acosta certainly agreed with this idea. In 1590 he wrote: 'I must say that I was astonished at the fowls which without doubt were kept there even before the coming of the Spaniards, this being clearly proved by the fact that the natives have names of their own for them, calling a hen *gualpa* and an egg *ronto*.'[74] The finding of a chicken-bone in a properly stratified and recorded pre-Columbian site would strongly support this case for what has been called rather scathingly the 'alleged South Pacific Regatta',[75] since the survival of domestic fowl would mean a swift deliberate voyage rather than accidental drifting. But for the moment one must wait the confirmatory evidence. In any case even without the additional step to the American continent the achievements of the ancient Pacific navigators in their own right remain a remarkable human and maritime feat.

# 16 The Americas

## THE AMERICAN CONTINENT

Ever since the Jesuit Joseph de Acosta first suggested the idea early in the seventeenth century, because it would have enabled the animals from Noah's Ark to get there dryshod,[1] orthodox opinion has held that the American continent was first peopled via the Bering Strait. Yet paradoxically, though this is assumed to have been a land route at the relevant period, of all the continents America has the richest range of surviving prehistoric craft. In addition to vast size, great variations in ecological conditions, and isolation, it was not until the arrival of the Spaniards in the sixteenth century that this continent felt the impact of the complicated development of European shipping. We have therefore had preserved for us, at least until recent times, an extraordinary range of aboriginal craft. This is of great importance to the nautical archaeologist because, while few would argue that exact parallels exist everywhere, we can see many of the solutions achieved by primitive peoples in different conditions and study some of the processes that in the old world are much more difficult to perceive under their elaborate layers of later events.

The reed-bundle *caballitos*, riding saucily through the surf off the west coast of South America, are probably the survivors of one of man's earliest constructed craft, which were used from North Africa through most of the temperate areas of the globe. The succeeding stage of technological evolution seems to have produced the bark canoe and the skin boat. The former is represented by the great birch canoe tradition of the North American Indians as well as the cruder craft of tropical South America and those of the Yahgans and Alacalufs in the far south; whilst skin was used for the floats of the Chonos, and the bull boat and *pelota*, as well as the brilliantly-adapted umiak and kayak of the Arctic north. In addition there were perhaps the most controversial of all aboriginal American craft, the sailing rafts, like the one sighted by Pizarro on his second voyage towards Peru (see below).

We have also on the American continent a separate version of that crucial event, the agricultural revolution. Though the domestication of crops and animals was primarily a land event, it had its repercussions at sea, which we can see reflected in central America in the evolution and use of the dug-out and, with interesting echoes of a similar course of events in the Mediterranean, the first steps towards a built craft.

### Birch bark

This richness of the American scene brings its own problems. The impossibility of telling from the archaeological evidence when and how the North American bark canoe evolved its special characteristics has already been mentioned. One would like to speculate that this craft dated at least as far back as the Indian painting 4 metres long of a black canoe with six men in it which Terence

16.1  *Canoes of Oonalashka, Aleutian Islands (National Maritime Museum)*

Grieder has recorded in Val Verde County, Texas.[2] From associated evidence, Grieder suggests a late palaeo-Indian or Early and Middle Archaic date for this work. On the other hand, without any discussion, he simply describes the craft as a dug-out. This on the face of it seems arguable. Both the decoration and shape of the bow and stern are reminiscent of Athabaskan canoes. If its southern location argues against a birch-bark construction, one could quote the possibility of higher river levels, which Grieder suggests, also reflecting a damper climate. Dug-outs, as we have seen, generally appear in more settled conditions with emergent or present agriculture. The Seneca Indians, in the third quarter of the eighteenth century, abandoned birch-bark canoes and took to making dug-outs when steel tools became available to them.[3] So it looks as if the more usual progression is that way, rather than from dug-out to birch-bark canoe.

Another cruder painting at Val Verde is surely too curved for a dug-out. So it is at least worth considering that these paintings reflect a possible age of a few thousand years for the birch-bark canoe. On the other hand, in conditions equivalent to the Old World Mesolithic, dug-outs may have already started to appear, so one cannot be certain.

## Skin boats

Much the same situation applies to the kayak. Here we have a craft superbly adapted to its purpose, built in a great many related forms, yet we can only speculate, as in chapter 4, how and where it evolved. As a type it must be at least several centuries old since one example was captured by a Danish expedition to north Russia in the seventeenth century.[4]

The canoe was made in the style of a gondola being 15 or 16 feet long by 2½ feet broad, very cleverly constructed of fish ribs [probably baleen or whalebone] covered with fish skins stitched together, thus making the canoe a purse, as it were, from one end to the other. Within it the two [paddlers?] were enclosed up to the waist in such a manner that not a single drop of water could get into their little vessel, so that they were enabled to expose themselves to every tempest without any danger.

Even earlier, if more uncertain, accounts of kayaks come from Claudius Clavus and Olaus Magnus.[5] Claudius Clavus reported that in AD 1430 a little hide vessel 'which had a pygmy in it' hung in the cathedral at Nidaros (Trondheim). As he also describes 'a long vessel of hides taken with pygmies in it', presumably a umiak, it seems highly likely the former was a kayak. Olaus

16.2  *Engraving on an ivory bodkin of the Western Thule Culture from House 7, Cape Krusenstern, Alaska (Giddings, Ancient Men of the Arctic, 1968)*

Magnus[6] claimed that in AD 1505 he had seen two small skin boats captured by King Haakon in the thirteenth century, which in turn suggests that the skin boats of the Skraelings which the Icelanders encountered in Greenland may have included kayaks.

There is some evidence from the Arctic regions of the American continent to expand the history of the kayak. A carving of a boat on a bodkin from House 7 at Cape Krusenstern, Alaska,[7] links the Eskimo skin-boat tradition to the Eurasian circum-Polar one which, as we have seen, goes back at least to Postglacial times. The distinguishing feature of this boat carving is that at the stern it has a double, and at the bow a single, upright line

(Figure 16.2). This is so contrary to modern umiak practice where the line of the gunwales is flat that it has even been suggested[8] that the carving is of a birch-bark canoe, despite its northerly and maritime provenance. If one looks at it beside the Scandinavian carvings from Evenhus (Figure 4.2) and Rødøy, however, a very different interpretation appears: the double line represents the familiar upright lifting handles. When one also considers that Captain Cook saw an Aleutian umiak with the same feature, then all these group themselves into a coherent type which, as Marstrander has argued,[9] was probably common to the entire circum-Polar world.

If the Western Thule Culture is given a broad dating bracket of AD 1000 to 1400, this, as well as the eighteenth-century Aleutian evidence, suggests that the modern umiak with its flat gunwales, which now ranges from Greenland to Siberia, was at least in some areas a comparatively recent development. Possibly the Baffin Island type of today which has an upright stern and stem fitted into the keelson with an open tenon, instead of the more usual sloping knees, represents a relic of the

16.3  *Wooden frame of a umiak dated to the fifteenth or sixteenth century discovered in 1949 at Herlufsholm, Greenland, and now in the National Museum of Denmark (Egil Knuth)*

older style of construction.[10] Howard Chapelle suggests that the current projection of the gunwales originally made building easier by giving a space for a retaining lashing when the gunwales were being bent. As the headboards became wider and the spring of the gunwales less pronounced, less strain was put on the lashings, but by then the Eskimo had become used to using the projecting ends as lifting handles.[11] These, then, which were originally developed for a quite different reason may thus have come to serve the same purpose as and replace the old upright pair of lifting handles of the early circum-Polar tradition.

How one wishes that the Vikings had described in a little more detail the 'hud-keipr', literally 'hide-rowlocks'[12] which Thorfinn Karlsefni saw approaching in such great numbers in Vinland in the eleventh century that the estuary looked as though it was covered with bits of charcoal.[13] This was a dramatic enough meeting in any case. Here were the finest evolutionary products of the skin-boat tradition, the deep-sea Viking ships, having crossed the north Atlantic, meeting the other wing of the tradition in its most eastern expression on the North American continent. Were they kayaks or umiaks? Did they have upright bows and sterns? One can hardly blame the fifteenth-century Icelandic scribe who wrote down Eirik's Saga in Skalholtsbok for concentrating on the Skraelings' lust for red cloth and the remarkable effect Freydis

slapping her bare breast with her sword had on them during the subsequent battle, rather than on details of their boats: but one does regret it.[14]

At the earlier end of the time scale, the maritime basis of Eskimo life seems fairly certain. To quote William E. Taylor Jr, it was a necessary precondition for their initial spread from Siberia to Greenland and their persistence for more than 5,000 years.[15] Therefore if one accepts that there is evidence for the Eskimo going back at least to the Denbigh Culture (c. 3000–1000 BC), if not to the earlier Onion Portage levels, then it seems likely that there is a minimum of 5,000 years development of the arctic skin boat.[16]

**Trans-oceanic voyages**

One thing there can be little doubt about is the feasibility of crossing from Asia to the American continent by sea once the long skin boat was evolved (Map 1.1). Well before Captains Cook and Clerke became the first Europeans to see the Eskimo of northern Alaska in 1778, records show that the peoples on the two sides of the Bering Strait were no strangers to one another. For instance in 1711 Sin Popow recorded[17] that in summer the Americans sailed over to Siberia in their skin boats in a single day. This merely confirms a situation which one suspects had existed for thousands of years, that the 90 kilometres

16.4 *Potsherds from Valdivia, Ecuador, dated to c. 3200 BC (Clifford Evans and Betty Meggers, Smithsonian Institution, Washington)*

between continents, with convenient stopping-places in the middle at St Lawrence Island and the Diomedes, was a very minor piece of navigation for a sea-going skin boat.

Although the Viking contacts with the American continent are now little doubted, other trans-oceanic contacts are more difficult to accept. Brendan and the Irish, Madog and the Welsh, Nicholas of Lynn, Henry Earl of Orkney, the Phoenicians of Ezion-Geber (whose circumnavigation of Africa it has been suggested took in the coast of Brazil)[18] and the Egyptians are some of the contenders. While it is certainly not impossible that one of these crossed the Atlantic, the evidence that they did has not so far won much in the way of scholarly acceptance.

Rather more relevant are the suggestions made by Alice B. Kehoe that the introduction of wood-making tools and fishing gear in the Laurentian Archaic culture of North America and of ground slate knives and points in Scandinavia and the Baltic in the third millennium BC could be explained by two-way diffusion across the north Atlantic. This would have occurred through deep-sea cod fishermen in skin boats being blown away from their home grounds. But the writer herself admits that this hypothesis is incapable of detailed demonstration without a great deal more work and evidence.[19]

Paradoxically it is an even longer and more difficult voyage across the other ocean which borders the American continent that has won most scholarly approval for a prehistoric inter-continental voyage, one which it is suggested brought the skill of pottery-making 8,000 miles from Japan to Ecuador five thousand years ago.[20] Pottery (Figure 16.4) found near the fishing village of Valdivia on the coast of Ecuador appears very abruptly in the archaeological record at about 3200 BC. What is more, this earliest so far known pottery of the New World is well made and has considerable assurance of form and decoration. As such it seemed more likely to be an introduction from somewhere else where there was a well-established pottery tradition, rather than a sudden and elaborate flowering of a local technology. Parallel evidence turned up on the other side of the Pacific in western and central Japan. Here pottery found in three shell-midden sites on the island of Kyushu seems to have almost all the characteristics of the Valdivia kind. The Jomon shellfish gatherers had been making pottery for some 4,000 years before it appeared at Valdivia. By that time Jomon pottery had nearly all the features found in the South American examples. The only explanation of this, Emilio Estrada and Betty Meggers suggest, is an accidental trans-pacific voyage 5,000 years ago from Japan to Ecuador.

This is a startling hypothesis, to say the least. The shortest Great Circle route between the two sites is some 8,200 miles. The two archaeologists argue that the pattern of winds, storms and ocean currents follow this route. The currents off the Kyushu coast, among the strongest in the Pacific, running at 24 to 32 miles a day towards the north-east, would be reinforced by typhoons whose tracks sweep past the Japanese islands from the Philippines. Then prevailing winds and gales follow a curving route north of Hawaii and southward along the American coast. Quite rightly they say that these fishermen of the Pacific must have been accustomed to exposure to sun and rain and have known the tricks of satisfying hunger and thirst at sea. There is no reason to suppose that accidental drifting voyages then would have been less likely than modern examples which have been known to last months, such as the 161-day voyage by the raft La Balsa which reached Australia from Ecuador in November 1970 after completing a journey nearly 3,000 miles longer than that of Heyerdahl's Kon-tiki. There is also the case of the nine stranded Japanese whom de Lesseps met in Kamchatka in the eighteenth century. He described how they had embarked in a ship of their own country with the intention merely of visiting the southern Kuril Islands to trade there. However, they were only a short distance from their own coast when they were overtaken by a violent gale which carried them out to sea and deprived them of all knowledge of where they were. Finally they had come ashore in the Aleutians.[21]

Then there is Kotzebue's account of finding in 1815 a distressed Japanese vessel off the Califor-

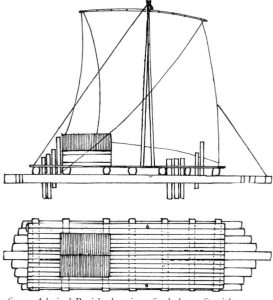

16.5   *Admiral Paris's drawing of a balsa raft with leeboards, from Guayaquil, Ecuador; length* c. *30 metres, beam 8 to 10 metres (after Paris, . . .* La Construction navale des peuples extra-européens, *Paris, 1841)*

nian coast, which had been driven by storms from the Japan sea and drifted across the Pacific for seventeen months. Only three of the crew of thirty-five were still alive. The rest had died of starvation.[22] According to Doran, of sixty recorded cases of Japanese junks being inadvertently swept away into the Pacific, at least six reached the coast of North America and another six ended up in Mexican waters, while Japanese slaves were reported to have been held by Salmon Indians of the north-west coast of America when the latter were first visited by Europeans.[23]

Finally, one might perhaps recall Stephen C. Jett's point that the Silk Road, the wandering of the Huns from Mongolia to France, the campaigns of Alexander the Great and the lengthy migrations of the Tupian Indians of South America all covered vast distances, up to 10,000 miles, on land. Yet sea travel in early times was generally easier than land travel, and water often joined places rather than separated them.[24] Nevertheless a drift voyage of 8,000 miles must have been hard going.

At the most optimistic rate it would have lasted a year and a half. Could they have landed en route and been pushed on rather than back when they set off again?

The voyages by which the Polynesian and Melanesian peoples occupied the Pacific islands were made in craft largely based on the dug-out. Presumably therefore the Jomon fishermen might have been as successful three thousand years or more earlier with a version of the same sort of craft. On the other hand one wonders whether the raft, whose early presence in Japan has been described, would not have provided better survival conditions in the suggested storm tracks and also account for the laisser-faire attitude to drifting which took them so far from their homeland. Simple rafts seem to have been used on the western coast of the American continent from very early times, and the evidence for the use of rafts in the Pacific has already been discussed in chapter 15.

## Rafts and sails

What now seems very likely is that a particular version of the sail crossed the Pacific. The great sailing rafts of the west coast of South America have possibly caught the imagination of a wider general public than any other primitive craft, partly because of the romantic vastness of the Pacific, but mostly because of the voyage of the *Kon-tiki*. One of the first European descriptions of the progenitors of Heyerdahl's craft was by Miguel de Estete during Pizarro's second voyage to Peru:[25]

These balsas are of some very thick and long wooden logs, which are as soft and light on the water as cork. They lash them very tightly together with a kind of hemp rope, and above them they place a high framework so that the merchandise and things they carry will not get wet. They set a mast in the largest log in the middle, hoist a sail, and navigate along all this coast. They are very safe vessels because they cannot sink or capsize, since the water washes through them everywhere.

Benzoni, the source of a famous early illustration of them (Figure 16.9), later emphasised their shape, which Estete had not mentioned:[26]

Along this entire seacoast the Indians are great fishermen. The craft which they use both for fishing and navigating are a kind of raft made of three, five, seven, nine or eleven very light logs, formed in the shape of a hand, in which the middle one is longer than all the others. They are made both long and short, and, according to their size and length, carry sails.

Models of pre-Columbian sail-less rafts are known from burials in northern Chile and, together with the *caballitos*, were probably the craft from which prehistoric fishermen dangled their shell or bone hooks and caught the fish whose bones make up the great characteristic middens along the coast. But by the time of the Inca Empire these early craft had developed into great trading rafts, whose continuing use after the arrival of the Spaniards is reflected in Dampier's description of them carrying 60 or 70 tons of goods on voyages of 500 to 600 leagues from Lima to Truxillo or Panama.[27] Early Spanish reports confirm that pre-Columbian versions were estimated to have a capacity for thirty large casks, or fifty men and three horses, and with their huts for shelter and bulwarks to protect the cargo were designed for large loads and lengthy voyages.[28] According to Clinton Edwards,[29] these rafts seem to have been more directly associated with the people of coastal Ecuador than the Inca-dominated Peruvians. This is borne out by a tale collected from the Indians by Sarmiento de Gamboa and Cabello de Balboa that the Inca ruler Tupac Yupanqui engaged both local seamen and local craft to go on a sea-going expedition from the Ecuador coast shortly before the Conquest. If these sailing rafts were limited to a relatively short area of coast, one arrives at the intriguing and controversial question whether the version with sails and centreboards was introduced to the American continent by sea across the Pacific.

That second voyage of Pizarro's, which provided Estete's account, also provided another which is very relevant to this particular controversy. This is the account signed by Juan de Samano, secretary to Charles V, but which was actually written by Francisco de Xerez. A ship sent south by Pizarro with Xerez on board met a local sailing raft, and Xerez described it like this: 'It carried masts and yards of very fine wood, and cotton sails of the same form as those of our ships, and very good rigging of henequen, which is like hemp'.[30] This would seem a straightforward enough account. Yet W. H. Prescott, influenced perhaps by later descriptions, interpreted this as 'two masts of sturdy poles, erected in the middle of

16.6 *Sixteenth-century Peruvian sailing raft as drawn by Richard Madox; British Library Cotton MS. Titus BVIII (British Library)*

16.7 *Detail from the early seventeenth century drawing of Paita Harbour, Peru, by George van Spilbergen; note the 'oceanic spritsails' and the three crewmen adjusting leeboards (Clinton R. Edwards)*

the vessel, sustained a large square-sail of cotton.'[31] H. Urteaga, S. K. Lothrop and P. A. Means, as well as Heyerdahl, all followed this lead of Prescott in accepting that the aboriginal craft used square sails.[32] It needed Edwards's perspicacious look at the original Spanish of Xerez to change this. The Spanish word for the yard of a lateen sail is '*antena*', and this was the word used rather than '*verga*', the yard of a square sail. Pizarro's ships were among the first dozen built by the Spanish on the west coast of the Isthmus. They had to be small as almost everything for their construction except timber had to be brought from Spain. As Edwards rightly points out, such small craft then would almost certainly have had lateen sails. So Xerez's use of the word '*antena*' and his likening of the raft's sail to that of his own ships could well mean that the

aboriginal sail was a triangular one.[33]

Edwards has found two more accounts and two illustrations which support this interpretation. Oviedo, who based his work on eye-witness accounts, twice described rafts met by the Conquistadores as having lateen sails.[34] So does Pedro Guitierrez de Santa Clara writing about central American life and customs a little later.[35] The first illustration (Figure 16.6) comes from the diary of Richard Madox, a chaplain on Edward Fenton's ill-fated voyage of 1582. There were some of Drake's former crew with Fenton and it was evidently from their descriptions that Madox learnt about his 'raffe' from Peru. The second one (Figure 16.7) illustrates George van Spilbergen's raid on Paita during his voyage round the world in 1619. What both illustrations show is not a lateen

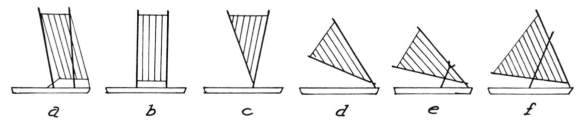

16.8 *Evolution of the Oceanic spritsail and Oceanic lateen, according to LeBaron Bowen. a, proto-Oceanic spritsail with two loose sprits; b, rectangular sail laced to the two sprits; c, two sprits converge; d, spritsail canted aft; e, primitive lateen with prop mast; f, fully developed Oceanic spritsail* (American Neptune, vol. 13, 1953, p. 110)

sail but the so-called Oceanic spritsail attached to a single spar which is both mast and yard. As LeBaron Bowen says,[36] the sail is one of the most easily diffused cultural traits known to man. According to him, the Oceanic spritsail evolved in the way shown in Figure 16.8. And if one accepts Edwards's evidence that a non-European type of triangular sail, reminiscent of but different from the lateen, was in use off the west coast of South America in the sixteenth century, then Bowen's suggestion that they were of Pacific origin seems highly likely.

The South Americans then seem gradually to have adopted elements from European ships. Benzoni's 1572 illustration (Figure 16.9) of an Ecuadorian raft seems to show a European-type square sail bent to a yard which is carried on a crossed pair of sheers. Dampier's seventeenth-century description of a Peruvian raft mentions a 'mast, to which is fastened a large sail, as in our West-Country Barges in the Thames'.[37] By the time Juan and Ulloa illustrated a Guayaquil raft in 1748, the mast, sail and rigging were almost entirely European. Captain Basil Hall, RN, in his journal of the early 1800s, was complimentary about this combination of aboriginal raft and European sail:[38]

The Balsa generally carries only one large sail, which is hoisted to what we call a pair of sheers, formed by

two poles crossing at the top, where they are lashed together . . . it is truly astonishing to see how fast these singular vessels go through the water; but it is still more curious to observe how accurately they can be steered, and how effectively they may be handled in all respects like any ordinary vessel.

A very similar form of raft called a *jangada* is found today off the coast of Brazil on the eastern side of South America (Figure 16.10). Bowen is definite that its sail and in fact the whole craft is derived from the Peruvian balsa.[39] Edwards is more cautious. While admitting the similarities in construction, tapered shape, logs secured by lashings, round pins, and triangular sails resembling those of the Madox and Spillbergen illustrations, he also quoted Cascudo who in a study of the Brazilian *jangadeiros* says that both the sail and the centreboard were introduced by Europeans probably after the end of the sixteenth century.[40] Cascudo stated this because various early descriptions (mainly Portuguese) make no mention of either sails or centreboards. However, this negative evidence is not strong, when one con-

16.9    *Rafts of the Puerto Viejo region, Ecuador, as drawn by G. Benzoni in 1572 (Clinton R. Edwards)*

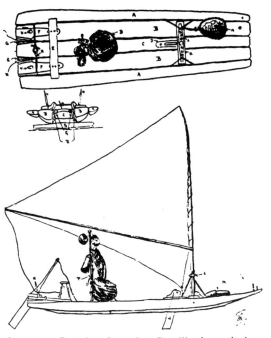

16.10    *(a) Drawing of a modern Brazilian* jangada *by Lane Poole (*MM, *vol. 26, 1940)*

16.10  *(b) A modern* jangada *under way off the coast of Brazil (Jesco von Puttkamer and Adrian Cowell)*

siders that the Portuguese were then ignorant of the use of centreboards and did not themselves use a triangular sail in which the upper yard and mast were one.

*Guares* or leeboards (centreboards) have been used in recent times on S. American rafts (Figure 16.11). Similarly-shaped wooden objects (Figure 16.12) have been excavated from pre-Columbian graves in Peru, and if these indeed are leeboards and not agricultural implements, then the Pacific coast examples are certainly aboriginal and pre-Columbian, and the Brazilian *jangada* ones poss-

ibly, but not certainly, so.[41] It has been argued that this widespread practice of both steering and reducing leeway by the use of leeboards on Formosan rafts as well as South American ones, despite differences in sails, hull-shape and construction material in the rafts involved, suggests a common origin. To quote Edwards:[42]

If further investigation should disclose real similarity of centreboard [leeboards] navigation techniques, the case for trans-Pacific dispersal would be very strong. The complex of raft, hull, sail, centreboards, and the sophisticated techniques of maintaining sailing

16.11  *Modern Peruvian sailing raft with leeboards (Clinton R. Edwards)*

16.12   Guares *or leeboards from tombs at Ica, Peru (Museum für Völkerkunde, Berlin)*

balance, preventing leeway, and manoeuvering and steering by changing the relationship of lateral plane to centre of effort, represents a set of ideas much more complicated than many that are generally accepted as evidence of dispersal rather than fortuitous parallel developments.

Such a trans-Pacific voyage would explain some of the often-quoted examples of Asian influence in pre-Columbian America, which Ekholm, Heine-Geldern, Jeffreys and others have collected.[43] These range from lotus motifs, tiger thrones and stylised elephant figures with mahouts riding them, to elaborate dicing games. They are found in the greatest strength in the later Mexican-influenced styles of Chichen Itza, Yucatan and Tula dating from about AD 1200, which suggests to these authors that these Asian influences may have appeared about AD 700. One would think that the probable date for any postulated sailing-raft voyages would also be in the fairly late pre-

Columbian period, because of the available radiocarbon dates for the most eastern Polynesian settlements, the late date (AD 1000) for the levels in which *guares* are found, and also because of the comparatively narrow stretch of coast, from Manabi in Ecuador to Sechura, where there is aboriginal evidence for the existence of sailing rafts with leeboards.[44]

The existence of pre-Columbian sailing rafts would also explain the pre-Spanish pottery found on the Galápagos Islands by Heyerdahl.[45] Ryden has said this could be of traditional style which persisted after the Conquest,[46] but it seems more reasonable to agree with Clifford Evans that it is too difficult to ascribe all the very large number of sherds to post-Spanish selection.[47]

To accept, however, that the sail and leeboard crossed the Pacific and reached central America through the agency of sailing rafts raises certain problems, of which the most important is the difference between the shaped raft of the South American coast and the square raft of the Chinese area. Of the ancient nature of the shaped raft in South America there is little doubt. In the models excavated at Arica in Chile (Figure 2.2), all the centre logs are longer to an almost exaggerated amount.[48] Nelson has traced the shaped raft across the Pacific, by way of such examples as the *konga* of Eddystone Island in the Solomons (Figure 15.15) and the raft of the Tonga, from east of New Ireland.[49] His view, admittedly rather tentative, is that the Polynesians need not have been the bringers of the raft to the Pacific, in view of the little use they made of it, and that the fragmented distribution of shaped rafts from India to Peru could represent a few late survivals of ancient migrations from raft-rich areas.[50] In this case, the more primitive shaped-raft-users presumably borrowed the idea of the sail either from square bamboo sailing-raft-users or outrigger peoples.

The unusual sailing raft of Mangareva could give a clue here. Hornell thought that this was a remnant, the roof in fact, of a double canoe with a large platform between the two hulls.[51] Nelson, however, disagrees. He suggests it could be a shaped sailing raft in its own right,[52] in which case its importance as a staging post, as it were, for the journey of the sail from the Pacific to South America is obvious.

It is perhaps time now to try and sum up this complicated and controversial subject. First, it is possible that both the sail and the use of leeboards for tacking and steering evolved independently in South America. Heyerdahl's view that Polynesia was populated from the American continent could perhaps be put alongside this, since the sailing raft is an important part of his thesis. The difficulty here, as has already been said, is supposing that such a highly complicated technical arrangement could have evolved separately in two different areas.

Alternatively, if one suggests that the sail and the leeboard were introduced to the American continent, one route it seems fairly safe to rule out is the northern one. No craft like the sailing raft has been found in the Bering-Aleutian area or along the west coast of North America,[53] and Barbeau

found no mention of it in his study of Indian legends about migrations to Alaska.[54] This is also only commonsense since it is unlikely that the raft would be used in the cold conditions of northern waters.

Then there is the possibility that the sail and centreboard were brought by a square-bamboo-type raft from Asia. If this did happen, it must have been a long voyage and little other impression was made on the way until the final point of arrival. Nevertheless these rafts are fine sea-worthy craft and might have used a Great Circle route.

Next there is perhaps the most likely possibility, that shaped rafts from Polynesia with a sail, like the Mangarevan example, and maybe leeboards as well, made the crossing eastwards. If they did, they did not leave any of the staple Polynesian food crops behind them along with the idea of the sail and leeboard. Rice, breadfruit, bananas and the Asian yam do not seem to have reached the American continent before 1492.[55] However, botanical arguments are complex: to illustrate this one could take the case of the sweet potato. One of Heyerdahl's arguments that Polynesia had been colonised by Amerindians is based on the similarity of the name for sweet potato in Peru and Polynesia.[56] This argument has now been rather intriguingly stood on its head by Patricia J. O'Brien,[57] who considers that the sweet potato originated in the New World and was not known elsewhere before the arrival of Columbus, except in Polynesia. Linguistic evidence and finds at Ventanilla in Peru and elsewhere suggest that it had been domesticated in the New World by 2000 BC. After the arrival of the Spaniards, it was rapidly dispersed through the Old World, but also it was found flourishing on a number of Pacific islands when they were first visited by Europeans. Poggeveen saw large plantations when in 1722 he became the first European to admire the spectacular statues of Easter Island. Cook found it was an important crop in Hawaii in 1778, and so did the first explorers of New Zealand in 1769. Recently, archaeological and botanical evidence has extended its presence to a good deal earlier. In Hawaii a carbonised sweet potato has been found in the ash of a fireplace given by radiocarbon the dating bracket of AD 1425 to 1765. On Easter Island one found in similar circumstances has the date of AD 1526 ± 100. In New Zealand the plant has had to develop into an annual rather than a perennial, because of the different climate there, and has also produced an amazing number of varieties (eighty at least); both facts suggest a considerable antiquity. Taking into account this evidence and linguistics which indicate that the Polynesian word 'kumala' was present before the final expansion of the Polynesian peoples, O'Brien argues that the plant probably arrived in the Samoa group about AD 1 (though about 500 BC in the Fiji area or about AD 400 in the Marquesas are alternatives) and thence was spread to the points of the Polynesian triangle where the Europeans found it in the eighteenth century. The similarity of the Peruvian word 'cumar' to the Polynesian 'kumala' she accounts for by 'armar' being an introduction by the Spaniards to Peru after their early travels in the Pacific. Donald W. Brand's study of the linguistic history of the Quechua people of Peru, who later used the word 'cumar', leads him to state positively that nowhere on the coast of Peru or Ecuador was there a people cultivating sweet potato under the name of 'cumar', so it could not have been taken from there to Polynesia or acquired by visiting Polynesian sailors.[58]

There still remains the problem how the plant got to Samoa nearly two thousand years ago. O'Brien suggests two possibilities: either an accidental drift voyage by a raft, whose crew might have been alive or dead on arrival, or, since the tuber does not float, the seeds might have been brought by birds in their digestive tracts or in mud sticking to their feet. The golden plover is a candidate, as it ranges over Polynesia and occasionally as far as South America, and cases have been known of new varieties of sweet potato being introduced into gardens in New Guinea by seeds dropped from birds.[59] If these possibilities are confirmed, the sweet-potato evidence might reinforce the suggestion that sail-less rafts existed on the west coast of the American continent in early times, but would not help to settle the question whether it was the Polynesians who introduced the ideas of the sail and leeboards to central America.

On a par geographically is another possibility – that Polynesian outrigger canoes brought the sail alone, as discussed in the last chapter. If they did, then the guares would have to be a local South American invention, duplicating what had happened much earlier in China.

Finally there is the 'big ship' theory, argued for on the basis that neither chance castaways, sailors nor merchants would have been the accomplished architects, sculptors or experts in cosmological lore necessary to introduce the shared traits of ancient Mexico and Asia. To this way of thinking, the trans-Pacific crossing would have been made by a wind-driven ship such as one of Nearchus's fleet, which traded between Ceylon and Indonesia in the first six centuries AD, or even a unit of the Emperor of China's fleet which under Hsu Fu was lost about 219 BC in a search for new medicinal drugs.[60]

One thing is certain: the already vast bibliography on the question of trans-Pacific contacts will get even larger before any general agreement on the subject is reached.

## THE WEST INDIES

On the eastern side of the American continent lies another area of interest and controversy, the Caribbean. In many ways this resembles the Mediterranean. Here was a sea virtually encircled by land and islands, in a warm climate with good sea-going conditions much of the time out of the hurricane season, and the agricultural revolution happening on the mainland from perhaps 6000 BC onwards. The Mayas and other advanced societies on the mainland had no equivalent of the River Nile, and no island obsidian trade is recorded so far with its stimulating effect on seafaring. Yet the similarities remain, and it is fascinating that at both ends of the time-scale the situation should have been so different in both places.

When the Spaniards arrived in the late fifteenth

century, they found the islands of the Caribbean occupied by Caribs and Arawaks, pottery-making agriculturalists, together with a few isolated pockets of more primitive people. In the local terminology, these are respectively Neo- and Meso-Indians, stages broadly comparable to the Old World Neolithic and Mesolithic. Since all these groups were active fishermen and skilled users of dug-outs, little thought was at first given to how the islands were reached by sea.

With the passage of time, a more detailed picture began to appear. Geologically, the islands seem to have been separated at an early time from the mainland, since they lacked continental mammals such as the glyptodon. Their fauna was assumed to have reached them largely by accidental rafting from South America, two of whose great rivers, the Magdalena and Orinoco, discharge debris with such force that it is caught up by the South Equatorial current and carried northwards to the islands.[61] Hence the comparative poverty of the island fauna: only one form of monkey, for instance, compared with the much greater numbers on the mainland. Man was at first thought to have arrived on the islands about the time of Christ and to have reached the Bahamas, via the Lesser and Greater Antilles, by about AD 1000.[62] However, in the 1930s, pre-pottery sites at Ile à Vache and Couri were found on Haiti and this was followed by the discovery in Hispaniola of the Cabaret complex of stone tools, which lacked ground stone artefacts and included projectile points, and thus could be classed as belonging to the so-called paleo-Indian stage.[63] This same island also provided, in 1963, a site called Mordan where in a deposit in which the top layers contained pottery and the lowest layer held, besides flint tools and fragments of animal- and fish-bones, enough charcoal to give radiocarbon dates which ranged from 2190±130 to 2610±80 BC.[64]

A short distance away from Mordan, the inland site of Rancho Casimira yielded even cruder and heavier flint tools.[65] Cruxent and Rouse claim that this could move human occupation of the Caribbean islands back as far as 5000 BC.[66] Through a somewhat complicated argument, they derive this early occupation from central America by way of the mid-Caribbean chain of islands. They reject South America as the source of this early paleo-Indian complex on Hispaniola because the transition from the early to the late paleo-Indian stage probably took place in Venezuela as long as 12,000 years ago. Florida is likewise ruled out because neither the gouge made from conch-shells nor the projectile points, which are characteristic of early paleo-Indian sites there, are present at Casimira. The two authors, however, are the first to admit the weaknesses of the case for the third possibility, central America. They have to infer from Neo-Indian examples that in the early paleo-Indian stage the right sort of tools to be ancestral to the Casimira ones were being made in central America. Neither have any prehistoric habitation sites of any kind been found on the mid-Caribbean chain or any paleo- or Meso-Indian ones on Jamaica.[67] On the other hand, not much systematic search has been made for them.

## Rafts

In a sense this argument is irrelevant as far as the maritime implications are concerned. Wherever they came from, the ancestors of the Casimira people reached Hispaniola by sea at a very early technological stage. Cruxent and Rouse have considered this question of sea travel and suggest that the Casimira people were tempted away from the mainland by the hunt for manatees and seals, which, according to the Spaniards, were once plentiful in the Caribbean.[68] They would have moved from island to island, more numerous then because sea levels were lower, until they reached Hispaniola where abundant supplies of flint, fresh water and vegetable food as well as sea mammals led them to settle. The craft they used would have been the raft fitted with mat sails.

The raft part of this thesis is certainly possible. Friederici and Suder describe primitive rafts in use in the Caribbean[69] and there is Lionel Wafer's seventeenth century description[70] of a Panamanian raft quoted in chapter 2. Further to the south-east, there is the exquisite pre-Columbian gold model of a raft (Figure 16.14) from Lake

16.13 *Nineteenth-century drawing of a raft from Gambier Island in the Tuamotu Archipelago (National Maritime Museum)*

Guatavita, Colombia, now in the Bogota Museum, and there was a rather similar one from the Lake of Siecha, which was lost in Germany in the Second World War. Then the Cenote at Chichen Itza has yielded a gold disc on which there is a raft as well as three dug-outs. Thompson sensibly points out that the hemispherical shapes under this latter may well be an attempt to represent a gourd raft, which could be an alternative to a balsa construction.[71]

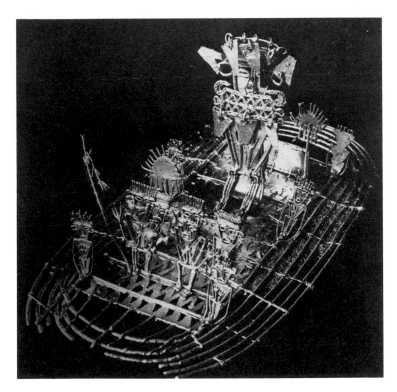

16.14 *Pre-Columbian gold model raft from Lake Guatavita, Colombia (Museo del Oro, Bogota, photo Hernán Díaz)*

## Sail

The sail part of Cruxent and Rouse's thesis is much less likely. The existence of an aboriginal sail as early as 5000 BC on the east side of the continent is hardly likely to have led to the situation already described on the west coast, where a trans-Pacific introduction is arguable but not proved, and in any case that arrival would seem more likely to be well into the first millennium AD. Some authorities such as McKusick have in fact argued that the Caribs had no knowledge of the sail in pre-Columbian times. McKusick's strongest argument comes from an account of a Franciscan friar who, when he was wrecked on the island of Dominica in 1605, saved his life by showing the island Caribs how to use sails.[72] According to Stoneman, who wrote down this story in 1625, the use of sails in canoes by these islanders had not been seen before.[73] On the other hand, Clinton Edwards sees more significance in Oviedo, who as early as 1526 specifically attributed knowledge of sailing to the islanders, and considered them to be accomplished canoe-sailors.[74] Bernard Diaz del Castillo described how, when the Cordova expedition reached Cabo Cotoche on the north-east coast of Yucatán, five canoes with sails came out to meet them, and later on he saw a trading vessel under sail off Honduras.[75]

Finally there is Thompson's linguistic point that the words 'bub' (a sail or to sail) and 'bubil' (to navigate with sails) are listed in the late sixteenth century Motul dictionary.[76] Since the South American peoples tended to adopt Spanish words for Spanish practices strange to them, just as the Arabs did with Portuguese naval terms, this confirms Thompson's belief that the case for aboriginal use of sail in the Caribbean is well established. But this by no means takes it back into the fifth millennium BC.

## Reed craft

An alternative to the sail-less raft in the early period is the reed-bundle craft or *caballito*. Since it existed in relatively early times on the west coast of the continent, there does not seem any theoretical

reason why it should not have been used on the east coast in the Caribbean. An early Spanish report describes reed floats in Mexico at Lake Chapalu, Lake Tlaxcala and in Mayarit, and examples have survived into modern times.[77] So suggesting that these craft were used a little further towards the east is not very challenging. Another point worth considering is that according to Edwards's distribution map of aboriginal craft on the west coast, dug-out canoes and reed-bundle craft are mutually exclusive,[78] and the same situation might have occurred in the Caribbean, just as in the Mediterranean, as we have seen in chapter 6, where the early evidence for reed boats was largely overlaid by subsequent developments.

## Dug-outs

When the Spaniards reached the Caribbean, there is no doubt that the dominant aboriginal craft there was the dug-out. Columbus described them:[79]

They have in all these islands very many canoes like our row-boats; some larger, some smaller, but most of them larger than a barge of 18 seats. They are not so wide, because they are made of one single piece of timber, but a barge could not keep up with them in rowing because they go with incredible speed and with these canoes they navigate among these islands, which are innumerable, and carry on their traffic. I have seen in some of these canoes seventy and eighty men . . .

In Bernaldez's account of Columbus's second voyage there is a description of an even bigger dug-out, off Jamaica: 'They have more canoes than in any other part of these regions, and the largest that have yet been seen, all, as had been said, made each from a single tree trunk . . . One of these large canoes which the Admiral measured was 96 feet long and 8 feet broad.'[80] So the widespread presence of these Carib and Arawak craft could explain the absence in the immediate pre-Columbian period of reed-bundle craft, and leave these as possibly handier contenders than sail-less rafts for the distinction of having taken the Casimira people to Hispaniola somewhere in the five millennia BC.

Despite this suggested sea-crossing almost as early as those in the Mediterranean, at the later end of the time-scale technological progress in the Caribbean seems to have slowed down. It is not even certain that the Caribs had achieved the basic practice of sewing on strakes to a dug-out base by the time the Spaniards arrived. Some authorities argue that since trees of a size to produce the big craft described by Columbus and Bernaldez do not come readily to hand in the West Indies, the islanders must have achieved these dimensions by lashing on planks. This process was certainly described by Jean Baptiste du Tertre in 1667:[81]

The barbarians made two kinds of boats in which they go to sea . . . Both types are made from whole trees which they trim, dig out, and then complete, with implements bought from Europeans such as axes, adzes and other tools. Prior to the trade with Europeans they spent entire years making their boats. They felled trees or burned them at the base. They hollowed out the log with stone axes and with a small fire, which progressed along the log hull until it had reached the desired shape.

Pirogues appear to be nothing more than two great planks joined to a base, and these boats have a width across the gunwales of 6 to 7 feet. Where the planks join at each end of the boat, the opening is closed with pieces of plank. This is especially true with the stern, which is almost always slightly higher than the bow.

Ordinarily, the pirogues are not high enough with just these first side planks and so they raise and build up the sides from one end to the other with some planks 15 to 16 inches wide. Without using nails they lash and fit these planks upon the pirogue with cordage made from 'mahot' fibre. They next caulk the joints with oakum made from the beaten bark of 'mahot'. Over this caulking they bind small sticks with 'mahot' cordage. This is indeed very water-tight, but it does not last long and must be done over and over again.

McKusick argues that it is reasonable to assume that, because the planks were lashed on, they must have been part of an aboriginal technique.[82] On the other hand, one could suspect that the Spaniards may have exaggerated the size of the dug-outs, and that lashing planks was the best the Caribs could do in the seventeenth century to imitate the nailed strakes of the Europeans. In which case, the use of added planks aboriginally is not proved.

Yet one can surely say, from their adoption of both techniques in the centuries after Columbus's arrival, that they would almost certainly have taken this step forward on their own accord in due course, if they had not done so by 1486. In which case, had the course of European civilisation gone differently and more slowly, it might well have been a captain from Hispaniola or Jamaica, with six millennia of sea-going traditions behind him, who followed the Atlantic westerlies and discovered Europe, instead of a Genoese doing it the other way round.

# Abbreviations used in the notes

| | |
|---|---|
| *AJA* | *American Journal of Archaeology* |
| *AJSL&L* | *American Journal of Semitic Languages and Literature* |
| BAR | British Archaeological Reports (Oxford) |
| *BCH* | *Bulletin de Correspondance hellénique* (Paris) |
| *IJNA* | *International Journal of Nautical Archaeology* |
| *JAOS* | *Journal of the American Oriental Society* (New Haven) |
| *JEA* | *Journal of Egyptian Archaeology* |
| *JPS* | *Journal of Pacific Studies* |
| *JRAI* | *Journal of the Royal Anthropological Institute* |
| *JRS* | *Journal of Roman Studies* |
| *MM* | *Mariner's Mirror* |
| *PPS* | *Proceedings of the Prehistoric Society* |
| *PSAS* | *Proceedings of the Society of Antiquaries of Scotland* |

# Notes

## Introduction

1 Vice-Admiral G. A. Ballard, 'The Sculptures of Deir el-Bahri: II', *MM*, vol. 6, July 1920, p. 216.
2 Lionel Casson, *The Ancient Mariners*, London, 1959, p. 3.
3 Stuart Piggott, *Ancient Europe*, Edinburgh, 1965, p. 2.
4 Notably in J. W. Needham, *Science and Civilisation in China*, vol. IV, part 3, Cambridge, 1971.

## Chapter 1 Earliest times

1 Grahame Clark and Stuart Piggott, *Prehistoric Societies*, Penguin, 1970, pp. 34–6.
2 K. W. Butzer, *Environment and Archaeology*, London, 1972, p. 453, Fig. 67.
3 ibid., p. 452.
4 Scales from a lemon sole are said to have been found in Derbyshire (A. L. Armstrong, 'Pin Hole Cave Excavations, Creswell Crags, Derbyshire', *Proceedings of the Prehistoric Society of East Anglia*, vol. 6, 1929–31, p. 27); and a site at Salzgitter-Lebenstedt in northern Germany has yielded remains of perch, pike, crabs and waterbirds (Butzer, op. cit., pp. 468–71).
5 P. A. Mellars, 'The Palaeolithic and Mesolithic', in C. Renfrew (ed.), *British Prehistory*, London, 1974, p. 56.
6 F. Ivanhoe, 'Was Virchow Right about Neanderthal?', *Nature*, vol. 227, 1970, pp. 577–9.
7 R. Virchow, 2. *Ethnel* 4, 1872, p. 157.
8 Ivanhoe, op. cit., p. 578 (quoting R. F. Sognnaes, *American Journal of Pathology*, vol. 32, 1956, p. 547, and C. A. Baud, S. Durif and P. W. Morgenthaler, *Arch. Suisses Anthrop. Gen.*, vol. 19, 1954, p. 37).
9 Ivanhoe, op. cit., p. 577.
10 J. M. Coles and E. S. Higgs, *The Archaeology of Early Man*, London, 1969 (Barma Grande, p. 252; La Ferrassie, p. 275).
11 Clark and Piggott, op. cit., p. 53.
12 This subject has inspired a very large amount of writing. For a useful list of references see Butzer, op. cit., pp. 491–5.
13 W. G. Hagg, 'The Bering Strait Land Bridge', *Scientific American*, 206, 1962, pp. 12–23.
14 D. J. Mulvaney, 'The Pleistocene Colonisation of Australia', *Antiquity*, vol. 38, 1964, pp. 263–7; D. J. Mulvaney, 'Prehistory from Antipodean Perspectives', *PPS*, vol. 37, pt 2, 1971, pp. 232–3; J. M. Bowler, Rhys Jones, Harry Allen and A. G. Thorne, 'Pleistocene Human Remains from Australia: a Living Site and Human Cremation from Lake Mungo, western New South Wales', *World Archaeology*, vol. 2, no. 1, 1970, pp. 39–60; A. G. Thorne, 'Preliminary Comments on the Kow Swamp Skeleton', Australian Institute of Aboriginal Studies, *Newsletter*, vol. 2, no. 10, 1969, pp. 6–7.
15 Mulvaney, 'Prehistory from Antipodean Perspectives', p. 232.
16 Clark and Piggott, op. cit., p. 98.
17 Butzer, op. cit., p. 38.

## Chapter 2 Raft and reed

1 James Hornell, *Water Transport*, Newton Abbot, 1970, p. 17.
2 ibid.
3 H. H. Brindley, 'The Sailing Balsa of Lake Titicaca and Other Reed Bundle Craft', *MM*, vol. 17, 1931, p. 9.
4 ibid., p. 10.
5 ibid.
6 S. Nishimura, *Ancient Rafts of Japan*, Tokyo, 1925, p. 29.
7 ibid., pp. 65–9.

8 ibid., p. 88.
9 J. G. Nelson, 'The Geography of the Balsa, no. 3', *American Neptune*, vol. 21, 1961, p. 166.
10 ibid., p. 163.
11 William Dampier, *A New Voyage Round the World*, 5th ed., London, 1703, vol. I, pp. 141–3.
12 C. R. Edwards, 'Aboriginal Watercraft on the Pacific Coast of South America', *Ibero-Americana* (Berkeley and Los Angeles), vol. 47, 1965, p. 95.
13 Nishimura, op. cit., p. 24.
14 Hornell, op. cit., p. 77.
15 Junius Bird, 'Excavations in Northern Chile', *Anthropological Papers of the American Museum of Natural History*, vol. 38, pt 4, 1943, p. 214.
16 L. Wafer, *A New Voyage and Description of the Isthmus of America*, Hakluyt Society, series 2, vol. 73, Oxford, 1933, p. 59.
17 G. Shelvocke, *A Voyage Round the World*, London, 1928, pp. 224, 226.
18 Edwards, op. cit., p. 95.
19 Ling Shun-Sheng, 'Formosan Sea-going Raft and its Origin in Ancient China', *Bulletin of the Institute of Ethnology* (Academia Sinica, Taiwan), vol. 1, 1946, p. 26.
20 Nishimura, op. cit., pp. 56–7.
21 Hornell, op. cit., p. 61.
22 ibid., pp. 51–4.
23 ibid., pp. 46–7.
24 Herodotus, II, 96.
25 Romola and R. C. Anderson, *The Sailing Ship*, London, 1963, p. 20.
26 B. Landström, *The Ship*, London, 1961, p. 13.
27 R. D. Barnett, 'Early Shipping in the Near East', *Antiquity*, vol. 32, 1958, p. 221.
28 Strabo, 16.1.33.
29 A. H. Layard, *Discoveries in the Ruins of Nineveh and Babylon*, London, 1853, p. 552.
30 Quoted in Hornell, op. cit., p. 58.
31 Brindley, op. cit., p. 15.
32 H. Lhote, *The Search for the Tassili Frescoes*, London, 1959, pp. 191–204.
33 J. Desmond Clark, 'Evidence for Agricultural Origins in the Nile Valley', *PPS*, vol. 37, pt 2, 1971, p. 66.
34 Hornell, op. cit., p. 55.
35 ibid., p. 54.
36 Brindley, op. cit., p. 15.
37 I am grateful to Professor Stuart Piggott for telling me about this interesting quotation. It occurs in J. J. Hatt, *La Tombe gallo-romaine*, Paris, 1951, pp. 66–9.
38 Brindley, op. cit., p. 12.
39 Hornell, op. cit., pp. 56–9.
40 Grahame Clark, *World Prehistory*, Cambridge, 1961, p. 242.
41 D. J. Mulvaney, 'The Prehistory of the Australian Aborigine', *Scientific American*, vol. 214, 1966, p. 95.
42 F. Péron, *Voyage de découvertes aux terres australes . . .*, vol. I, Paris, 1807, p. 224; A. Lane-Fox, 'On Early Modes of Navigation', *JRAI*, vol. 4, 1875, p. 414. See also H. Ling Roth, *The Aborigines of Tasmania*, 2nd ed., Halifax, 1899, pp. 154–9.
43 Elsdon Best, *The Maori Canoe*, Dominion Museum (Wellington), Bulletin no. 7, 1925, pp. 137–8.
44 ibid., p. 143.
45 Brindley, op. cit., p. 10.
46 G. H. S. Bushnell, 'The Birth and Growth of New World Civilisation', in S. Piggott (ed.), *The Dawn of Civilisation*, London, 1961, p. 385.
47 Edwards, op. cit., p. 1.
48 Hornell, op. cit., p. 45.
49 Personal communication from Professor J. C. Spahni of Lima University.
50 Edwards, op. cit., p. 116
51 Quoted by Edwards, op. cit., pp. 3–4.
52 Edwards, op. cit., p. 15.
53 ibid., p. 112.
54 S. K. Lothrop, 'Early Migrations to Central and South America', *JRAI*, vol. 91, 1961, p. 110.
55 George Coggeshall, *Thirty-six Voyages to Various Parts of the World . . . between . . . 1799 and 1841*, 3rd ed., New York, 1855, pp. 333–4.
56 Edwards, op. cit., p. 7.
57 Vincent J. Maglio, 'Vertebrate Faunas and Chronology of Hominid-bearing Sediments East of Lake Rudolph, Kenya', *Nature*, 239, 1972, p. 379.
58 J. D. Clark, 'Human Ecology during the Pleistocene and Later Times in Africa South of the Sahara', *Current Anthropology*, vol. 1, 1960, pp. 307–24.
59 Edwards, op. cit., p. 166.

## Chapter 3 Bark

1 Grahame Clarke, *Prehistoric Europe: the Economic Basis*, London, 1952, pp. 207–8.
2 ibid., p. 208.
3 H. Shetelig and H. Falk, *Scandinavian Archaeology*, London, 1937, p. 149.
4 J. Hornell, *Water Transport*, Cambridge, 1970, p. 181.
5 ibid., pp. 181–3.
6 D. J. Mulvaney, 'The Prehistory of the Australian Aborigine', *Scientific American*, 214, 1966, p. 93.
7 Hornell, op. cit., p. 186.
8 ibid., pp. 181–9.
9 ibid.
10 C. R. Edwards, 'Aboriginal Watercraft on the Pacific Coast of South America', *Ibero-Americana* (Berkeley and Los Angeles), vol. 47, 1965, p. 21.
11 Quoted in ibid., pp. 22–3.

12  Maud D. Brindley, 'The Canoes of British Guiana', *MM*, vol. 10, 1924, p. 125.

13  David Livingstone, *Missionary Travels in South Africa*, London, 1857.

14  R. A. Jubb, 'Primitive African Fishing Methods', *African Wild Life*, vol. 23, p. 306.

15  P. Vinnicombe, 'A Fishing Scene from the Tsoelike River, South Eastern Basutoland', *S. African Archaeology Bulletin*, vol. 15, 1960, pp. 15–19.

16  E. T. Adney and Howard I. Chapelle, *The Bark Canoes and Skin Boats of North America*, Washington, 1964, p. 7.

17  ibid., pp. 15–17.

18  ibid., pp. 36–57.

19  ibid. (kayak-form canoes, pp. 158–68; emergency skin boats, p. 219).

20  ibid., p. 98.

21  D. MacRitchie, 'The Kayak in North-West Europe', *JRAI*, vol. 42, 1912, p. 506.

22  Hornell, op. cit., p. 184.

23  Adney and Chapelle, op. cit., p. 172.

24  H. H. Brindley, 'Notes on the Boats of Siberia', *MM*, vol. 5, 1919, pp. 104–6.

25  Clark, op. cit., p. 284.

26  P. Humbla and L. von Post, *Galtabäcksbåten och Tidigt Båtbyggeri i Norden*, Gothenburg, 1937, p. 11.

27  Quoted by R. Bosi, *The Lapps*, London, 1960, p. 51.

28  H. C. Folkard, *The Sailing Boat*, London, 1870, pp. 213–14.

29  Brindley, op. cit., p. 141.

30  Edwards, op. cit., p. 25.

31  Quoted in ibid.

32  ibid., p. 27.

33  ibid., p. 32.

34  ibid., p. 33.

35  ibid., pp. 33–4.

36  J. M. Cooper, *Analytical and Critical Bibliography of the Tribes of Tierra del Fuego and Adjacent Territory*, Smithsonian Institution Bureau of American Ethnology, Washington, bulletin 63, 1917, pp. 203–4.

**Chapter 4 Skin**

1  J. G. D. Clark, *Prehistoric Europe: the Economic Basis*, London, 1952, p. 283. Grahame Clark says that a skeleton in an oval basket in the clay of the Ancholme Estuary, Lincolnshire, may have been a coracle burial.

2  Chapter 7 in James Hornell, *Water Transport*, Newton Abbot, 1970, pp. 111–48.

3  J. G. D. Clark, 'Star Carr: a Mesolithic Site in Yorkshire', in R. L. S. Bruce-Mitford (ed.), *Recent Archaeological Excavations in Britain*, London, 1956, p. 16.

4  J. G. D. Clark in ibid., p. 9; J. J. Wymer, 'Excavations at the Maglemosian Sites at Thatcham, Berkshire, England', *PPS*, vol. 28, 1962, pp. 352–3.

5  In Bruce-Mitford (ed.), op. cit., p. 16.

6  Grahame Clark and Stuart Piggott, *Prehistoric Societies*, Penguin, 1970, p. 104.

7  Vilhjalmur Stefansson, *Ultima Thule*, London, 1942, pp. 37–8.

8  ibid., p. 39.

9  Hornell, op. cit., p. 179. See also Timothy Severin, *The Brendan Voyage*, London, 1978, which describes an Atlantic crossing by a twentieth-century skin boat.

10  James Hornell, 'The Curraghs of Ireland, Part III', *MM*, vol. 24, 1938, p. 13.

11  M. Graham, 'The Annual Cycle in the Life of the Mature Cod in the North Sea', *Fishery Invent*, II.6. 6, 1924, pp. 1–77.

12  J. G. D. Clark, *Prehistoric Europe*, pp. 84–5.

13  H. L. Movius, 'An Early Post-Glacial Archaeological Site of Cushendun, Co. Antrim', *Proceedings of the Royal Irish Academy*, vol. 46, 1940, p. 5.

14  J. M. Coles, 'The Early Settlement of Scotland: Excavations at Morton, Fife', *PPS*, vol. 37, pt 2, 1971, pp. 284–366.

15  ibid., pp. 350–3.

16  J. G. D. Clark, 'Notes on the Obanians', *PSAS*, vol. 89, 1955–6, pp. 92–100.

17  P. R. Ritchie, 'The Stone Implement Trade in Third Millennium B.C. Scotland', in J. M. Coles and D. D. A. Simpson (eds), *Studies in Ancient Europe*, Leicester, 1968, pp. 121–3.

18  Ole Klindt-Jensen, *Denmark before the Vikings*, London, 1957, pp. 20–2.

19  ibid.

20  J. G. D. Clark, *Prehistoric Europe*, pp. 84–6.

21  A. W. Brøgger and Haakon Shetelig, *The Viking Ships*, Oslo, 1951, p. 14.

22  ibid., pp. 14–18.

23  Strabo, *Geography* (trans. H. L. Jones), London, 1923, 3.3.7.

24  A. Arribas, *The Iberians*, London, 1963.

25  Emmanuel Anati, *The Camonica Valley*, London, 1964, p. 132.

26  J. Hornell, 'British Coracles', *MM*, vol. 21, 1936, pp. 294–5.

27  Hornell, *Water Transport*, p. 176.

28  ibid., p. 16.

29  ibid.

30  ibid. p. 9.

31  ibid. (see pp. 13 and 16 for references).

32  ibid., p. 28.

33 Quoted in ibid.
34 ibid., pp. 14, 28, 30.
35 ibid., p. 92.
36 J. Maringer and H. G. Bandi, *Art in the Ice Age*, London, 1953, p. 147.
37 op. cit., p. 265.
38 Maringer and Bandi, op. cit., p. 147; Marija Gimbutas, 'Middle Ural Sites and the Chronology of Northern Eurasia', *PPS*, vol. 24, 1958 (Bor III, p. 145, Fig. 17, no. 3; fishing objects, p. 123).
39 Reported in 'Record of the Rocks', *Soviet Weekly* (London), 1 April 1967, pp. 8–9.
40 H. H. Brindley, 'Notes on the Boats of Siberia', *MM*, vol. 5, 1919, p. 137.
41 ibid., pp. 66–78, 101–7, 130–42, 184–7; *MM*, vol. 6, 1920, pp. 15–18, 187.
42 Brindley, *MM*, vol. 5, p. 67.
43 Sverre Marstrander, *Ostfolds Jordbrukaristninger-Skjeberg*, Oslo, 1963, vol. II, p. 446.
44 E. T. Adney and H. I. Chapelle, *The Bark Canoes and Skin Boats of North America*, Washington, 1964, pp. 219, 220.
45 Hornell, *Water Transport*, p. 152.
46 ibid., p. 32.
47 Adney and Chapelle, op. cit., pp. 184–6.
48 ibid., p. 176.
49 ibid., p. 192.
50 ibid., p. 180.
51 Julius Caesar, *De Bello Civile*, Book I, chapter II.
52 Holinshed, The last volume of the *Chronicles of England, Scotland and Ireland*, 1577, p. 1171.
53 F. R. Chesney, *The Expedition for the Survey of the Rivers Tigris and Euphrates*, London, 1850, vol. II, p. 643.
54 J. Hornell, 'The Coracles of South India', *Man*, vol. 33, 1933, p. 160.
55 Stuart Piggott, *Ancient Europe*, Edinburgh, 1965, p. 17.
56 D. MacRitchie, 'The Kayak in North-Western Europe', *JRAI*, vol. 42, 1912, pp. 493–510.
57 Hornell, *Water Transport*, p. 10.
58 ibid., p. 176.
59 Lionel Casson, 'Sewn Boats', *Classical Review*, vol. 13, n.s. 1963, pp. 257–9.
60 Colin Renfrew, *Before Civilisation*, London, 1973, p. 109.
61 Bridget Allchin, *The Stone-tipped Arrow*, London, 1966, pp. 58–9.
62 Maringer and Bandi, op. cit., pp. 157–9.
63 Marstrander, op. cit., p. 447.
64 op. cit., p. 264.
65 ibid., p. 135.
66 F. J. Pohl, *The Viking Explorers*, New York, 1966, p. 43.
67 Hornell, *Water Transport*, pp. 151–2.
68 op. cit., pp. 60–80.
69 ibid., p. 64, p. 75.
70 H. Kuhn, *Die Felsbilder Europas*, Vienna, 1952, Fig. 38.
71 Maringer and Bandi, op. cit., p. 122.
72 H. Breuil, *Les Peintures rupestres de l'Espagne*, Paris, vol. IV–V, 1912, p. 551, Fig. 10.
73 See for instance, S. Piggott, *Ancient Europe*, Edinburgh, 1965, p. 34.
74 H. Breuil and M. Burkitt, *Rock Paintings of Southern Andalusia*, Oxford, 1929, p. 16.
75 C. Renfrew, 'Colonialism and Megalithismus', *Antiquity*, vol. 41, 1967, p. 283, Fig. 3(c).
76 Beatrice Blance, 'Early Bronze Age Colonists in Iberia', *Antiquity*, vol. 35, 1961, p. 199.
77 Breuil and Burkitt, op. cit., p. 28.

## Chapter 5 Dug-outs and the evolution of the plank-built boat

1 For a useful summary of sewn-plank craft, see E. V. Wright and D. M. Churchill, 'The Boats from North Ferriby, Yorkshire, England', *PPS*, vol. 31, 1965, pp. 18–24.
2 C. R. Edwards, 'Aboriginal Watercraft on the Pacific Coast of South America', *Ibero-Americana* (Berkeley and Los Angeles), vol. 47, 1965, p. 108.
3 ibid., pp. 53–8.
4 J. E. S. Thompson, 'Canoes and Navigation of the Mayas and their Neighbours', *JRAI*, vol. 79, 1949, pp. 69–76.
5 Marshall B. McKusick, 'Aboriginal Canoes in the West Indies', Yale University, Department of Anthropology, paper no. 63, 1960, pp. 3–11.
6 D. F. Thomson, 'Notes on some Primitive Watercraft in Northern Australia', *Man*, vol. 52, January 1952, p. 5.
7 Grahame Clark, *World Prehistory*, Cambridge, 3rd ed., 1977, p. 385.
8 James Hornell, *Water Transport*, Newton Abbot, 1970, p. 263.
9 Jean Baptiste du Tertre (1667) (trans. M. B. McKusick and M. S. Verin), quoted in McKusick, op. cit., p. 6.
10 Elsdon Best, *The Maori Canoe*, Dominion Museum (Wellington), Bulletin no. 7, 1925, p. 42.
11 E. V. Wright, *The North Ferriby Boats*, National Maritime Museum, monograph no. 23, Greenwich, 1976.
12 S. McGrail, 'Dating Wooden Boats', in J. Fletcher (ed.), *Dendrochronology in Northern Europe*; BAR, no. S 51, 1978, pp. 239–58.
13 S. McGrail, *The Logboats of England and Wales*, BAR, no. 51, 1978, p. 9; S. McGrail, 'Searching for a Pattern among the Logboats of England and Wales', in S. McGrail (ed.), *Sources and Techniques*

14  S. McGrail, *The Logboats*, p. 109.

15  Cyril Fox, 'A Dug-out Canoe from South Wales: with Notes on the Chronology, Typology, and Distribution of Monoxylous Craft in England and Wales', *Antiquaries Journal*, vol. 6, 1926, pp. 121–51.

16  S. McGrail, *The Logboats*, pp. 28–37.

17  A. Lane Fox, 'On Early Modes of Navigation', *JRAI*, vol. 4, 1875, p. 403.

18  S. McGrail, *The Logboats*, pp. 38–9, 44–55.

19  R. J. C. Atkinson, *Stonehenge*, London, 1956, pp. 106–14.

20  M. L. Boczar, 'The Craft in Use at the Rivergate of Dunajec', *MM*, vol. 52, 1966, pp. 211–22. For other examples of dug-outs in multiples bigger than two, see Ole Crumlin-Pedersen, 'Parallel to Dunajec Craft', *MM*, vol. 53, 1967, p. 31.

21  ibid., pp. 216–21.

22  S. McGrail, *The Logboats*, pp. 44–51, 314.

23  J. G. D. Clark, *Prehistoric Europe: the Economic Basis*, London, 1952, p. 288.

24  S. McGrail, *The Logboats*, pp. 38–41.

25  O. Crumlin-Pedersen, 'Skin or Wood?', in O. Hasslof *et al.* (eds), *Ships and Shipyards, Sailors and Fishermen*, Copenhagen, 1972, pp. 208–34.

26  J. G. D. Clark, op. cit., p. 288.

27  S. McGrail, *The Logboats*, pp. 51–5, 314.

## Chapter 6 The earlier Mediterranean

1  J. R. Cann and C. Renfrew, 'The Characterization of Obsidian and its Application to the Mediterranean Region', *PPS*, vol. 30, 1964, p. 111.

2  G. Durrani, S. A. Khan, C. Renfrew and J. Taj, 'Obsidian Source Identification by Fission Track Analysis', *Nature*, vol. 233, 1971, p. 242.

3  A. Aspinall, S. W. Feather and C. Renfrew, 'Neutron Activation Analysis of Aegean Obsidian', *Nature*, vol. 237, 1972, p. 333.

4  J. R. Cann, J. E. Dixon and C. Renfrew, 'Obsidian in the Aegean', *Annual of the British School of Archaeology at Athens*, vol. 60, 1965, p. 225.

5  C. Renfrew, J. E. Dixon and J. R. Cann, 'Obsidian and Early Cultural Contact in the Near East', *PPS*, vol. 32, 1966, p. 53.

6  T. W. Jacobsen, 'Excavations at Porto Cheli and Vicinity', *Hesperia*, vol. 38, 1969, pp. 343–81.

7  Durrani *et al.*, op. cit., p. 243.

8  S. J. de Laet, *The Low Countries*, London, 1962, p. 55.

9  J. Geikie, 'Discovery of an Ancient Wreck in the Old Alluvium of the Tay at Perth', *Scottish Naturalist*, vol. 5, 1879, pp. 1–7; V. G. Childe, *The*

*Prehistory of Scotland*, London, 1953, p. 18; A. D. Lacaille, *The Stone Age in Scotland*, Oxford, 1954, p. 66; S. McGrail, *The Logboats of England and Wales*, BAR, no. 51, 1978, p. 108.

10  Jacobsen, op. cit., p. 343, and personal communication.

11  V. Stefansson, *Ultima Thule*, London, 1942, pp. 37–40.

12  J. G. D. Clark, *Prehistoric Europe*, London, 1952, p. 277.

13  Grahame Clark, *World Prehistory*, 3rd ed., Cambridge, 1977, p. 230; R. Reed, *Ancient Skins, Parchments and Leathers*, Seminar Press, London and New York, 1972, p. 48.

14  S. Marinatos, 'La Marine creto-mycénienne', *BCH*, 1932, p. 217.

15  C. S. Coon, *The History of Man*, London, 1967, pp. 193–5.

16  Lionel Casson, *Ships and Seamanship in the Ancient World*, Princeton U.P., 1971 (paktons, p. 342; Strabo 17.818; Megara to Epidaurus, p. 4; Diodorus 19.54.3; Corsican timber raft, p. 4; Theophrastos *Hist. Plant.* 5.8.2; Hercules, p. 5; Metellus, p. 5; Pliny, *Nat Hist.* 8.16).

17  Lucien Basch, 'Graffites navals à Delos', *BCH*, supplement 1, 1973, pp. 65–76.

18  D. Woolner, 'Graffiti of ships at Tarxien, Malta', *Antiquity*, vol. 31, 1957, pp. 60–7.

19  Clinton R. Edwards, personal communication, 21 December 1967.

20  C. R. Edwards, 'Aboriginal Watercraft on the Pacific Coast of South America', *Ibero-Americana* (Berkeley and Los Angeles), vol. 47, 1965, pp. 107–11.

21  ibid., p. 108.

22  R. J. Rodden, 'Excavations at the Early Neolithic Site at Nea Nikomedeia, Greek Macedonia', *PPS*, vol. 28, 1962, pp. 267–88.

23  Pliny, VII. 2, quoted by C. Torr, *Ancient Ships*, Cambridge, 1895, p. 118.

24  ibid., p. 118.

25  B. Landström, *The Ship*, London, 1961, pp. 27–8.

26  C. Tsountas, *Ephemeris Archaiologike*, 1899, p. 91.

27  A. Evans, *The Palace of Minos*, vol. II, London, 1928, p. 240.

28  Jacquetta Hawkes, *Dawn of the Gods*, London, 1968, p. 27; Sinclair Hood, *The Home of the Heroes*, London, 1967, p. 46; R. D. Barnett, 'Early Shipping in the Near East', *Antiquity*, vol. 32, 1958, p. 224.

29  Quoted by S. Marinatos, op. cit.

30  ibid., p. 186.

31  For full bibliography see Casson, op. cit., p. 41, n. 3.

32  C. Doumas, *Korphi t'Aroniou, Archaeologikou Deltion*, 1965, p. 49 and Fig. 11.

33  C. Doumas, in E. Anati (ed.), *Val Camonica Symposium*, 1970–1, pp. 285–90.
34  C. Renfrew, 'Cycladic Metallurgy and the Aegean Early Bronze Age', *AJA*, vol. 71, 1967, p. 5.
35  Casson, op. cit., pp. 30–2, 41–2.
36  I owe this suggestion to Lieutenant-Commander A. F. Tilley, RN.
37  Evans, op. cit., vol. IV, p. 950, Fig. 917.
38  J. S. Morrison, review of L. Casson, *Ships and Seamanship in the Ancient World*, *IJNA*, vol. 1, 1972, pp. 230–3.
39  Basch, op. cit., p. 74.

## Chapter 7 The later Mediterranean

1   Copper trade: C. Renfrew, 'Cycladic Metallurgy and the Aegean Early Bronze Age', *AJA*, vol. 71, 1967, p. 16; animal bones in Cyprus: J. H. Schwartz, 'The Palaeozoology of Cyprus: a Preliminary Report on Recently Analysed Sites', *World Archaeology*, vol. 5, no. 2, 1973, pp. 215–20.
2   R. LeBaron Bowen Jr, 'Eastern Sail Affinities', *American Neptune*, vol. 13, 1953, p. 82.
3   R. C. Anderson, *Oared Fighting Ships*, London, 1962, p. 1; C. Torr, *Ancient Ships*, Cambridge, 1895, p. 2.
4   V. G. Kenna, *Cretan Seals*, Oxford, 1960, p. 12. For a contrary view see J. Betts, 'Ships on Minoan Seals', in D. J. Blackman (ed.), Colston Papers no. 23, *Marine Archaeology*, London, 1973, pp. 325–38.
5   F. Benoit, *L'Épave du grand congloué à Marseille*, XIV, Supplement to *Gallia*, Centre National de la Recherche Scientifique, Paris, 1961, p. 123.
6   Colin Renfrew, 'New Configurations in Old World Archaeology', *World Archaeology*, vol. 2, no. 2, 1970, p. 206.
7   W. F. Edgerton, 'Ancient Egyptian Ships and Shipping', *AJSL&L*, vol. 39, no. 2, 1923, p. 133.
8   B. Landström, *Ships of the Pharaohs*, London, 1971, p. 23.
9   Herodotus, II. 96.
10  Abdel Moneim Abubakr and Ahmed Youssef Moustafa, *The Funerary Boat of Khufu*, Beitrage zur Ägyptischen Bauforschung und Altertumskunde, 12, 1971, pp. 2–6.
11  R. Lepsius, *Denkmaeler aus Aegypten und Aethiopen*, vol. II, Leipsig, 1849–50, p. 108.
12  Landström, op. cit., p. 39.
13  ibid., p. 90.
14  ibid., p. 35.
15  T. Save-Söderbergh, *The Navy of the Eighteenth Egyptian Dynasty*, Uppsala, 1946, pp. 10, 29.
16  Quoted in Landström, op. cit., p. 89 (G. Posener *et al.*, *Dictionnaire de la civilisation égyptienne*, Paris, 1970, p. 184).

17  Save-Söderbergh, op. cit., p. 72.
18  L. Casson, 'Sewn Boats', *Classical Review*, vol. 57, 1963, pp. 257–9.
19  J. S. Morrison and R. T. Williams, *Greek Oared Ships, 900–322 B.C.*, Cambridge, 1968, p. 50.
20  L. Casson, 'The River Boats of Mesopotamia', *MM*, vol. 53, 1967, pp. 286–8; L. Casson, *Ships and Seamanship in the Ancient World*, Princeton U.P., 1971, pp. 25–8.
21  S. Piggott, 'The Earliest Wheeled Vehicles and the Caucasian Evidence', *PPS*, vol. 34, 1968, pp. 278, 274.
22  C. Aldred in E. J. Holmyard and C. Singer (eds), *History of Technology*, vol. I, London, 1954, p. 683.
23  Piggott, op. cit., p. 305.
24  J. Deshayes, *Les Outils de bronze de l'Indus au Danube*, Paris, 1960, p. 301.
25  Piggott, op. cit., p. 270; Casson, *Ships and Seamanship*, p. 218.
26  W. B. Emory, *Great Tombs of the First Dynasty*, vol. II, Oxford, 1952, p. 53.
27  Flinders Petrie, *The Wisdom of the Egyptians*, London, 1940, pp. 122–3.
28  Casson, *Ships and Seamanship*, p. 203.
29  G. Kossack, 'The Construction of the Felloe in Iron Age Spoked Wheels', in J. Boardman, M. A. Brown and T. G. E. Powell (eds), *The European Community in Later Prehistory*, London, 1971, pp. 141–64.
30  A. C. Western, 'A Wheel Hub from the Tomb of Amenophis III', *JEA*, vol. 59, 1973, pp. 91–4.
31  V. Karageorghis, *Excavations in the Necropolis of Salamis*, vol. I, 1967, pp. 6–85.
32  Kossack, op. cit., p. 159.
33  Casson, op. cit., p. 222, quoting Strabo, 15.691.
34  R. LeBaron Bowen Jr, 'Egypt's Earliest Sailing Ships', *Antiquity*, vol. 34, 1960, pp. 117–20.
35  See, for instance, *National Geographic Magazine*, vol. 130, 1966, p. 679.
36  LeBaron Bowen, 'Egypt's Earliest Sailing Ships', pp. 119–20.
37  Landström, op. cit., p. 35.
38  ibid., p. 50.
39  LeBaron Bowen, 'Egypt's Earliest Sailing Ships', p. 131.
40  ibid., p. 130.
41  Landström, op. cit., p. 141.
42  Lucien Basch, 'Phoenician Oared Ships', *MM*, vol. 55, 1969, pp. 142–3.
43  ibid., p. 144.
44  A. S. Murray, A. H. Smith and H. B. Watters, *Excavations in Cyprus*, London, 1900, p. 112, Fig. 164.
45  Basch, op. cit., pp. 150–1.
46  Homer, *Odyssey* (trans. E. V. Rieu), London, 1957, pp. 94–5, 200.

47 E. Linder, 'Naval Warfare in the El-Amarna Age', in D. J. Blackman (ed.), op. cit., p. 319.
48 C. H. Gordon, *Ugaritic Textbook*, 1968, p. 7.
49 Linder, op. cit., pp. 317–24.
50 Morrison and Williams, op. cit., p. 153.
51 Basch, op. cit., p. 143.
52 *New Scientist*, 16 September 1965, p. 674.
53 Basch, op. cit., p. 150.
54 Morrison and Williams, op. cit., p. 51.
55 ibid., p. 279.
56 M. Nour, Z. Iskander, M. S. Osman and A. Youssef, *The Cheops Boats*, Cairo, 1960, p. 4.
57 Morrison and Williams, op. cit., pp. 55, 301.
58 Nour *et al.*, op. cit., p. 43.
59 Morrison and Williams, op. cit., pp. 50, 52.
60 Casson, *Ships and Seamanship*, p. 37.
61 Morrison and Williams, op. cit., pp. 62–4.
62 M. L. Katzev, 'The Kyrenia Ship', in G. Bass (ed.), *A History of Seafaring*, London, 1972, pp. 50–2; Morrison and Williams, op. cit., p. 63.
63 Casson, *Ships and Seamanship*, pp. 281–91.
64 Homer, *Odyssey* (trans. Rieu), p. 95.
65 Morrison and Williams, op. cit., p. 135; Landström, op. cit., p. 79.
66 Morrison and Williams, op. cit., p. 312.
67 G. Kapitan, 'Greco-Roman Anchors', in D. J. Blackman (ed.), op. cit., pp. 383–94; Honor Frost, *Under the Mediterranean*, London, 1963, p. 34.
68 Honor Frost, 'Anchors: The Potsherds of Marine Archaeology', in D. J. Blackman (ed.), op. cit., p. 402; Casson, *Ships and Seamanship*, p. 36.
69 Frost, *Under the Mediterranean*, p. 50; Casson, *Ships and Seamanship*, p. 254.
70 G. Bass, 'The Cape Gelidonya Wreck: Preliminary Report', *AJA*, vol. 64, 1961, pp. 267–76.
71 Katzev, op. cit., pp. 6–14; D. E. Owen, 'Picking up the Pieces', *Expedition* (Philadelphia), vol. 13, no. 1, 1970.
72 Morrison and Williams, op. cit., pp. 294–8.
73 ibid., pp. 200, 294–8.
74 Casson, *Ships and Seamanship*, p. 211.
75 Benoit, op. cit., pp. 128–9.
76 L. Basch, 'Un modèle de navire romain au Musée de Sparte', *L'Antiquité classique* (Brussels), vol. 37, pt 1, 1968, pp. 154–7.
77 Morrison and Williams, op. cit., p. 297; Apollonius Rhodius, I, 367–9.
78 Casson, *Ships and Seamanship*, p. 205, quoting Procopius, *Bell. Goth.* 4.22.10; Anderson, op. cit., p. 41.

## Chapter 8 The Atlantic

1 E. G. R. Taylor, *The Haven-finding Art*, London, 1956, p. 142.
2 ibid., p. 131.
3 ibid., pp. 104–21.
4 Strabo, 3.5.3, quoted by Jules Tontain, *The Economic Life of the Ancient World*, London, 1930, p. 132.
5 V. Gordon Childe, *Prehistoric Communities of the British Isles*, London and Edinburgh, 1940, p. 46.
6 C. Renfrew, *Before Civilisation*, London, 1973, pp. 120–9.
7 H. N. Savory, *Spain and Portugal*, London, 1968, p. 51.
8 C. Renfrew, 'Colonialism and Megalithismus', *Antiquity*, vol. 41, 1967, pp. 282–3.
9 Savory, op. cit., pp. 78, 123.
10 Strabo, *Geography* (trans. H. J. Jones), London, 1923 (skin boats, 3.2.3; dug-outs, 3.3.7).
11 Julius Caesar, *The Conquest of Gaul* (trans. A. Handford), London, 1967, pp. 98–9.
12 R. Y. Creston, 'Considerations techniques sur la flotte des Vénètes et des Romains', *Annales de Bretagne* (Rennes), vol. 63, no. 1, 1956.
13 ibid., p. 91.
14 A. Jal, *Glossaire nautique*, Paris, 1848, p. 1201; C. de la Roncière and G. Clerc-Rampel, *Histoire de la marine française*, Paris, 1934, pp. 2–3.
15 L. Casson, *Ships and Seamanship in the Ancient World*, Princeton U.P., 1971, p. 159, n. 9.
16 D. Ellmers, 'Rheinschiffe der Romerzeit', *Beitrage zur Rheinkunde*, 2nd series, vol. 25, 1973, p. 40.
17 P. R. V. Marsden, *A Roman Ship from Blackfriars, London*, London, 1966, p. 47.
18 Notably by Lucien Basch, *Archéologie navale et archéologie sous-marine*, vol. 20, 1968, pp. 38–53.
19 ibid., pp. 40–52.
20 Marsden, op. cit., pp. 30–1. Fragments are in the Museum of London.
21 ibid., pp. 22–3.
22 ibid., pp. 34–5.
23 O. Crumlin-Pedersen, 'Cog-Kogge-Kaag', *Handels og Sjøfartsmuseets pa Kronberg Årbog*, Copenhagen, 1965, p. 142.
24 P. R. V. Marsden, 'Ships of the Roman Period and After in Britain', in G. Bass (ed.), *A History of Seafaring*, London, 1972, p. 123.
25 P. R. V. Marsden, 'A Boat of the Roman Period Found at Bruges, Belgium, in 1899, and related types', *IJNA*, vol. 5, 1976, pp. 23–55.
26 D. Ellmers, 'Keltischer Schiffbau', *Jahrbuch des Romisch-Germanischen Zentralmuseums, Mainz*, vol. 16, 1969, pp. 73–122.
27 Ellmers, 'Rheinschiffe der Romerzeit', p. 25.
28 T. C. Lethbridge, *Boats and Boatmen*, London, 1952, pp. 116–19.
29 P. Johnstone and A. F. Tilley, 'An unusual Portuguese Fishing Boat', *MM*, vol. 62, 1976, pp. 15–21.

30 P. Stewart (ed.), *Deae Nehelenniae*, Rijksmuseum van Outheden, Leiden, 1971, Plate 44A.

31 I am grateful to Lieutenant-Commander A. F. Tilley, RN, who first pointed this out to me.

32 Strabo, 11.3.4 (quoted by C. Torr, *Ancient Ships*, Cambridge, 1895, p. 113).

33 For rumours in Classical writers that this had in fact happened, see M. Cary and E. H. Warmington, *The Ancient Explorers*, London, 1963, p. 223.

34 R. D. Barnett, 'Early Shipping in the Near East', *Antiquity*, vol. 32, no. 128, 1958, p. 229.

35 D. Ellmers, 'Keltischer Schiffbau', pp. 96–7.

36 J. Déchelette, *Manuel d'archéologie*, vol. II, part 1, Paris, 1924, p. 441, Fig. 182.

37 Barnett, op. cit., p. 228.

38 Torr, op. cit., pp. 113–14 (Sophocles, *Andromeda* Fr. 2 apud *Athenaeum*, XI. 64; Strabo, 2.3.4; Pliny, 7.57).

39 A. F. Tilley, 'An Ancient Gondola', *MM*, vol. 55, 1969, p. 76.

40 G. B. Rubin de Cervin, 'The Evolution of the Venetian Gondola', *MM*, vol. 42, 1956, p. 207.

41 ibid., pp. 203, 206.

42 A. F. Tilley, 'Venice, Malta and the Phoenicians', *Ships Monthly*, no. 7, 1972, pp. 237, 241.

43 Rubin de Cervin, op. cit., pp. 211–15.

44 Jal, op. cit., p. 790.

45 A. F. Tilley, 'A Phoenician Survival', *MM*, vol. 55, 1969, pp. 467–9.

46 For further evidence, see O. L. Filgueiras, 'The *Xavega* boat', in S. McGrail (ed), *Sources and Techniques in Boat Archaeology*, BAR, no. S 29, 1977, pp. 77–111.

47 Ellmers, 'Rheinschiffe der Romerzeit', p. 37.

48 Beatrice Blance, 'Early Bronze Age Colonists in Iberia', *Antiquity*, vol. 35, 1961, p. 200.

49 Savory, op. cit., p. 112.

50 C. F. C. Hawkes, 'Las Relaciones entre la Peninsula Iberia y las Isles Britainias' *Ampurias*, vol. 14, 1952, p. 96.

51 George Coffey, *New Grange and other Incised Tumuli in Ireland*, Dublin, 1912, p. 30.

52 H. Case, 'Neolithic Explanations', *Antiquity*, vol. 43, 1969, p. 180.

53 S. Piggott, *Ancient Europe*, 1965, p. 97; Grahame Clark, *World Prehistory*, London, 1961, p. 139. Savory, op. cit., p. 233.

54 C. D. Darlington, *The Evolution of Man and Society*, London, 1969, esp. pp. 45–65.

55 L. V. Luce, *The End of Atlantis*, London, 1969; A. G. Galanopoulos and E. Bacon, *Atlantis*, London, 1969.

## Chapter 9 Scandinavia

1 A. W. Brøgger and H. Shetelig, *The Viking Ships*, Oslo, 1951, p. 13.

2 ibid., p. 16.

3 A. Hagen, *Norway*, London, 1967, p. 110.

4 H. Shetelig and H. Falk, *Scandinavian Archaeology* (trans. E. V. Gordon), Oxford, 1937, p. 110.

5 Hagen, op. cit., p. 23.

6 ibid., p. 26.

7 ibid., p. 33.

8 ibid., p. 34.

9 Shetelig and Falk, op. cit., p. 20.

10 ibid., pp. 44–5.

11 J. G. D. Clark, *Prehistoric Europe: the Economic Basis*, London, 1952, p. 174; Hagen, op. cit., p. 50.

12 Hagen, op. cit., p. 67

13 G. Hallström, *Monumental Art of Northern Sweden from the Stone Age*, Stockholm, 1960, p. 353.

14 ibid.

15 Hagen, op. cit., p. 38.

16 ibid., p. 40.

17 ibid., p. 43.

18 Brøgger and Shetelig, op. cit., p. 15.

19 James Hornell, *Water Transport*, Newton Abbot, 1970, p. 145.

20 S. Marstrander, *Østfolds Jordbruksristninger-Skjeberg*, Oslo, 1963, p. 118.

21 Hallström, op. cit., p. 34.

22 Marstrander, op. cit., pp. 442–3.

23 ibid., pp. 448, and 131, Fig. 33.

24 J. Hornell, 'The Curraghs of Ireland, Part III', *MM*, vol. 24, 1938, p. 5.

25 Marstrander, op. cit., p. 448, p. 96.

26 ibid., p. 136, Fig. 37, nos 3 and 5.

27 For a detailed account of this experiment see Paul Johnstone, 'Bronze Age Sea Trial', *Antiquity*, vol. 46, 1972, pp. 269–74; and S. Marstrander, 'Building a Hide Boat', *IJNA*, vol. 5, 1976, pp. 13–22.

28 E. T. Adney and H. I. Chapelle, *The Bark Canoes and Skin Boats of North America*, Washington, 1964, p. 184.

29 W. Reeves (ed.), *Life of St Columba*, Edinburgh, 1874, p. 170. For a recent experimental building and voyage of a skin boat, see T. Severin, *The Brendan Voyage*, London, 1978.

30 Adney and Chapelle, op. cit., p. 180.

31 E. Arima, 'How the Umiak was Built at Ivugivik', *Arctic Circular*, vol. 13, no. 4, 1961.

32 Hagen, op. cit., p. 50.

33 A. Eskeröd, 'Early Nordic Arctic Boats: a Survey and Some Problems', *Arctica* (Studia Ethnographica Upsaliensis, XI), 1956, pp. 57–87.

34 F. Nansen, *In Northern Mists*, London, 1911.

35 Brøgger and Shetelig, op. cit., pp. 25–34.

36 Hallström, op. cit., p. 354.
37 ibid., p. 345.
38 ibid., p. 304.
39 Hornell, op. cit., p. 197.
40 Shetelig and Falk, op. cit., pp. 186–7; G. Rosenberg, 'Hjortspringfundet', *Nord Oldtidsminder*, vol. III, part 1, Copenhagen, 1937.
41 Herodotus, 1. 194. 2.
42 A. E. Christensen, 'Scandinavian Ships from Earliest Times to the Vikings', in G. Bass (ed.), *A History of Seafaring*, London, 1972, pp. 160–1.
43 O. Crumlin-Pedersen, 'Skin or Wood?', in O. Hasslof *et al.* (eds), *Ships and Shipyards, Sailors and Fishermen*, Copenhagen, 1972, pp. 208–34.
44 Shetelig and Falk, op. cit., p. 353.
45 H. Åkerlund, *Nydamskeppen*, Goteborg, 1963.
46 Crumlin-Pedersen, op. cit.
47 Crumlin-Pedersen, op. cit., pp. 225–6; O. Klindt-Jensen, 'Rejsen til dødsriget', *Skalk*, no. 1, 1960; E. H. Hansen, 'Baden der var syet sammen', *Skalk*, no. 4, 1962.
48 Crumlin-Pedersen, op. cit., pp. 226–7.
49 ibid., p. 228; Åkerlund, op. cit., pp. 117–22.
50 Crumlin-Pedersen, op. cit., p. 231.
51 S. Marstrander, review of O. Crumlin-Pedersen, 'Skin or Wood?', *IJNA*, vol. 1, 1972, pp. 234–6.
52 For a good discussion of this point, see P. H. Sawyer, *The Age of the Vikings*, London, 1962, p. 76.
53 Shetelig and Falk, op. cit., p. 345; *Tacitus on Britain and Germany* (trans. H. Mattingly), Penguin, 1948, p. 137.
54 R. C. Anderson, *Oared Fighting Ships*, London, 1962, pp. 90–9.
55 B. Landström, *The Ship*, London, 1961, p. 182.
56 See C. R. Edwards, 'Aboriginal Sail in the New World', *Southwest Journal of Anthropology* (Albuquerque), vol. 21, no. 4, 1965, pp. 352–3.
57 Adney and Chapelle, op. cit., p. 65.
58 S. Fliedner, *Die Bremen Kogge*, no. 2 Hefte des Focke Museums, Bremen, 1964; H. Abel *et al.*, *Die Bremen Hanse-Kogge: Fund, Konservierung, Forschung*, Bremen, 1969.
59 O. Crumlin-Pedersen, 'Cog-Kogge-Kaag', *Handels og Sjøfartsmuseets pa Kronberg Årbog*, Copenhagen, 1965, p. 143.
60 E. P. von de Porton, 'Wrecks, Archives and Living Tradition', *MM*, vol. 51, 1965, p. 145.
61 Crumlin-Pedersen, 'Cog-Kogge-Kaage', p. 141.
62 O. Crumlin-Pedersen, 'The Vikings and the Hanseatic Merchants: 900–1450', in G. Bass (ed.), op. cit., p. 187.
63 J. P. W. Philipsen, 'The Utrecht Ship', *MM*, vol. 51, 1965, pp. 35–46.
64 ibid., p. 37.
65 ibid., pp. 44–5.
66 Crumlin-Pedersen, 'The Vikings and the Hanseatic Merchants', p. 189.
67 Crumlin-Pedersen, 'Cog-Kogge-Kaage', p. 143.

## Chapter 10 The British Isles: skin boats

1 See for instance, E. D. Evans, I. F. Smith and F. S. Wallis, 'The Petrological Identification of Stone Implements from South-Western England: Fifth Report of the Sub-committee of the South-Western Federation of Museums and Art Galleries', *PPS*, vol. 38, 1972, pp. 235–75 (for details of previous reports, see bibliography of above article), G. de G. Sieveking, P. T. Craddock, M. J. Hughes, P. Bush and J. Ferguson, 'Characterization of Flint Mine Products', *Nature*, vol. 228, 1970, pp. 251–4.
2 G. Clark, 'Traffic in Stone Axe and Adze Blades', *Economic History Review*, vol. 18, 1965, p. 5.
3 H. J. E. Peake, 'The Final Insulation of Britain', *PPS*, vol. 4, 1938, p. 344.
4 Clark, op. cit., p. 11.
5 T. H. McK. Clough and B. Green, 'The Petrological Identification of Stone Implements from East Anglia', *PPS*, vol. 38, 1972, pp. 108–55.
6 L. Keen and J. Radley, 'Report on the Petrological Identification of Stone Axes from Yorkshire', *PPS*, vol. 37, 1971, p. 49.
7 F. E. Zeuner, *Discovery*, vol. 16, no. 187, 1945, p. 199.
8 The passage quoted is from A. Berthelot (ed.), Festus Avienus, *Ora Maritima*, Paris, 1934, p. 34, lines 98–108, trans. in W. F. Skene, *Celtic Scotland*, vol. I, p. 168. Early dating implied by use of 'Oestrymnis' is proposed by Berthelot, op. cit., p. 57; *c.* 500 BC in M. Cary and E. H. Warmington, *The Ancient Explorers*, rev. ed., London, 1963, p. 224; no later than 545 BC in T. C. Lethbridge, *Boats and Boatmen*, London, 1952, p. 117; around 600 BC in Stuart Piggott, *Ancient Europe*, 1965 p. 194.
9 Johannes Brondsted, *The Vikings*, London, 1960, p. 132; Romola and R. C. Anderson, *The Sailing Ship*, London, 1926, p. 75.
10 J. M. Coles, 'European Bronze Age Shields', *PPS*, vol. 28, 1962, p. 165.
11 Christopher Hawkes, 'Tartessos y sus Problemas', *V. Symposium Internacional de Prehistoria Peninsular*, Barcelona, 1969, pp. 190–2.
12 H. N. Savory in L. L. Foster and Glyn Daniel (eds), *Prehistoric and Early Wales*, London, 1963, p. 83; J. X. W. P. Corcoran, 'The Caergwrle Bowl: a Contribution to the Study of the Bronze Age', in *Ber. V. Internat. Kongr. Vor- und Frühgeschichte im Hamburg, 1958*, 1961, p. 202.

13  Corcoran, op. cit., p. 202.

14  Paul Johnstone, 'A Medieval Skin Boat', *Antiquity*, vol. 36, 1962, p. 34.

15  Lethbridge, op. cit., p. 111.

16  A. Hartman, *Prähistorische Goldfunde aus Europa*, Berlin, 1970, p. 29; A. W. Farrell and S. Penny, 'The Broighter Boat: a Re-assessment', *Irish Archaeological Research Forum*, vol. 2, part 2, 1975, pp. 15–28.

17  Paul Johnstone, 'The Bantry Boat', *Antiquity*, vol. 38, 1964, pp. 277–8, Plate XLVb.

18  Françoise Henry, *Irish Art in the Early Christian Period*, London, 1940, p. 108.

19  Laird Clowes and Cecil Torr, *The Story of Sail*, London, 1936, p. 49.

20  Sverre Marstrander, *Ostfolds Jordbrukaristninger-Skjeberg*, Oslo, 1963, vol. II, pp. 447–8.

21  Stuart Piggott, op. cit., p. 63.

22  Humphrey Case, 'Neolithic Explanations', *Antiquity*, vol. 43, 1969, pp. 182–3.

23  Quoted by Stuart Piggott, *Neolithic Cultures of the British Isles*, Cambridge, 1954, p. 298.

24  Dutch dates: Grahame Clark and Stuart Piggott, *Prehistoric Societies*, London, 1970, p. 235.

25  J. G. D. Clark, *Prehistoric Europe: the Economic Basis*, London, 1952, pp. 244–5.

26  P. R. Ritchie, 'The Stone Implement Trade in Third Millennium B.C. Scotland', in J. M. Coles and D. D. A. Simpson (eds), *Studies in Ancient Europe*, Leicester, 1968, pp. 121–3.

27  Case, op. cit., pp. 176–86.

28  Piggott, *Neolithic Cultures*, pp. 324–36.

29  Piggott, *Ancient Europe*, p. 64.

30  P. A. Mellars, 'The Palaeolithic and Mesolithic' in C. Renfrew (ed.), *British Prehistory*, London, 1974, p. 89.

31  R. Raikes, *Water, Weather and Prehistory*, London, 1967, pp. 87–116.

32  Quoted in William Reeves (ed.), *Life of St Columba*, Edinburgh, 1874, Book 2, chap. XLII, p. 170 notes.

33  P. O'Sullivan Beare, *Historia Catholicae Iberniae Compendium, Ulyesiphone*, Lisbon, 1621, vol. 3, Book 7, C.IX, fol. 190, 191.

34  J. Hornell, *Water Transport*, Newton Abbot, 1970, p. 139.

35  ibid., p. 132.

36  ibid., pp. 122–5.

37  ibid., p. 135.

38  ibid., p. 158.

39  James F. Kenney, *The Sources of the Early History of Ireland*, vol. I, Oxford, 1929, pp. 412–14.

40  Hornell, op. cit., p. 140.

41  For instance Geoffrey Ashe, *Land to the West*, London, 1962; see also Timothy Severin, *The Brendan Voyage*, London, 1978.

42  *Life of St Columba (Columb-Kille), AD. 521–597: Founder of the Monastery of Iona and First Christian Missionary to the Pagan Tribes of North Britain, by Saint Adamnan, A.D. 679–704, 9th Abbot of the Monastery of Iona* (trans. Wentworth Huyshe), London, 1924 (encounter with a sea monster, p. 40; . . . in Loch Ness, p. 136; haul barges, p. 177; shelter for a thief, p. 72 C.XLI).

43  ibid. (hard labour, p. 17; whirlpool of Breccan, p. 25; bilge water, p. 110).

44  ibid. (mast stepped, p. 40; skin bag, p. 156).

45  ibid., p. 23.

46  T. C. Lethbridge, *Herdsmen and Hermits*, Cambridge, 1950, p. 73.

47  Huyshe, op. cit., pp. 168–72.

48  Nora K. Chadwick, *St Columba: Fourteenth Centenary*, Glasgow, 1963, p. 14.

49  Lethbridge, *Herdsmen and Hermits*, p. 2.

50  Dicuil, *De Mensura Orbis Terrae*, Parthey edition, Berlin, 1870, chap. 7, p. 44.

51  Discussed by Vilhjalmur Stefansson, *Ultima Thule*, London, 1942, p. 50.

52  Gildas, *De Excidio et Conquestu Britanniae* (trans. T. Habington), 1638, quoted by Hornell, op. cit., p. 141.

53  Hornell, op. cit., p. 142.

54  Giraldus Cambrensis, *Topographia Hibernica*, vol. III, p. 26.

55  Hornell, op. cit., p. 114.

## Chapter 11 The British Isles: wooden craft

1  S. McGrail, *The Logboats of England and Wales*, BAR, no. 51, 1978.

2  T. Sheppard, 'An Early Scandinavian Model Boat and Crew', *MM*, vol. 6, 1920, pp. 300–1.

3  S. Lundquist, 'The Boat Models from Roos Carr', *Acta Archaeologica* (Copenhagen), vol. 13, 1942, pp. 235–42.

4  A. Arribas, *The Iberians*, London, 1963, Fig. 19, p. 80.

5  C. F. C. Hawkes and J. E. Bartlett, 'A Barbed Bronze Spearhead from North Ferriby, Yorkshire, England', *PPS*, vol. 31, 1965, pp. 370–2.

6  J. G. D. Clark, *Prehistoric Europe*, London, 1952, p. 186.

7  C. Zervos, *La Civilisation de la Sardaigne*, Paris, 1954, p. 323.

8  J. E. Gillespie, 'A Canoe Found in Loch Lotus, Kirkcudbrightshire', *PSAS*, vol. 11, 1874–6, pp. 21–3.

9  E. V. Wright and C. W. Wright, 'Prehistoric Boats from North Ferriby, East Yorkshire', *PPS*, vol. 13, 1947, pp. 114–38; E. V. Wright and D. M. Churchill, 'The Boats from North Ferriby,

Yorkshire, England, with a Review of the Origins of the Sewn Boats of the Bronze Age', *PPS*, vol. 31, 1965, pp. 1–24; E. V. Wright, *The North Ferriby Boats*, National Maritime Museum, Monograph no. 23, Greenwich, 1976.

10 S. McGrail and R. Switsur, 'Early British Boats and their Chronology', *IJNA*, vol. 4, 1975, pp. 191–200.

11 E. V. Wright and C. W. Wright, op. cit., pp. 134–5.

12 J. Thropp, 'An Ancient Raft Found at Brigg', *Architectural Societies Papers*, vol. 19, 1887–8, pp. 95–7.

13 S. McGrail, 'The Brigg "Raft" Re-excavated', *Lincolnshire History and Archaeology*, vol. 10, 1975, pp. 5–13.

14 Rev. Prebendary Cross and A. Atkinson, 'Discovery of a Prehistoric Ship at Brigg', *Architectural Societies Papers*, vol. 18, 1885–6, pp. 33–5; T. Sheppard, Review, *Transactions of the East Riding Antiquarian Society*, vol. 16, 1943, p. 42; Wright and Churchill, op. cit., p. 12; S. McGrail, *The Logboats of England and Wales*, catalogue entry no. 22.

15 H. E. Dudley, 'A One-tree Boat at Appleby, Lincolnshire', *Antiquity*, vol. 17, 1943, pp. 156–61; McGrail, *The Logboats of England and Wales*, catalogue entry no. 5.

16 D. Ellmers, 'Rheinschiffe der Romerzeit', *Beitrage zur Rheinkunde*, 2nd series, vol. 25, 1973, p. 29.

17 ibid., p. 31 and Fig. 5.

18 Wright and Churchill, op. cit.; E. V. Wright, 'The Boats of North Ferriby', in *Three Major Ancient Boat Finds in Britain*, National Maritime Museum, Maritime Monographs and Reports no. 6, 1972, p. 6.

19 C. E. Dove, 'The First British Navy', *Antiquity*, vol. 45, 1971, p. 16.

20 Romilly Allen, *The Early Christian Monuments of Scotland*, Edinburgh, 1903, part 3, p. 216, Fig. 230b; R. Feachem, *A Guide to Prehistoric Scotland*, London, 1963, p. 196.

21 P. H. Sawyer, *The Age of the Vikings*, London, 1962, p. 76.

22 C. MacLagan, *PSAS*, vol. 11, 1876, pp. 115–17, Plate 4.

23 T. C. Lethbridge, *Boats and Boatmen*, London, 1952, p. 124.

24 Shetland County Museum, registered no. ARC66129. See also *Catalogue of Shetland County Museum*, Lerwick, 1967, pp. 9–10 and Plate 4.

25 For an interesting discussion of this passage in Vegetius, *De Re Militari*, IV, c.37, see N. K. Chadwick, 'The Name Pict', *Scottish Gaelic Studies*, vol. 8, 1958, p. 164.

26 C. F. C. Hawkes, 'New Thoughts on the Belgae',

*Antiquity*, vol. 42, 1968, p. 14.

27 See, for instance, the review by J. N. L. Myres of Charles Green's *Sutton Hoo: the Excavation of a Royal Ship-burial*, *English Historical Review*, vol. 80, 1965.

28 C. F. C. Hawkes, *Pytheas* (eighth J. L. Myres Memorial Lecture), Oxford, 1975.

## Chapter 12 European river craft

1 J. G. D. Clark, *Prehistoric Europe: the Economic Basis*, London, 1952, p. 282.

2 ibid., pp. 241–2, 282.

3 A. C. Leighton, *Transport and Communication in Early Medieval Europe A.D. 500–1100*, Newton Abbot, 1972, pp. 125–6; Strabo, IV, I.22 (trans. Hamilton and Falconer), London, 1852.

4 L. Casson, 'Harbour and River Boats of Ancient Rome', *JRS*, vol. 4, 1965, p. 32.

5 O. Testaguazza, 'The Port of Rome', *Archaeology*, vol. 17, 1964, pp. 173–9.

6 Casson, op. cit., p. 30.

7 J. le Gall, *Revue archéologique* (Paris), vol. 22, 1953, pp. 42–3.

8 Casson, op. cit., p. 37.

9 ibid.

10 ibid.

11 ibid., pp. 38–9.

12 H. Dragendorff and E. Kruger, *Das Grabnal von Igel*, Trier, 1924, pp. 46–9.

13 Albert Grenier, *Manuel d'archéologie gallo-romaine*, Paris, 1934, vol. VI, part 2, *Navigation*, p. 590.

14 L. Bonnard, *La Navigation intérieure de la Gaule à l'époque gallo-romaine*, Paris, 1913, p. 238.

15 H. de la Tour, *Atlas de monnaies gauloises*, Paris, 1892, nos 8743–4, Plate XXXV.

16 A. Houbigant, *Recueil des antiquités bellovaques conservées dans le cabinet de M. Houbigant à Nogent-les-Vierges*, Paris, 1860, p. 14.

17 Grenier, op. cit., p. 348.

18 ibid., p. 528.

19 D. Ellmers, 'Rheinschiffe der Romerzeit', *Beitrage zur Rheinkunde*, 2nd series, vol. 25, 1973, p. 40.

20 ibid., p. 41.

21 Grenier, op. cit., p. 536.

22 Strabo, V. C.218 (ed. Loeb, 1921, vol. II, pp. 24–5).

23 M. D. de Weerd and J. K. Haalebos, 'Schepen voor het Opscheppen', *Spiegel Historiael* (Bussum), nos 7–8, 1973, pp. 386–97.

24 Ellmers, op. cit., p. 37.

25 P. Marsden, 'The County Hall Ship', *Transactions of the London and Middlesex Archaeological Society*, 21, part 2, 1965, pp. 109–17.

26 S. Muller, *Verslag van het Verhandelde in de Algemene*

*Vergadering van het Provinciaal Utrechtsch*, Utrecht, 1895, pp. 129–42, 160–1.

27  J. D. van der Waals, 'Neolithic Disc Wheels in the Netherlands', *Palaeohistoria*, vol. 10, 1964, pp. 103–46.

28  ibid., p. 122, Fig. 25.

29  D. Ellmers, 'Keltischer Schiffbau', *Jahrbuch des Romisch-Germanischen Zentralmuseums* (Mainz), vol. 16, 1969, pp. 73–122.

30  de Weerd and Haalebos, op. cit., pp. 386–97.

31  L. Casson, *Ships and Seamanship in the Ancient World*, Princeton U.P., 1971, p. 210 n. 39.

32  ibid., p. 209, n. 39.

33  B. Arnold, 'La Barque gallo-romaine de la Baie de Bevaix', *Cahiers d'archéologie subaquatique* (Fréjus), no. 3, 1974, p. 138.

34  ibid., pp. 132–50.

35  ibid., pp. 139–41.

36  ibid., p. 141.

37  G. de Boe and F. Hubert, 'Une installation portuaire d'époque romaine à Pommeroeul', *Archaeologia Belgica*, vol. 192, 1977, pp. 5–57.

38  D. Ellmers, 'Nautical Archaeology in Germany', *IJNA*, vol. 3, 1974, p. 144.

39  Ellmers, 'Rheinschiffe der Romerzeit', p. 25.

40  ibid., p. 26.

41  ibid., p. 25.

42  ibid., p. 28. For a comment on this theory see O. Crumlin-Pedersen in a review of D. Ellmers's 'Keltischer Schiffbau', *IJNA*, vol. 2, 1973, pp. 397–8.

43  Ellmers, 'Keltischer Schiffbau', p. 92.

44  Ellmers, 'Rheinschiffe der Romerzeit', p. 33; 'Keltischer Schiffbau', pp. 95, 109.

45  Muller, op. cit., p. 131; Ellmers, 'Rheinschiffe der Romerzeit', p. 37.

46  Ellmers, 'Rheinschiffe der Romerzeit', p. 39.

47  Suetonius (trans. Robert Graves), London, 1965, p. 218.

48  Leighton, op. cit., p. 129.

49  Bonnard, op. cit., p. 134.

50  Ellmers, 'Rheinschiffe der Romerzeit', p. 25.

51  G. B. Rubin de Cervin, 'Mysteries and Nemesis of the Nemi Ships', *MM*, vol. 41, 1955, pp. 38–42.

52  J. Needham, *Science and Civilisation in China*, vol. IV, part 3, Cambridge, 1971.

53  R. Engelmayer, *Die Felsgravierierungen von Sayala*, Vienna, 1965, Plates XI and XLV.

54  George F. Bass (ed.), *A History of Seafaring*, London, 1972, pp. 14, 18.

55  Casson, *Ships and Seamanship*, p. 29.

56  Casson, 'Harbour and River Boats of Ancient Rome', p. 39.

57  Sidonius Apollinaris, Epist. II. 10 (quoted by A. Grenier, op. cit., p. 556).

## Chapter 13 The Indian Ocean and Arabian Gulf

1  J. Hornell, *Water Transport*, Newton Abbot, 1970, pp. 2, 5, 34–6, 9–12, 22–4, 92–8, 59–60, 61–8, 192.

2  R. Mookerji, *A History of Indian Shipping*, London, 1912, pp. 20–32.

3  E. H. J. Mackay, *Further Excavations at Mohenjo-Daro*, New Delhi, 1938 vol. I, p. 340; vol. II, Plates LXIX–4, LXXXIX-A; G. F. Dales, 'New Investigations at Mohenjo-Daro', *Archaeology*, vol. 18, 1965, p. 147.

4  Mackay, op. cit., vol. I, p. 340.

5  Hornell, op. cit., pp. 252–3.

6  S. R. Rao, 'Shipping and Maritime Trade of the Indus People', *Expedition* (Philadelphia), vol. 7, 1965, pp. 35–6.

7  ibid., pp. 36–7.

8  G. F. Dales, 'Harappan Outposts on the Makran Coast', *Antiquity*, vol. 36, 1962, p. 192.

9  A. L. Oppenheim, 'The Seafaring Merchants of Ur', *JAOS*, vol. 74, 1954, pp. 6–17.

10  For instance, see Sir Mortimer Wheeler, *The Indus Civilisation*, Cambridge, 1968, p. 81; S. N. Krarmer, 'Dilmun, Quest for Paradise', *Antiquity*, vol. 37, 1963, pp. 111–15; G. Bibby, *Looking for Dilmun*, New York, 1969.

11  Oppenheim, op. cit., p. 15.

12  M. Cary and E. H. Warmington, *The Ancient Explorers*, rev. ed., London, 1963, p. 77.

13  G. Bibby, op. cit., pp. 176–82, 252–3. I am grateful to Mr Michael Rice for drawing my attention to these photographs of the seals, and allowing me to publish them.

14  R. LeBaron Bowen Jr, 'Primitive Watercraft of Arabia', *American Neptune*, vol. 12, 1952, p. 194.

15  H. A. Winkler, *Rock Carvings of Southern Upper Egypt*, London, 1939, vol. I, p. 38; B. Landström, *The Ships of the Pharaohs*, London, 1970, p. 16.

16  E. J. Baumgartel, 'Predynastic Egypt', in *The Cambridge Ancient History*, vol. I, part 1, 3rd ed., Cambridge, 1970, p. 476.

17  ibid., p. 481.

18  ibid., p. 478.

19  See for instance R. W. Ehrich (ed.), *Relative Chronologies in Old World Archaeology*, Chicago, 1956.

20  C. Boreux, *Études de nautique egyptienne*, Cairo, 1924, pp. 45, 80.

21  LeBaron Bowen, op. cit., p. 192; G. Hourani, *Arab Seafaring*, Beirut, 1963, p. 7.

22  LeBaron Bowen, op. cit., pp. 193–4.

23  Pliny, *Natural History*, VI. 24, 82.

24  S. Zwemer, *Arabia: the Cradle of Islam*, Edinburgh, 1900, p. 101.

25  A. H. J. Prins, 'Maritime Art in an Islamic Context: Oculus and Therion in Lamu Ships',

26 LeBaron Bowen, op. cit., p. 213.
27 Hornell, op. cit., pp. 234–5.
28 ibid., p. 235.
29 A. Villiers, *Sons of Sinbad*, London, 1940, p. 54.
30 A. H. Hill, 'Some Early Accounts of the Oriental Boat', *MM*, vol. 44, 1958, pp. 207–8.
31 Mookerji, op. cit., p. 32.
32 E. V. Wright and D. M. Churchill, 'The Boats from North Ferriby, Yorkshire, England', *PPS*, vol. 31, 1965, pp. 22–3.
33 Hourani, op. cit., p. 95.
34 T. M. Johnstone and J. Muir, 'Portuguese Influences on Shipbuilding in the Persian Gulf', *MM*, vol. 48, 1962, pp. 58–63.
35 R. LeBaron Bowen Jr, 'Boats of the Indus Civilisation', *MM*, vol. 42, 1956, pp. 284–5.
36 B. Greenhill, 'The Karachi Fishing Boats', *MM*, vol. 42, 1956, pp. 54–66.
37 E. J. H. Mackay, 'Excavations at Chanhu-Daro', *Journal of the Royal Asiatic Society*, vol. 85, 1937, p. 542. I am grateful to Professor Stuart Piggott for this interesting reference.
38 ibid., p. 541.
39 LeBaron Bowen, 'Boats of the Indus Civilisation', p. 286.
40 Greenhill, op. cit., pp. 60–6.
41 Hourani, op. cit., p. 91.
42 Johnstone and Muir, op. cit., p. 60.
43 F. E. Paris, *Essai sur la construction navale des peuples extra-européens*, Paris, 1841, pp. 7–8.
44 S. B. Haines, 'Memoirs of the South and East Coasts of Arabia', *Geographical Journal*, vol. 15, 1845, p. 110.
45 LeBaron Bowen, 'Primitive Watercraft of Arabia', p. 210.
46 Hourani, op. cit., p. 90.
47 Kramer, op. cit., p. 112.
48 ibid.
49 Hourani, op. cit., p. 91.
50 See description in Bibby, op. cit., pp. 306, 316.
51 LeBaron Bowen, 'Primitive Watercraft of Arabia', pp. 198, 204.
52 LeBaron Bowen, 'Boats of the Indus Civilisation', pp. 288–9.
53 Hill, op. cit., p. 209.

**Chapter 14 China and Japan**

1 R. Mookerji, *A History of Indian Shipping*, London, 1912, p. 185.
2 ibid., pp. 191–3.
3 J. W. Needham, *Clerks and Craftsmen in China and the West*, Cambridge, 1970, pp. 50–2, 54.
4 Mookerji, op. cit., p. 39; J. W. Needham, *Science and Civilisation in China*, vol. IV, part 3, Cambridge, 1971, pp. 454–5.
5 Needham, *Clerks and Craftsmen*, p. 41.
6 ibid., p. 42.
7 S. Nishimura, *Ancient Rafts of Japan*, Tokyo, 1925, p. 122.
8 ibid., p. 114; Needham, *Science and Civilisation*, p. 390.
9 J. Hornell, *Water Transport*, Newton Abbot, 1970, p. 99; Needham, *Science and Civilisation*, p. 379.
10 Hornell, op. cit., p. 25.
11 Nishimura, *Skin Boats*, Tokyo, 1931, p. 180; H. Chattey, 'Water Transport in China', *China Journal* (Shanghai), vol. 10, no. 5, 1939, p. 228.
12 Kwang-chih Chang, 'The Beginnings of Agriculture in the Far East', *Antiquity*, vol. 44, 1970, p. 176.
13 ibid., p. 180.
14 ibid., p. 179.
15 ibid.
16 C. R. Edwards, 'Aboriginal Watercraft on the Pacific Coast of South America', *Ibero-Americana* (Berkeley and Los Angeles), vol. 47, 1965, p. 93.
17 ibid.
18 R. Suggs, *The Island Civilisations of Polynesia*, New York, 1960, p. 57.
19 G. R. G. Worcester, *Sail and Sweep in China*, Science Museum, London, 1966, p. 1; Needham, *Science and Civilisation*, pp. 395–6.
20 Kwang-chih Chang, op. cit., p. 181.
21 G. R. G. Worcester, 'Four Small Craft of Taiwan', *MM*, vol. 42, 1956, pp. 308–10.
22 Kwang-chih Chang, *The Archaeology of Ancient China*, New Haven and London, 1963, p. 281.
23 Needham, *Clerks and Craftsmen*, p. 63 and *Science and Civilisation*, p. 379.
24 Worcester, *Sail and Sweep*, p. 3.
25 Chattey, op. cit., p. 228.
26 Needham, *Clerks and Craftsmen*, p. 64 and *Science and Civilisation*, pp. 395–6; Hornell, op. cit., p. 90; Worcester, *Sail and Sweep*, p. 1.
27 Hornell, op. cit., pp. 89–90; Needham, *Science and Civilisation*, p. 394.
28 B. Greenhill, *Archaeology of the Boat*, London, 1976, pp. 103–4.
29 E. Sigant, 'A Northern Type of Chinese Junk', *MM*, vol. 46, 1960, pp. 161–2.
30 N. Matsuomotu, 'Some Remarks on Ancient Sea Navigation in South-East Asia', *Journal of the Hong Kong Archaeological Society*, vol. 1, 1968, p. 31; Needham, *Science and Civilisation*, pp. 424–5.
31 Needham, *Science and Civilisation*, p. 469.
32 J. W. Needham, *The Development of Iron and Steel Technology in China*, London, 1954, p. 3.
33 ibid., pp. 4, 5.
34 Worcester, *Sail and Sweep*, p. 8.

35 A. Christie, 'An Obscure Passage from the "Periplus" ', *Bulletin of African and Oriental Studies*, vol. 19, 1957, pp. 345–53.
36 ibid., p. 350.
37 ibid.
38 Needham, *Clerks and Craftsmen*, p. 67.
39 Quoted by C. R. Edwards, op. cit., pp. 98–9.
40 Needham, *Clerks and Craftsmen*, p. 66.
41 Quoted by C. R. Edwards, op. cit., p. 100.
42 Needham, *Clerks and Craftsmen*, p. 254.
43 ibid., p. 253.
44 ibid., p. 258.
45 J. Muir, 'Early Arab Seafaring and Rudders', *MM*, vol. 51, 1965, p. 358.
46 O. Crumlin-Pedersen, 'Two Danish Side Rudders', *MM*, vol. 52, 1966, pp. 251–3; Needham, *Clerks and Craftsmen*, p. 629.
47 Needham, *Clerks and Craftsmen*, p. 360.
48 J. Poujade, *La Route des Indes et ses navires*, Paris, 1946, p. 166.
49 R. LeBaron Bowen Jr, 'Eastern Sail Affinities', *American Neptune*, vol. 13, 1953, pp. 81–211.
50 Needham, *Clerks and Craftsmen*, p. 68.
51 ibid., p. 67, and *Science and Civilisation*, pp. 664, 431.
52 Needham, *Clerks and Craftsmen*, p. 25.
53 ibid., p. 26.
54 ibid., p. 241.
55 ibid., p. 240.
56 ibid., p. 248.
57 Poujade, op. cit., p. 163.
58 Needham, *Clerks and Craftsmen*, p. 63.
59 G. R. G. Worcester, 'The Origin and Observance of the Dragon Boat Festival in China', *MM*, vol. 42, 1956, pp. 127–31.
60 C. W. Bishop, 'Long-Houses and Dragon-Boats', *Antiquity*, vol. 12, 1938, pp. 411–24.
61 J. E. Kidder, *Japan before Buddhism*, London, 1959, p. 27.
62 J. M. Coles and G. E. S. Higgs, *The Archaeology of Early Man*, London, 1969, p. 410.
63 Kidder, op. cit., p. 34.
64 W. Watson, 'Neolithic Japan and the White Races of Today', in E. Bacon (ed.), *Vanished Civilizations*, London, 1963, p. 96.
65 Kidder, op. cit., p. 51.
66 ibid.
67 ibid.
68 N. H. Munro, *Prehistoric Japan*, Edinburgh, 1911, p. 138; Matsuomotu, op. cit., p. 29.
69 Kidder, op. cit., p. 59.
70 Watson, op. cit., p. 98.
71 Nishimura, *Ancient Rafts of Japan*, p. 56.
72 ibid., p. 127; J. G. Nelson, 'The Geography of the Balsa', *American Neptune*, vol. 31, 1961, p. 177.
73 Kidder, op. cit., p. 40.
74 W. Jochelson, *Archaeological Investigations in Kamchatka*, Washington, 1928, p. 70.
75 Watson, op. cit., p. 96.
76 H. G. Bandi, *Eskimo Prehistory*, London, 1964, pp. 50–1.
77 Kidder, op. cit., p. 57.
78 Bandi, op. cit., p. 86.
79 S. Nishimura, *Skin Boats*, Tokyo, 1931, pp. 165–6.
80 ibid., p. 130.
81 ibid., p. 133.
82 ibid., p. 155; Munro, op. cit., p. 138.
83 Nishimura, *Skin Boats*, p. 166.
84 ibid., p. 207.
85 ibid., pp. 204–5.
86 S. Nishimura, *Kumano-No-Morota-Bune*, Tokyo, 1920, p. 20.
87 Nishimura, *Ancient Rafts of Japan*, p. 115; see also Kidder, op. cit., p. 102.
88 Bishop, op. cit., p. 419; W. G. Aston, *Nihongi: Chronicles of Japan*, vol. 1, London, 1924, p. 68.
89 Nishimura, *Ancient Ships of Japan*, 10 vols.
90 Kidder, op. cit., p. 163.
91 ibid., p. 164.
92 ibid.

## Chapter 15 The Pacific

1 Elsdon Best, *The Maori Canoe*, Dominion Museum (Wellington), Bulletin no. 7, 1925, p. 3.
2 See for instance: E. W. Gifford, 'Archaeological Excavations in Fiji', *University of California, Anthropological Records*, vol. 1, no. 3, 1951; K. P. Emory, *Archaeology of the Pacific Equatorial Islands*, B.P. Bishop Museum (Honolulu), Bulletin 123, 1930; J. Golson, 'New Zealand Archaeology', *JPS*, vol. 66, 1957, pp. 271–3. A. Spoehr, 'Marianas Prehistory', *Fieldiana: Anthropology Papers* no. 48, 1957; W. R. Ambrose and R. C. Green, 'First Millennium B.C. Transport of Obsidian from New Britain to the Solomon Islands', *Nature*, no. 237, 1972, p. 31.
3 R. C. Suggs, *The Island Civilisations of Polynesia*, New York, 1960, pp. 112–13. For a suggested later date see C. S. Smith, review of *Prehistoric Culture in Oceania*, ed. I. Yawata and Y. H. Sinoto, *Science*, vol. 162, pp. 1375–9.
4 Sir Peter Buck, *Vikings of the Pacific*, Chicago, 1938, p. 283.
5 Suggs, op. cit., p. 113.
6 A. Spoehr, 'A Close Look at the Kon Tiki', *Chicago Natural History Museum Bulletin*, vol. 12, 1951.
7 Suggs, op. cit., p. 61.
8 ibid., p. 62.
9 T. Heyerdahl, *Early Man and the Ocean*, London,

1978, ch. 2.

10   Best, op. cit., p. 251.

11   J. Garanger, 'La Préhistoire des Iles polynesiennes', *Archéologia*, vol. 3, 1966, p. 15 (trans. Frances McGrail).

12   Quoted in Best, op. cit., p. 265.

13   William Dampier, *A New Voyage Round the World*, London, 1689.

14   Best, op. cit., p. 253.

15   ibid., p. 227.

16   ibid., p. 236.

17   Suggs, op. cit., p. 73.

18   K. P. Emory, *Pacific Islands*, Council for Old World Archaeology Survey (Cambridge, Mass.), Area 21, no. 1, 1958, pp. 3–5.

19   Best, op. cit., p. 37.

20   The following account of the building of a Maori war canoe is taken from Best, op. cit., pp. 36–119.

21   Buck, op. cit., p. 124.

22   A. Metraux, *The Ethnology of Easter Island*, B.P. Bishop Museum (Honolulu), Bulletin 160, 1940, p. 204.

23   Best, op. cit., p. 230.

24   Buck, op. cit., p. 93.

25   Best, op. cit., pp. 269, 161.

26   Buck, op. cit., p. 40.

27   Suggs, op. cit., p. 81.

28   Buck, op. cit., p. 41.

29   Suggs, op. cit., p. 83.

30   J. Hornell, 'Was there Pre-Columbian Contact Between the People of Oceania and South America?' *JPS*, vol. 54, 1945, p. 170.

31   Quoted by Katherine Luomala, review of Andrew Sharp, *Ancient Voyagers in the Pacific*, *American Antiquity*, vol. 60, 1955, pp. 776–8.

32   A. Sharp, *Ancient Voyagers in the Pacific*, London, 1957. For a good summary of other views and bibliography, see D. R. Finney, 'New Perspectives on Polynesian Voyaging' in *Polynesian Cultural History*, Hawaii, 1967, pp. 141–66.

33   Buck, op. cit., p. 63.

34   Suggs, op. cit., p. 84.

35   Luomala, op. cit., p. 778.

36   See for instance A. Thom, *Megalithic Sites in Britain*, Oxford, 1967.

37   Buck, op. cit., p. 98.

38   Best, op. cit., p. 268. Thomas Gladwin in his very interesting study of navigation on Puluwat in the Carolines, *East is a Big Bird* (Harvard U.P., 1970), found no evidence of latitude-finding, but David Lewis, in *We, the Navigators* (Wellington, 1972, pp. 233–47), found sparse evidence in Tonga, the Tikopias and Ninigo.

39   D. E. Sopher, *The Sea Nomads*, Singapore, 1965, p. 30.

40   ibid., p. 29

41   ibid., p. 19.

42   ibid., pp. 55–6.

43   ibid., p. 186.

44   C. W. Bishop, 'Long-Houses and Dragon Boats', *Antiquity*, vol. 12, 1938, p. 417.

45   ibid.

46   ibid., pp. 422–3.

47   B. A. G. Vroklage, 'Das Schiff in den Megalithculturen Südostasiens und der Südsee', *Anthropos*, vol. 31, 1936, pp. 712–57.

48   T. Harrisson, 'New Archaeological and Ethnological Results from Niah Caves, Sarawak', *Man*, vol. 59, 1959, p. 7; T. Harrisson, 'The Prehistory of Borneo', *Asian Perspectives*, vol. 13, 1970, pp. 17–45.

49   Bishop, op. cit., p. 423.

50   J. Hornell, *Water Transport*, Newton Abbot, 1970, pp. 263–71.

51   J. Hornell, 'Some American Balanced Canoes: Stages in the Invention of the Double Outrigger', *Man*, vol. 28, 1928, pp. 129–33.

52   Hornell, *Water Transport*, p. 269. But, for a contrary view, see E. Doran, *Nao, Junk and Vaka*, Texas A&M University Press, 1973, pp. 42–3.

53   Hornell, *Water Transport*, pp. 270–1.

54   Sopher, op. cit., pp. 194–5; N. Matsuomotu, 'Some Remarks on Ancient Sea Navigation in South-East Asia', *Journal of the Hong Kong Archaeological Society*, vol. 1, 1968, p. 30.

55   J. Hornell, *The Outrigger Canoes of Indonesia*, Madras Fisheries Bulletin no. 12, 1920, pp. 76, 81, 86.

56   Suggs, op. cit., p. 78.

57   T. Barthel, 'Grundlagen zur Entzifferung der Osterinselschrift', *Abhandlung aus dem Gebiete der Auslandskunde*, vol. 64, Reihe B, Hamburg, 1958; E. S. C. Handy, *Marquesan Legends*, B.P. Bishop Museum (Honolulu), Bulletin 69, 1930, p. 30; T. Henry, *Tahiti aux temps anciens*, publication de la Société des Oceanistes, no. 1, Paris, 1951, pp. 196–7.

58   P. E. Buck, 'The Disappearance of Canoes in Oceania', *JPS*, vol. 51, 1942, p. 195.

59   J. Hornell, 'South American Balsas: the Problem of their Origin', *MM*, vol. 17, 1931, p. 353.

60   A. C. Haddon and J. Hornell, *The Canoes of Oceania*, B.P. Bishop Museum, Special Publications, no. 27, 1936, p. 144.

61   C. Nooteboom, 'The Study of Primitive Sea-going Craft as an Ethnological Problem', *Internationales Archiv für Ethnographie*, vol. 45, nos 4–6, 1947, p. 218.

62   H. Rusenfeld, *The Megalithic Culture of Melanesia*, Leiden, 1950, p. 252.

63   J. G. Nelson, 'The Geography of Balsa', *American Neptune*, vol. 21, 1961, p. 192.

64 ibid., pp. 187–95.
65 C. R. Edwards, *New World Perspectives on Pre-European Voyaging in the Pacific*, University of Wisconsin, Milwaukee Center for Latin American Studies, reprint no. 6, New York, 1969, p. 26.
66 Sopher, op. cit., p. 383.
67 A. Christie, 'The Sea-locked Lands', in S. Piggott (ed.), *The Dawn of Civilization*, London, 1961, p. 293.
68 Edwards, op. cit., p. 32.
69 ibid., p. 34.
70 Suggs, op. cit., p. 68.
71 Handy, op. cit., p. 131.
72 Suggs, op. cit., pp. 208–9.
73 G. F. Carter, 'Pre-Columbian Chickens in America' in C. L. Riley *et al.* (eds), *Man Across the Sea*, Austin and London, 1971, pp. 178–218.
74 ibid., p. 202.
75 P. G. Mangelsdorf and D. L. Oliver, *Whence Came Maize to Asia?*, Harvard University Bot. Mus. leaflet, 14 (10), 1951, p. 263.

**Chapter 16 The Americas**

1 José de Acosta, *Historia Natural y Moral de las Indias*, Madrid, 1849.
2 Terence Grieder, 'Periods in Pecos Style Pictographs', *American Antiquity*, vol. 31, 1966, pp. 710–20.
3 W. N. Fenton and E. N. Dodge, 'An Elm Bark Canoe', *American Neptune*, vol. 9, 1949, p. 201.
4 A. Martinière, *Voyages des pais septentrionaux*, Paris, 1671, pp. 150–3 (trans. D. MacRitchie).
5 F. Nansen, *In Northern Mists*, vol. II, London, 1911, p. 127.
6 Olaus Magnus, *Historia de Gentibus Septentrionalibus*, Rome, 1555, Lib. II, C.9.
7 J. Louis Giddings, *Ancient Men of the Arctic*, London, 1968, p. 91, Plate 24(d).
8 ibid., p. 92.
9 S. Marstrander, *Ostfolds Jordbrukaristninger-Skjeberg*, Oslo, 1963, p. 446.
10 E. T. Adney and H. I. Chapelle, *The Bark Canoes and Skin Boats of North America*, Washington, 1964, p. 189.
11 ibid., p. 190.
12 I am grateful to Magnus Magnusson for translating and clarifying the use of this phrase. Rowlock is used here as a part for the whole. 'Hud' is usually used for the hide of cattle but occurs for 'sealskin' in places and can be used for hides of all kinds.
13 Magnus Magnusson and Hermann Palsson, *The Vinland Sagas*, London, 1965, p. 100.
14 ibid., pp. 30–1, 99–100.

15 William E. Taylor Jr, 'An Archaeological Perspective on Eskimo Economy', *Antiquity*, vol. 40, 1966, p. 119.
16 Giddings, op. cit., p. 274.
17 ibid., p. 46.
18 See for instance F. J. Pohl, *The Viking Explorers*, New York, 1966, p. 227.
19 Alice B. Kehoe, 'Small Boats upon the North Atlantic', in C. L. Riley *et al.* (eds), *Man Across the Sea*, Austin and London, 1971, p. 287.
20 Betty Meggers, Clifford Evans and Emilio Estrada, 'The Early Formative Period, in Coastal Ecuador: the Valdivia and Machalille Phases', *Smithsonian Contributions to Anthropology*, vol. I, Washington, 1965.
   Betty J. Meggers, *Ecuador*, London, 1966, pp. 42–7.
21 J. G. Nelson, 'The Geography of the Balsa, no. 3', *American Neptune*, vol. 21, 1961, p. 164.
22 E. Best, *Polynesian Voyagers: the Maori as a Deep-sea Navigator Explorer and Colonizer*, Dominion Museum (Wellington), Monograph no. 5, 1954, p. 24.
23 E. Doran Jr, 'The Sailing Raft as a Great Tradition', in Riley *et al.* (eds), op. cit., p. 155.
24 Stephen C. Jett in ibid., p. 26.
25 'Historia de las Guerras Civiles de Peru (1544–1548) y de Otros Sucesos de las Indias', in *Colección de Libros y Documentos Referentes a la Historia de America*, vol. III, Madrid, 1905, pp. 527–8 quoted by C. R. Edwards, 'Aboriginal Watercraft on the Pacific Coast of South America', *Ibero-Americana* (Berkeley and Los Angeles), vol. 47, 1965, p. 70.
26 Girolamo Benzoni, *Historia del Mondo Nuovo*, 2nd Italian ed., Venice, 1572, p. 165, quoted in Edwards, op. cit., p. 71.
27 William Dampier, *A New Voyage Round the World*, 5th ed., London, 1703, vol. I, pp. 141–3.
28 Edwards, op. cit., p. 105.
29 ibid., p. 113.
30 'La Relacion Samano-Xerez', in Raul Porras Barrenechea, *Las Relaciones Primitivas de la Conquista del Peru*, Paris, 1937, p. 66, quoted in ibid., p. 67.
31 W. H. Prescott, *History of the Conquest of Peru*, London, 1847, vol. I, p. 244.
32 Edwards, op. cit., p. 67.
33 ibid.
34 ibid., p. 68.
35 'Historia de las Guerras Civiles de Peru (1544–1548) y de Otros Sucesos de las Indias', pp. 527–8.
36 R. LeBaron Bowen Jr, 'Eastern Sail Affinities', *American Neptune*, vol. 13, 1953, p. 82.
37 Dampier, op. cit., pp. 141–3.
38 Basil Hall, *Extracts from a Journal Written on the Coasts of Chili, Peru and Mexico*, 2nd ed.,

Edinburgh, 1824, vol. II, pp. 80–1.

39 LeBaron Bowen, op. cit., 1953, p. 91.
40 Edwards, op. cit., p. 97.
41 ibid., pp. 110, 96–7.
42 ibid., p. 100.
43 For an excellent summary of these views see R. Wauchope, *Lost Tribes and Sunken Continents*, Chicago, 1962, pp. 93–4.
44 Edwards, op. cit., pp. 110–12; Jett, op. cit., p. 12.
45 T. Heyerdahl and A. Skjokvold, 'Archaeological Evidence of Pre-Spanish visits to the Galapagos Islands', *Mem. Soc. Amer. Arch.*, no. 12, 1956.
46 S. Ryden, review of T. Heyerdahl and A. Skjokvold, op. cit., *American Antiquity*, vol. 24, 1956, p. 88.
47 C. Evans, comment on Ryden's review, *American Antiquity*, vol. 24, 1956, p. 189.
48 Junius Bird, *The Cultural Sequence of the North Chilean Coast, II: Handbook of South American Indians*, Smithsonian Bulletin no. 143, 1946, p. 388.
49 Nelson, op. cit., pp. 183, 185.
50 ibid., p. 192.
51 J. Hornell, *Water Transport*, Newton Abbot, 1970, p. 77.
52 Nelson, op. cit., p. 187.
53 ibid., p. 165.
54 M. Barbeau, 'The Aleutian Route of Navigation into America', *Geographical Review*, vol. 35, 1945, pp. 424–43.
55 B. Pickersgill and A. H. Bunting, 'Cultivated Plants and the *Kon-Tiki* Theory', *Nature*, vol. 222, 19 April 1969, p. 227.
56 T. Heyerdahl, *American Indians in the Pacific*, London, 1952, p. 429.
57 Patricia J. O'Brien, 'The Sweet Potato: its Origins and Dispersal', *American Anthropologist*, vol. 74, 1972, pp. 342–65.
58 Donald W. Brand, 'The Sweet Potato: an Exercise in Methodology', in Riley *et al.* (eds), op. cit., pp. 359–63.
59 O'Brien, op. cit., pp. 354–5.
60 Wauchope, op. cit., pp. 89–95; Doran, op. cit., p. 135.
61 I. Rouse, *The Entry of Man into the West Indies*, Yale University Publications in Anthropology, no. 61,

New Haven, 1960, p. 5; G. G. Simpson, *Zoogeography of West Indian Land Mammals*, American Museum Novitates no. 1759, New York, 1956.
62 I. Rouse, 'Prehistory of the West Indies', *Science*, vol. 144, 1964, pp. 499–513.
63 J. M. Cruxent and I. Rouse, 'Early Man in the West Indies', *Scientific American*, vol. 221, 1969, p. 45.
64 ibid., p. 46.
65 ibid., p. 49.
66 ibid.
67 ibid., pp. 49–51.
68 ibid., p. 52.
69 G. Friederici, *Die Schiffahrt der Indianer*, Stuttgart, 1907, p. 22; H. Suder, *Von Einbaum und Floss zum Schiff*, Institut für Meereskunde, Berlin, 1930, p. 85.
70 L. Wafer, *A New Voyage and Description of the Isthmus of America*, Hakluyt Society, series 2, vol. 73, Oxford 1933, p. 59.
71 A. Emerich, 'Gold Raft from Lake Siecha', in *Sweat of the Sun and Tears of the Moon*, Washington, 1965, p. 86; J. E. S. Thompson, 'Canoes and Navigation of the Mayas and their Neighbours', *JRAI*, vol. 79, 1949, p. 70.
72 M. B. McKusick, 'Aboriginal Canoes in the West Indies', Yale University, Department of Anthropology, paper no. 63, 1960, p. 5.
73 John Stoneman, 'The Voyage of M. Henry Challons Intended for the North Plantation of Virginia, 1606, Taken by the Way, and Ill Used by Spaniards', in *Purchase his Pilgrimes*, ed. Samuel Purchas, vol. IV, London, 1625, pp. 1832–6.
74 C. R. Edwards, 'Aboriginal Sail in the New World', *Southwest Journal of Anthropology* (Albuquerque), vol. 21, 1965, p. 352.
75 Thompson, op. cit., p. 71.
76 ibid., p. 72.
77 ibid., p. 74; Edwards, 'Aboriginal Watercraft', p. 85.
78 Edwards, 'Aboriginal Watercraft', p. 107.
79 McKusick, op. cit., p. 8.
80 ibid., p. 7.
81 ibid., p. 6.
82 ibid., p. 9.

# Index

Abipones tribe, 41
Abu Sayd, 178
*actuaria* (galley), 88
Adhamas, Melos, 55
adzes, *see* axes
Aeschylus, 80
Afghanistan, 12
Agauna, R., Japan, 196
Ahrensburg Culture, 105
Ainu, 25, 45, 195, 196, Fig. 14.10
Ajanta, India, 185, Fig. 14.1
Alacalufs tribe, 19, 24, 25
Alaska, 32, 195, Fig. 4.8, Map 1.1
Albania, 30
Aleutian, Aleuts, 32, 33, 195, Figs 4.8,
    16.1
Aliseda, Spain, 94, Fig. 8.11
Allectus coin, 151–3, Fig. 11.15
Althiburus, Tunisia, 88, 161
Amara Indians, 14
Amathous, Cyprus, 78, Fig. 7.13
ambach tree, 7
amber, 96
Amiens Cathedral, 160, Fig. 12.8
Amoy, Stavanger, Norway, 125, Fig.
    10.5
Amur, R., 8, 18, 196
Ancholme, R., Humberside, 148
anchors, 82
Andaman Islands, 12
animal figureheads, 94, 114, 142, 175,
    176, 194, Fig. 14.2
animals, transport of, 49, 121
Anula tribe, 24
Appleby, Lincs, 149
Aran Islands, 27
Araucanians, 25
Arctic, 32, 36, 103
Ardnamurchan, Skye, 28
Arica, Chile, 230, Fig. 2.2
Ari the Learned, 138
art, farmers', 103, 107
Ashanti, 7

*ashi-bune* (reed canoe), 13
Ashur-nasir-pal II, 31, Fig. 4.6
Åskekarr, Sweden, 117
Askola, Finalnd, 105
Assyria, 72
Atacama Culture, 14, Fig. 2.9
Athens, 57
Atrebates, 88
Aulus Gellius, 72
Aurignacian, 42
Australia, 5, 17–18, 24, Figs 3.1, 3.2
Aveiro lagoons, Portugal, 93
Avienus, 26, 123
axes and adzes, 56, 71, 81, 201
axe factories, 121

Bab el-Mandeb, 175, Map 13.1
Babelthusp raft, 195
Bad Junkerath, 98
Badarians, 175
Baganda people, 45
Bahrain, *see* Dilmun
*baidar and baidarka* (skin boats), 33, 38
Balaton, Lake, Hungary, 12
Balawat, 94, 95, Fig. 8.13
ballast, 22, 87
bamboo, 188–9
Bantry pillar, Co. Kerry, Ireland,
    128–30, 153, Fig. 10.10, Map 11.1
*barco rabelo* (boat), 120
barge, 89, 156–8, 161, 168
Bari region, Uganda, 7, 76
bark (boats and canoes), 17–25, 196–8,
    219–20, Figs 3.1, 3.2, 4.9, 14.10,
    14.11
Barma Grande, 4
basket work, basket boats, 32, 34, 58,
    108, 134, 175
Bayeux Tapestry, 124
beaching, 32, 65, 92, 98, 112, 147
*beden-seyed* (boat), 180–1, Fig. 13.15
Beothuk tribe, 22
Bering Strait, 4, 33, 34, Map 1.1

Bet She'arim, Israel, 59, Fig. 6.4
Bevaix, Switzerland, 150, 164, 166, Fig.
    12.14
*bhum* (Arabian Gulf boat), 177
Birka, Sweden, 119
bitumen, 11
Bjornstad, Norway, 107, Fig. 9.8
Blackfriars ship, 89–90, 98, 153, 163,
    Figs 8.2, 8.3, 8.4, Map 11.1
Blasket Islands, Ireland, 139
Blessey, France, 88, 159, Fig. 12.5
Blussus (boatman), 166, 191, Fig. 12.16
boat-handling qualities: curragh, 137;
    multiple dug-out, 48; umiak, 57
Bohuslän, Sweden, 28, Fig. 4.1
Bømlo, Norway, 28, 131
Borobodur, Java, 215, Fig. 15.14
Boyne coracle, 134, Fig. 10.15
Brazil, 17, 227
Brigg: dug-out, 148–9, Fig. 11.12;
    'raft', 147–8, Figs 11.10, 11.11
Broighter boat model, 127–8, 153, 166,
    Fig. 10.9, Map 11.1
Bronze Age, 33, 60, 67, 77, 99, 107–8,
    143, 161, 187; carving, Fig. 9.24
Bruges boat, 90, Fig. 8.5
Brumby, nr Scunthorpe, 125
building, boats, *see* bark; dug-outs;
    raft; skin
building, descriptions of: bark canoes,
    19, 21, Fig. 3.5; *caballitos*, 14;
    'Celtic', 91, 162–6; coracles, 133–4;
    curraghs, 133; dhows, 180; dug-outs,
    47; Humberside, 149–51; Kuwait,
    reed boats, 174; Maori canoes,
    206–9, Fig. 15.3; Noah, Fig. 10.7;
    Pacific, 209–10; *pelota*, 41; *pirogues*,
    235; Roman, 89–90; *saveiros*, 92–3;
    skin boats, 133–4, Fig. 10.15; umiaks,
    34, 134, Figs 4.11, 4.12
building, planked boats, *see* carvel or
    flush planking; clinker planking;
    shell sequence; skeleton sequence

building, time taken: dug-out, 46; Maori canoe, 206
bull-boat (skin boat), 34
buoyancy of multiple dug-out, 48
Bushmen, 20, Fig. 3.4

Cabárceno, Spain, 99
*caballito* (reed-bundle boat), 14, 219, 225
Cabrières d'Aygues, Var, France, 158, Fig. 12.3
Caergwrle bowl, 124–7, Figs 10.1, 10.2, Map 11.1
canals, 167
Canary Islands, 57
Canton, 191
cargo, 21, 31, 72, 79, 82, 89, 118, 156, 225; *see also* trade
Carib, Caribbean, 232
carvel or flush planking, 89–90, 118
carvings and engravings, 29, 32, 33, 38, 40, 59, 63, 66, 77, 102, 104, 107, 113, 151–3, 175, 221, Figs 4.1, 4.2, 4.7, 6.3, 6.4, 6.6, 6.7, 6.11, 7.3, 9.1, 9.2, 9.5, 9.6, 9.7, 9.8, 9.10, 9.15, 9.16, 9.17, 10.4, 10.5, 11.8, 12.2, 12.3, 13.7, 16.2
casks and coopers, 161–2, Fig. 12.10
castles, ships', 118
caulking, 25, 89, 120, 144, 147–8, 149, 163–4, 190, 196
Celtic shipbuilding, 87–92, 150, 155, 161–6
centreboards, *see* leeboards
Chad, Lake, 9
Chanhu-Daro, Pakistan, 172, 180
Chasséen, 131
Chenchu people, India, 40
Ch'éng-Tzu-Yai, Shantung, 186
Cheops ship, 71, 74, 75, Figs 7.4, 7.5
*chhien Han Shu*, 185
Chichen Itza, Mexico, 229, 233
Chikapa, R., 20
Chile, 14
Chimu Culture of Peru, 14
Chios, 56, 64
Chiyoi Jyu Island, 8
Chukchi Peninsula, Siberia, 4, 33, Map 1.1
Cissbury, Sussex, 121, Maps 4.2, 10.1
Claudius, Emperor, 156
cleats, 146, 147
climatic changes, 17, 186, 195
clinker planking, 116, 120
coastal and cross-channel boats, 27, 119–20
*codicaria* (boat), 157–8, Fig. 12.2
coffins, 187, Fig. 14.2
cog, 118–19, Figs 9.25, 9.26
coins, 58, 94, 151–3, 159, Figs 8.12, 11.15, 12.6; Contorniate, 58, Fig. 6.2
Colombia, 45

comb or boat?, 42, Fig. 4.14
Connemara, 27
coracle, 26, 30, 32, 37, 38, 105, 186
Corfu, 12
Coromandel, 178
County Hall ship, London, 162
Couri, Haiti, 232
Crete, 63, 67–9, 75, 101, Fig. 6.3
cross-beams, 71
culture contact, 40
curragh or navog, 26, 129, 132–7, Figs 8.17, 10.11, 10.12, 10.13, 10.16
Cyclades, 60, 61, Fig. 6.5
Cyprus, 67, 79, Fig. 7.12

Dahomey, 7
Dakkas, 7
*dalca* (sewn boat), 25, 45
Danube, R., 30, 60
Dashur boats, 71, 72, 75, Fig. 7.7
dating: *see* dendrochronology; radiocarbon
Deir el-Bahari, Egypt, 167
Delaware Indians, 47
Delos, 66, Fig. 6.10
Denbigh Culture, 222
dendrochronology, 85, 140, 146
Desna, R., 42
*dghaisa* (boat), 93, 95–7, Fig. 8.16
Dhehemenegaki, Melos, 55
dhow, 178–80
diffusionist theory, 39, 97
Dilmun (Telmun), Bahrain, 173–4, 176, Figs 13.5, 13.6, 13.8, 13.9
Dinka people, 76
discovery, voyages of, 56, 57
distribution: of skin boats, 36, Map 4.1; of skin and planked boats, 153–5, Map 11.1
Dniester, R., 42
Dobrizhoffer, Martin, 41
Dolgans tribe, 33
Dolmen de Antelas, Visieu, Portugal, 42, 98, Fig. 4.14c
Don, R., 42
Dong S'on Culture, 213, Fig. 15.11
Dorestadt, 119, Fig. 9.28
double-ended boats, 64, 97, 98, 151, 176, Fig. 6.9
dragon boats, *see* lung chhuan
drift voyages, 100, 223
dug-outs (logboats), 45–51, 60, 113–14, 140–3, 148–9, 186–7, 194, 203, 212–14, 220, 234–5, Figs 6.5, 14.2, 15.12, 15.13; heat treatment, 47, 49, 50, 116, 206, 212, Fig. 5.5; *see also* expanded dug-outs; multiple dug-outs; stability; washstrakes
Dunajec, R., Poland, 48, 49, Fig. 5.3

Eadwine Psalter, 160, Fig. 12.7
Easter Island, 231

Ecuador, 45, 226–7
Egtved, Denmark, 17
Egypt, 7, 39, 69–72, 79, 175–6
Erik's Saga, 222
El-Gebelein, Egypt, Fig. 2.4
Elbe, R., 60
elephants, 161
Erasthones, 123
Ertebølle people, Denmark, 28
Eskimo, 109, 222
'esping' or 'aspen', 116
Eudoxus, 93
Euphrates, R., 10, 30, 31
Evenhus, Norway, 29, 102, 104, 105, 125, 221, Figs 4.2, 10.4
expanded dug-outs, 49, 50, 116, 212, Figs 5.5, 5.6, 5.7
experimental skin boat, *see* Kalnes
Ezinge, Netherlands, 162

*faering* (boat), 116
Falaika, 174
fastenings, see lashings; mortise and tenon; nails; skewers; trenails
fenestration of rudder, 191
Ferriby, Humberside, 46, 141, 143–7, 153, Figs 11.2, 11.4, 11.5, 11.6, 11.7, 11.8, 11.9, Maps 4.2, 11.1
ferries, ferrying, 37
Finistère, 41
Finns, 24, 45
fish, fishing and fishermen, 3, 11, 13, 27, 28, 41, 60, 99, 103, 186, 194, 201, Figs 3.4, 4.1
flat-bottomed boats, 64, 72, 89, 91, 98, 150, 164
Floamanna Saga, 41
Formosa, 188, 195, Fig. 14.5
Fortetsa, Crete, 78
Fosna, Norway, 103
fowls, domestic, evidence from in Pacific, 218
frames, *see* ribs
Franchthi cave, Greece, 56, 60
freeboard, 49, 50, 118, 176, 203
Friarton, Perth, Scotland, 56

Gades (Cadiz), 85, 93, 97, 98; *see also* Tartessus
Gallinazo Culture, Peru, 14
Ganges, R., 172
Gåshopen, Norway, 106, Fig. 9.6
Gebel el-Arak, 175
Gelidonya, Cape, wreck, 82
Genghis Khan, 31
Gokstad ship, 116, Fig. 9.22
Goldi tribe, 18
gondola, 93, 95–7, Fig. 8.15
Gontsi, Russia, 42
Gotland, Sweden, 28
graffiti, drawings and pictograms, 65, 130, 171, Figs 10.13, 13.12, 13.14,

13.16, 13.17, 14.3
Graig Llwyd, Gwynedd, Wales, 121, Map 10.1
Gran Chaco, 41
Grand Pressigny, France, 156
Gravettian, 42
Great Langdale, 121, Map 10.1
Guadalquivir, R., 60, 87
Guardafui, Cape, E. Africa, 93
*guares* (leeboards), 228–30, Fig. 16.12
Guatavita, Colombia, 233, Fig. 16.14
Gujarat, India, 173
gunwales, 21, 35
*gurgurru*, 81
Guyana, 17, 19

Ha'atuatua, Marquesas, 200–1
*hai-ku* (ship), 189
al-Hariri, 177, 191, Fig. 13.10
Han dynasty, 188
Haniwa pottery, Japan, 199, Fig. 14.14
Hannibal, 31
Harappa, 12, 171, 173–4, 176, 179, 182
harbours, 82
Hatshepsut, Queen, 9, 77, 167
Hawaii, 210
Heilbronn-Böckingen, Germany, 161
Hembury, Devon, 121, Maps 4.2, 10.1
Henry V, 36
Hercules, 58, 85
Herodotus, 10, 31, 71, 81, 82, 183
Hespriholmen, Norway, 103, 106
Heyerdahl's theories, 100–1, 201–3
Hio (Pontevedra), Spain, 99
*hippos* (boat), 93–5, Figs 8.11, 8.13
Hjortspring (Als), Denmark, 109, 115, 116, 117, Fig. 9.20
Hognipen, Norway, 103, 104
Hokkaido, Japan, 195
Holinshed, 36
Homer, 72, 75, 80, 81
*Homo erectus*, 3–4
Hou Han period, 191
Hoxne, Essex, 3
Huaca Prieta, Peru 13
Huanchaco, Peru, 15
Huang Ho, 32, Fig. 4.5
Huelva, Spain, 99
hulk (ship), 119–20, Figs 9.27, 9.28, 9.29
Humber, R., 143
Humboldt current, 15
Hungary, 12
hunting, 38, 103, 195, Fig. 14.8
*hupozoma*, see truss

Ibn Battutah, 189
Ibn Jubayr, 181
Igel, Trier, 166
Ile à Vache, Haiti, 232
Illyrians, 12
Indus, R., 171–4, 180, Figs 13.1, 13.3

Iona, 135
Irish monks, 26, 132; voyages to Iceland, 138–9
Irrawaddy, R., 214
Iscuande, R., Colombia, 214
Istorp, Sweden, 24
Ivugivik, Canada, 110
Iwajuka, Gumma, Japan, 194

*jangada* (sailing raft), 190, 227, Fig. 16.10
Japan, 8, 194–9, Fig. 14.3
Jarlshof, Shetland, 153, Fig. 11.18
Jemdat Nasr, 10, Fig. 2.5
Jerusalem, tomb of Jason, Fig. 7.16
Jomon people, 194–5, 223
Jonathan's cave, East Wemyss, Scotland, 152–3, Fig. 11.17, Map 11.1
Julius Caesar, 36, 87–8, 90, 98, 159
junk, 185, 188–9, Figs 14.1, 14.6; characteristics of, 189; development of, 192–3

*Kaahua* (legendary canoe), 218
*kabang* (expanded dug-out), 212
Kalnes boat, 108–12, Figs 9.12, 9.13, 9.14
Kamchatka, 33, 195, 196, Fig. 14.9
Kapel Avazaath (Netherlands), 164
Karam, R., 39
Karelia, 33
Kathiawar, India, 173
Kaveri, R., India, 171
kayak, 24, 26, 34, 36, 37, 105–6, 220, Figs 4.9, 4.13
Kentmere boat, Fig. 5.9
Kerry, Ireland, 27
Khorsabad, Iraq, 94, 96, Fig. 8.14
Killary, Co. Meath, Ireland, 128
*kirkarah, kerkouros*, 81
Kistna, R., 171
Klamath Indians, 14
Knossos, 56, 62
Kobystan, Azerbaijan, 33
Komsa, Norway, 32, 103, 105
*konga* (raft), 217
Koryak tribe, 33
Krefeld, Germany, 166
Krusenstern, Cape, Alaska, 221
Kumano, Japan, 198
Kuril Islands, 25, 45
Kutch, 173
Kyrenia ship, 75, 81, 82

La Ferrassie, Dordogne, 4
La Tène, 166
Ladrone Islands, 203, Map 15.1
lakes and rivers, boats for, 21, 24, 27, 150, 156, 166–7; trade, 161
Lambas of Zambia, 18
Lamu, Kenya, see *mtepe*

land-bridges, 4, 219
Lapps, 24, 45
Larnian people, 27, 28, Map 4.2
Las Figuras, cave, Andalusia, 42, Fig. 4.14a
lashings, 9, 34, 36, 48, 71, 115, 190, 208; see also needles; sewing
launching, 92
leather, *see* skins
leeboards, 190–1, 227–30, Figs 16.5, 16.12
Lepenski Vir, 46
Lesotho, 20
*liburnian* (ship type), 12, 81
Linear B, 80
Limfjorden, 119
Lindos, Rhodes, 83
Lingones tribe, 12
*lintres* (boat type), 159
Lipari, Liparite, 56
Liria vase, Spain, 141–2, Fig. 11.1
Livy, 159
Llyn Llangorse dug-out, 47, Map 4.2
Lofoten Islands, 29
logboats, see dug-outs
Lois (Leon), Spain, 99
long-boats, see *lung chhuan*
Lothal, India, 172, Fig. 13.4
Lotus, Loch (Arthur), Dumfries, Scotland, 114, 142
Loughcrew, Co. Meath, Ireland, 99
Lucan, 30
Lucus, R., Morocco, 100
Luli, King, see Tyre and Sidon
*lung chhuan*, dragon boat, long-boat, 193–4, 198, 212–14, Fig. 14.7
Lung-Shan culture, 186

*madarata* (boat type), 178
Maelstrom, 29
magnetic compass, 192
*mahadalpura* (boat of Ceylon), 179, Fig. 13.13
Mainz, 166, Fig. 12.16
'*Maison aux stucs*', Delos, 66, Fig. 6.11
Makkan, 173
Malta, 56
*manche* (R. Ganges vessel), 172
Mané Lud, Brittany, 99, 130
Mangareva, 230
Maoris, 200–10, Figs 15.3, 15.4, 15.5, 15.6, 15.7; war canoes, 205–9
Marco Polo, 185, 189
Marquesas, 200–1, 218, Map 15.1
Marseilles (Massalia), 26, 159
Mas d'Aire, France, 160
mast, sail and rigging, 75–6, 120, 151, 168, 176, 190, 203, Figs 8.5, 12.4; bipod mast, 10, 70; mast-step, 90, 164; see also sail
al-Masudi, 181
*masula* (sewn boat), 178–9, Figs 13.11, 13.12

medieval ships in N. Europe, 118–20
Medinet Habu (Thebes), 77
Medway, R., Kent 3
megalithic monuments/period, 85–6,
    98, 123; distribution, Map 8.1
*meia lua* (boat), 91–3, 127, Figs 8.6, 8.7,
    10.8
Mekong, R., 186, 214
Melos, 55–7, Fig. 6.1
'Meluhha', 173
Menapii, 159, Fig. 12.6
Merobriga, Spain, 158
Meshurashi tomb, Japan, 199
Mesolithic period, 28, 33, 41, 46, 56,
    60, 87, 121
Mesopotamia, 10, 30, 39, 58
metallurgy, 64
Mezin, Russia, 42
Midau el-Tahrir, Cairo, Fig. 2.3
Midorikawa tomb, Japan, 199, Fig.
    14.13
migration, 5, 15, 104, 132
Mika Hiva Island, Marquesas, 200
military uses of vessels, 36, 79, 80
Minateda, Albacete, Spain, 42
Minoan, 63, 68, 81, Fig. 7.1
Mochica Culture, Peru, 14
Mochlos, Crete, 59, Fig. 6.3
models, 64, 65, 77, 94, 124, 129, 142,
    171–2, Figs 6.1, 6.8, 7.15, 10.1, 10.2,
    10.6, 10.9, 13.4, 14.5
Mohenjo-Daro, 171, Fig. 13.2
*mokihi* (New Zealand floats), 13
*moliceiro* (boat), 93
Montgaudier baton, 4
Morbihan, 87
Mordan, Hispaniola, 232
*morota-bune* (sewn boat), 196–8, Fig.
    14.11
mortise and tenon (plank fastening),
    51, 78, 89, 90, 150, 163
Morton, Fife, Scotland, 27, 28, 42,
    Map 4.2
Mousterian, 4
Mozambique, 20
*mtepe* of Lamu, Kenya, 177–8
Muge, Portugal, 87
Mullerup, Denmark, 17
multiple dug-outs, 47, 48, 202–10, 214,
    Figs 5.3, 5.4, 15.2
al-Muqaddasi, 191
Murray–Darling Rivers, 17
Mycenae, 85, 86

*nabe buta* (log raft), 8
nails, metal, 51, 189
Nämforsen, Sweden, 113
Naqada, 175; pot, 76, Fig. 7.10
Navestad Pytelund, Norway, 106, Fig.
    9.7
navigation, *see* seamanship
Naxos, Greece, 64, Figs 6.7, 6.8

Nea Nikomedia, 56, 60, Map 6.1
Neanderthal, 4
needles and awls, 39, 40, 41, 58, 82
Nemi, Lake, Italy, 89, 167, Fig. 12.17
Neolithic, 55–6, 60, 121–3, 131–2, 200
Nero, Emperor, 167
Neuchâtel, Switzerland, 150, 164, 191
Neumagen, Trier, 158, 167, Fig. 12.4
New Grange, Co. Meath, Ireland, 99
New Guinea, 5, Map 1.1
New Guy's House ship, 89–90, 163,
    Fig. 8.4
New Shoreham, Sussex, 119, Fig. 9.27
New South Wales, 17
New Zealand, 45, 206, 230–1
Newfoundland, 22
Ngadju Dyaks of Borneo, 214
Niah caves, Sarawak, 213, Fig. 15.10
Nile, R., 7–8, 11, 26, 58, 60, 72, 76
Nineveh, 78
Nogent-les-Vierges (Nogent-sur-Oise),
    159
Nors, Thy, Denmark, 126, Fig. 10.6
Nøstvet people, Norway, 28, 103
Nydam boat, 115–16, Fig. 9.21

oars, 62, 66, 76, 81, 97, 100, 129, 151,
    168
Obanian, Oban, 27, 41, Map 4.2
obsidian, obsidian trade, 55, 60
oculus, 57, 127, 177, Figs 10.1, 10.8
Odoric, Friar, 178
Odysseus, *Odyssey*, 57, 72, 75, 78, 132
Oestrymnides, 123
Ohthere, 24
Oishi village, Japan, 198, Fig. 14.12
Okavango swamps, 11
Olaus Magnus, 24, 221
Onega, Lake, 32, 33
Onion Portage, 222
open sea voyages, 22, 26–7
*Ora Maritima*, 123
Orkney, 85, 132
Oronsay, 27
Orrabeinsstjup, Thorkils, 41
Ostia, 158
outriggers, *see* stabilisers

Pacific, 13, 200–18, Map 15.1;
    chronology, 217–18; evolution of
    craft, 211–12
paddle-wheel, 192
paddling, paddles, 28, 60, 100
paintings, 11, 20, 42, Figs 3.4, 6.5, 7.2,
    7.16, 11.1, 12.2
Pakistan, 31
'pakton' (basket boat), 58
Palau Islands, 8
Paleolithic, 1–6, 28, 40, 42, 194
Pao-lun-yuan, China, 187, Fig. 14.2
Papataettur, Iceland, 138
Pasyryk, Upper Altai, 74

Patagonia, 34
*pelota* (skin boat), 34, 41, 219
*pentekontor*, 80, 81
*Periplus*: Erythraean Sea, 32, 39, 178;
    Massiliote, 26, 123
Persia, Iran, 12, 31
Peru, 13
Pesse, Netherlands, 46, 56
Phaistos disc, Crete, 63, Fig. 6.6
Phoenicia, 77, 81, 94
*pi-chuan* (skin boat), 186
Picts, 152, 153
Pinneburg/Lyngby, 105
*pirogue*, 235
planked boats, evolution of, 45–6, 50–1,
    98, 155, 180–4
planking, strakes, 50, 51, 79, 90, 115,
    144–6, 147–8, 150–1, 161, 179, 189;
    *see also* fastenings; washstrakes
Plato, 100
Pleistocene (Postglacial), 17, 18
Pliny, 26, 32, 39, 60, 72, 96, 176
Po, R., 30
*po* (ocean-going ship), 189–90
Pommeroeul, Belgium, 164
Pompey, 31
*ponto* (ship type), 87
Porticello ship, 75, 82
pot rafts, 58
potato, sweet, spread of, 230–1
Praestelyngen, Denmark, 47
'pram' (boat type), 120
*prer* (boat type), 8
Prescelly Mountains, Wales, 48, Map
    4.2
propulsion, *see* oars; paddles; sail;
    towing
Ptolemy, 123
*pu fa* (reed boat), 13, 186
Pungwe, R., 20
Punt, Red Sea, 183, Fig. 13.16

Queensland, 7
Quentovik, 119
*quffa*, 32, 134

*Ra II*, 100
radiocarbon dating, 46, 47, 68, 85, 90,
    103, 121, 131, 140, 146, 148, 149,
    164, 200, 206, 231, 232, Map 15.1
raft: bulrush, 12, 13; log, 7–9, 147, 171,
    182–6, 194–5, 216–17, 224–30,
    232–3, Figs 2.1, 2.2, 13.16, 15.15,
    16.5, 16.6, 16.11, 16.13, 16.14
ram, 23, 32, 60, 77, 78, 80, 81
Rameses III, 9, 79
Rancho Casimira, Hispaniola, 232
Ras ed-Dura lagoon, Morocco, 11
Rathlin Island, Co. Antrim, 121, Map
    10.1
reed, types of, 9, 12, 13, 60
reed boats, 7–16, 58, 60, 69, 87, 100–1,

174, 186, 219, 225, 234, Figs 2.3, 2.4, 2.8, 2.9, 2.10, 13.6
representations of boats, *see* carvings; coins; graffiti; models; paintings; seals
Rhine, R., 166–7
Rhône, R., 60, 159
ribs (frames), 24, 35, 96, 102, 116, 120, 126, 164, Fig. 5.9
rigging, *see* mast
Rinyo, Orkney, 132
Risby Warren, Lincs, 132
Risga, Strathclyde, Scotland, 27, 28
rivers, boats for, *see* lakes and rivers
Rødøy, Helgeland, Norway, 102, 104, 105
Roos Carr, Yorks, 114, 126, 140, Fig. 9.18, Map 4.2
rudder, 61, 166, 190–1; axial, 191; balanced, 191

Sag, R., Norway, 103
Sahul Shelf, 5, Map 1.2
sail, 65, 75–7, 79, 81, 98, 117, 155, 158, 224–5; bush or branch, 117; Caribbean, 234; cotton, 225; earliest, 76; evolution in Pacific, 218, Fig. 16.8; hemp, 225; lateen, 226–7; Fig. 16.8; matting, 191–2, 204; skin, 19, 87; sprit, Fig. 16.8; triangular, 226–7
St Brendan, 110, 133, 135
St Columba, 135, 138
St Cormac, 132, 135
St Orland, Scotland, 152–3, Fig. 11.16
St Paul, 66
Santorini, 100, 101
Salween, R., 214
Salzgitter-Lebenstedt, Germany, 4
Samian ware, 163
Samoyeds, 33
sampan, 187–8, Fig. 14.4; development of, 192–3
Sanchi, 171, 179, 180
Santa Cruz Islands, 204
Saône, R., 159
Saqqara, Egypt, 71
Satakunta, Finland, 116, Figs 5.5, 5.6, 5.7
*saveiro* (Portuguese coast craft), 91–3, 127, 150–1, Figs 8.8, 8.9, 8.10, 11.14
saws, 71
Sayala, Nubia, 168, Fig. 12.18
Scala di Boes, 142
sea-level changes, 5, 41
seals, engravings on, 68, 171, 176, Figs 7.1, 13.5, 13.8, 13.9
seamanship and navigation, 81, 85; in Pacific, 210–11
seaworthiness, 34, 36, 79, 117
Seine, R., 159
Seneca Indians, 220
Sennacherib, 77

Seostris III, 71
Seri Indians, California, 14
Seward Peninsula, Alaska, 4, Map 1.1
sewing, sewn boats, 19, 24, 35, 36, 40, 51, 70, 72, 111, 144, 149, 178–9, 196–8, 210, Figs 9.23, 13.11, 13.13; *see also* lashings; needles
Shang Dynasty, 75, 188, Fig. 14.3
*shaskah* (boat), 175
shell sequence, 72, 115
Shewalton Moor, Ayrshire, 133
shields, 76, 124–5, Fig. 10.3
Shilluk people, 8
Siberia, 32, Map 1.1
Sicoris, R., Spain, 36
Sidonius Apollinaris, 26, 168
sinew, 35
Skail Bay, Orkney, 132
Skara Brae, Orkney, 132
skeleton sequence, 74
skewers, 18
skin boats, 26–44, 56, 87, 99–100, 102–12, 124, 134, 186, 195–6, 220–2; Figs 8.17, 9.1, 9.2, 9.3, 9.4, 9.6, 9.9, 9.12, 9.13, 9.14; advantages of, 27; distribution, 153–5; waterproofing, 35; *see also* bull-boat; coracle; curragh; *pelota*; umiak
skin float, 26, 34, 161, Figs 4.5, 12.9
skins (hides, leather), 35, 57
Skjeberg, Norway, 107
Skjomen, Ofoten, Norway, 102, 104, 105
Skraelings, 221
Skyros, 56, 60, 64, 94
Slusegård, Bornholm, Denmark, 116
Solinus, 26
Somme, R., 162
Soroka, Russia, 104
speed: of Kalnes boat, 112; in Roman period, 82
Split (Salonae), Jugoslavia, 158
stabilisers and outriggers, 48, 50, 203–4, 214–15, Figs 5.4, 5.8, 15.12, 15.13
stability in dug-outs, 47, 49, 77
Star Carr, Yorks, 17, 23, 26, 46, Map 4.2
stitches, stitching, *see* lashings; needles; sewing
Strabo, 11, 58, 75, 85, 87, 93, 95, 97, 99, 156
strakes, *see* planking
Stonehenge, 48, Map 4.2
Stuppatores (Guild of Caulkers), 164
Sulu Sea, 211
Sumer, Sumerian, 10, 57, 72, 171
Sunda Shelf, 5, Map 1.2
Surnuinmäki, Finland, Fig. 5.4
Susuya, R., Japan, 196, Fig. 14.8
Swiderian, 105
Syr-Darya, Russia, 13
Szechwan, 187, Fig. 14.2

Tagus, R., Portugal, 41, 87
Tahiti, 210
Tana, Lake, 9
Tartar, 30
Tartessus, Tarshish, Tarsis, 91, 98, 123; *see also* Gades
Tarxien, Malta, 59, 68, 77
Tasmania, 12
Tassili paintings, 11
*tek-pai* (raft from Formosa), 189, Fig. 14.5
Terenouthis stele, 65, Fig. 6.10
Thames, R., 3, 89–90
Thang dynasty, 192
Thatcham, Berks, 26
Thebes, 9
Thera (Santorini), 68, Fig. 7.2
Thompson Indians, B. Columbia, 14
Thule, 138, 221, Fig. 16.2
thwarts, 19, 20, 209
Tiber, Father, 157, Fig. 12.1
Tibet, 37
Tievebulliagh, 121, Maps 4.2, 10.1
Tigris, R., 10, 30, 31
Til Barsip, Assyria, 80
Tinevelly, India, 171
*tiradas* (black boats), 11
Tiryns, 59
Titicaca, Lake, 14, 16
Tonga, 205, 216
tools: bone, 21, 26, 39; metal, 24, 67, 161, 175; stone, 7, 17, 26, 28, 40, 48, 56, 60, 131, 186, 194, 206
towing (tracking), 77, 157–8, 168, Fig. 12.18
towing-mast-step, 168
trade, 67, 96, 172–4; stone axe, 121–3, 131; timber, 182; tin, 123, 127; *see also* obsidian
Transcaucasus, 74
trees, selection of, 50, 206
trees, species, 21, 24, 35, 81
trenails and pegs, 51, 71, 82, 89, 120, 164, 180
*trieris*, 80, 81, 167
Trondheim (Nidaros), Norway, 220
truss, 70, 71, 77, 83, 193, Figs 7.6, 7.17, 14.7
Tuamotu Islands, Figs 15.2, 16.13
Tungabhadra, R., 171
Tungus people, 18, 33, 196
Turkana, (Rudolf), Lake, 16
Tutankhamun, 70, 75
typhoons and cyclones, 211
Tyre and Sidon, 78, 80, 125

Uadji, Egypt, 74, Fig. 7.9
Uganda, 7
Ugarit and Ugaritic texts, 79, 82
Ulkestrop, Denmark, 28
umiak, 26, 27, 30, 34, 38, 42, 103, 109–10, 134, Figs 4.4, 4.11, 4.12

Untersberger Moor, Salzburg, 166
Ur, 174, Fig. 2.6
uses of boats, *see* ferries; fish;
  migration; military; trade
Utrecht, 119–20, Fig. 9.29

Vaaler-Moor, Germany, 116
Val Camonica, Italy, 29
Val Verde, Texas, 220
Valdivia, Ecuador, 223; potsherds
  from, Fig. 16.4
vanes, wind, 61
vases, 79, Figs 6.5, 7.12, 7.14
Vechten, Netherlands, 162, 167
Vedda people, India, 40
Veneti, ships of, *see* Celtic
Venezuela, 34
Venice, Venetian, 10, 93, 95–7, Fig.
  8.15
Vetulonia, 142
Victoria, Lake, 9, 11, 45
Vikings, 84, 102, 116, 128, 222; ship-
  building, 124, 128
Virgil, 45, 72, 82
Viste, Norway, 28

Vistula, R., Poland, 48
vitamin D deficiency, 4
Volos, Greece, 79
voyages, sea, 132, 135, 138, 173,
  210–11, 216–17, 222–4
Vyg, R. Russia, 32, 33, 104, 106, 113,
  Figs 9.2, 9.5, 9.16

Wadi Hammamat, Egypt, 175
*waka-puhara* (reed float), 13, Fig. 2.8
Wanzenau, Alsace, 166
Warring States period in China, 186
war-ships, 84; *see also* military uses
*Wasa*, 116
washstrakes, 49, 60, 116, 203, 235, Figs
  5.7, 5.9; *see also* planking
waterfowl, evidence from, 43
weapons, 141, 195, Fig. 11.2
Weissenburg, Bavaria, 150, Fig. 11.13
Wellington, Duke of, 36
wheels, 73–5, 162, 180, Figs 7.8, 12.11
Winchester, font, 191

*xavega, see saveiro*
Xenophon, 32

Yahgans of Chile, 19, 24
Yakut tribe, 18, 33
Yalu, R., 8
Yalung, R., 186
Yangh-Shao culture, 186
Yangtze, R., 186, 193; dragon boat,
  Fig. 14.7
Yap raft, 195
Yassi Ada wreck, 81
Yayoi Culture, Japan, 194, 199
Yellow River, *see* Huang Ho
Yenesei, R., 33
*yuloh* oar, 192
Yurak tribe, 33
Yverdon, Switzerland, 150, 166, Fig.
  12.15

Zawyet el-Mdin, 71, Fig. 7.6
Zedelghem, font, 191
Zuider Zee, 119
Zwammerdam, 91, 98, 150, 162–3, 166,
  168, Figs 12.12, 12.13